INSIGHT ⊙ GUIDES

ARGENTINA

◉ Walking Eye App

YOUR FREE DESTINATION CONTENT AND EBOOK AVAILABLE THROUGH THE WALKING EYE APP

Your guide now includes a free eBook and destination content for your chosen destination, all for the same great price as before. Simply download the Walking Eye App from the App Store or Google Play to access your free eBook and destination content.

HOW THE WALKING EYE APP WORKS

Through the Walking Eye App, you can purchase a range of eBooks and destination content. However, when you buy this book, you can download the corresponding eBook and destination content for free. Just see below in the grey panels where to find your free content and then scan the QR code at the bottom of this page.

Destinations: Download your corresponding essential destination content from here, featuring recommended sights and attractions, restaurants, hotels and an A–Z of practical information, all for free. Other destinations are available for purchase.

Ships: Interested in ship reviews? Find independent reviews of river and ocean ships in this section, all available for purchase.

eBooks: You can download your free accompanying digital version of this guide here. You will also find a whole range of other eBooks, all available for purchase.

Free access to travel-related blog articles about different destinations, updated on a daily basis.

HOW THE DESTINATION CONTENT WORKS

Each destination includes a short introduction, an A–Z of practical information and recommended points of interest, split into 4 different categories:

- Highlights
- Accommodation
- Eating out
- What to do

You can view the location of every point of interest and save it by adding it to your Favourites. In the 'Around Me' section you can view all the points of interest within 5km.

HOW THE EBOOKS WORK

The eBooks are provided in EPUB file format. Please note that you will need an eBook reader installed on your device to open the file. Many devices come with this as standard, but you may still need to install one manually from Google Play.

The eBook content is identical to the content in the printed guide.

HOW TO DOWNLOAD THE WALKING EYE APP

1. Download the Walking Eye App from the App Store or Google Play.
2. Open the app and select the scanning function from the main menu.
3. Scan the QR code on this page – you will then be asked a security question to verify ownership of the book.
4. Once this has been verified, you will see your eBook and destination content in the purchased ebook and destination sections, where you will be able to download them.

Other destination apps and eBooks are available for purchase separately or are free with the purchase of the Insight Guide book.

CONTENTS

LEGEND
℗ Insight on
◙ Photo story

THE BEST OF ARGENTINA: TOP ATTRACTIONS

△ **Iguazú Falls.** Getting up close to these Niagara-beating cataracts, which run for 2.5km (1.5 miles) along the Argentina–Brazil border, is one of the most thrilling spectator experiences the natural world has to offer. See page 208.

▽ **Perito Moreno glacier.** Larger than Buenos Aires, and taller than that city's Obelisk, this ice behemoth is Patagonia's most awe-inspiring sight. Seeing shards break off the main wall and crash to the lake below is an unforgettable experience. See page 289.

△ **Palermo Viejo.** A seemingly endless array of pleasures awaits in Buenos Aires' most fashionable barrio, from browsing the racks in hip boutiques to sampling the city's most adventurous cuisine. See page 158.

△ **Quebrada de Humahuaca.** This gorge of many colors in northwest Argentina was once part of the Camino Inca and is now a Unesco World Heritage Site. See page 231.

△ **San Antonio de Areco.** With its quiet streets lined by one-story buildings housing *pulperías* (a kind of rural bar), silversmiths, fodder and fertilizer stores, and, increasingly, B&Bs, San Antonio is the archetypal gaucho town. See page 171.

◁ **Mendoza's wine country.** Irrigated by melt water from high up in the Andes, Mendoza's wineries now produce world-class wines along with the rough stuff that accompanies every good *asado* (barbecue). Many of the best of them are open to tourists. See page 252.

▷ **Nahuel Huapi National Park.** Extinct volcanoes, turquoise lakes, thick temperate forests, ski centers, luxury accommodations, and Patagonia's liveliest city, Bariloche – just a few of the attractions in this, Argentina's oldest national park. See page 277.

△ **Península Valdés.** Jutting out into the Atlantic Ocean, this bleak promontory is one of the world's greatest marine wildlife sanctuaries. Southern right whales (in season), penguins, sea lions, and (if you're very lucky) orca are among the animals you may spot here. See page 283.

▽ **The Beagle Channel.** Cutting through the heart of Tierra del Fuego, this wild and beautiful strait joins the world's two great oceans. A boat trip along the channel from Ushuaia is an exhilarating voyage to the "end of the world." See page 300.

△ **Ruta 40.** Traversing the country from tip to toe, this legendary 5,000km (3,107-mile) route is one of the longest in the world. Several stretches, including ones in the provinces of Salta and Santa Cruz, pass through some of the country's most sublime landscapes. See page 288.

THE BEST OF ARGENTINA: EDITOR'S CHOICE

The imposing façade of MALBA, Buenos Aires.

BEST NATIONAL PARKS

Parque Nacional Los Glaciares, southern Patagonia. This well-managed park is home to some of the country's most spectacular natural landmarks, including the Perito Moreno glacier and the Fitz Roy mountain range. See page 289.

Parque Nacional Lanín, Neuquén Province. Named for its most imposing feature, the cone-shaped Lanín volcano, this park protects some of the northern Lake District's most gorgeous landscapes. See page 276.

Parque Nacional Talampaya, La Rioja. With its red sandstone cliffs rising sheer from the desert floor, this Unesco World Heritage Site is worth taking the trouble to reach. See page 263.

Parque Nacional Tierra del Fuego. Trails lead through southern beech forests to hidden lakes in this huge coastal reserve, which can be reached from Ushuaia on the Tren del Fin del Mundo. See page 301.

Trekking on the Perito Moreno glacier.

BEST MUSEUMS AND GALLERIES

Museo de Arte Latinoamericano de Buenos Aires (MALBA). This world-class museum exhibits an unrivaled collection of 20th-century Latin American art and its temporary shows always make waves. See page 156.

Fundación PROA, Buenos Aires. An avant-garde venue in an old-world barrio (La Boca), PROA hosts the city's best temporary exhibitions and has a terrific restaurant and library too. See page 165.

Museo Evita, Buenos Aires. This museum details the life of Eva Perón through artifacts, photographs, and film, as well as exquisite items from her wardrobe. See page 67.

Museo de Arqueología de Alta Montaña, Salta. The museum houses the perfectly preserved remains of three Inca children found frozen at the peak of Mount Llullaillaco in 1999. See page 227.

Museo de la Patagonia, Bariloche. This old-school museum, with its dioramas, scale models, and information panels, is the best place to learn about Patagonia's history, culture, and wildlife. See page 277.

Museo James Turrell, Bodega Colomé, Salta. This purpose-built space high up in the mountains exhibits many of Turrell's most hauntingly beautiful "light and space" installations. See page 236.

BEST FESTIVALS AND EVENTS

Festival Nacional del Folklore. January is the month for Argentina's most important folkloric music festival, which takes place in Cosquín, Córdoba. See page 199.

Fiesta Nacional de la Vendimia. Beginning in February and climaxing in March, Mendoza's annual wine harvest festival offers a full program of bacchanalian activities. See page 247.

Festival Internacional de Cine Independiente. Held in April, Buenos Aires' annual independent film festival is no Cannes or Sundance, but it gets bigger and better every year. See page 312.

Arte BA. Held each May in Buenos Aires, this art fair has grown to become one of the most important cultural events in South America. See page 312.

Día de la Tradición. This celebration of the gaucho and his way of life takes place on November 10, with San Antonio de Areco the epicenter of festivities. See page 172.

BEST OUTDOOR ACTIVITIES

Lake safaris in Esteros del Iberá. Covering large swathes of Corrientes province, the Iberá wetlands are an essential destination for wildlife lovers. See page 214.

Trekking near El Chaltén. This mountain village in Santa Cruz province is Argentina's official trekking capital. A day's hike will get you to the base of Mt Fitz Roy, while longer, more arduous walks take you deep into the back country. See page 290.

Horseback riding in the Lake District. There's no better way to explore the lakes and valleys of the Andean foothills than on horseback. Book an excursion in towns like Bariloche and El Calafate. See pages 277 and 288.

Snowboarding at Las Leñas. If it is not snowing in the northern hemisphere, there's a good chance it is here, at Mendoza's top ski resort. See page 258.

White-water rafting in Mendoza. The Atuel Canyon has a number of exciting rapids to shoot, classified between Class II and IV. See page 257.

Trekking up into the Andes.

White-water rafting near Uspallata, Mendoza province.

BEST ESTANCIAS

Estancia Los Dos Hermanos, near Buenos Aires. One of the best day trips from the capital is to this small but handsome ranch, where horseback rides across the pampas are followed by a belt-busting *asado* (www. estancialosdoshermanos. com).

Estancia Villa María, near Buenos Aires. If you want to watch the gaucho lifestyle rather than sample it, this luxurious mock-Tudor country estate could be what you're looking for (www. estanciavillamaria.com).

Dos Lunas, Córdoba. This is one of the best ranches for serious horseback riders in the Americas. There's no better place than the saddle from which to view Argentina's central sierras (http:// doslunas.com.ar).

Rincón del Socorro, Corrientes. Offering plush amenities and delicious organic food, this modernized ranch is the perfect base for exploring the Esteros del Iberá wetlands (www. rincondelsocorro.com.ar).

Peuma Hue, near Bariloche. Activities ranging from yoga to kayaking are on offer at this renowned lakeside estancia, which feels much more remote than it really is (www.peuma-hue.com).

Gaucho in San Antonio de Areco.

Bandoneon player, La Boca, Buenos Aires.

*Fiesta de la Tradición,
San Antonio de Areco.*

Palacio San José in Concepción del Uruguay, northeast Argentina.

Tango in the street, Buenos Aires.

GO SOUTH

Slip on your tango shoes, your walking boots, or your riding spurs, and lose yourself in one of the world's most beautiful countries.

Wine-tasting at a Mendoza finca.

Argentines have a lovely habit of making international visitors feel like guests rather than tourists. They are solicitous and sociable ("How do you like Argentina?" so often leads into "Why don't you come round for a barbecue?") and they never tire of hearing travelers tell them how wonderful their country is. And travelers never tire of telling them. Argentina is the eighth largest country in the world, and surely one of the most beguiling and diverse. A fantasy itinerary makes the case. If you were to leave Buenos Aires (something many people find hard to do) and move counterclockwise around the country, you would pass through dry plains and muggy jungle, see – and hear – one of the world's greatest waterfalls at Iguazú, traverse the cactus-studded uplands and deep valleys of the Northwest, roam down the Andean mountain range whose highest peaks look up only to the Himalayas, dip your toes into lakes that were once glaciers, all but press your nose up against glaciers that remain glaciers, hack your way through the primeval forests of Tierra del Fuego, and complete the circuit by returning northwards along the austere Atlantic coastline, much of whose marine wildlife is in the must-see-before-you-die category.

Iguazú Falls.

That this itinerary is less implausible than it sounds is a testament to how far Argentina's tourism industry has progressed over the last decade. The country has not rested on its clichés. The steaks you can cut with a spoon and the remote estancias where you can hang out with gauchos are still here (and still celebrated). But they have been joined by all manner of high-concept gastronomy and lavish design hotels.

Put another way, Argentina is ready for prime time. But it is far from tamed. The pampas grasslands, proverbially flat, are still best crossed on horseback. The perpetual gales that flay the Patagonian steppe can cause the hardiest gaucho to grimace. Even Buenos Aires, that most civilized of South American cities, has an epic, impalpable quality. So don't expect to conquer Argentina. Better to let it conquer you.

Hikers on their way to Lago Torre, Patagonia.

Llama in Purnamarca, Jujuy.

LANDSCAPES AND WILDLIFE

From the humid subtropics to the windswept Patagonian steppe, Argentina's diverse landscapes contain a dazzling array of exotic plants and animals.

Argentina is enormous – the eighth largest country in the world. If it could be stretched out over Europe, with its northwest corner positioned over London, the country's easternmost point would lie roughly over Budapest. Its southernmost tip, Tierra del Fuego, would be roughly over Timbuktu in Mali, about a third of the way down the African continent.

As one might expect, a country covering this much terrain possesses a great diversity of topography and climate. This may come as a surprise to anyone crossing Argentina by car or (more rarely these days) train, who will find themselves frequently looking through the window and wondering where the next tree is coming from. Most of the country is flat and featureless; the pampas grasslands dominate much of Argentina's central region, the Patagonian steppe and much of the south. It is on the fringes of these great plains that Argentina is at her most photogenic. But life is everywhere.

We have divided the country into seven geographical zones reflecting the areas tourists are most likely to visit: the fertile central pampas, of which Buenos Aires (both the city and the province) is a part; the marshy Northeast or Litoral, which encompasses the Iguazú Falls, the Jesuit ruins, and what little the loggers have spared of the once-mighty Atlantic rainforest; the forested Chaco region of the central north; the high plateau of the Northwest, including Salta and the Quebrada de Humahuaca; the mountainous west, known also as the Cuyo, where the winegrowing region of Mendoza shelters in the lee of the highest peaks outside the Himalayas; the Patagonian Andes range, which stretches from Neuquén through Río Negro,

Condor over Iguazú Falls.

Chubut, and Santa Cruz before ducking its head beneath the waves of the South Atlantic off the coast of Tierra del Fuego (it re-emerges further south to form the Antarctic Peninsula); and the rugged Atlantic coastline, famous worldwide for its marine wildlife.

THE PAMPAS

Even those going no further than Buenos Aires can, on a day trip, get out into the terrain for which Argentina is best known – the pampas. These fertile alluvial plains were once the home of the legendary gaucho (cowboy), and today they are the base for a large percentage of the nation's wealth. They cover much of central Argentina, stretching south, west, and north in a radius of 970km (600 miles) from the capital.

The pampas have two subdivisions: the humid pampa *(pampa húmeda)* and the dry pampa *(pampa seca)*. The humid pampa lies in the easterly part of the country, mostly in the province of Buenos Aires. This wetter area supports much of the nation's agriculture: grains, primarily wheat and (increasingly) soya, are grown here. The humid pampa is also the heart of the cattle industry. The grass-feeding of cattle gives Argentine beef its celebrated flavor and tenderness. The pampas' development took a large leap with the British building of a railroad system during the late 19th century and the importing of British cattle breeds.

Virtually all the *pampa húmeda* has been carved up and cultivated, and the original wildlife of this area – described so evocatively by the writer W.H. Hudson (see page 51) – has struggled in the face of these changes. Many of the birds mentioned in Hudson's writings are still to be seen, but mammals have

Cows grazing in the pampas.

⊘ FAR AWAY AND LONG AGO

In an age of rapid communications, it can be hard to imagine what life was like for the earliest European settlers on the pampas. One way to find out is to read *Far Away and Long Ago*, written by the novelist and naturalist William Henry Hudson. Hudson was born near Buenos Aires in 1841, and grew up on a sheep farm. In his book, he describes what often sounds like an idyllic childhood, with a vast natural playground full of wildlife on his doorstep, waiting to be explored. Hudson actually wrote the book in his seventies, when he was living in England, but his reminiscences of pampas life proved to be a lasting bestseller.

coped less well with the alterations produced by over a century of intense farming, and, as a consequence, many of them are now scarce.

Perhaps the most representative pampas left today, largely because of the absence of ploughing, is the area surrounding General Lavalle and south to Madariaga. Between Lavalle and San Clemente there is a wildlife sanctuary, managed by Fundación Vida Silvestre Argentina, where some of the last surviving pampas deer can be seen in the wild.

Northwards from Buenos Aires, Parque Nacional El Palmar (see page 218), near Concordia in Entre Ríos province, gives a flavor of a different kind of habitat, where the open pampas is replaced by palm-studded savannah. The park preserves only a few square kilometers of the palm-and-grassland landscape, but its wildlife makes the trip well worthwhile. Among its inhabitants are viscachas, nocturnal burrowing rodents that were once common throughout the pampas. They can weigh up to 9kg (20lbs), and their nighttime calls are loud, varied, and unnerving. The viscachas at El Palmar are unusually tame, but campers here must be tidy, as the animals may steal anything that is left out at night and cart it quickly off to their dens.

The economy in the north is based on agriculture, with the principal crops being a form of tea, yerba mate, and various types of fruit. Enormous tracts of virgin forest have been lost to a lumber business that has become increasingly important to the Argentine economy.

Toward the northern tip of Misiones province in the Northeast, a plateau of sandstone and basalt rises from the lowlands. The landscape here is characterized by a rough relief combined with fast-running rivers. Straddling the northern border with Brazil are the magnificent Iguazú

El Palmar National Park.

THE LITORAL

The isolated northeast area of Argentina – the Litoral – is occasionally referred to as Mesopotamia (Greek for "between rivers"), as most of it lies between the Paraná and Uruguay rivers. The whole area is cross-cut by waterways, and much of the land is marshy and low, receiving a lot of rainfall.

The southern sector, comprising the provinces of Santa Fe and Entre Ríos, with their swamps and low, rolling hills, has an economy supported by sheep farming, horse breeding, and cattle raising. This is one of the major wool-producing areas of the country.

Toward the north, into Misiones province, the climate becomes subtropical and very humid.

Falls (see page 208), which have more than 270 separate cascades, falling more than 60 meters (200ft) through the lush sub-tropical forest.

Once the thrill of watching the cataracts has worn off, the surrounding forest has much to offer: some 2,000 species of flowering plants, nearly the same number of butterflies and moths, 100 species of mammals including the elusive jaguar, and nearly 400 kinds of birds including hummingbirds and toucans. However, this kind of habitat is notorious for hiding its inhabitants, so seeing its richness requires time and patience. If you want to train your binoculars on the wildlife, your best strategy is to book a stay in a jungle lodge such as Yacutinga (see page 211).

THE GRAN CHACO

The Gran Chaco is a vast low-lying region that straddles northern Argentina, as well as parts of Bolivia and Paraguay. The climate here becomes drier from east to west, splitting the Chaco into two merging parts. The Dry Chaco, in the west, is likely to appeal only to the most adventurous of travelers. Its wildlife is hugely diverse – reputedly including some exceptionally large snakes – but, even for reptile-lovers, getting about in this region is a daunting task. The country is covered with dense thorn thickets crossed by very few roads, and there are no amenities for visitors.

The Wet Chaco to the east is easier to visit. Although it has undergone some major clearance for agriculture over the past 25 years, it still contains some beautiful tracts of woodland interspersed with marshes, and is rich in wildlife. Traveling west from Corrientes or Resistencia, RN16 is worth exploring at least as far as Chaco National Park.

The wet season in the summer (from December to March) is best avoided, for the heat is intense and the roads become impassable. Between April and November, conditions are more congenial, making it a good time to visit the national park. There are howler monkeys and many other mammals, but the main attraction for most visitors is the park's bird life, which includes guans, chachalacas, whistling herons, jabirú storks, jacanas, and ducks galore.

From Corrientes, both east and south, there are some very rich woodlands interspersed with wide-open grasslands and enormous marshes. RN12 is paved in both directions, but the tougher earth roads which run northeast–southwest between the paved stretches, through places such as Mburucuyá and San Luis del Palmar, generally venture into far more interesting wildlife habitats.

In Corrientes, in the region of the headwaters of the Esteros del Iberá wetlands (see page 214), where grass seas stretch from horizon to horizon, visitors sometimes catch a glimpse of the rare maned wolf. More closely related to foxes than to wolves, this slender member of the canine family has very long legs, making it look like it's on stilts. Marsh deer also survive here – albeit in small numbers – and on larger estancias that are run with conservation in mind, the endangered pampas deer can be seen.

Yacare caiman, Esteros del Iberá wetlands.

⊙ A BARREN LAND

There is little vegetation that is native to the pampas. In some areas there is a fine grass that grows low, while in other places there are tall, coarse grasses mixed with low scrub. The only tree that grew here as a native, the ombú, is not even really a tree: it's a weed. Although it grows to a substantial size, its moist fibers are useless as fuel for burning. Historically, its most useful function was to provide shade for tired gauchos as they rested beneath its branches to sip their mate tea. Over the years, many non-indigenous plants have been introduced. Tall rows of trees serving as windbreaks are everywhere and break the monotony of the landscape.

THE ANDEAN NORTHWEST

The provinces of Jujuy, Salta, and Tucumán have a mixture of extraordinary scenery and fascinating wildlife, spread over a dizzying range of altitudes. All three have wet, subtropical regions, while Salta and Jujuy also contain much higher and drier areas as the land rises to the Andes mountains. Along with cattle ranching, there are vineyards, olive and citrus groves, and tobacco and sugar-cane plantations. Vegetable farms lie in the valleys and piedmonts.

Parque Nacional Calilegua lies on the eastern slopes of the Andes, between 600 and 4,500 meters (2,000–15,000ft), in the province of Jujuy. Visits are only practicable during the dry season (June through October or November) as the roads are frequently washed out the rest of the year. The road through the park rises steeply, crossing through a series of vegetation zones in rapid succession. The lowest is the Chaco vegetation, with its silk floss trees (*Chorizia*), known locally as *palos borrachos*. This zone also has jacarandas and tabebuias – trees that often burst into bloom while they are still leafless, toward the end of the dry season. Their spectacular lilac, yellow, or pink flowers are an impressive sight, attracting pollinating insects. Higher up, the journey continues through a jungle dominated by tipa trees (*Tipuaria*) and into the cloud forest of coniferous podocarp trees (*Podocarpus*) and moisture-loving alders (*Alnus*).

The forest's animal life also changes with altitude, although many of the larger predators range throughout the park. Wildcats, including jaguars, pumas (cougars), ocelots, and jaguarundi all live here, although it takes skill and luck to spot them. They prey on deer, tapirs, peccaries, agoutis, and even capuchin monkeys, as well as many local birds.

The higher parts of Salta and Jujuy are best approached slowly to avoid mountain sickness, or *soroche*, and an ideal way to do it is to travel up the Quebrada de Humahuaca in Jujuy (see page 231). The journey begins in lush subtropical farmland and ends in the thin and stunningly clear air of the Altiplano, more than 3,000 meters (10,000ft) up. In this part of the Andes water is often in short supply, and plants and animals have to cope with drought as well as intense sunlight by day and often chilling cold at night.

One animal – the vicuña – is quite at home in these conditions. Despite its dainty appearance, this smallest wild relative of the llama can survive at over 5,000 meters (16,400ft), and it can run effortlessly in mountain air that leaves visitors gasping for breath. For a grazing animal, its hearing is not particularly good, but its large Bambi-like eyes give it superb long vision, allowing it to spot movement from a great distance.

The road up the *quebrada* (gorge) eventually leads to the dusty town of Abra Pampa, where

Argentina has over 40 national parks and reserves, containing everything from astonishing waterfalls and glaciers to teeming bird life. They make a good place to start exploring wild Argentina.

Talampaya National Park.

the level landscape is ringed by distant mountains. At this altitude, the climate is too harsh for trees to thrive, but there is no shortage of wildlife. The region's woodpeckers and owls are particularly interesting, because they have had to adapt to a habitat without any cover. The owls dig burrows, while the woodpeckers peck nest holes into earth banks – both can often be seen from the road.

DINOSAUR COUNTRY

Roughly 800km (500 miles) south of the Abra Pampa region is an equally spectacular part of the Argentine Andes that sees far fewer visitors from abroad. In this stark landscape, erosion has carved out bizarre formations in sediments laid down millions of years ago. At Parque Nacional Talampaya in La Rioja province, deep-red cliffs flank a precipitous gorge – ideal country for the condors that soar overhead. In neighboring San Juan, the Parque Provincial Ischigualasto contains a moonscape of eroded clay with rocky pillars and cliffs (see page 259).

Country like this has yielded a treasure-trove of fossilized animals over many decades. Discoveries at Ischigualasto have included Herrerasaurus, an early meat-eating dinosaur that lived over 200 million years ago, and many other rep-

The Cuyo area is blessed with mineral wealth. Oil discovered here and in Patagonia, and the mining of copper, lead, and uranium, have made Argentina nearly self-sufficient in these vital resources.

with many peaks reaching over 6,600 meters (21,780ft). West of Mendoza lies Aconcagua, at 6,980 meters (23,030ft) the highest peak in the western hemisphere. Just south of Aconcagua is

Vineyard in Lujan de Cuyo in front of Mount Aconcagua, the highest peak in the Andes.

tiles alive at that time. Further east on the pampas, Argentine paleontologists have unearthed fossils of what may be the largest flying bird ever to have existed. Named *Argentavis magnificens*, it had a wingspan of about 7.5 meters (25ft), and measured over three meters (10ft) from beak to tail. Like today's condors, this gigantic creature probably flew by soaring, a technique that works well in open, sunny landscapes that generate currents of rising air.

THE CUYO

The central-western section of Argentina, comprising the provinces of San Juan, Mendoza, and San Luis, is known as the Cuyo. The Andes here become a single towering range,

the Uspallata Pass (a former Inca road), which at its highest point of 3,800 meters (12,540ft), crosses into Chile.

Fingers of desert extend eastward from the glacial mountains and down into the plains. A great deal of the land here is dry, wind-eroded, and dotted with scrub vegetation. Rivers nourished by the melting snows of the Andes cut through the desert.

It is these same rivers which, with the help of an extensive irrigation system, allow for large-scale agriculture in the region. The Cuyo is the heart of Argentina's wine country; the arid climate, sandy soil, and year-round sunshine provide the ideal conditions for viticulture (see page 245). Citrus fruits are also grown here.

PATAGONIA – THE NORTHERN LAKE DISTRICT

The Andes and their foothills make up no more than a fraction of Patagonia's total surface area, but it is in this mountainous ribbon of land, running down the country's western spine from Neuquén to Tierra del Fuego, that some of Argentina's most sublime landscapes can be seen and explored.

North of Santa Cruz, in the provinces of Neuquén, Río Negro, and Chubut, is the region is known as the "Lake District" (or sometimes the "northern Lake District" to distinguish it from its southern counterpart). The lacustral valleys that account for the name were carved out over millions of years by glacial activity; when the glaciers retreated, the ice left behind melted to form the vast, turquoise lochs that so dazzle visitors today.

Limpid they may be when lapping against the shore, but these waters run deep. Lago Nahuel Huapi, located within the national park of the same name, has a maximum measured depth of 438 metres (1,437ft) and a surface area of 529 sq km (204 sq miles). You would need ten Manhattans to cover it. This is plenty enough space for a mythical water beast to hide in, hence the legend of Nahuelito, a Nessie-like giant serpent which has been "sighted" on numerous occasions since the early years of the 20th century.

Thanks to the region's impressive tourist infrastructure, the northern Lake District is easy to explore. Bariloche (see page 277) sits on the shore of Lago Nahuel Huapi, while the smaller San Martín de los Andes (see page 275) occupies a breathtaking natural harbor on the eastern tip of Lago Lácar. Farther north is Lago Huechulafquen, famous for its trout fishing and easily reached from Junín de Los Andes (see page 276).

PATAGONIA – THE SOUTHERN LAKES AND GLACIERS

Around 1,800km (1,118 miles) south of Bariloche, in the province of Santa Cruz, is El Calafate (see page 288), a popular tourist resort and the gateway to Parque Nacional Los Glaciares. Several of the continent's most spectacular glaciers are contained within the national park and, for many visitors, seeing them up close is the experience of a lifetime.

The glaciers spill down from the Southern Patagonian Ice Field, which straddles the Andes and covers large tracts of Argentina and Chile. The world's largest ice field outside the poles, it feeds dozens of glaciers in both countries. The best known on the Argentine side are the Upsala, the Viedma, and, most celebrated of all, the Perito Moreno (see page 289).

WILDLIFE IN THE PATAGONIAN ANDES

The Patagonian Andes are a stronghold of many of the country's native plants and animals.

Male Magellanic woodpecker, Patagonia.

Among the animals visitors can expect to see are foxes, deer, geese, and parakeets, while native plants include southern beeches (*Nothofagus*), an attractive broad-leaved tree that is covered with small scallop-edged leaves.

Southern beeches are a living legacy of South America's very distant past. At one time, South America formed part of Gondwanaland, a southern supercontinent that included Antarctica and Australasia. The southern beech family evolved when Gondwanaland was still intact, but its member species became separated as Gondwanaland broke up, and the continents drifted apart. This explains the remarkable distribution of southern beeches today: as well as growing in South America, they also grow in Australia, New

Zealand, and New Guinea – thousands of miles away on the other side of the Pacific.

The high regions are home to large flocks of upland geese in grassy valleys, ashy-headed geese in clearings in woods near lake shores and rivers, and noisy buff-necked ibises nearly everywhere. The woods also contain rich and colorful flocks of austral parakeets and hummingbirds called greenbacked firecrowns. Both seem out of place in such surroundings, but they have successfully adapted to the region's cool conditions. This area is also the home of the

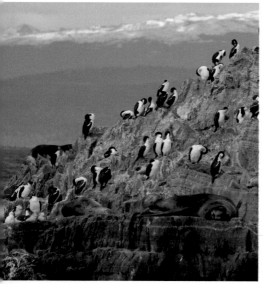

Sea lions and sea birds on an island in the Beagle Channel.

torrent duck, which, as its name implies, is only seen in white-water rivers and streams.

One of the most spectacular birds in the Patagonian Andes is the Magellanic woodpecker, the giant of its family. The male sports a bright scarlet head with a small crest, while his all-black mate has a very long and floppy crest that curls forward.

You probably won't spot a Magellanic woodpecker (you have a much better chance of hearing one) but you have every chance of clapping eyes on a condor. These emblematic vultures, easily distinguished by the ruff of white feathers around their dark necks, have the largest wingspan (over three meters/10ft) of any land bird. Central to the folklore and mythology of

many indigenous Andean religions, the condor is considered "near threatened" by the International Union for Conservation of Nature. However, those who make the journey to the trekking center of El Chaltén (see page 290) are almost guaranteed to spot one.

The South Andean deer, by contrast, has an official status of critical – estimates of the remaining population in Argentina range from 400 to 600. Known in Argentina as the huemul, this mid-sized deer ranges across rocky upland terrain and open scrubland. Its only natural predator is Argentina's national animal – the puma or cougar.

TIERRA DEL FUEGO

When Charles Darwin sailed up the Beagle Channel in 1832, Tierra del Fuego was almost unknown to the outside world. Since then, European settlers have done much to transform the ecology of this remote and stormy region. Sheep and rabbits arrived in the 19th century, and beavers and muskrat were introduced in the 1940s, creating havoc in the island's woodlands by felling trees and damming streams.

More recently, unrestrained development has turned Tierra del Fuego's southernmost town, Ushuaia, into a busy, sprawling city, complete with the most southerly traffic jams in the world.

Despite this, Tierra del Fuego is a fascinating destination for anyone interested in wildlife. The Beagle Channel is as beautiful as it was in Darwin's day, and its cormorants, sea lions, and fur seals can be seen at close quarters by taking a boat trip from Ushuaia. The Channel also has small colonies of Magellanic penguins, together with the occasional gentoo, a larger penguin species with a bright-red beak. There's a good chance you might also come across kelp geese, as well as flightless steamer ducks. These remarkable birds get their name from the dramatic paddle-wheel-like spray they generate as they chase or escape from their rivals.

Where they are still intact, Tierra del Fuego's southern beech forests have a sombre and otherworldly feel. The winds this far south can be fierce and unrelenting, and growth is a slow business, with bleached branches showing where trees have lost their battle against the elements. But despite the hostile conditions, these forests are far from lifeless: austral parakeets fly among the trees, and condors often soar overhead. The Parque Nacional Tierra del Fuego is a good place not only to see these trees, but also glaciers and bare tundra. It offers many trails, such as the Senda Costera (Coast Trail) with the chance to get a glimpse of abundant wildlife, such as the famous giant woodpeckers.

THE PATAGONIAN DESERT

Turning northward once more, the journey back to Buenos Aires crosses hundreds of miles of Patagonian steppe – a vast windswept plateau that rises gently from east to west. In this part of South America, the Andes intercept most of the moisture carried by the prevailing westerly winds, creating a rain shadow in their lee. As a result, Patagonia is unusually dry for somewhere so far south – the inland city of Colonia Sarmiento, for example, receives just 13cm (5ins) of rain a year.

This desert is the seventh largest in the world, occupying 673,000 sq km (260,000 sq miles) or roughly the area of the US state of Texas. It's one of the harshest environments imaginable, but a number of animal species still manage to scrape out a living here, including the armadillo, gray fox, iguana, skunk, burrowing owl, guanaco, and puma.

THE ATLANTIC COAST

The continental shelf in the South Atlantic east of Argentina is bathed by a nutrient-rich current flowing up from the south, and so inevitably attracts prodigious numbers of marine mammals, as well as sea birds. At one time many of these were ruthlessly hunted, but today the whales, seals, and penguins breed here largely unmolested.

In Chubut province, two reserves – Punta Tombo and Cabo Dos Bahías – are home to hundreds of thousands of Magellanic penguins during the summer breeding season. Further north, the Península Valdés is famous for its sightings of whales and seals. There is something to see on the coast throughout the year, with southern sea lions hauling out to breed between January and March, migrating southern right whales arriving in June, and elephant seals beginning to breed from September. By December they have given birth, and the adults can be seen lazing on the shingle, flicking flipper-loads of shells over their bodies to help dislodge their molting fur.

In the shallows, a spectacular presence is the marauding orcas (killer whales), which create a threatening atmosphere between the months of March and May, as they lie in wait for young sea lions that venture innocently beyond the beach.

MOVING INLAND

Away from the starkly beautiful coast, the protected status of Península Valdés benefits land animals as well. This is an ideal place to see guanacos, rheas, and maras – long-legged rodents that look something like a cross

Guanacos, relatives of the llama, can survive in the Patagonian desert.

between a hare and a small deer. The peninsula also teems with the well-known tinamous, dumpy ground-feeding birds that can often be seen on the side of the road. Despite their squat shape, biologists conclude that tinamous are probably more closely related to ostriches and rheas than to the game birds they resemble.

Heading north along the South Atlantic coast, the Patagonian plateau blends gradually with the pampas, and leads back to Buenos Aires. After the vast space and solitude of the far south of the country, the bustling crowds and hectic traffic can come as a shock. Nevertheless, even here you can be assured that the varied wildlife of Argentina is never far away.

The prehistoric Cueva de las Manos (Cave of the Hands), in Santa Cruz province.

DECISIVE DATES

PRE-COLUMBIAN PERIOD

c.10,000 BC
Nomadic tribes reach Argentina from the north.

500 BC–AD 600
Ceramic cultures emerge in Jujuy and San Juan.

600–1480
Development of Diaguita-Calchaquí culture – including the Quilmes and Tafí tribes – in northwest Argentina.

1480
The Incas conquer northwestern Argentina.

THE SPANISH EMPIRE

1516
Spaniard Juan Díaz de Solis claims the Río de la Plata for Spain.

1536
Pedro de Mendoza founds the settlement of Nuestra Señora de Santa María del Buen Ayre (Buenos Aires). It is wiped out by disease and attacks from local indigenous tribes.

1580
Buenos Aires is founded a second time by Juan de Garay.

Pucará del Titiconte, a pre-Columbian fort near Tilcara.

1776
Buenos Aires is made capital of the fourth Spanish viceroyalty in the Americas.

1806–7
British troops invade Buenos Aires, but are twice expelled.

THE INDEPENDENT REPUBLIC

1810
An independent junta of government is named in Buenos Aires on May 25.

1816
Argentine Congress formally declares itself a state on July 9.

1817
General José de San Martín leads Argentine troops to fight Spanish loyalists in Chile.

1826–7
Bernardino Rivadavia is elected president.

1829–52
Argentina is dominated by the caudillo Juan Manuel de Rosas, who rules continuously from 1835 to 1852.

1853
Argentina's constitution is adopted on May 1.

1879
The "Conquest of the Desert" – General Roca defeats remaining indigenous tribes and pushes back southern frontiers. Roca elected president.

1890
Radical Party (Radical Civic Union) is formed.

1916–30
Radical Party comes to power. Hipólito Yrigoyen is president 1916–22 and 1928–30.

1930
Military step into politics for the first time in 20th century, under General José F. Uríburu.

1943
Government is overthrown by the military GOU (Group of United Officers), one of whom is Colonel Juan Domingo Perón.

PERONISM AND AFTER

1945
Juan Perón is arrested in October after the formation of the General Confederation of Labor (CGT), then released after huge rally.

1946
Perón, now married to Eva Duarte (Evita), is elected Argentine president on February 24.

1951
Perón is re-elected with 67 percent of vote. A year later Evita dies from cancer.

1955
Protests from Catholic church and unrest among armed forces leads to coup. Perón flees into exile.

1958
Arturo Frondizi (Radical Party) becomes president.

1962–3
Military government returns to power.

President Mauricio Macri.

ARGENTINE DEMOCRACY

1983
Raúl Alfonsín is elected president after collapse of the military government.

1985
Nunca Más report documents almost 9,000 cases of people secretly abducted during the dictatorship.

1989
Peronist candidate Carlos Saúl Menem is elected president.

1991
The peso is pegged to the US dollar. Economic stability is restored after three decades.

1993
Constitution is changed to allow re-election of president.

1995
President Menem is re-elected.

1999
Fernando de la Rúa, of the Radical Party, wins election.

2001
President de la Rúa resigns after protests in which 39 protesters are killed.

2003
Néstor Kirchner, governor of Santa Cruz province, takes office as president.

2005
Supreme Court approves repeal of amnesty laws protecting military junta members suspected of human rights abuses.

2007
Cristina Fernández, the wife of Néstor Kirchner, is elected president.

1966
Armed forces intervene again; General Juan Carlos Onganía is made president.

1970
Growing unrest leads military to oust Onganía.

1973
Peronists win elections.

1974
Perón takes over as president with Isabel, his third wife, as vice president. Perón dies on July 1; Isabel is declared president of an increasingly divided nation.

1976
Military junta overthrows Isabel Perón on March 24. "Dirty war" is launched to suppress opposition. Between 9,000 and 30,000 Argentines are abducted, tortured, and killed by security forces.

1977–83
Succession of military governments known as the "Proceso."

1978
Host nation Argentina wins its first World Cup.

1982
General Galtieri sends troops to occupy the Falkland Islands/ Malvinas. Argentina surrenders with the loss of 600 soldiers to Great Britain.

2010
Néstor Kirchner dies of a heart attack. Former head of the Argentina junta Jorge Videla receives a life sentence for crimes against humanity.

2011
Cristina Fernández de Kirchner is re-elected by a landslide.

2013
Jorge Mario Bergoglio is elected pope. Anti-corruption demonstrations take place across the country.

2014
Argentina defaults on its external debts after it fails to reach agreement with so-called "vulture fund" investors.

2015
Mauricio Macri, conservative mayor of Buenos Aires, is elected president and embarks on ambitious reforms.

2016
A settlement between Argentina and US "vulture fund" investors is reached over bond repayments.

2017
President Macri's coalition wins parliamentary elections widely seen as a referendum on his reformist policies. Argentinian submarine ARA *San Juan* – with 44 crewmen on board – goes missing in South Atlantic.

2018
The centre-right government hints for the first time that it might hold a referendum on legalizing abortion. A congress committee is set up to investigate the disappearance of the ARA *San Juan* submarine.

Pucará de Tilcara.

PRE-COLUMBIAN PERIOD

Swept aside by successive waves of European conquerors, Argentina's early inhabitants have left behind only traces of their culture, revealing them to be self-sufficient and highly creative peoples.

According to a theory accepted by most archeologists, the first inhabitants of the Americas came from Asia. During one of the many ice ages, the Bering Strait between Asia and Alaska became a land bridge which human beings crossed in their search for new lands in which to live and hunt.

Somewhere between 30,000 and 25,000 BC, these Asiatic people, the theory goes, gradually spread southwards through the American landmass. It is possible that these early inhabitants reached the southern tip of South America by about 11,000 BC. Artifacts and human remains excavated at the Los Toldos site in Santa Cruz province seem to support this theory.

More recently, some archeologists have suggested that the first South Americans may have crossed the Pacific from Australia, settling the Amazon and other areas before pushing up into North America.

CLIMATE CHANGE

The last advance of the ice sheet in South America occurred between 9000 and 8000 BC, provoking different effects from those in North America. No ice sheets covered the pampas of Argentina or the jungles of Brazil. The principal manifestation was that the Andes, the great chain of mountains that forms the spine of South America, had more ice covering it then than it does today.

The environment was also different, since many more lakes existed than is the case today, and the sea level was lower; many areas that are now under water were then inhabitable. The Atlantic side of the continent, which today has a large and not very deep submarine platform, was likely much wider, extending outward from

Aguada vase, 640–850 AD.

today's pampas and Patagonia to form a still larger plain. The rainfall pattern was also different and areas such as now-arid Patagonia were then covered with grass.

For many thousands of years the natives of this area developed separately from the inhabitants of other continental landmasses. Furthermore, it seems, they had relatively little contact with the great civilizations of the Central Andes.

When the first Spaniards finally entered Argentina during the 16th century they did not find the great cities and pyramids of Meso-America or a splendid empire such as the one the Peruvian Incas had built in only 100 years. Rather, they found a sparsely populated landmass carved up between a number of contrasting societies.

HUNTER-GATHERERS

Although there are a large number of archeological sites throughout Argentina, the dating of many of them has still not been satisfactorily settled, and only a few can be ascribed to the end of the Pleistocene and beginning of the Holocene Period, about 10,000 to 9000 BC.

Many archeologists call the earliest-known cultural tradition the "hunting tradition" or the

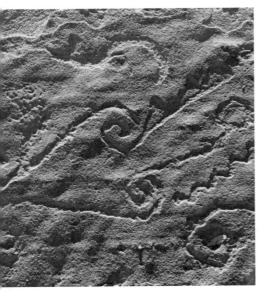

Rock paintings, Talampaya National Park.

⊘ CAVES OF KNOWLEDGE

Bones and other items found in caves have yielded much information about Argentina's early history. The Fells and Pailli Aike caves, located on the southern tip of the continent, contain horse, guanaco (llama family), and ground-sloth bones, together with those of humans. In southern Chile, the Eberhardt cave has remains of the Mylodon (giant sloth) and Onohippidon (early horse). The Los Toldos site is a group of caves containing horse bones. All these sites contain stone tools; some of them have bone tools and Eberhardt has worked hides. The sites represent a pattern of seasonal nomadic occupation that followed the food resources.

"hunting and gathering tradition." As the names suggest, these early groups roamed the country, hunting big game and gathering plants, seeds, and fruits. Many of the animals hunted and eaten are now extinct.

These nomads sheltered in caves. The so-called Cueva de las Manos (Cave of the Hands), in Santa Cruz province, has walls and ceilings covered with paintings; those which give the site its name are hands done in what is called "negative technique" (the hand is placed on the wall and the paint applied around it, like a stencil), but there are also depictions of human beings hunting animals such as guanaco (camelid similar to the llama) and rheas. The oldest paintings are thought to date back around 9,500 years, while the stenciled hands have been dated to 550 BC, or around the time Pythagoras was thinking about right-angled triangles.

The hunting tradition survived for several thousand years – even until European contact in some areas. The related archeological sites have certain common characteristics: the absence of ceramics and metal, no clear sign of the practice of agriculture (although by 2500 BC, some milling stones are present in some of the places), and the presence of stone and bone tools and objects for personal decoration.

LIFE AT THE END OF THE WORLD

Development was uneven throughout the country and certain areas within the Patagonia and Tierra del Fuego zones never moved beyond the hunting tradition stage. The Tunel site, on the Beagle Channel, on the southern coast of Tierra del Fuego, testifies to that. After a first occupation, oriented on guanaco hunting, the Fuegians – comprising the Ona, Haush, Yaghan and Alacaluf tribes – gradually converted to a sea-oriented economy.

For 6,000 years – until their full contact with the Europeans in the late 1800s – their economy and way of life remained mostly within a sea-based hunting and gathering pattern, complemented by hunting and seed and fruit collection. The lack of revolutionary changes does not reflect primitiveness or cultural backwardness but a successful and, with time, comfortable adaptation to the local environment by people who knew their resources and how to exploit them. (The story of the Fuegian civilizations is explored in more depth in several good museums in Ushuaia; see page 298.)

THE DAWN OF AGRICULTURE

In other areas the hunting tradition gave way to agriculture. The transformation was from a pattern of collecting fruits, seeds, and leaves when and where they could be found to an organized pattern of planting, tending, and collecting the fruits within a more restricted area. If nomadism was an inevitable consequence of the hunter-gatherer regime, the process of settling flowed naturally from the agricultural way of life.

Within the New World, Mexico and the Andean area were the centers of domestication of wild plants. The vegetables and fruits that, with time, became the main staples of all the pre-Columbian societies and later of the European settlements – maize, potatoes, squash, beans, peppers – appear in either Meso-America or the Andean area by approximately 5000 BC.

POTTERY AND STONE SCULPTURES

The advent of agriculture is often closely followed by the development of ceramic skills. It is possible that the harvesting of crops and the new phenomenon of surplus food were an incentive for the making of containers which could hold and store seeds and fruits. Although pottery appeared in the New World during the 4th millennium BC, it is not seen in Argentina's archeological record until c.500 BC. Most ceramic cultures occurred in the northern half of what is now Argentina.

To the Early Ceramic Period, which extended from about 500 BC to AD 600, belong several cultures which occupied an arch extending from the center of Jujuy to the eastern part of San Juan province. One of the early complexes is the Tafí culture of Tucumán, which is noted for its stone sculptures. Some of these beautiful carved monoliths (which reach three meters/10ft in height) have stylized human faces.

The people of the area lived in settlements formed by groups of houses arranged around a central square. Their diet included quinoa (an Andean cereal), potatoes, and possibly maize,

and they practiced llama herding. Mounds have been found which were used either for burials or as platforms for special structures.

Another extraordinary example of excellent stone sculpture is found at the site of the Alamito culture, on the Tucumán–Catamarca border. The statues here (both of women and men) reached an unusual level of development, with an almost abstract style both powerful and expressive.

In contrast to these stone-oriented cultures there is Condorhuasi, a culture in which

Stone face of unknown significance, from the Parque de los Menhires, Tucumán province.

ceramic art reached levels of expression not known in any other groups. Strange figures, often with both animal and human characteristics, are shown sitting and crawling, usually with globular bodies and legs, painted in a variety of white and red, cream and red, or black and red combinations.

SETTLEMENT DEVELOPMENT

The Middle Ceramic Period, dating from AD 650 to 850, witnessed the development and continuation of the advances made by preceding cultures, the existence of full agricultural communities living in permanent settlements, and the herding of llama and alpaca.

Architecture was still not impressive – at times just clay walls, probably with straw or wood roofs. Ceramic art continued to be developed, but stonework declined. Metalworking was by then highly developed, with the making of bronze and copper axes, needles, tweezers, bracelets, and disks with complicated designs. The distinct differences in the number of artifacts found in graves is a clear indication that by now social stratification existed. The lack of monumental works or clear examples of organized labor points to a

Pre-Columbian-inspired sculpture, Quilmes.

still simple political organization. The Aguada complex (mostly from Catamarca and La Rioja) is a good representative of this period.

The Late Ceramic Period, AD 850–1480, witnessed some changes. Settlements became larger, some in defensible locations, and thick walls made of round stones are found in many sites. Roads, cemeteries, irrigation works, and what were probably ceremonial centers gradually began to appear.

The ceramic urn (used for the burial of children) is one of the markers of the period. These vessels (40–60cm/16–24ins in height) often have painted human faces showing what could be tear marks. Other markers are beautiful metal disks or breastplates lavishly decorated with human head and snake motifs.

The region which encompasses the southern half of the country, from Santa Fe and Córdoba to the southernmost islands, had very little permanent architecture. Many of the groups here were nomadic and erected temporary settlements with simple houses of branches or hides. Almost no agriculture was practiced, with hunting (both on land and at sea) and gathering playing important roles. Pottery was either not known or, when made, very crude.

CIVILIZATION IN THE NORTHWEST

What is now Argentina's Northwest was unquestionably the most culturally developed area. Throughout the centuries this area received the influences that diffused from Bolivia (during the peak of the Tiahuanaco Empire, about 1,000 years ago) and Peru (especially during the expansion of the Inca Empire, which incorporated northwestern Argentina within its great realm).

The early 16th century found the natives of the Northwest living in architecturally simple stone houses, in towns with populations that might have reached 5,000 people in some cases (such as at Quilmes, the largest known pre-Columbian settlement in the country; see page 235), making this area the most densely inhabited.

Many of the towns were walled, located on hill tops for defense purposes, and had their own ceremonial buildings. Intensive agriculture and irrigation were practiced everywhere and domestic animals, mostly camelids such as the llama and alpaca, were widely used for transportation, wool, and meat.

Most of the arts had reached a high level of development by the 16th century; good ceramics, woodcarvings, excellent metalworking (mostly consisting of copper and bronze pieces), and stone sculptures have been found, relics of the different groups living in the area. Tribes and confederations of tribes were the units of political organization.

FROM THE CENTRAL MOUNTAINS TO THE NORTHEAST

The Central Mountains and the region around Santiago del Estero were less developed. Small villages existed in this region, in some cases with semi-subterranean houses. Although agriculture was practiced, hunting and gathering still played an important role. Ceramics were made but were rather crude, and little or no metal was worked in the area. Many of the metal pieces were imported from the Northwest.

Life in the northeastern region of Argentina had many of the characteristics of that in the Central Mountains, except that the presence of two major rivers, the Paraná and the Uruguay, added a new dimension to the region's economies: fishing. Although pottery was known, metallurgy seems to have been absent. Unfortunately, to date this is one of the less archeologically studied areas of the country.

ENTER THE INCAS

Finally, in AD 1480, the invading forces of the Incas arrived, led by Topa Inca. This period saw the peak expansion of the vast Inca Empire, as they conquered what was to become the northwest region of Argentina. Remains of Inca roads, *tambos* (places of rest, supply, and storage), and *pucarás* (forts) can be found in the region. The Incas introduced their well-formed styles and artistic values and many of the pieces of this period are little more than local reproductions of original Inca pieces.

One interesting aspect of the Inca ascendancy, shared with the Roman Empire of earlier times, is that the conquerors were more concerned with dominating their new subjects in the political and economic spheres than with imposing their cultural and religious norms on them. Within limits, the indigenous population of the

Northwest was allowed to keep its time-honored rituals. One aspect of Inca culture that did penetrate the region was the rite of child sacrifice, as vividly illustrated by the mummified remains of the so-called "Children of Llullaillaco" exhibited in Salta's MAAM museum (see page 227).

THE CONQUEST

When the first Spaniards arrived in Argentina in the early 16th century, it is thought that there were perhaps 500,000 indigenous people, living in numerous scattered groups. Two-thirds of

Ruins of the Quilmes civilization, a Diaguita culture.

them were estimated to live in the Northwest of the country, or in the central highlands of Córdoba and San Luis, which is where the Comechingones lived. Further south were the Tehuelche tribes, referred to by the Spaniards as "Pampa Indians," and the "Patagones" of Patagonia.

The first native inhabitants to encounter the Spaniards were probably the nomadic Querandí of the pampas, who lived in temporary shelters and hunted with bolas, weighted balls on leather thongs. In common with all the other indigenous groups, they had no horses, did not use the wheel for transport, and had no gunpowder or firearms. This meant that though they resisted the Europeans for several decades, their technology was no match for the invaders.

ENAS AERES

A satirical view of the conflicts between the Spanish conquistadors and the Amerindians.

FROM CONQUEST TO INDEPENDENCE

The Spanish invasion brought European civilization to Argentina, but by the 19th century the people were keen to break free from their distant rulers.

The first half of the 16th century was a period of intense exploration on behalf of the Portuguese and Spanish crowns. Not quite 10 years after Columbus' first voyage to the New World, Amerigo Vespucci was probing the eastern shores of South America. Today, many credit him with the European discovery of the Río de la Plata, although standard Argentine accounts cite Juan de Solís as the first European to sail these waters.

Solís reached the Río de la Plata estuary in 1516 and named the river Mar Dulce, or Sweet Sea. Not long after, while Solís was leading a small party ashore, he was killed by Charrúa tribesmen, along with all but one of the sailors accompanying him. After killing the Spaniards, the natives proceeded to eat them in full view of the rest of the crew still on board ship.

In 1520, Ferdinand Magellan, on his voyage to the Pacific, was the next explorer to reach what is now Argentina. Then came Sebastian Cabot. Sailing under the Spanish flag, and drawn by rumors of a mountain of silver, he was the next to venture into the Río de la Plata region in 1526. He reached modern-day Paraguay, where Guaraní tribespeople gave him some metal trinkets. Thus inspired, Cabot named the muddy stretch of water the Rio de la Plata (River of Silver).

Also drawn by reports of great wealth in the region, the Spanish nobleman Pedro de Mendoza led a large expedition to the area. On February 3, 1536, he founded Santa María del Buen Ayre. The natives were at first helpful, but then they turned furiously against the Spaniards. As one of Mendoza's soldiers wrote: "The indians attacked our city of Buenos Aires with great force... There were around 23,000 of them... While some of them were attacking us, others

Mural depicting the resettlement of Buenos Aires.

were shooting burning arrows at our houses..." The natives finally retreated under the fire of Spanish artillery.

Mendoza and his men never did locate any great mineral wealth and left Buenos Aires to eventually found Asunción in Paraguay.

A second group of Spaniards, this time approaching overland from Chile, Peru, and Upper Peru (today's Bolivia), was more successful in founding lasting settlements. The Northwest towns of Santiago del Estero, Catamarca, Mendoza, Tucumán, Córdoba, Salta, La Rioja, and Jujuy were all founded in the second half of the 16th century, with Santiago del Estero being Argentina's oldest outpost (founded in 1551).

DOMINANCE OF THE NORTHWEST

Throughout the 17th century and during most of the 18th, the Northwest was the center of activity in Argentina. This was mostly due to protectionism on the part of the King of Spain, who in 1554 prohibited traffic on the Río de la Plata. Manufactured goods from Spain and enslaved Africans were shipped in a South American triangular trade via Panama and then Peru. The king's ruling was of great benefit to the Spanish colonial cities of Lima (the capital of the Viceroyalty of Peru) and Mexico City but meant that the

Rampant Spaniards on the hunt in 1586.

> The University of Córdoba is Argentina's oldest university (and the second oldest in South America). It was founded by the Jesuits in 1613 to instruct pupils in philosophy and theology.

Río de la Plata estuary remained isolated and commercially backward.

While Argentina was part of the Peruvian viceroyalty until 1776, two areas of the colony became important centers. Tucumán developed into a successful agricultural region, supplying wheat, corn, cotton, tobacco, and livestock to neighboring Upper Peru. Somewhat later, Córdoba

attained status as a center of learning, with the establishment of the Jesuit university in 1613.

Córdoba also prospered economically, owing to its central location and fertile lands. By contrast, Buenos Aires, which had been refounded in 1580 by Juan de Garay, was a small town that relied on smuggling for its income. Because all manufactured goods had to come the long route from Spain via Panama, prices were very high, and this led to flourishing contraband traffic.

THE VICEROYALTY OF RÍO DE LA PLATA

The decline of the Andean mining industries, coupled with growing calls for direct transatlantic trade, finally persuaded the Spanish Crown to establish the new viceroyalty of Río de la Plata, with its administrative center at Buenos Aires.

With a new viceroyalty, which included Argentina, Uruguay, Paraguay, and parts of Upper Peru, Spain hoped to exert greater control over a region that was growing in importance. Buenos Aires experienced an explosion in population, increasing its numbers from 2,200 in 1726 to more than 33,000 by 1778. Upwards of a quarter of this rapidly growing population was Afro-Argentine and still held in bondage. Many others were of mixed Amerindian and Spanish parentage, a consequence of the fact that the Spanish population in the viceroyalty was predominantly male.

Some of these mixed-race Argentines settled on the pampas, where they lived off the many thousands of cattle that ran wild, becoming superb horsemen thanks to the huge numbers of horses that had also escaped. In time, these horsemen became the famous gauchos, whose free, nomadic lifestyle was in strong contrast to the niceties of Buenos Aires.

The growing importance of the viceroyalty of the Río de la Plata did not go unnoticed in Europe. The Franco-Hispanic alliance during the Napoleonic Wars (1804–15) resulted in a loosening of Argentina's ties with the motherland when Spain's fleet was destroyed by the British Navy. This meant that the Spanish colonies in Latin America were open for British attention.

THE BRITISH INVASIONS

In 1806, and again the following year, the British invaded Buenos Aires. During the first invasion, the inept Spanish viceroy fled to Montevideo, across the Río de la Plata, taking with him many of his troops. The retaking of the city was left to Santiago de Liniers, a French officer serving in the Spanish Army, who organized the remaining Spanish troops and the local inhabitants. The British were quickly routed but were to return soon afterwards.

After seizing Montevideo in spring 1807, the British tried to recapture Buenos Aires with an army of 10,000. They were met by Liniers and his men, and by women pelting them with roof tiles and (legend has it) pouring boiling water on them from above. The English commander of the expedition promptly evacuated his troops.

Aires deposed the Spanish viceroy and created a revolutionary junta to rule in his stead.

Bernardino Rivadavia, Manuel Belgrano, and Mariano Moreno were three criollo intellectuals

> *When British troops invaded Buenos Aires for the second time in 1807, the city's streets were turned into what they later called "pathways of death" and the British were forced to surrender.*

The first British invasion, 1806.

Beyond the immediate consequences of repelling the invaders, a number of important effects stemmed from the confrontations with the British. Pride in the colony was a natural outcome of having defeated a large and well-trained army with a mostly local militia. In addition, tensions arose between the criollos (Argentine-born colonists) and the Spanish administration. Thoughts of developing an economy without the strictures and regulations of a distant Crown in Spain began to enter the minds of leading criollos.

INDEPENDENCE AND ITS AFTERMATH

Napoleon Bonaparte's invasion of Spain in 1808 provided the final push for a rupture in relations; a *cabildo abierto* (open town council) in Buenos

who, inspired by European liberal thought, channeled their energies toward the creation of a new nation based on a re-ordering of colonial society. Naturally enough, the old order – rich merchants, *estancieros* (large landowners), members of the clergy, and, indeed, the whole colonial administration – was violently opposed to anything that might compromise its status in the country.

This lack of unity made the realization of an independent nation much more of a tortured process than the criollo intellectuals could have imagined. Indeed, a civil war was in the making following what the Argentines call the May Revolution. On May 25, 1810, an autonomous government was set up in Buenos Aires. This date is still celebrated in Argentina as the birthday of independence, although a formal declaration was not made until six years later.

These early years were not easy; the people of the viceroyalty were split along political, class, and regional lines, setting a Buenos Aires elite against the loyalists from the interior provinces. The *Unitarios* (Unitarians) were intent on having a strong central government, to be based entirely in offices in the capital, Buenos Aires. Meanwhile, the *Federales* (Federalists) campaigned for a loose confederation of autonomous provinces.

The formal declaration of independence on July 9, 1816, in Tucumán.

A confusing series of juntas, triumvirates, and assemblies rose and fell, as one group gained the upper hand for a brief period only to lose the advantage to another. The eight original jurisdictions of the viceroyalty dwindled to three, and these then fragmented into seven provinces.

A congress was called to maintain whatever unity was left. On July 9, 1816, the congress at Tucumán formally declared independence under the blue and white banner of the United Provinces of South America.

JOSÉ DE SAN MARTÍN

The task of ridding the continent of Spanish armies remained. José de San Martín was to execute one of the boldest moves of the South American wars of independence. Gathering a large army, San Martín crossed the icy Andes at Mendoza in 21 days (a feat English essayist and near contemporary Thomas Carlyle compared to Hannibal's march over the Alps) and met and defeated Spanish soldiers at Chacabuco in Chile (1817). He again engaged the Spaniards, this time at Maipú (1818), where he ended Spanish rule in Chile once and for all.

San Martín then amassed a fleet of mostly British and US ships to convoy his army the 2,400km (1,500 miles) to Lima in Peru. The Spanish army evacuated the city without fighting, wishing to keep their forces intact. It was at this time, in 1822, that San Martín met the other great liberator of South America, Venezuelan Simón Bolívar, at Guayaquil. What was discussed at this meeting is not known and has kept historians speculating ever since. The upshot, though, was San Martín's retirement from battle, leaving the remaining honors to be garnered by Bolívar.

San Martín was posthumously elevated to a position of sainthood by the Argentines. Today, every town in Argentina has a street named after him and every classroom a portrait of the general crossing the Andes on a gallant white horse.

It was a different story, however, when he returned to Buenos Aires in 1823 from his campaigns on behalf of Argentina. He received no acknowledgment for the services he had rendered his country. Soon afterwards San Martín left for France, where he was to die in obscurity in Boulogne.

⊘ A CHARISMATIC LEADER

Basil Hall, a contemporary of José de San Martín's, described him thus: "There was little, at first sight, in his appearance to engage attention; but when he rose up and began to speak, his great superiority over every other person...was sufficiently apparent...a tall, erect, well-proportioned, handsome man, with a large aquiline nose, thick black hair, and immense bushy whiskers...his complexion is deep olive, and his eye, which is large, prominent and piercing, jet black; his whole appearance being highly military...The contest in Peru, he said, was a war of new and liberal principles against prejudice, bigotry and tyranny."

THE CASE OF THE AFRO-ARGENTINES

Argentina's once sizable black population had all but vanished by the turn of the 20th century. What happened to them?

Argentina's greatest puzzle is the vanished Afro-Argentines. Historians throughout the years have offered diverse explanations, while curious laypersons are ready with stories that range from the plausible to the ludicrous.

Argentines of African heritage existed in large numbers – comprising 30 percent of the Buenos Aires population for almost 40 years (1778–1815). Slaves were first brought to Argentina in the 16th century by their Spanish owners. Due to the peculiar trading arrangements with the Spanish Crown, most slaves were imported to Buenos Aires via Panama and Peru and then overland from Chile, thereby greatly increasing their price. Others were brought in illegally, directly to Buenos Aires or from Brazil.

Argentine slaves were generally domestic servants but also filled the growing need for artisans in the labor-short colony. While the degree of their labor differed greatly from that of plantation workers in Brazil and the United States, they suffered similarly. Families were torn apart, gruesome punishments awaited runaways, and the status of black people in society was kept low, even after emancipation.

Black Argentines are recorded as having fought bravely in the struggle for independence and in San Martín's armies. Partly as a result of this, black and mixed-race slaves were declared free in 1813, although formal legislation was only passed in 1853. One early-1800s law stipulated that the children of slaves would be free upon birth, though their mothers would remain slaves. However, it was not unusual for slave owners to spirit their pregnant slaves to Uruguay, where slavery was still legal, and then bring both mother and child back to Argentina as slaves.

The North American professor George Reid Andrews has done much research to uncover the fate of the black population in his important work, *The Afro-Argentines of Buenos Aires, 1800–1900* (1980). He offers no definitive conclusions, but he has explored in depth some of the more likely theories.

Reid Andrews offers four possible explanations for the disappearance of the Afro-Argentines. The first is that many of the men were killed fighting in the wars of independence, and in the War of the Triple Alliance against Paraguay in 1865. Another reason could be their gradual absorption into the general population with the arrival of European immigrants from the

An Afro-Argentine street vendor, a common sight in mid-19th-century Buenos Aires.

1860s onwards. The great yellow fever epidemic of 1871 and the general ill health and horrendous living conditions of the black population is also cited as a possible factor. Finally, Andrews explores the decline of the slave trade (outlawed in 1813) and its impact on a community that would not have its numbers refreshed with new shipments of human chattel.

Census figures for Buenos Aires from 1836 to 1887 show a steep decline in the numbers and percentages of black people, from a figure of 14,906 or 26 percent of the total population to 8,005 or 1.8 percent.

After the early 19th century, Afro-Argentines to all intents and purposes disappeared. One must sift through prints and photographs of the late 1800s to discover that this group, although in decline, remained a part of the greater community. In these pictures we see Afro-Argentines working as gauchos, street vendors or artisans in Buenos Aires. Most modern Argentines would be surprised by these images: the contributions black people made to Argentine society have, for the most part, been written out of history.

Morning mate in an upper-class salon.

TRAVELERS' TALES

Travelers in the 18th and 19th centuries painted a colorful picture of Argentina as a country where wild-west violence was a part of daily life.

Today's traveler to Argentina follows in some illustrious footsteps. While Magellan and the early Spanish discoverers left vivid records of their voyages, it was in the 19th century that scientists such as Alexander von Humboldt and Charles Darwin began to take a closer scientific interest in the land, its inhabitants, and its flora and fauna. The impressions that they and others recorded in their essays and travel diaries are fascinating because they give an outsider's perspective on what was then an obscure country at the end of the known world.

The reader of travel literature, especially of the 18th- and 19th-century vintage, discovers many of the wonders of Argentina that no longer exist. These fabulous tales need to be approached somewhat cautiously because many of the travelers neither spoke the language nor necessarily understood the events unfolding before them. Nonetheless, these accounts provide the color and flavor that is sometimes missing from published scientific diaries.

Travelers in the late 19th-century.

THE CITY OF GOOD AIR – AND PUBLIC EXECUTIONS

The 19th-century traveler would often commence his or her itinerary in Buenos Aires. Charles Darwin, in 1833, described the city as "large and I should think one of the most regular in the world. Every street is at right angles to the one it crosses, and the parallel ones being equidistant, the houses are collected into solid squares of equal dimensions, which are called *quadras*."

Writing 10 years after Darwin, Colonel J. Anthony King commented that: "The market place of Buenos Ayres [*sic*] is... the center of all public rejoicings, public executions, and popular gatherings. It is in the market place

that Rosas hung up the bodies of many of his victims, sometimes decorating them... with ribbons of the Unitarian color [blue], and attaching to the corpses labels, on which were inscribed the revolting words, 'Beef with the hide'."

J.P. and W.P. Robertson wrote a series of letters from South America, which they published in 1843. What first impressed them were the methods of transportation in the city. "Nothing strikes one more on a first arrival in Buenos Aires than the carts and carters. The former are vehicles with large wooden axles, and most enormous wheels, so high that the spokes are about 8 feet [2 meters] in diameter, towering above both horses and driver; he rides one of these animals... The first sight you have of these clumsy vehicles is on your landing. They drive off like so many bathing-machines to your hotel, a dozen carters, just like a dozen porters here, struggling...for the preference in carrying ashore passengers and their luggage."

Even in the mid-19th century, travelers to Buenos Aires were impressed by how much of a melting pot the city was. Writing in 1853, Scottish traveler William McCann expressed his amazement: "The varieties of complexion and costume, including specimens of the human race from almost every country of the world, and the Babel of tongues from all nations, so confound the senses that it is difficult to describe the effect. Surely no other city in the world could present such a motley assemblage; and the diversity of physiognomy is so great that one might doubt if mankind are all descended from a common stock." (From *Two Thousand Mile Ride Through the Argentine Provinces*.)

LIFE ON THE FRONTIER

Dangers on the road were certainly plentiful for both traveler and native alike. Francis Bond

Boleadora-wielding Amerindians on the pampas.

⊘ A MINISTER'S MUSINGS

G.L. Morrill, a US minister who wrote about Buenos Aires in his *To Hell and Back: My Trip to South America* (1914), had this to say about the cosmopolitan nature of the Argentine capital: "An afternoon walk shows the city very much like Paris in its architecture, fashionable stores, cafés and sidewalks filled with little tables where males and females flirt and gossip. There are newspaper kiosks and flower girls selling violets on the corners. The side streets are crowded with cars and carts and the main avenues with taxis which rest in the center or rush up and down either side. At nights it is a big white way with electric lights blazing a trail to the cafés and theaters."

Head, an English mining engineer who spent two tempestuous years, 1825–6, in the Argentine outback, and whose book *Rough Notes Taken During Some Rapid Journeys Across the Pampas and Among the Andes* is one of the best travelogues on Latin America, was well prepared for the violence he knew he would face.

Head wrote that, "In crossing the pampas it is absolutely necessary to be armed, as there are many robbers or *saltadors*, particularly in the desolate province of Santa Fe. The object of these people is of course money, and I therefore always rode so badly dressed, and so well armed that although I once passed through them with no one but a child as a postilion, they thought it not worth their while to attack me. I always carried two brace of detonating pistols in a belt, and a short detonating double-barreled gun in my hand. I made it a rule never to be an instant without my arms, and to cock both barrels of my gun whenever I met any gauchos."

Head, aptly named "Galloping Head," describes the dangers Amerindians posed. "A person riding can use no precaution, but must just run the gauntlet, and take his chance, which, if calculated, is a good one. If he fall in with them, he may be tortured and killed, but it is very improbable that he should happen to find them

One of Galloping Head's fondest wishes was to be able to spend time with the native South American. "His profession is war, his food simple, and his body is in that state of health and vigor that he can rise naked from the plain on which he has slept, and proudly look upon his image which the white frost has marked out upon the grass without inconvenience. What can we 'men in buckram' say to this?"

E. Lucas Bridges, whose *Uttermost Part of the Earth* (1948) chronicles his encounters with and impressions of the natives of Tierra

Indigenous settlement on the Sierra de la Ventana pampas.

on the road; however, they are so cunning, and ride so quick, and the country is so uninhabited, that it is impossible to gain any information."

ENCOUNTERS WITH AMERINDIANS

Meeting an Amerindian could be a high point of a journey, as Lady Florence Dixie related in her *Across Patagonia* (1881). "We had not gone far when we saw a rider coming slowly towards us, and in a few minutes we found ourselves in the presence of a real Patagonia Indian. We reined in our horses when he got close to us, to have a good look at him, and he doing the same, for a few minutes we stared at him to our hearts' content, receiving in return as minute and careful a scrutiny from him."

del Fuego (the Yamana), noted "the fair division of labor between the sexes. The men gathered fuel and fungus for food, while the women cooked, fetched water, paddled the canoes and fished...Being in charge of the canoes...the women were also good swimmers, but it was a rare thing to find a male Yamana who could swim."

COUNTRY LIFE

The gauchos were often perceived as being as wild as the Amerindians – and just as interesting. Additionally, the gauchos and others living in the countryside were noted for their hospitality. Colonel King writes that, "whether in health or sickness, the traveler is always welcome to their houses and boards, and they would as soon as think of charging for a cup of water, as for a meal of victual or a night's lodging."

Darwin, too, was greatly struck by their manners. "The gauchos, or countrymen, are very superior to those who reside in the towns. The gaucho is invariably most obliging, polite, and hospitable. I did not meet with even one instance of rudeness or inhospitality." And once, when Darwin inquired whether there was enough food for him to have a meal, he was told, "We have meat for the dogs in

limb. Little hairless dogs are in great request to sleep at the feet of invalids."

Travelers were greatly impressed by the skills gauchos showed as they worked their horses, threw bolas to fell cassowaries – the South American ostrich – or lassoed cattle. Darwin witnessed such a sight: "I was amused by the dexterity with which a gaucho forced a...horse to swim a river. He stripped off his clothes, and jumping on its back rode into the river till it was out of its depth; then slipping off over the crupper, he caught hold of the tail, and as often as

Nineteenth-century engraving of gauchos in Tucumán.

Darwin described the trials of the terrain. "Changing horses for the last time, we again began wading through the mud. My animal fell, and I was well soused in black mire – a very disagreeable accident."

the horse turned around, the man frightened it back by splashing water in its face. As soon as the horse touched bottom on the other side, the man pulled himself on, and was firmly seated, bridle in hand, before the horse gained the bank. A naked man on a naked horse is a fine spectacle; I had no idea how well the two animals suited each other. The tail of a horse is a very useful appendage."

UNTAMED LANDSCAPE

our country, and therefore do not grudge it to a Christian."

In the country, far from doctors and hospitals, the people often relied on an assortment of folk medicine. Darwin was appalled at the remedies: "One of the least nasty is to kill and cut open two puppies and bind them on each side of a broken

The size of the country and the rough paths made the traveler's trip through Argentina a very long one indeed. E.E. Vidal, another early 19th-century traveler, quotes the unnamed author of *Letters from Paraguay*, who describes his trip from Buenos Aires to Mendoza, at the foot of the Andes, as taking 22 days in a large cart drawn by oxen. "We set off every afternoon about two, and sometimes three hours before sunset, and did not halt till about an hour after sunrise."

Having a sufficient supply of water was one of the obstacles the writer faced in his journey. "We were obliged to halt in a spot, where even the grass seemed to have been burned to the very roots, and nothing was presented to the eye but barrenness and desolation... We had but

Many travelers commented on the seemingly endless flat pampas. W.J. Holland, a US scientist on an expedition to Argentina in 1912, described the scene from his train compartment. "I have crossed the prairies of Minnesota and the Dakotas, of Kansas and Nebraska, of Manitoba and Alberta; I have traveled over the steppes of Russia; but in none of them have I seen such absolutely level lands as those which lie between Rosario and Irigoyen. The horizon is that of the ocean; an upturned clod attracts attention; a hut looks like a house; a tree looms up like a hill."

Darwin's research vessel, the HMS Beagle.

one small jar of water left, our thirst seemed to increase every moment."

Some of the most poetic descriptions of Argentine rural life in the 19th century were written by W.H. Hudson. Born in Argentina of a family from New England, as an old man he recalled his childhood on the pampas in books such as *Far Away and Long Ago*: "We see all around us a flat land, its horizon a perfect ring of misty blue color where the crystal-blue dome of the sky rests on the level green world. Green in late autumn, winter, and spring, or say from April to November, but not at all like a green lawn or field: there were smooth areas where sheep had pastured, but the surface varied greatly and was mostly more or less rough."

LIFE IN BUENOS AIRES

In 1870 the Scottish writer and cattle rancher Robert Cunninghame Graham wrote of a central hotel in Buenos Aires: "Just at the corner of the streets called Twenty-fifth of May and Calle de Cangallo stood Claraz's hotel...The life of Buenos Aires ran before the door. Only three squares away, the two great Plazas, with their palaces and barracks, basked in the sun, or shivered in the wind, according as the Pampero whistled, or the hot north wind blew. The Stock Exchange was near, and up the deep-cut Calle de Cangallo, which looked more like a dry canal than a great thoroughfare, stood several of the principal hotels."

For female travelers, however, the capital was not always so welcoming. The North

American Katherine S. Dreier described what she had to contend with in Buenos Aires in 1918. "Before leaving for Buenos Aires everybody in New York told me that the Plaza Hotel was the only hotel in Buenos Aires, and that of course I would make it my headquarters during my sojourn there. But my information had been given me by men, and neither they nor I expected to find that the Plaza did not take women unaccompanied by their husbands or supposed husbands. Not even sisters accompanied by their brothers, or wives heat of argument, smoke cigarettes between the courses, and even while a course of which some of them do not partake is serving – a soothing habit which stimulates expectoration and provokes discussion – use the same knife and fork for every course – fish, entree, or joint, in a word, the studied deportment of the street is, in the house, exchanged for the coarse manners of the tap-room."

Turner was also shocked at the way politics dominated discussions, something that still is prevalent. "Although forbidden subjects are

A pulpería – multi-purpose saloon, general store, and community social center on the pampas.

whose husbands have to travel, or widows, are made welcome. Much less respectable maiden ladies!"

FOOD AND POLITICS

Thomas Turner, describing one well-known and wealthy family at supper in the 1880s had this to say: "Of the domestic habits of the Argentines, their manners at table, *en famille*, it is impossible to give an attractive description. Their manners at table are ultra-Bohemian. They read the papers, shout vehemently at each other, sprawl their limbs under and over the table, half swallow their knives, spit with true Yankee freedom on the carpeted floor, gesticulate and bend across the table in the discussed by both sexes with zest and freedom, the staple topic of conversation is politics. Everybody talks politics... Even children talk politics, and discuss the merits of this, that or other statesmen with parrot-like freedom of opinion and soundness of judgment."

Argentina has always attracted travelers, drawn to its vast empty spaces and to the mix of people living there. Whether positive or critical, these wanderers and explorers have passed on the country's lore through their writing, which might otherwise have been lost to us. Taken together, they chart the rise of the nation from being an insignificant part of a vast empire to a modern, outward-looking country with a rich heritage.

A 19th-century gentleman farmer.

Two 19th-century gentlemen in traditional dress.

CAUDILLOS, TYRANTS AND DEMAGOGUES

The dark side of Argentina's 200-year march toward liberty and democracy has been the all-too-common descent into dictatorship and military rule.

The years from independence to the start of the dictatorship of Juan Manuel de Rosas in 1829 were difficult for the United Provinces of the Río de la Plata. Bernardino Rivadavia, a man of great vision, valiantly but vainly attempted to shape the country's future.

Rivadavia was interested in establishing a constitution for the nation, forming a strong central government, dividing up the land into more equitable shares, and attracting immigrants to settle in the United Provinces. His plans were quickly sidetracked, however, both by caudillos in the interior, who were none too anxious to surrender any of their power, and by the draining Cisplatine War (1825–8) with Brazil over the status of Uruguay. When Rivadavia resigned from the presidency of the United Provinces in 1827 and went into exile, there remained little to show for his years of effort.

JUAN MANUEL DE ROSAS: CAUDILLO AND TYRANT

Juan Manuel de Rosas, who ruled much of Argentina as his personal fiefdom for more than 20 years, is one of the most intriguing, if bloodthirsty, figures in Latin American history. In his quest for power, Rosas forged a coalition of gauchos, wealthy landowners, and others.

Although born in Buenos Aires in 1793, Rosas was a product of the open pampas. It was here on his family's estancia that he learned to ride and herd cattle. Rosas became as skilled in these pursuits as any of the gauchos with whom he kept company, gaining their respect and later their support.

Rosas became wealthy in his own right at an early age. By his mid-twenties, he owned thousands of acres of land and was a successful

The tyrant Juan Manuel de Rosas.

businessman. He chose well when he married María de la Encarnación Escurra, the daughter of another rich family.

To stem the rising tide of anarchy that followed the exile of Rivadavia, Rosas was asked to become the governor of the province of Buenos Aires in 1829. Rosas, a powerful caudillo and experienced military man, seemed the perfect individual to restore order and stability.

The problem with the Federalists was that there was little unity among the various factions. Those in the provinces demanded autonomy and an equal footing with Buenos Aires, while those espousing the Federalist cause in Argentina's major city were not willing to surrender their premier position. As governor with extraordinary powers, in 1831 Rosas signed the Federal Pact, which tied together the provinces of Buenos Aires, Entre Ríos, Santa Fe, and Corrientes.

The opposition to Rosas, the Unitarian League, was dealt a severe blow when its leader, José María Paz, was unhorsed by a Federalist soldier wielding *boleadoras*. Paz was jailed by Rosas. By 1832, the Unitarians had suffered a number of reverses on the battlefield and, for the moment, did not pose a great threat to the Federalists.

When Rosas' first term as governor ended in 1832, he refused to accept another stint in office

A Rosas soldier in Federalist colors.

⊘ THE KILLING GAME

Under Juan Manuel de Rosas, horrific methods of silencing opponents became institutionalized. Castration and tongue extraction were common means of torture. The favored manner of despatching prisoners was throat-cutting, reflecting the tradition of the gauchos. W.H. Hudson, naturalist and chronicler of the pampas, wrote that the Argentines "loved to kill a man not with a bullet but in a manner to make them know and feel that they were really and truly killing." Another method employed was lancing: two executioners standing on either side of the prisoner would plunge lances into the body. The dead were then disposed of in mass unmarked graves.

because the council of provincial representatives was unwilling to allow him to maintain his virtually unlimited authority.

ROSAS REDUX

Even out of power, Rosas continued to fight. He took command of the campaign against the native Argentine tribes in the south, and earned himself even more dubious glory by wiping out thousands of Amerindians.

While Rosas was campaigning in the south, his wife waged an underground campaign to have her husband reinstated as governor of Buenos Aires, forming the *Sociedad Popular Restauradora* and its terror wing, the *mazorca*. Doña Encarnación effectively hampered the efforts to rule of the three governors who followed Rosas.

The junta finally acquiesced to Rosas' demands and he assumed his post as Restorer of the Laws and governor in a regal ceremony on April 13, 1835. The red color of the Federalists became a distinguishing factor. Women wore scarlet dresses, while men wore red badges that proclaimed "Federation or Death." Decorating in blue, the color of the "savage Unitarians," could be cause for imprisonment or even execution.

ROSAS' REIGN OF TERROR

While Rosas did not create the brutal methods of repression that so characterized his regime, he did give a certain order and system to them in making himself supreme dictator. Generally speaking, Rosas' victims were not massacred wholesale but rather executed on an individual basis. Long lists of suspected Unitarians and the property they possessed were drawn up by Rosas' effective spy network, the police, the military, and justices of the peace. The actual numbers of those who perished remains unclear, but estimates range in the thousands. Whatever the number, Rosas created and maintained a climate of fear for more than 20 years.

With Rosas at the helm, Argentina did not prosper. He meddled in the affairs of neighboring Uruguay, but was never able to conquer its capital, Montevideo.

In response to the atmosphere of terror and lack of freedom, Argentines organized in secret, and some in exile, to overthrow Rosas. These intellectuals, whose ranks included such luminaries as Bartolomé Mitre, Juan

Bautista Alberdi, and Domingo Faustino Sarmiento, provided the rhetoric which galvanized the opposition.

Justo José de Urquiza, a caudillo who had long supported Rosas, turned against the Restorer and organized an army that soon included thousands of volunteers, and even many Uruguayans and Brazilians. On February 3, 1852, Urquiza's army engaged Rosas' demoralized and rebellion-weary troops at Caseros, near Buenos Aires. "The battle," as Mitre later wrote, "was won before it was fought." A new age in Argen-

was held in the city of Santa Fe and this meeting produced a document modeled on the Constitution of the United States.

The Argentine constitution was accepted by the convention on May 1, 1853. Not surprisingly, Urquiza was chosen as the first president. During his tenure he established a national bank, built schools, and improved transportation in the republic. But the role of Buenos Aires was still uncertain. There were, in fact, two Argentinas, one in wealthy Buenos Aires and the other in the interior with its capital at Paraná. A con-

Amerindians captured during the Desert Campaign.

tina's history had begun, with Urquiza intent on consolidating the nation as one unit and not a collection of semi-independent provinces; progress in all areas came quickly.

STATE FOUNDATIONS

The period from Rosas' downfall to 1880 was a time of organizing the nation-state and establishing the institutions required to run it. The major conflict of this period was an old one: the status of Buenos Aires in relation to the interior. This issue was finally settled in 1880 by federalizing the city and making it something like the District of Columbia in the United States.

Urquiza's first task was to draw up a constitution for Argentina. A constitutional convention

gress met in Buenos Aires in 1862 and decided that Buenos Aires would become the capital of both the republic and the province.

WAR AND PEACE

Bartolomé Mitre, historian and former governor of the province of Buenos Aires, became the next president. Although the task of creating a national infrastructure was of great importance to Mitre, he found himself distracted by the Paraguayan War (1865–70). It took five years of bloody fighting for the triple alliance of Brazil, Uruguay, and Argentina to subdue the Paraguayan dictator Francisco Solano López.

Mitre was succeeded by Domingo Faustino Sarmiento, whose role in promoting education in Argentina has taken on mythic proportions. It was during Sarmiento's administration (1868–74) that Argentina's progress soared. Hundreds of thousands of immigrants poured into the city of Buenos Aires, railroads were built, and the use of barbed-wire fencing spread, controlling the open range. Sarmiento continually stressed the need to push for a removal of the "barbaric" elements within Argentine society, namely the caudillos and the gauchos.

Following Sarmiento came President Nicolás Avellaneda, whose inauguration in October 1874

GOLDEN AGE

The next three decades saw a golden age in Argentina. New methods for chilling and then freezing meat, innovations in shipping, and the construction of rail networks all made possible intensive ranching and farming. The amount of cultivated land multiplied 15 times from 1872 to 1895, and cereal exports exploded between 1870 and 1900. Behind this accelerated economic growth lay the increased demand for foodstuffs in Europe. By the 1880s, the territory of Argentina had

Military college students and citizens celebrate the revolution of September 6, 1930, in which General Uriburu ousted President Hipólito Yrigoyen.

almost did not happen. Mitre, fearing a decline in Buenos Aires' prestige at the hands of such non-*porteños* (non-residents of Buenos Aires) as Sarmiento, Avellaneda, and Julio Roca (none of whom lived in the capital), led a revolt against the government. It took three months to crush this rebellion.

As Avellaneda's minister of war, Roca headed a series of expeditions against the natives of Patagonia in the infamous Conquest of the Desert which was concluded by 1879. Many thousands of square miles were opened up for settlement and exploration after this war, but the indigenous population never recovered.

almost reached the boundaries of today, although it would be many more years before the exact borders with Chile in Patagonia and Tierra del Fuego were settled.

The new meat and cereals economy required workers, and by the 1890s Argentina was receiving thousands of immigrants – mostly Italian and Spanish. The population grew from 1.8 million in 1869 to more than 4 million by 1895. These immigrants were attracted to Argentina because of the promise of "land, a house, and a job." However, families often had to live in crowded tenements known as *conventillos*, while the men went out to try to find the third thing promised: a job.

There was a corresponding growth in the intellectual field as well. Newspapers were founded, political parties sprang up, books were published, and a world-class opera house, the Teatro Colón, opened in Buenos Aires.

This is not to say that all was well in Argentina. Politics remained closed to most Argentines; a few had taken it upon themselves to run the country. The middle class, supporting the new political party, the Radical Civic Union, pressed for entry into what had been a government run by a small group of conserva-

to fill domestic demand as imports fell by 50 percent. This industrial boom revealed weaknesses in the Argentine economy – dependence on imported raw materials, lack of energy resource development, and a lack of capital – that would become crucial during the Great Depression, when the nation once more relied on local production.

The Radical Party came to power for the first time in 1916. Under Hipólito Yrigoyen, the Radicals introduced social security and other measures that benefited the middle and work-

Perón and Evita soak up their supporters' adulation from the balcony of the Casa Rosada.

tive families. Workers also became politicized and were attracted to the Socialist Party and the anarchists. Strikes hit Argentina at the turn of the 20th century and labor unrest grew. The workers found themselves expendable as the country struggled to pay back international loans and as imports began to exceed exports.

THE EFFECTS OF WORLD WAR I

The war in Europe stimulated the Argentine economy in two ways. First, the belligerents' need for agricultural products skyrocketed. Second, the paralysis of European trade in manufactured goods encouraged local production. Impoverished urban artisans began

ing classes. These liberal policies were seen as a threat by the more conservative sectors of Argentine society, and in 1930 President Yrigoyen was toppled by a military coup. This military intervention set a sad precedent that was to be followed throughout the next half-century.

Weak civilian governments were allowed back after 1937, but by the time of the outbreak of World War II, Argentina was very divided politically and socially. The armed forces largely supported Italy and Germany, and in 1943 carried out another coup when it appeared that a pro-Allies president would be elected. The new military government appointed a young colonel as Minister for War and Labor: Juan Domingo Perón.

THE PERONIST REVOLUTION

Perón's background certainly indicated no pro-labor tendencies. He attended a military college and rose through the ranks as a career officer. While stationed in Italy in 1939 as a military observer, he was impressed by the nationalism of the fascists. He also thought the state's intervention in Italy's economy to be logical. On his return to Argentina, Perón involved himself deeply in the secret military organization, the GOU (*Grupo Obra de Unificación* or Unification Task Force), which was

Duarte, and labor leaders were behind these actions, rallying support for the imprisoned Perón. Within weeks he was free. He would soon marry Eva to legitimize their relationship in the eyes of the voters and the church. Perón sensed correctly that his moment on the national stage had arrived. In the presidential elections of 1946, Perón won with a majority of 54 percent.

In the years immediately following World War II, Argentina's agricultural exports were in great demand throughout Europe. Perón used the economic surplus to nationalize many

The masses turn out for Loyalty Day, 1946.

composed of young agitators bent on remodeling Argentina's political system along the lines of those in Germany and Italy.

Perón used his position to build his power base. His labor reforms – job security, child labor laws, and pensions among them – were immensely popular with the working class. Furthermore, Perón tied union and non-union members together through the national welfare system, a move that assured him control over and allegiance from most workers.

The military became uneasy with Perón's growing power and arrested him. This led to a series of demonstrations, capped by a gigantic display in the Plaza de Mayo by the *descamisados* (the shirtless ones). Perón's consort, Eva

industries – in 1948, he paid the largest check ever known to buy back the railway system from its British owners. Although storm clouds were gathering on the economic horizon, nobody seemed to notice: this was a golden age when every family could eat steak twice a day, and Perón was re-elected in 1951 with a massive 67 percent majority.

It was to be Perón's high-water mark. Severe droughts and a decrease in international prices of grain led to a 50 percent increase in Argentina's trade deficit. Eva Perón's death shortly after her husband's second inauguration left him without one of his most successful organizers and contributed to the malaise of the nation. Perón seemed to lose his willpower and left many decisions to his increasingly radical acolytes.

MIDDLE-CLASS REVOLT

Opposition to Perón grew. As inflation rose and other economic problems mounted, the middle classes became increasingly concerned. To many, he seemed like a dictator, imposing his views through class violence. The church hierarchy felt threatened by Perón's secular views on education, divorce, and prostitution. As in 1930, the armed forces responded by

remained inefficient, costly, uncompetitive, and unable to provide sustained growth. At the same time, continued dependence on imported raw materials and capital goods, vulnerability to agricultural price cycles, and the burden of a state sector designed to provide high levels of employment and social welfare led to a series of balance of payment crises, beginning in the late 1950s.

SERIES OF WEAK GOVERNMENTS

For the next 18 years, the armed forces tried to rule Argentina without Perón and Peron-

President Lanusse meets with his generals in 1972 to discuss Perón's return from exile.

seizing power. In September 1955, a church-sponsored demonstration drew 100,000 to the center of Buenos Aires. This was soon followed by the rebellious air force's bombing of the Casa Rosada and the Plaza de Mayo. The army struck back against the dissident air force while Peronist mobs burned churches.

Events were rolling out of control as the navy then rebelled, joined by some army units in the interior. Perón spared his country enormous bloodshed by not making good his promise to arm the workers, and instead fleeing to Paraguay.

Economically, Peronism left a contradictory heritage that was only dismantled under President Menem in the 1990s. Under strong protection from imports, local manufacturing grew but

ism. Weak civilian governments were tolerated, but Peronists were not allowed to stand in any elections. The Peronist trade unions were forced underground, and at the first sign of any social unrest, the armed forces intervened again.

Arturo Frondizi was the first president elected after Perón, in February 1958. His tenure was marked by a state of siege, an economic downturn, and some 35 coup attempts.

What brought Frondizi down was his decision to allow Peronists to participate in the congressional elections of 1962. Frondizi's attempts to accommodate the Peronists disturbed the Argentine military; they ordered him to annul the election results and when he refused to declare all Peronist wins illegal, the army stepped in.

Arturo Illia did not fare much better when he won the presidential elections in 1963. Although the economy was stronger than under Frondizi's administration, inflation remained oppressively high. Illia's minority government stood little chance of survival; the military was apprehensive over the president's inability to hold back the increasingly popular Peronist Party.

The next in line to try his hand at governing Argentina was General Juan Carlos Onganía,

Perón's third wife, Isabel.

⊘ PERÓN STILL AT LARGE

Although Juan Domingo Perón served as president for only 11 years, his shadow remains over Argentina. Ever since his death in 1974, the man and his ideology have remained strongly influential. He elicits the most powerful and polarized of responses from the citizenry: complete adoration or utter revulsion. Perón managed to be all things to all people, and in his name governments have fallen, terrorist acts have been committed, and workers organized. His greatest achievement was to harness the energy of the Argentine laborer. Through the workers Perón established a political party that is still a force to be reckoned with.

leader of the 1966 coup against Illia. Onganía ushered in a repressive era: political parties were banned; congress was dissolved; and demonstrations were outlawed.

The *Cordobazo* (Córdoba riots) of 1969 precipitated Onganía's departure from government. Argentina's second largest city was the focus of anti-government activity among a new alliance of students, workers, and businessmen, all of whom had been badly hurt by Onganía's policies. Córdoba became a war zone, as soldiers battled with demonstrators. Over 100 were killed or wounded in the street fighting.

Onganía was ousted by General Lanusse and other military representatives. An obscure general assumed the presidency, lasting only nine months in office before Lanusse himself took charge. Yielding to the inevitable, he prepared the nation for a return to civilian elections, which were to be held in 1973.

Argentine society became increasingly divided. Lanusse introduced repressive measures to combat the activities of left-wing guerrilla groups, in particular the Peronist Montoneros and the Marxist People's Revolutionary Army (ERP). The struggle became increasingly violent, with more than 2,000 political and trade-union prisoners languishing in prison.

It was in this climate that the presidential election of 1973 took place. Perón chose Héctor Cámpora to run as his proxy as the head of the Peronist Justicialist Party. On a platform of national reconstruction, Cámpora won just less than half the vote. It was time for Perón to end his exile.

ROUND TWO FOR PERÓN

Perón's return to Argentina did not have auspicious beginnings. Two million were on hand at the international airport to greet the aging man they thought could restore order to the economy and dignity to the working classes. Riots among different groups of demonstrators and security police at the airport turned into pitched battles that left hundreds dead.

Cámpora resigned from office and in the new presidential elections Perón won with ease. Following past form, his third wife, Isabel, was given political power, as vice president.

The sudden death of Juan Domingo Perón on July 1, 1974 brought Isabel to the supreme position in the land, but her administration was an unmitigated disaster. She was no Evita and she had little to offer Argentina except her husband's name. Her government was marked by ultra-conservatism, corruption, and repression.

Additionally, Isabel came to rely for advice on one of Argentina's most bizarre and sinister figures, the ex-police corporal José López Rega. This Rasputin-like character wielded great power and founded the infamous right-wing terrorist group, the Alianza Argentina Anticomunista. Reportedly, under Lopéz Rega's

the four successive juntas made a point of co-ordinating efforts among the various branches of the armed forces. The first junta tried to lend legitimacy to its leadership by amending the constitution. This amendment, the Statute for the National Reorganization Process, called for the junta to shoulder responsibility of executive and legislative functions of the state. The period of military rule from 1977 to 1983 has come to be known as the "Proceso".

General Jorge Rafael Videla was chosen as the first president and he attacked the problem

The Mothers of the Plaza de Mayo, whose children "disappeared" during the military dictatorship of 1977–83.

influence, Isabel even took to employing astrological divination as a means to determine national policy.

Isabel Perón's inability to get a grip on Argentina's chronic economic problems, and her failure to curb rising terrorism, led the military to intervene yet again. In a move that was widely expected and hoped for by many, they removed the last Perón from the Casa Rosada on March 24, 1976.

THE PROCESO

Although the military had never proved itself any more able to solve the nation's problems, there seemed to be a different attitude with this band of uniformed men steering the nation. Each of

of left-wing guerrilla action through a campaign dubbed the "dirty war" (the actions of the military junta during the 1970s' dictatorship). The military had set about "cleansing" Argentine society of any left-wing influence, whether real or imagined, by eliminating union leaders, intellectuals, and student radicals – even executing a group of high-school students who had staged a protest against rising bus fares. The whole campaign was conducted secretly, abductions often occurring at night. The rule of law was completely flouted. The authorities never admitted capturing anyone, and very few people were ever charged with any offense. Alongside this repression, the armed forces took control of the universities, schools, and the television, radio, and other media. Few people in Argentina realized at the time the scale of the human-rights violations being carried out in their name.

International condemnation, the pleas of human-rights groups, and the efforts of the mothers of the disappeared – the Madres de la Plaza de Mayo (see page 139) – did not alleviate state-sponsored terrorism.

The military dictatorship in Argentina was different from the one in Chile under General Pinochet during the same period, because none of its members sought to take all power for themselves. The original junta of the different branches of the armed forces made decisions together, and stepped down together in 1980.

Videla was succeeded by General Viola who was then forced from office and replaced by General Galtieri. In economic matters, the military fared no better. Foreign debt soared to US$45 billion while the inflation rate went from bad to worse, unemployment increased, and the peso was constantly devalued. It was in this climate that General Galtieri and his junta chose to try something new.

General Galtieri makes a public address in 1982.

⊘ THE DESAPARECIDOS

It was while General Videla held office that the majority of the *desaparecidos* (disappeared) vanished. Anyone who was suspected of anti-government activity, as broadly defined by the military, could be made to disappear. Nuns, priests, intellectuals, journalists, Jews, schoolchildren, and whole families were kidnapped, raped, tortured, and then murdered by a nefarious coalition of the military, police, and right-wing death squads acting in the dubious name of Christianity and democracy. Estimates of the numbers of *desaparecidos* range from 10,000 to 30,000 people, of whom only the tiniest fraction had actually been involved in any kind of terrorist activities.

THE MALVINAS CONFLICT

It was ironic that the Argentine military, having won its dirty war against its own people, was forced from power through waging – and losing – a conventional conflict. Galtieri hoped to divert public attention from the growing domestic crisis by the traditional method of turning people's attention to foreign matters, in this case the British-occupied Malvinas (Falkland Islands).

The ensuing South Atlantic War was brief but bloody, beginning on April 2, 1982 with the Argentine invasion of the islands and ending with their surrender at the capital, Port Stanley, on June 14.

The disputed archipelago appeared the perfect target for Galtieri: the tiny and sparsely populated islands lay more than 13,000km (8,000 miles) from the United Kingdom; Galtieri and the other military commanders did not consider the possibility that Britain would fight to retain its claim.

This major miscalculation was one of many that the Argentine junta was to make during the following weeks. Technically, tactically, and politically, Argentina's rulers blundered badly. The conscripted army was ill-prepared for battle against trained professionals and did not put up much of a fight, while the navy stayed in

and other city centers reminded him and the other military leaders that the only task left for them was to organize free and fair elections as quickly as possible.

END OF MILITARY POWER

The military, knowing its days in power were numbered, sought to protect itself from anticipated criminal prosecution for human-rights abuses by issuing its own study, *The Final Document of the Military Junta on the War Against Subversion and Terrorism*. This white paper praised

Crosses in the Plaza de Mayo representing the 17 soldiers fallen while protecting the Argentinian Patagonic Litoral in 1982.

port after a British submarine sank the cruiser *General Belgrano* on May 2. Only the efforts of the Argentine Air Force salvaged some military honor for the country.

Taught since school that the "Malvinas are Argentine," many people at first supported their armed forces' efforts to regain the islands. It soon became clear that the military claims about the conflict were untrue, however, and the eventual defeat dealt the whole nation a crushing blow.

General Galtieri resigned three days after the Argentine surrender and was replaced a week later by the retired general Reynaldo Bignone. Frequent demonstrations in the Plaza de Mayo

the efforts of the armed forces in combating and defeating terrorism and denied any involvement by the administration in the barbaric actions undertaken during the "dirty war." As an extra protection, the government proclaimed a general amnesty for all those involved in the "extralegal" efforts to crush the opposition.

The election campaign of 1983 was full of surprises. Many analysts expected a Peronist return to power or possibly a coalition government. A majority of voters, however, selected Raúl Alfonsín and his Radical Party to lead the nation out of repression. Alfonsín was sworn in as president on December 10, one day after the military junta dissolved itself.

EVITA

María Eva Duarte de Perón, known throughout the world as Evita, lived in the limelight only briefly but her impact on Argentine politics was enormous and continues today, more than five decades after her death.

Evita at her dazzling peak.

Evita was venerated by the Argentine working class, mocked and vilified by the *grandes dames* of Buenos Aires society (who called her a whore and worse), and misunderstood by the military establishment. Through all of this, she came to symbolize a wealthy Argentina, full of pride and with great expectations following World War II.

Her meteoric rise from her beginnings as a poor villager in the backwaters of the interior to a status as one of the most intriguing, engaging, and powerful figures in a male-dominated culture is a tale worth retelling.

Evita was born in the remote village of Los Toldos in 1919, one of five illegitimate children her mother bore to Juan Duarte. After her father's death, the family moved to the provincial town of Junín de los Andes, under the patronage of another of her mother's benefactors.

It was in Junín that Evita, at the age of 14, became determined to be an actress. In the company of a young tango singer, she ran off to Buenos Aires, the cultural mecca of Latin America, where she faced almost insurmountable odds in landing jobs in the theater. Her opportunities took a dramatic leap forward when a rich manufacturer fell for her and provided her with her own radio show. Shortly thereafter, Evita's voice became a regular feature on the airwaves of Radio Argentina and Radio El Mundo.

Evita's energy was boundless; her work pace became frenetic and she made powerful friends. Her lack of acting talent and sophistication did not seem to hinder her ability to attract important people to her cause. Among her admirers were the president of Argentina and, more importantly, the Minister of Communications, Colonel Imbert, who controlled all radio stations in the country.

Evita met Colonel Juan Domingo Perón, the reputed power behind the new military government, at a fundraising event for victims of the devastating 1944 San Juan earthquake. She left the event on the widowed colonel's arm.

Despite being exactly half Perón's 48 years when they met, Evita assisted his rise to power in ways that were beyond the imagination of even the most astute politicians. When Perón became Minister of Labor and Welfare, Evita convinced him that his real power base should be the previously ignored masses of laborers living in the horrible *villas miserias* (slums) that still ring the capital city.

A stream of pronouncements issued forth from the ministry instituting minimum wages, better living conditions, salary increases, and protection from employers. Additionally, and most brilliantly, Perón won the support of the giant Confederación General del Trabajo (CGT or General Confederation of Labor), which embraced many of the trade unions. In the process, however, recalcitrant labor leaders were picked up by the police and sent to prisons in Patagonia.

It was not long before Evita called Perón's constituency to his aid. In 1945, an army coup was on the point of success when Evita called in all her chips. Upwards of 200,000 *descamisados* – the shirtless ones – entered the capital city and demanded that Perón be their president. The colonel accepted the mandate of the Argentine people.

Evita, now married to Perón, cemented her ties with the workers by establishing the Social Aid Foundation. Through this charity, scores of hospitals and hundreds of schools were built, nurses trained, and money dispensed to the poor. Evita also formed the first women's political party, the Peronista Feminist Party.

Although a cult was developing around her personality, she always told the people in her countless speeches that all credit should go to her husband and that she would gladly sacrifice her life for him, as they should sacrifice theirs. Perhaps Evita's finest hour came with her long tour of Europe, during which she

had to hold her up as she spoke to the *descamisados*. Evita's death on July 26, 1952 brought the whole of Argentina to a standstill. Her body was embalmed, and at her wake hundreds of thousands paid their last respects.

Death brought no respite, however, and in 1955, Evita's corpse disappeared, stolen by the military after they had deposed Juan Perón. It was carried to Germany and then Italy, where it was interred for 16 years under another name. After negotiations, it was returned to her husband in Spain. Evita's long odyssey came to an end when Juan Perón died in Argentina in 1974. Her coffin was brought from Spain and lay in state next to that of the one she had said she would die for.

Evita addresses a crowd of women workers.

met Franco, the dictator of Spain, Pope Pius XII, and the Italian and French foreign ministers. She dazzled postwar Europe with her jewels and elegant gowns. Her rags-to-riches story was told and retold in the press, and she was even on the cover of *Time* magazine.

On the negative side, Evita would brook no criticism of her husband. Newspapers were closed, careers destroyed, and opponents jailed on trumped-up charges. She could be extremely vindictive, never forgetting an insult, even if it lay years in the past. Family and friends were placed in positions well above their levels of competence.

The people's heroine was dying by 1952, a victim of uterine cancer. Despite suffering severe and almost constant pain, she kept up her intense work schedule. During her last speech, on May Day, her husband

Even though efforts to have her canonized by the Roman Catholic church have been met with polite refusal, Evita still holds near-saint status in Argentina. Graffiti proclaiming *¡Evita Vive!* (Evita lives!) can be seen everywhere. At the Duarte family crypt in the Recoleta Cemetery (see page 151), devotees still leave flowers and written tributes. The Museo Evita in Palermo, housed in a former home for single mothers run by the Eva Perón Foundation, has interesting exhibits relating to her life and work.

Evita's epitaph, famously paraphrased in the Andrew Lloyd Webber–Tim Rice rock opera *Evita* and in Alan Parker's subsequent film of the musical, reads: "Don't cry for me, for I remain quite near to you, and I am an essential part of your existence." It still rings true, more than half a century after her premature death.

CRISIS AND RECOVERY

The three and a half decades since the fall of the military dictatorship have witnessed alarming fluctuations in the country's fortunes, yet hard-won democracy has endured.

For many Argentines, the collapse of the military government in 1983 marked the end of a cycle of armed forces' interference in political life which had begun in 1930. There was great enthusiasm for civilian rule, which brought new freedom in the press, in literature, and in general discussions. Many thousands of Argentines who had fled military rule to live in exile returned, helping to add to the sense of a fresh start in political and social life.

This was combined with an attempt to explain and come to terms with what had happened during the military dictatorship. In 1984 the Radical Party and its president, Raúl Alfonsín, set up a commission to report on the political violence and its victims. The result was *Nunca Más* (Never Again), which detailed how the military dictatorship had kidnapped, tortured, and killed at least 9,000 Argentines whom they had regarded as "subversive." The evidence gathered led to the public trial of the leaders of the military juntas, and the historic decision to condemn five of them to imprisonment for crimes against humanity.

Menem supporters at a rally in the run-up to the 2003 presidential election.

Soon after his election as president, Menem's picturesque long hair and sideburns were shortened to more conventional lengths and his gaucho's poncho was left for special visits to the interior.

The civilian government's determination to prosecute the military leaders caused great unease among the armed forces. There were several military uprisings against Alfonsín, which were put down only thanks to popular support for him, and the loyalty of the new military commanders. In response to this pressure, President Alfonsín brought in two laws, one which limited responsibility for the "disappeared" to the military high command, and the other which declared the time for prosecutions for human-rights abuses to have a definite end.

INFLATION AND DEBT

Another legacy from the military dictatorship which President Alfonsín found hard to cope with was its economic mismanagement. The juntas had borrowed money internationally to fund huge projects and to balance their budgets. Now inflation and debt, combined with the

Radical Party's lack of experience in government, undermined President Alfonsín's popularity. To try to remedy matters, a new currency, the *austral*, was introduced but within months, inflation of several hundred percent wiped out many people's savings, and restricted the government's ability to plan coherently.

This was the situation in 1989, when Argentines were called on to vote for a second time in their newly restored democracy. By now, many of the voters thought that the Radical Party had failed in its attempt to bring prosperity and good

flood Argentina. But his boldest and most controversial move was to pass a law which put the Argentine peso on a par with the US dollar. This was intended to solve all of Argentina's chronic inflation problems. The value of the Argentine currency was guaranteed by government reserves, which were boosted by strong exports and the revenues from privatization.

PROSPERITY UNDER MENEM

President Menem attempted to change Argentina's relations with the rest of the world. Great

Students protest against education reforms, 2003.

government to Argentina. So they turned once more to the Peronists, and voted for Carlos Saúl Menem. The flamboyant Menem appeared to represent traditional Peronist economic and social values: support for working people and national industry, and an "anti-imperialist" stance in foreign affairs.

It soon became clear that Menemism was very different from traditional Peronism. From the start of his administration, Menem followed the recipes for success suggested by the International Monetary Fund. He began to sell off much of Argentine industry, from the nationalized oil concern to the telephones and railways. He removed all tariff protection for Argentine industry, allowing cheaper foreign imports to start to

efforts were made to heal the rift with the United Kingdom – although the question of sovereignty over the Falkland Islands remained unresolved. Argentina left the Non-Aligned Movement, and declared that its interests were the same as those of the developed Western world. At the same time, the president declared an amnesty for the military personnel and the guerrillas who had been involved in the political violence of the 1970s, thus attempting to draw a line under this tragic episode in the country's history.

The early 1990s were boom years for Argentina. Buenos Aires once again rivaled the cities of Europe and North America not only for the choice of goods in the huge new shopping malls, and its glitzy restaurants and elegant cafés, but also in the quality and range of its films, plays, and books. The chattering classes often looked down on President Menem, with his love of fast cars and his taste for the celebrity lifestyle (memorably characterized as "pizza with champagne") but they enjoyed being consumers of the newly available goods.

This sense of satisfaction helped Menem to win a second period in office easily in 1995. However, problems soon began to mount. The fact that the Argentine peso was the same value as the US dollar made the country's exports

distant relative of the elected representative, brought in to support the Peronists, to accusations that the president and other high-ranking officials had been involved in multimillion-dollar illegal arms sales. A lot of the money earned through privatization had ended up in the politicians' pockets.

The discontent led to the creation of an anti-Peronist alliance of parties, including the Radical Party and the FREPASO (Front for a Country of Solidarity). This alliance was triumphant in the 1999 presidential elections.

Then-President Kirchner in front of the Perito Moreno glacier.

overpriced compared to those of its regional rivals. The imported goods that middle-class Argentines enjoyed so much were also very costly, making it hard for the government to balance the books. Many thousands of Argentines had been put out of work by the sell-off of state concerns, and could find no other employment. All this put a great strain on social security and pension provisions, which in turn made it hard for the central government to achieve stability.

THE END OF MENEMISM

The administration was increasingly mired in corruption. The press revealed all kinds of scandals, from the discovery that one of the congressmen voting for the government was a

The new president was Fernando de la Rúa of the Radical Party. Once again there was optimism that things might change. In the event, de la Rúa and his allies failed to grasp the opportunity. His biggest mistake was to continue with the policy of parity between the Argentine peso and the US dollar.

FROM MENEM TO KIRCHNER: ECONOMIC FREEFALL

The crisis came to a head in December 2001. Exasperated unemployed workers and government employees, who had not been paid in many months, joined with Peronist trade unionists in violent street protests. As many as 39 people are thought to have died in the demonstrations, and the situation was so unstable that President de la Rúa resigned, fleeing the presidential palace in a helicopter to avoid the angry crowds.

At the end of 2001, Argentina had four presidents in two weeks. Eventually it was the head of congress, Eduardo Duhalde, who was appointed interim president and had sufficient authority to calm the situation. His government declared it would not meet the payments due on foreign debt, and, to re-activate exports and reduce debts, he ended the peso-

of malnutrition. Many turned against all politicians: *"Que se vayan todos"* (Get rid of them all) was the rallying cry at the continuing street protests.

Presidential elections in 2003 saw Carlos Menem, who was seeking a third term in office, facing the little-known governor of the remote Patagonian province of Santa Cruz, Néstor Kirchner. Menem won most votes in the first round but not enough to guarantee success; he pulled out of the second round, leaving Kirchner as president-elect, although

Protestors carry a banner marked nunca más (never again) at a demonstration on the 37th anniversary of the 1976 dictatorship.

dollar parity. This led to a huge devaluation, with the peso soon having only one third of its previous international value. Controversially, to avoid the complete collapse of the economy, the government froze all the dollar deposits that Argentines had in their local banks, and the middle classes, whose savings in many cases had been wiped out overnight, joined the demonstrations.

The emergency measures brought some financial stability but did not solve the underlying problems. The years of unemployment and underinvestment had led to unprecedented poverty and economic hardship and Argentines were shocked to see pictures of children dying

he had polled only a little over 20 percent of the vote in the first round. A familiar South American scenario ensued: when judges tried to have him arrested over allegations of fraud, Menem fled to Chile, returning at the end of 2004 when the warrants were canceled.

REBUILDING CONFIDENCE

Néstor Kirchner, sworn into office in May 2003, faced a daunting challenge in salvaging the country's economy and trying to reduce the poverty affecting almost half of all Argentines. The country had hit economic rock bottom, and the only way was up. The cheap peso greatly boosted the country's exports. The surplus generated was used to pay off IMF loans, freeing Argentina from the incubus of debt that had weighed it down for so long.

In the eyes of both his critics and his admirers, Kirchner governed as an old-style Peronist. He re-nationalized some industries and promulgated a range of redistributive government programs. He also surrounded himself with a clique of trusted associates. Declining to stand for re-election in 2007, Kirchner only had to turn over in bed to find his successor. His wife, Cristina Fernández, a formidable politician in her own right, ran for the presidency and won it by a landslide.

Fernández's presidency got off to a shaky start. In 2008 she announced a new taxation system for agricultural exports, cutting into the profits made by the farming sector. This led to a nationwide series of strikes by farming associations. After an unprecedented defeat in congress – which included her own vice-president voting against the farming bill – Fernández was forced to compromise, and her approval ratings began to rise thereafter.

Fernández's administration recovered strongly in 2009 and 2010, but personal tragedy was around the corner. On October 27, 2010, Néstor Kirchner died of a massive heart attack. Many wondered whether Fernández would stand for re-election in 2011. But she did – and won an even bigger landslide than she had achieved in 2007.

However, her efforts to stabilise the country's economy proved elusive, and inflation continued to increase. In 2014 Argentina again defaulted on its international debt. Fernández's presidency was also marred by controversial decisions, such as the nationalization of the biggest oil company, YPF, as well as a series of corruption scandals which sparked countrywide demonstrations in 2013. Demonstrators carried banners denouncing government corruption and urging Argentina to "wake up".

Fernández's reputation was further tarnished by a scandal triggered by the mysterious death of prosecutor Alberto Nisman in January 2015. A few days before his death, Nisman had accused Fernández and members of her cabinet of protecting Iranian agents suspected of the terrorist attack on the AMIA

Jewish center in Buenos Aires in 1994 that left 85 people dead. The Argentine court later dismissed Nisman's accusations. 2015 also saw tensions in relations with the UK rise as the Argentine president denounced British oil exploration off the Falkland Islands and the British government's decision to boost its military presence on the islands.

Presidential elections in the same year were won unexpectedly by the conservative mayor of Buenos Aires and former president of Boca Juniors football club, Mauricio Macri, who

President Mauricio Macri in a 2017 TV interview.

beat the Férnandez-endorsed Peronist candidate, Daniel Scioli. Macri quickly embarked upon a program of ambitious reforms, starting by removing currency controls and liberating exchange rates of the Argentinian peso (which quickly lost 30 percent of its value), and slashing subsidies and import tariffs. He also managed to settle the long-term multi-billion dollar dispute with US hedge funds and substantially curbed the inflation rate (hovering around 25 percent at the beginning of 2018) – the second highest in Latin America after Venezuela. Next steps for Macri will see him endeavour to reform the labour market and tax system before the next presidential elections in 2019.

Gauchos in Mercedes,
Corrientes province.

Che Guevara mural in San Telmo, Buenos Aires.

THE ARGENTINES

Most Argentinians today are of European and not Amerindian descent, and the country's large and varied immigrant populations make for a colorful and diverse national identity and cultural life.

Visit Bariloche in July and the Fiesta de las Colectividades (Community Festival) will give you a taste of the different immigrant groups that make up Argentina. There you'll see people of Spanish, Italian, German, Russian, and Danish (to name but a few) descent celebrating an often dormant sense of ethno-cultural identity and entering a bustling melee around colorful stalls that sell typical food from pizzas to blinis. It's a vibrant celebration, but when the bunting is taken down and the stalls packed away, everyone goes back to being what they truly are – Argentine. For while it's true that Argentines celebrate diversity, what they aspire toward is unity.

That sense of oneness – fragile and subject to numerous caveats – has been centuries in the making. The original inhabitants of Argentina were divided into many distinct peoples, but their numbers were few. The first European settlers, in the 16th century, were almost all Spanish, as were those arriving over the next 300 years. A minority population of mestizos (people of Amerindian and Hispanic descent) developed early. A large number of enslaved Africans were brought in during the 17th and 18th centuries, and mulattos (people of black and Hispanic descent) and people of Amerindian/Afro-American descent formed a significant part of the population.

Yet the 19th century saw great changes in this ethnic make-up of Argentina. Many Amerindians died at the hands of the Argentine army, and many more died from smallpox and other Old World diseases to which they had no resistance. This freed the land for European settlers. After the abolition of slavery, the black population also faded from view (see page 45).

European immigrants in Buenos Aires, 1910.

EUROPEAN IMMIGRANTS

At the end of the 19th century and turn of the 20th century, there was another wave of immigration across the Atlantic from Europe. By 1914, the population of Argentina was about 30 percent foreign-born, and in some of the larger cities the foreigners outnumbered the so-called natives. These new hands were put to work filling positions in the expanding agricultural industry, in cattle raising and processing, and in the developing economies of the big cities.

Argentina's population increased fourfold between 1860 and the start of World War II. Most of the newcomers were agricultural workers, who had been promised "a job, a house, and land." They often found that none of these promises was fulfilled, and so were forced to live in Buenos Aires and the other cities, in crowded tenements or *conventillos*. The countryside remained in the hands of a few criollo landowners, which led to many of the political and social tensions between city and countryside throughout the 20th century.

Many of these newcomers came from Spain and Italy, but there were significant numbers from other nationalities. Many thousands of Jewish people fled persecution in Eastern Europe and Russia and came to Argentina. Some

Quechua children in the town of Humahuaca, Jujuy.

of them went to live on land bought for them by a Baron Hirsch, and became the famous "Jewish gauchos," while most of these pioneers ended up in the cities. As a result of this, Buenos Aires has the highest proportion of Jewish inhabitants of any city outside Israel apart from New York.

Many thousands of Germans also came. Some of them headed south for the mountains and lakes that reminded them of home, and there are towns and villages in the Andes that look distinctly German still.

One of the most influential foreign communities in Argentina were the British. Although in Argentina they are known as the *ingleses*, many of these arrivals were in fact Welsh or Scottish in origin, or even Irish – neither British nor English).

THE WELSH IN PATAGONIA

The Welsh, who left their native valleys to pursue this opportunity (see page 284), must have had their doubts when the first arrivals in the 1860s walked for days across Patagonia's barren wastes in search of fresh water, until they reached the River Chubut.

The initial co-operation of the indigenous peoples, and their own tenacity, eventually yielded a string of prosperous settlements along the Chubut valley, and so with legitimate pride, the Welsh cling to their national identity more fiercely than most. One of these Welsh towns, Gaiman, brings over someone from Wales each year to preserve and protect the native culture, and the annual *eisteddfod* is celebrated with great enthusiasm.

MORE ENGLISH THAN THE ENGLISH

The first British settlers came to administer the building of the country's infrastructure, and their services helped to make Argentina one of the world's 10 richest countries by the beginning of the 20th century. To a large extent, it was British capital that built the Argentine railroad and banking systems in the 19th century. British money also helped develop the cattle industry, with modern methods of refrigeration, packaging, and transportation. Some Englishmen bought huge tracts of land in the south to raise sheep and, for a time, southern Patagonia seemed an extension of the British Empire.

⊘ INDIGENOUS SURVIVORS

Argentina has a huge immigrant population, each one maintaining parts of its culture. Indigenous populations survive in pockets, and while some native languages continue and traditional crafts enjoy a revival of interest, few tribes practice traditional lifestyles in more than a ceremonial sense. Quechua is still spoken in the Northwest, where the Colla are the largest group. Chiriguan, Choroti, Wichi, Mocovi, and Toba are spoken in the Chaco; the Chiriguan are the principal tribe of Mesopotamia. The Araucano-Mapuches and the Tehuelche were the major groups in Patagonia and the pampas, but very few pure-blooded descendants survive today.

The 1982 war over the Malvinas (Falkland Islands) was inevitably a tense time for Anglo-Argentines. Some left but for most, loyalty to Argentina triumphed. Argentines remain convinced of the legitimacy of their claim to the islands: even in the most remote and unlikely places stand large signs proclaiming "*Las Malvinas son Argentinas.*"

British schools such as St. Andrew's and St. George's continue to thrive in Argentina, as does the British hospital. Polo and cricket continue to be played at weekends on the manicured lawns of the exclusive Hurlingham Club outside Buenos Aires. Rugby and football are other British imports, as evidenced by the English names of soccer clubs such as River Plate and Racing.

NON-EUROPEAN ARRIVALS

Many groups have also come to Argentina from outside Europe. From the former Turkish Empire there are many people of Syrian or Lebanese origin (popularly known as *turcos*). The best-known of these was former President Menem, although he had to convert to Catholicism to become president.

Unlike many other Latin American countries, Argentina does not have a large Chinese community, but Buenos Aires can boast one Japanese neighborhood, while Koreans have taken over many corner shops in the cities and towns.

ECONOMIC MIGRANTS

For many years, Argentina's standard of living was much higher than that of its neighbors. Its education system and universities were also much more developed. This has meant that people from Bolivia, Paraguay, Uruguay, and Chile have frequently sought a better life in Argentina. These immigrants, as well as internal migrants from Argentina's poorer provinces in the north and west, tend to do the jobs most other Argentines shun: in the service sector, as laborers on building sites, or in agriculture. They are the first to suffer from any economic downturn.

THE NATIONAL IDENTITY

The fact that all these groups of incomers usually live alongside each other in harmony is a tribute above all to the Argentine education system. From the earliest years, schools insist that everyone is first and foremost Argentine – religions and languages other than Spanish are left for the individual to pursue. This has created a strong sense of national identity, although tensions remain.

For a start, there is the contrast between urban and rural life, all the more sharply drawn in a nation where suburbia scarcely exists. Of a total population of over 44 million, more than 15 million live in Buenos Aires.

The *porteño*, as the resident of Buenos Aires is known, thrives on the pace and bustle of life in the capital. Walk along Florida, Buenos Aires'

Grocery store, Valle de Uco.

busiest shopping street, and the sleek sophistication is palpable, further accentuated by the inherent stylishness of the people. The latest trends may sometimes be slow to cross the Atlantic, but the Argentines do not need anyone to tell them how to look good, and elegant shopping malls continue to open in the capital.

Outside the capital, dress is generally more relaxed, though stylish nonetheless. Designer jeans are more commonplace than suits. Ties for men are not de rigueur.

COFFEE HOUSE CONVERSATION

In the coffee houses of Buenos Aires one thing is clear. The Argentines love to talk. People are articulate and lucid, confident in expressing their opinions. All matters, small or large, are worthy of comment. The most routine of meetings can erupt in animated discussion. Teenagers are rarely reticent. The problem is not

> In family, social, and even formal situations there is rarely any of that agonized Anglo-Saxon uncertainty about the right greeting. People just kiss.

Enjoying a drink in the Palermo Soho district of Buenos Aires.

getting people to talk, but rather to listen, with a rich and expressive vocabulary of gestures jostling with words for attention.

Soccer and politics are among the topics most likely to ignite conversation. Soccer is the big national sport, and team allegiances are strong. At a fairly early age most Argentines decide where those allegiances lie.

IN THE COUNTRY

Outside the big cities, it's a different story. The archetypal male is taciturn, especially in mixed company. He will still hold firm his opinions, often tinged with a wry melancholy, but he will waste fewer words on them.

Here the social lubricant is not coffee but mate (see page 118). The thirst-quenching qualities of this home-brewed tea are of secondary importance to its social role. Passing the mate around is a decorous ritual. Traditionally the water is heated in a crude tin or kettle over an open fire, brewed in a small gourd, and sipped through a perforated metal straw called a *bombilla*. It's a convivial part of life, and not only in the country.

So too is the *asado* (barbecue), where Argentines indulge their passion for meat to the full. Barbecues are usually communal affairs where everyone will be expected to put away about half a kilo (one pound) of meat. Nowhere more than at an *asado* is Argentine machismo apparent. Preparing the *asado* is a male preserve and involves a certain way of positioning and timing of the meat to ensure it is cooked to perfection. Men stand around the fire cutting hunks of meat from the carcass with showy *asado* knives, while women sit at a rustic table and chat together. When all have eaten their fill the men continue their discussions over a mate, while the women depart to wash the dishes.

Nonetheless, Argentine family life has undergone a striking metamorphosis. Women now comprise nearly half of the workforce; 40 percent of Argentine households are supported by female breadwinners; and 50 percent of students at university are women. Argentina was the first country in Latin America to introduce quotas for women in elective congressional posts. As a result, women now hold about 42 percent of seats in the upper chamber of Congress and nearly 39 percent in the lower compared to 6 percent in 1991, and Brazil, Bolivia, Venezuela, Peru, and Ecuador have followed this radical lead. In 2017, Congress passed a parity law which requires all political parties to have 50 percent of their electoral lists filled by women as of 2019.

THE EXTENDED FAMILY

Although old-fashioned chauvinism and its counterpart, chivalry, still exist, the overwhelming flavor of society, especially among the young, is of freedom and informality. This is in part a reaction, some say, to the years of military repression. It's also a reflection of the strength of the extended family.

Young people often live at home until they get married, and even then may only move a few blocks away. Students do not often move out when they enter university, as they frequently attend schools in their home towns. The generation gap is far less apparent than in some countries. Young and old are used to each other's company, sharing news and ideas comfortably in contexts like family *asados*. Cousins are often best friends. The cool and studied indifference of adolescence exists, of course. But the overall impression is of people visibly enjoying life.

When a child reaches school-leaving age, most parents will put considerable effort into planning and preparing the class celebration. It is a milestone, a shared occasion among families and classmates, and just one telling demonstration of how much the Argentines know about the art of celebration. Nightlife, for example, is vigorous. Many clubs do not even get going until the early hours, and the music does not finish until daybreak.

GROUP MENTALITY

Among young people, there is a keen sense of the individual, and yet there is also a very strong feeling of group identity. Children will pass through school with virtually the same classmates throughout. Usually all will share their birthday celebrations together. All will take part in a week-long school trip to mark the end of their secondary schooling and, by the time they emerge, the common bond of shared experience is enough to cement relationships for a lifetime. Besides, Argentines are by nature gregarious. Find an idyllic quiet picnic spot and, if a car should happen to pass, the occupants are as likely to join you as search for their own patch of solitude. Or witness the streets of Bariloche or Carlos Paz, popular destinations of these *viajes de egresados* (school-leaving trips), when students move in packs singing and chanting, crowding into group photographs, all sporting matching hats or jackets.

Tactile behavior in Argentina is the norm. Not just a polite social peck, but touching, kissing, hugging, and linking arms, all with an easy, uninhibited warmth that no one in the country will misconstrue.

TAKING THEIR TIME

The relaxed social approach also applies to time frames. If it doesn't get done today it will surely get done tomorrow – the infamous Spanish "*mañana*." When waiting for an Argentine to keep an appointment, whether for a cup of coffee or a business meeting, allowance should be made for benign tardiness. It's a way of life. Beware of being asked to wait "*un momentito*," literally a little moment – which might be considerably more; or of being assured that something is about to happen "*ya*," or right

Gaucho on an estancia.

away, which is similarly elastic. If you ask the mechanic when your car will be ready, the answer is usually "*última hora*" – closing time, whenever that might be.

This is partly due to a different work ethic. Here people are always ready to sacrifice a little efficiency for the sake of making work more enjoyable with a chat, a mate, and a few *facturas* (pastries).

CHURCH AND BUREAUCRACY

The church is still a pervasive, if nominal, influence. Constitutional reforms in 1994 continue to guarantee religious freedom, but Catholicism is no longer the state religion, nor does the president have to be a Catholic. About 70 percent of the Argentine population is Catholic, but less than 23 percent are practicing. Strict faith no longer seems to have a firm grip on the national psyche and only periodic observances remain, like catechism classes and First Communion.

> *A traditional Argentine cure for stomach ache (empacho) is to deftly pull the skin covering the lower vertebrae – tirando el cuero.*

La Bombonera stadium in La Boca, Buenos Aires, is home to Boca Juniors, one of Argentina's most famous football clubs.

However, it was only in 2002 that the government managed to pass a law to allow family-planning advice and free birth control. Until then the move was resisted strongly by Catholic groups in a country where abortion is still illegal. In 2012, however, the Argentine Supreme Court upheld a ruling decriminalizing abortion in cases of rape or where the woman's life is at risk, and in 2018 the government hinted for the first time that it might hold a national referendum on liberalization of the abortion law.

Argentina is a country which operates on a low level of trust. It may be because a chancer (vivo) who gets away with something is more likely to evoke grudging admiration here than moral indignation. As a result, bureaucracy has had to build in elaborate and often cumbersome systems of verification and security to reduce the scope for dishonesty. The public sector often lacks the resources to implement modern systems and is frequently unwieldy and inefficient. Obtaining a simple document may involve trips to the bank, the post office, and the police station, all in pursuit of the appropriate array of rubber stamps and validated papers. To open a business in Argentina demands 13 separate bureaucratic procedures and takes 24 days. A paper chase that would drive many other nationalities wild is met with resigned acceptance by the otherwise volatile Argentines.

HEALTH MATTERS

Visiting the doctor also requires this patience in abundance. Even children rise to the occasion, waiting passively, with neither toys nor books to distract them. But health matters are ready fuel for conversation. People exchange news of their ailments with remarkable openness. Virtual strangers will pat a pregnant woman's stomach as they make inquiries and pass judgment on the likely sex of the impending arrival.

Sophisticated medical care is available in Buenos Aires, less so in the provinces. There is also a growing interest in alternative medicines, and many traditional remedies are held dear.

Psychology, too, is something of a national hobby. A school may not have a photocopier or even stationery, but it will certainly have an educational psychologist. The study and practice of psychology was suppressed during the years of the Proceso (military rule from 1977 to 1983). Military authorities viewed the field as subversive, and books on the subject were removed from public and private shelves. University departments were cut or closed down.

LIVING WITH THE PAST

Ironically, repression in the Proceso era, together with the dirty war's legacy of harrowing memories, has contributed to the resurgence of interest in psychology. While the government's policy has been to draw a line under the past and move forward, with an early amnesty for many military offenders of the period, public pressure has challenged this approach.

For many years, the mothers of the "disappeared" (see page 139) rallied in the Plaza de Mayo every Thursday, their white headscarves neatly embroidered in blue with the names of their lost children. Long years of steadfast campaigning have met with success that at times is bittersweet. Grandparents have been united with grandchildren they never knew – children taken from women abducted while pregnant and placed for adoption with childless couples (some in the militia), whose natural mothers were then killed. Some of these chil-

years a number of major trials involving military men accused of kidnapping, torturing, and murdering detainees have been concluded, with dozens of former army officials sentenced to life imprisonment. Some of the accused decided to break the silence and assist prosecutors in locating execution sites and common graves where many of the *desaparecidos* were clandestinely buried. Argentines will never forget this dark period in their history but the arc of history, as Martin Luther King phrased it, is at last bending toward justice.

Argentina has a long history of protest marches and demonstrations.

dren, brought up in loving homes, have been, and are being, torn apart by the truth.

Argentina is still trying to come to terms with the savage political repression of the 1970s. The truth about what happened to the thousands of "disappeared" is slowly becoming known, and a number of high-profile human-rights violators were tried and convicted in 2011. In 2012 former military dictators Jorge Videla and Reynaldo Bignone received posthumous prison sentences of 50 and 15 years respectively for their participation in a scheme to steal the babies of political opponents detained by the military regime. It is estimated some 500 children were stolen and raised by families sympathetic to the regime. In recent

⊙ IN PAPAL FOOTSTEPS

The former cardinal of Buenos Aires, Jorge Mario Bergoglio – better known as Pope Francis – is a popular figure in Argentina. He is revered as both a spiritual leader and reformer of the Catholic Church, and as a fellow Argentine who has shared many of his compatriots' miseries and passions. For many years he lived like an ordinary *porteño*, traveling on buses and cheering on his beloved local football club, San Lorenzo. Argentines and tourists alike flock to see the house in Barrio de Flores where he was born, the local basilica, his first school, or the Devoto Penitentiary where he used to celebrate Mass for the inmates.

Tango dancers in San Telmo.

THE TANGO

Conceived by immigrants, born in the brothel, and raised in the ballroom, the fiery tango is Argentina's greatest gift to popular culture.

A music filled with nostalgia, sexiness, drama, and kitsch, tango is the soul of Argentina. Like the blues in the United States, it can express sadness and hard times, and yet it has survived triumphantly for more than a century. As a dance, it is enjoying a huge revival in Argentina and around the world, with tango world championships being held every year in Buenos Aires. But the music has also moved into the electronic era, with groups such as Gotan Project and Bajofondo Tango Club incorporating new sounds from rap to dub beats into its typical 5/8 rhythms.

But what are the origins of this sensual and melancholy music, so intimately identified with Argentina and its nerve center and capital, Buenos Aires? The story begins just as the 19th century was ending. At this time, the whole Río de la Plata region, in Uruguay as in Argentina, began to receive great waves of European immigrants. Most of them settled in and around the growing ports of Buenos Aires and Montevideo.

The mixture of Italian, Spanish, East European, and Jewish newcomers mingled with the local population, itself a combination of Hispanics, blacks, and indigenous Americans. Each of these groups had its own musical heritage.

In the rough-and-tumble world of the predominantly male immigrants and working poor, the pulsing rhythm known as the *candombe* that arrived with African slaves mixed with the haunting melodies of Andalusia and southern Italy and the locally popular *milongas* (traditional gaucho songs). Sometime during the 1880s, all these cultural elements fused to give rise to something completely new – the tango.

Taking tango to the streets.

MUSIC OF THE NIGHT

Exactly when and where is both a mystery and a hotly disputed controversy. The most important gathering place for the working classes in this period was the brothel. In the parlors, as customers waited their turn, musicians played and sang suggestive and often obscene lyrics that gave the tango its early fame for ribaldry. Because of the context, only fragments of the earliest tango lyrics survived, and their authors remain anonymous or known only by colorful nicknames. It wasn't until 1896 that pianist Rosendo Mendizabal put his name to *El Enterriano (The Man from Entre Ríos)*, the first signed tango.

But the men who spent their nights listening to tangos in the brothels lived by day in the overcrowded tenements that were concentrated in the older, southern areas of Buenos Aires. Inevitably, the tango began to spill out into the patios, there to be played by the local

> *A number of clubs located in San Telmo feature tango music and professional dancers who provide tourists with the variety of tango flavors that made the dance a successful exotic export.*

Plaza Dorrego in the San Telmo district holds a weekly Sunday market, attracting tango dancers and folk singers.

musicians, and to become part of other popular cultural forms, such as the much-attended theatricals known as *sainetes*.

A NEW AUDIENCE

By the turn of the 20th century, the tango had increased its audience to include all but the still disapproving upper classes. During these early years, the configuration of a tango orchestra varied greatly. As many of the musicians were poor, they relied on whatever instruments could be hired. Guitars, violins, flutes, and the less transportable piano were joined by that most special of all tango instruments, the bandoneon, a close relative of the accordion.

In the 20th century's first decade, Buenos Aires, and with it the tango, underwent a transformation. Gradually the tango moved out of the poorest areas and into the salons of the rich. The dancing became more stylized, the lyrics less openly bawdy. But it was not until the music traveled back across the Atlantic and was taken up by the smart set in Paris that its fame became international. This international acceptance in turn reinforced its success back in Argentina: what was good for Paris had to be good enough for Buenos Aires.

CARLOS GARDEL

Another source of change was the arrival of the recording industry. By 1913 a limited number of local recordings were being made, and in 1917 Victor Records captured the young voice of Carlos Gardel singing *Mi Noche Triste (My Sad Night)*. It was the end of one era and the beginning of another.

Carlos Gardel became tango's first international superstar. His career shows the most important developments of the genre in its first golden era. Despite the debate among aficionados, it seems likely that Gardel was born in Toulouse in France sometime around 1891. What transformed Gardel into a star and the tango into music with a far wider appeal, were recordings, radio, and cinema. Gardel went to France in 1929 and made films at Joinville, and in 1934 he signed a contract with Paramount in Hollywood, where he made five films.

By the time of his death in a plane crash in Colombia in 1935, Gardel had become the personification of the tango. When his body was taken to Buenos Aires, thousands gathered to say goodbye to the *"pibe de Abasto"* (kid from Abasto), the neighborhood around the old Central Market. In 1984 the local subway stop was renamed in his honor.

AFTER GARDEL

Gardel's tragic early death seemed to many a confirmation that tango music and life were inextricably intertwined. Throughout the difficult 1930s, songwriters like Enrique Santos Discépolo wrote poetic lyrics of loss, betrayed hope, and nostalgia for a golden age that had never really existed: "tango is a sadness to dance to," wrote Discépolo.

Thousands of world-weary *compadritos* (small-time crooks) adopted the Gardel uniform: a felt fedora hat, white scarf, and tuxedo, as they danced to increasingly sophisticated rhythms from ever-larger tango orchestras. This was the second golden age of tango, when the radio and dance bands in every city provided the backdrop for celebrations by every Argentine, and young-sters learnt the intricate dance steps almost as soon as they could walk.

jazz, and although it had its followers, the old dance halls fell into decay.

It was nostalgia that once again saved the tango. Many of the thousands forced into European exile

---

Edmundo Rivero, one of the great tango singers of all time, said: "When all is said and done, the tango is no more than a reflection of our daily reality."

Tango is enjoyed by both young and old in Argentina.

Tango shoes have different heels from normal shoes, plus a smooth sole to allow the dancer to slide.

In the late 1940s, tango became increasingly associated with Peronism and his kind of stri-dent nationalism. In consequence, it suffered when Perón was toppled and went into exile, giving way to more international styles such as pop and rock. In the 1960s, the last thing young Argentines wanted to be seen doing was dancing the old-fashioned, stale tango.

TANGO RENAISSANCE

But tango music not only survived, it thrived. Musicians such as Astor Piazzolla, who spent most of his childhood in New York, brought in influences from jazz and classical music, cre-ating what was called *nuevo tango* (new tango). This was tango to be listened to, like modern

in the late 1970s listened to the music, crooned Gardel's *Mi Buenos Aires Querido* with tears in their eyes, and encouraged a new generation of sing-ers to revisit the 1930s classics. As the political scene opened up again in Argentina, tango made a triumphal return along with the exiles.

In Buenos Aires now there are several 24-hour tango radio stations. Argentines try to outdo each other by finding the most "authentic" *milonga* or ballroom where the music is played. Thousands of tourists come to see the tango shows and to learn the intricate dance steps. New groups have revitalized the music, and there are fans of its unmistakable rhythms from Japan to Finland.

📷 A TANGO TOUR OF BUENOS AIRES

From the buskers and street dancers of La Boca to the glitzy dinner shows of San Telmo, tango is as popular as ever in the Argentine capital.

The tango dance was born in the port of Buenos Aires more than a hundred years ago. Nobody is sure of its origins: its rhythms are a mixture of Spanish, African, Cuban, and indigenous Argentine dances. For many years it was banned from polite society in Argentina, because it was a product of the brothels and other low dives of the port area. Only when it became all the rage in France just before World War I was it taken up by everyone in Argentine society.

PURE PASSION

Close in spirit to jazz and the blues, tango has been in and out of fashion over the past century, but has always survived and been taken up by another generation of young Argentines who recognize it as a true expression of their emotions. Argentines argue as passionately about their favorite tango orchestras and eras as they do about their football teams. Some say that tango should be danced to and not sung; others argue that tango reaches its highest expression when the nostalgia and longing of the music are put into words. One tango writer has called its rhythms "sadness you can dance to," but the intricate steps and subtle interplay between the two partners is exhilarating – and incredibly good exercise!

Several of the old dance-halls in downtown Buenos Aires from tango's 1940s heyday have been restored to cater for the new devotees of the dance. Confiteria Ideal, near Avenida Corrientes, is a historic bar and dance hall which holds shows, classes, and milongas.

There are many styles of tango dancing, but Argentine tan is quite different from "ballroom" tango. The man leads the woman in a series of steps, often improvised, and the two hold their bodies in a continuous close embrace.

Tango dancers depicted in a filete-style painting.

There are numerous organized tango tours of Buenos Aires and part of the trail is likely to focus on tango legend Carlos Gardel. One renowned venue, Esquina Carlos Gardel, is located on the site of the Chanta Cuatro restaurant where Gardel and friends once met to sing and while away the hours. Gardel died in 1935 but is still the idol of all Argentine tango devotees: "Gardel sings better every day" is a common expression.

The language of love

Many of the songs played by tango orchestras are written in the slang of the Buenos Aires port area known as *lunfardo*. This is thought to have originated in Genoa, where many of the Italian immigrants to Argentina came from, but in Buenos Aires words from Spanish, Portuguese, from the indigenous Indians of the pampas, as well as words of backslang (in which, for example, the word "tango" becomes "gotan"), have been added to the mix. As with the tango itself, *lunfardo* began in the poorest areas of the port on the margins of respectable society, but over the years, many new words and expressions have been added, and some of them, such as *mina* (a girl or woman) or *gil* (a stupid idiot), have passed into everyday language. The tangos of the 1930s and 1940s are full of *lunfardo* lines and images, which are often impenetrable to other Spanish-speaking Latin Americans. The ability to speak *lunfardo* (the word itself is thought to mean "outside the law") is proof that you are a genuine *porteño* (someone from the port of Buenos Aires), and it continues to thrive. Nowadays there are even *lunfardo* hip-hop artists proudly making up fresh *lunfardo* verses.

e bandoneon is the most important instrument of tango chestras. A button accordion, it is thought to have ought to Argentina by German sailors during the second lf of the 19th century.

ural in the Caminito area of La Boca, which inspired the mposer of the Caminito tango, one of the most famous ngos in the world.

Dressing for tango performances sees the men as "compadritos," a style copied from the immigrants who dressed up to dance in their finest fedoras, with a white scarf over a dark jacket.

A gaucho in Salta province.

THE GAUCHO

A vital presence in Argentina's history, culture, and mythology from the 17th century to the present day, the lone cowboy of the pampas continues to grip the imagination.

So potent is the gaucho as a symbol of Argentine rural culture, that people who have never even visited the country will form a picture in their mind's eye when the word is dropped. A man (it is always a man) on horseback (always on horseback, unless he is by a campfire), long knife tucked into his belt, silhouetted against the horizon of a flat, infinite plain, oblivious to the hot sun beating down on his head, alone, homeless and, most importantly, free.

That in any case is the gaucho of song, poem and silver screen. Like the North American cowboy, he is an endlessly mythologized and sentimentalized figure. Most gauchos these days would view themselves as working men, not idealistic loners. Nonetheless, what is probably the most surprising and sensational aspect of the gaucho myth is that a great deal of it is based on historical truth.

PAMPEAN ORPHANS

The mystery begins with the word: from what language is "gaucho" derived? Various exotic theories have traced it back to everything from Arabic and Basque, to French and Portuguese. The most likely answer is that the word has joint roots in the indigenous dialects of Quechua and Araucanian, a derivation of their word for orphan.

The first gauchos were mostly *mestizos*, of mixed Spanish and native American descent. As with the North American cowboy, some also had varied amounts of African blood, a legacy of Argentina's slave trade.

CATTLE HIDES

Cattle and horses that had escaped from early Spanish settlements in the 16th century had,

Gaucho riding near Purmamarca in the Quebrada de Humahuaca valley, northwest Argentina.

over the decades, proliferated into enormous feral herds, and it was this wild, unclaimed abundance that was the basis for the development of the gaucho subculture. The horses were first caught and tamed, and then used to capture the cattle.

Beef at that time did not have any great commercial value; there was more meat than the tiny population of Argentina could consume, and methods to export it had not yet been developed. This surplus led to waste on a grand scale: once a cow had been skinned, its carcass was left to rot on the plain or be torn apart by vultures.

The primary value of the cattle was in the hides and tallow they provided, which were non-perishable exportable items. The first gauchos made their living by selling these in exchange for tobacco, rum, and mate (gauchos were said to be so addicted to this stimulating tea that they would rather have gone without their beef). Their existence was fairly humble, with few needs. Most did not possess much beyond a horse, a saddle, a poncho, and a knife. A day spent chasing down cattle would often be followed by a night spent drinking and gambling. Sometimes a knife fight would break out, though the idea that the gaucho was a man of constant

borrowed from the indigenous peoples. *Boleadoras* consisted of three stones or metal balls attached to the ends of connected thongs. Thrown with phenomenal accuracy by the gauchos, this weapon was designed to trip the legs of the fleeing prey.

The great emphasis placed on equestrian skills led to competition. Strength, speed, and courage were highly prized, and the chance to demonstrate these came often.

In one event, the *sortija*, a horseman would ride full tilt with a lance in his hand to catch

Early gaucho, with distinctive toe-held stirrups.

violence largely derived from the prejudices of city folk, who looked upon the freewheeling, often lawless lifestyle of the pampean cowboy with both horror and disdain. The animosity was mutual. The gaucho scorned what he saw as the fettered and refined ways of the urbanite.

AN EQUESTRIAN ELITE

The primary reputation of the gaucho, however, was that of a horseman, and this was well deserved. It is still said that when a gaucho is without his horse, he is without his legs.

Almost all of the gaucho's daily chores, from bathing to hunting, were conducted from atop his steed. The first gauchos hunted with lassoes and *boleadoras*, both of which were inventions

a tiny ring dangling from a crossbar. Another test, the *maroma*, would call for a man to drop from a corral gate as a herd of wild horses was driven out beneath him. Tremendous strength was needed to land on a horse's bare back, bring it under control, and return with it to the gate.

RANCH HANDS

Profound change came to the gauchos' way of life as increasing portions of the pampas came under private ownership. The gauchos, with their highly independent ways, were seen as a hindrance to the development of the land. Increasing restrictions were put on their lives, in order to bring them under authoritarian control and to put them at the service of the new landowners.

It was not only the land which came under private ownership, but the cattle and horses that were found on it, making them inaccessible to the free riders. The gauchos were suddenly put in the position of being trespassers and cattle thieves. This rendered their situation similar to that of the remaining tribes of plains Amerindians.

With such an obvious conflict of interests, there had to be a resolution, and it was, pre-

THE COWBOY CAVALRY

However, while the gaucho ceased to present an independent threat, he still had a role to play in the new social structure of the rural areas, and soon new bonds of loyalty were formed between the worker and his master. Powerful caudillos were gaining control over large parts of the interior, backed up by their gauchos, who served as irregular troops in private armies. This formation of regional powers was in direct contradiction to the goals of centralized government.

Riding flat out on an estancia near the town of Guemes in Salta province, northwest Argentina.

dictably enough, in favor of the landowners. The open prairie lands were fenced off, and the disenfranchized gauchos were put to work at the service of the *estancieros*. Their skills were employed to round up, brand, and maintain the herds.

However, the gauchos maintained their pride. They refused to do any unmounted labor, which was seen as the ultimate degradation. Everyday chores such as the digging of ditches, mending of fences, and planting of trees were reserved for the immigrants who were arriving in increasing numbers from Europe. Yet when barbed-wire fencing was put up, fewer hands were needed to maintain the herds. Combined with the increase in agriculture, this led to even harder times.

⊘ LIFE FOR LAS CHINAS

The family life of the gaucho was never a very settled one. Supposedly, the women of their early camps were captives from raids on nearby settlements. This primitive theft was perhaps one of the practices that made the gauchos so unpopular with city folk. Even when women later moved voluntarily out onto the pampas, the domestic arrangements were somewhat informal, with common-law marriages being the norm. These *chinas* (from the Spanish for servant or mistress), were rarely welcome on the estancias where the gauchos worked. The few that were allowed were employed as maids, wet nurses, laundresses, and cooks.

Gauchos were also, at various times, put to work in the defense of the central government. These skilled horsemen were first used in the armies that routed the British invasion forces in 1806 and 1807, and by all accounts, their services were invaluable. Gaucho squadrons were next employed in the war of independence from Spain, and again they displayed great valor. The last time that the gauchos fought as an organized force in the nation's army was during the Desert Campaign of the 1870s (see page 58).

Working cattle on Huechahue estancia in Patagonia.

GAUCHO GARB

Although gaucho clothing was originally designed simply for comfort and practicality, the men of the pampas were proud of how their dress distinguished them from the common farm laborer, and their traditional outfits were always worn with a certain amount of flair.

The *chiripá*, a loose diaper-like cloth draped between the legs, was very suitable for riding. It was often worn with long, fringed leggings. These were later replaced by *bombachas*, pleated pants with buttoned ankles that fitted inside their boots.

Although store-bought boots with soles became popular with gauchos in later years, the first boots were home-made, fashioned from a single piece of hide, slipped from the leg of a horse. Often the toe was left open. This had a practical function, as the early stirrups were nothing more than a knot in a hanging leather thong.

Around his waist the gaucho wore a *faja*, a woolen sash, and a *rastra*, a stiff leather belt adorned with coins. This leather belt provided support for the back during the long hours in the saddle. At the gaucho's back, between these two belts, was tucked the *facón* (knife), a gaucho's most prized possession after his horse.

> *Such is the gaucho's reputation for helping strangers in distress that when an Argentine needs a favour from someone, they will often ask for "una gauchada."*

The outfit was completed with a kerchief, a hat, a set of spurs, and a vest, for more formal occasions. Over all this, a gaucho wore his poncho, which also served as a blanket at night.

The gaucho saddle was a layered set of pads, braces, and molded leather, on top of which sat a sheepskin that made the long rides more comfortable. In the region of the pampas where high thistles grew, a set of stiff, flared leather guards called *guardamontes* were used to protect the legs. The *rebenque*, a heavy, braided fine leather crop, was always carried in the riding gaucho's hand.

MARTÍN FIERRO

Just as the traditional gaucho way of life was fading in reality, it was being preserved in art. Poetry and music had always been popular with the gauchos, and the songs, stories, and poems of the *gauchesco* tradition were gradually absorbed into mainstream Argentine culture.

A masterpiece of Argentine literature is a two-part epic poem, *El Gaucho Martín Fierro*. Written by José Hernandez, and published in the 1870s, the work is a defense of the proud, independent ways of the gaucho, and a diatribe against the forces that conspired to bring him down, from greedy landowners to corrupt policemen and conscription officials.

Such works as *Martín Fierro* and, later, Ricardo Güiraldes' *Don Segundo Sombra* (1926) served to elevate the stature of the gaucho in the minds of the public, but not enough and not in time to save him. The free-riding gaucho passed into the realm of myth, a folk hero who was the object of sentimentality and patriotic pride in a nation searching for cultural emblems.

THE 21ST-CENTURY GAUCHO

Although the historical line places the demise of the gaucho in the late 19th century, there is

their lunchtime *asado* barbecue, lead them on long *cabalgatas* (horseback rides), and, if they are lucky and he is musical, play them a selection of folk songs on his guitar or *charango* (an Andean variant on the lute, made from an armadillo shell). On a visit to an estancia, you might perhaps see a *domador* breaking horses, or men riding at breakneck speed with lassoes flying.

Estancia owners rarely treat their gauchos with anything other than great respect, often addressing them using the honorific "Don," a custom that has all but died out in other contexts.

Gaucho with a boleadora, used to trip the legs of fleeing prey.

much that remains of gaucho culture in Argentina today. While the reduction of labor requirements in the countryside forced many gauchos into the cities, many remained on the estancias to work under the new established order.

Wherever cattle- and sheep-ranching is done in Argentina, you will find ranch hands working at the rough chores of herding and branding. Most are settled with a regular wage, but there are still itinerants who provide services such as fence mending and sheep shearing.

The most straightforward way to meet a gaucho is to book a stay on an estancia. Aside from performing his regular duties around the farm, the modern gaucho will often have a role entertaining guests. He will prepare the fire for

THE RODEO

One of the biggest treats is to see a rodeo. Some of these are large organized events, with an accompanying fiesta of eating, dancing, and singing. Bowlegged men gather at these celebrations, dressed up in hats, *bombachas*, and kerchiefs, with their *chinas* (women) by their sides.

With some investigation and a little luck, it is possible to find more informal rodeos in the villages of the outback, where the gauchos will come from miles around to compete in rough tests of skill and bravery. Amid flying dust and spirited whooping you will see gauchos barrel racing and lassoing cattle with as much panache and pride as their ancestors ever had.

📷 A DAY IN THE COUNTRY – GAUCHO-STYLE

Argentina grew rich on its agricultural output, and a visit to a traditional ranch provides an insight into the gaucho's livelihood – and often, the chance to join in.

One of the options for a day trip out of the city is a visit to an estancia (ranch). Many of these receive either day visitors or weekend guests, although most are also still active in their traditional livestock and agricultural work. There are a number of these establishments, particularly within a couple of hours' drive of Buenos Aires. Most were founded early in the 20th century and follow a similar layout: a tree-lined entry and main residential area (the trees forming a windbreak in the flat and often bare pampas), with a large main house in traditional criollo or imitation English, French, or Italian style, surrounded by gardens and lawns.

ESTANCIA ACTIVITIES

Although agricultural methods have obviously changed since the 1920s heyday of the estancias, it is still possible to see traditional methods demonstrated for visitors. For those who can spare only one day for the outing, most estancias offer transport, and a traditional *asado* lunch composed of empanadas, grilled meat, sausage, and sweetbreads, usually accompanied by red wine. Thereafter, most offer a gaucho display of horsemanship and roping in the best rodeo style; in many cases, it is also possible to go horseback riding or take a ride in a sulky (open carriage). Estancias near the coast or one of Buenos Aires' many lakes may also provide fishing, and all offer fresh air, blue sky, green grass, and a glimpse of the endless pampas.

Gauchos customarily drank yerba mate from a specially seasoned gourd through a metal straw called a bombilla.

Huechahue estancia in northern Patagonia. A 15,000-acre working estancia, Huechahue has Criollo horses (the local Argentine breed) guests can ride in the foothills of the Ande

Riding at Estancia Peuma Hue. Most estancias have horses and rides to suit both beginners and experienced riders, as well as activities for non-riding partners.

A traditional decorative gaucho belt, complete with silver-handled facón (knife).

Tools of the trade

Argentine gauchos have always been proud of the tools of their trade, and these have become a highly decorative part of their wardrobe.

The traditional gaucho knife (*facón*) is used for butchering, skinning, and even castrating animals, but also for self-defense and eating. The handle is usually of ornately carved silver. Spurs may also be made of silver and – like the ornamental silver belt buckles – are designed to stand out as well as to serve a practical purpose. The wide crops are made of braided leather with a loop at the end to make a sharp cracking noise.

The *boleadoras*, a set of three balls linked by rope, are used to capture and bring down livestock; the throwing of *boleadoras* was an indigenous art learned by the gaucho, and is a highly skilled task that requires infinite practice.

Also essential is the traditional mate gourd and *bombilla* (straw), used to drink the tea-like mate, though nowadays these are often made of ornately carved silver or alpaca.

...aff at Estancia Los Potreros. Gauchos on estancias that ...e open to visitors do anything from breaking young ...orses to rounding up mares and foals to protect them ...om pumas. They often lead the guests on rides, which ...n vary from an all-day picnic ride to long-distance pack ...ips of a week or longer.

...ack room at Los Potreros estancia in Córdoba province, ...howing the different style of saddlery used.

A gaucho demonstrates his equestrian skills in a sortija, where the horseman rides full tilt with a twig to catch a tiny ring dangling from a crossbar.

Floralis Generica sculpture by architect Eduardo Catalano, on Plaza Naciones Unidas in Recoleta, Buenos Aires. The flower's petals close at night.

THE ARTS

The challenge of creating a distinctive national culture is one that Argentine writers, artists, and film makers have taken up with relish.

What does it mean to be Argentine? This is a question that the country's writers, artists, musicians, and film directors have wrestled with in the two centuries since Argentina became an independent nation.

A few, such as Jorge Luis Borges, the greatest of Argentine writers, have chosen (or at least pretended) not to wrestle with it at all. "As I think of the many myths," he said, "there is one that is very harmful, and that is the myth of countries. I mean, why should I think of myself as being an Argentine, and not a Chilean, and not an Uruguayan."

Borges liked to provoke. But his statement illuminates a tension between two traditions, the cosmopolitan and the home-grown, which has marked and ultimately enriched Argentine culture, and which persists to this day.

PAINTING ARGENTINA

You can see the fruits of this tension by visiting Buenos Aires' National Fine Arts Museum (see page 155). At first glance it looks like Argentina's visual arts tradition is a purely cosmopolitan one. The works of 19th-century painters like Erneste de la Cárcova and Angel Della, and those of modernist successors like Emilio Pettoruti, Antonio Berni, Xul Solar, and Lino Enea Spilimbergo, seem to align closely, even slavishly, with European styles. Movements that began in Paris – Realism, Impressionism, Cubism – were taken up on the Río de la Plata, where they flourished.

Look more closely, however, and you will see that towards the end of the 19th century, and into the 20th, specifically Argentine themes, if not forms, become more sharply defined. In Cárcova's *Sin pan y sin trabajo*

Writer Jorge Luis Borges, Argentina's most famous literary son.

(Without bread and without work), a classic work of social realism, we see a rural laborer with his wife and baby living in the most wretched poverty, and this during the country's most prosperous era. Antonio Berni used styles developed in Europe to create his wrenching depictions of social inequality, but in works like *Desocupados (The Unemployed)*, *Manifestación (Demonstration)* and his Chaco series, his subject is his homeland.

Not all representations of "Argentine-ness" are so serious. In photographer Marco López's brilliant and hilarious *Asado criollo*, Leonardo da Vinci's *Last Supper* is recast as a typically messy and raucous Argentine barbecue.

FROM FIERRO TO FUNES

Argentine writers were quicker to develop a home-grown tradition than the painters. The 19th century saw the rise of *literatura gauchesca*, a genre grounded in the language, stories, and lifestyle of the Argentine gaucho. Estanislao del Campo, Bartolomé Hidalgo, Leopoldo Lugones, and, into the 20th century, Ricardo Güiraldes were among the poets and novelists whose works so vividly evoked life on the pampas. The master of this style was José Hernández, whose 2,316-line narrative poem

The ornate interior of the El Ateneo Grand Splendid bookstore.

Martín Fierro (1872), the story of a heroic gaucho fighting for independence and justice, is considered to be Argentina's national epic.

Jorge Luis Borges (1899–1986) wrote that *Martín Fierro* was the pinnacle of Argentine literature, and then went on to produce a body of work that arguably superseded it. The short stories that Borges wrote in the 1940s and 1950s, collected in *Fictions* (1944) and *The Aleph* (1949), altered the landscape of world literature. In them we meet vain caudillos, knife-wielding gauchos, and ordinary citizens of Buenos Aires (including the writer himself). But we also meet (among others) a blind immortal who turns out to be Homer, a librarian who works in a library of infinite dimensions, and Funes, a man who remembers everything and understands nothing.

Some have argued that Borges is the least Argentine of Argentine writers; others have asserted the opposite. A lover of paradox, Borges would have been content with the idea that both judgements are probably equally valid.

ARGENTINE THEATER

Buenos Aires' first theater was built at the instigation of the Spanish viceroy in 1783, and for almost a century thereafter, Argentine theater was dependent on European works. Then, in the 1880s, a new and largely indigenous style of theater emerged: *circo criollo*. Combining acrobatics, clowning, and straight acting, it was a huge success – and it was uniquely Argentine.

Mirroring developments in art, the early to mid-20th century found playwrights like Florencio Sánchez and Roberto Arlt writing searing works of social criticism. However, the 1970s dictatorship would tolerate not a scintilla of dissent; it banned such productions and blacklisted their authors. After the return of democracy in 1983, Argentine theater carried on where it had left off, and if anything became more transgressive and avant-garde than ever before.

Currently, the Argentine theater is thriving, with dozens of revivals and fresh productions opening every week, in venues great and small. The modern successor to the *circo criollo* is the *revista porteña*, with showgirls (known as *vedettes*) and comedians in place of clowns and acrobats. Its home, both spiritual and actual, is Avenida Corrientes in Buenos Aires, although productions often transfer to the Atlantic coast during the summer high season (see page 179).

SONG AND DANCE

All *revistas porteñas* incorporate music and dance routines, of which at least one must be a tango. The dance, which emerged toward the end of the 19th century, reversed the usual polarity of cultural influence: for once Parisians took up a style that had begun in Buenos Aires, rather than vice versa (see page 86).

Other distinctly Argentine music and dance styles either predate tango or have developed in parallel to it. Folkloric singers and musicians like Jaime Torres, Mercedes Sosa, and Raúl Barboza did much to popularize the music of rural Argentina during the 20th century, and this remains a country where real men dance in public.

And then there is *rock nacional*. Tired of hearing their parents' tango records, young Argentines in the 1960s formed their own rock and roll bands, aping the sounds and styles of their heroes The Beatles and The Rolling Stones, but singing in Spanish and addressing Argentine themes in their lyrics. Figures like Sandro, Pappo, and Charly García loomed large in the culture, and even though the dictatorship disapproved of rock as they did everything else, songwriters like García were able to smuggle coded anti-military messages into their songs.

HOE DOWN, PAMPAS STYLE

Dances and music that are particular to gaucho culture are the *chacarera*, the *gato*, and the *escondido*. These forms descended from old colonial and modern European culture and are known as "creole" dance.

Both the *chacarera* and the *gato* resonate with the repetitive beat of large drums and employ guitar and accordion accompaniments as well as a soloist storyteller. The *escondido* is a particularly entertaining dance for visitors to watch as man and woman act out a pantomime of hide and seek (the name of the dance means "the hidden or lost one"). The woman hides by crouching down on one knee and shielding her eyes, while the man-protector struts around in spurred boots, snapping his fingers in the air as he mimics a frantic search for her.

FILMING ARGENTINA

The dictatorship paid far closer attention to the content of movies than it did to that of rock songs, and the 1970s was a long dark night for Argentine cinema, just as it had been for the theater. Then, in 1983, dawn broke – and the decades since the return of democracy have witnessed a great flowering of the country's film industry.

An almost immediate success was Luis Puenzo's *The Official Story* (1985), the harrowing story of a mother (played by Norma Leandro, who had to flee the country during the 1970s) coming to terms with the fact that her adopted child is the daughter of a woman who was kidnapped and murdered by the military junta. It won the Oscar for Best Foreign Film in 1986, the first such triumph by an Argentine movie.

Numerous successes, both artistic and commercial, have followed. Directors like Daniel Burman (*Lost Embrace*, *Family Law*),

Dancer performs the chacarera.

Lucrecia Martel (*The Swamp*, *The Headless Woman*, *Zama*), and Pablo Trapero (*Crane World*, *Lion's Den*) are now familiar names on the international independent film circuit, as are actors such as the brilliant Ricardo Darín (*Nine Queens*, *Son of the Bride*, and *Wild Tales*).

Argentina's second Oscar triumph came in 2009, with Juan José Campanella's *The Secret in Their Eyes*. Like *The Official Story*, it's set during the nightmare years of the 1970s. This fact, perhaps, points us towards the greatest achievement of the Argentine arts: unable to change history, they can at least present it in a fresh way to the viewer, the reader, or the listener, and in doing so, help ensure that its worst aspects are never repeated.

Kayaking on Lake Gutierrez in
Patagonia's Lake District.

Climbing Volcán Lanín.

OUTDOOR ADVENTURE

Whether you want to stand on the top of the world or sail around the end of it, catch a big brown trout or release your inner cowboy, Argentina will allow you to do it (and much more besides).

With snowcapped mountain ranges, dense forests, and more than 2,000km (1,240 miles) of coastline, Argentina is the proverbial big outdoors – only bigger.

The problem is knowing where to start. If you have serious, off-the-beaten-track adventure in mind, have a plan inked in before you arrive and bring all the equipment you need with you (imported gear is very expensive to buy). From the lush rainforests of Misiones to bare and windswept Tierra del Fuego, there is abundant wilderness to experience and explore, but no expedition into the backcountry should be taken lightly. On the other hand, if you regard adventure as a side dish to your trip rather than the main course, there are plenty of things you can do on a whim and a string of developed and developing outdoor activity centers around the country where you can do them.

Be assertive when it comes to your personal health and safety, since some activity organizers can be rather *laissez-faire* in this regard. Many estancias, for example, do not offer riders helmets as a matter of course before setting out on a ride.

CLIMBING AND TREKKING

The Andes mountains, which run the length of Argentina's western border with Chile, have long attracted climbers from around the world. One of the main centers for climbing is in the province of Mendoza, about 1,300km (800 miles) west of Buenos Aires, where the highest peak in the western hemisphere – Aconcagua (6,962 meters/22,840ft) – is found. Scores of expeditions have scaled Aconcagua (the "Stone Sentinel") since Matias Zurbriggen of Switzerland first conquered it in 1897.

Trekking on Perito Moreno glacier in Los Glaciares national park, near El Calafate.

There are 10 recognized routes up the mountain, the northern approach being the most popular. It is possible to reach the top without any technical climbing expertise, although a guide and appropriate acclimatization for the altitude are essential. A somber warning for those less prepared is the small cemetery at the foot of Aconcagua in Puente del Inca, the burial place of a number of climbers who have lost their lives in the attempt. Aventuras Patagonicas (www.patagonicas.com) is a climbing service with decades of experience of guiding international travelers to the summit of Aconcagua, as well as to those of other peaks in the region.

The main center for trekking and climbing in this area is Villa Los Penitentes en route from Mendoza to the frontier. The Tupangato peak – a volcano reaching 6,650 meters (21,000ft) – is also difficult, and can be reached only by riding mules part of the way. Less demanding peaks in the Andes include Catedral, Cuerno, Tolosa, Cúpula, Almacenes, and Pan de Azúcar, all between 5,300 meters and 5,700 meters (17,390–18,700ft).

The Patagonian Lake District region around Bariloche is an increasingly popular destination for trekkers. Many trails of varying difficulty

planet, and a serious challenge) should base themselves in or near El Calafate. To organize a longer trek (up to 10 days), contact an outfitter like Andes Cross (www.andescross.com). If, however, you simply want to walk on (and, if the conditions are right, *inside*) a glacier, book a Big Ice tour, either through your accommodations or with the Hielo y Aventura agency in downtown El Calafate.

Some 230km (140 miles) from Calafate lie the spectacular Monte Fitz Roy (3,440 meters/ 11,000ft) and Cerro Torre. Professional climb-

Horseback-riding on the shores of Lago Gutiérrez.

tion for trekkers. Many trails of varying difficulty can be attempted, including ones leading to the summit of Tronador, the extinct stratovolcano that is the region's highest peak (3,500 meters/11,500ft). For maps and advice on trails, mountain refuges, and how to hire the right guide, drop in for a chat at the Club Andino Bariloche (www.clubandino.org).

If you want to climb the celebrated Lanín volcano (3,776 meters/12,389ft), you will need a permit from the national park office in San Martín de los Andes. They can also advise you on equipment requirements, as well as where and how to hire a guide.

Those keen to explore the Southern Patagonian icecap (the largest non-polar icecap on the

ers regard Fitz Roy and the surrounding peaks as among the most difficult in the world to climb. It was scaled for the first time in 1952 by Lionel Terray and Guido Magnone. Cerro Torre (3,128 meters/9,500ft) and its neighbors are right on the fringe of the Patagonian icecap, and as the westernmost peaks of the Fitz Roy chain they receive the full force of winds blowing in from the Pacific.

Those keen to explore the area more fully stay in the rapidly developing settlement of El Chaltén, now officially designated Argentina's "trekking capital." Although it lacks some of the tourist facilities of El Calafate, it obviously gives much readier access to the mountains. Buses leave El Calafate for El Chaltén early in the morning, giving an ideal opportunity to see rheas and guanaco en route. Serious climbers should visit website www.pataclimb.com which provides essential information on nearby climbing areas, including Fitz Roy, Cerro Torre, and Cerro Catedral massifs.

SKIING AND SNOWBOARDING

Still poor compared to the best of the northern hemisphere resorts, Argentine's skiing and snowboarding destinations are getting better all the time. Although the snowfall is unpredictable, the best season is generally June to October, with August the busiest month on the slopes.

The two main centers are Cerro Catedral, near Bariloche (so popular with Brazilian skiers that it's been nicknamed "Brasiloche") and the newer Las Leñas resort, in Mendoza province. The former is South America's biggest skiing resort, with more than 30 chairlifts and ski tows. It has runs for all levels as well as ski schools, kids' clubs, a snowboard park, and several restaurants and accommodations. The season runs from July through September. Las Leñas has 29 pistes and a first-rate infrastructure that includes artificial snow cannons and ski schools. Argentina's other, lesser resorts are: Cerro Chapelco, near San Martín de los Andes; Cerro Castor, near Ushuaia; Cerro Bayo, near Villa La Angostura; Caviahue, near Copahue Volcano; and La Hoya, near Esquel.

HORSEBACK RIDING

Aside from trekking, horseback riding is probably the most popular outdoor activity for people traveling in Argentina.

The simplest way to guarantee yourself plenty of time in the saddle is to book yourself a stay on an estancia. The per person room rate invariably includes as much horseback riding as your backside will allow, and most of the best days spent on an estancia follow the pattern ride–lunch–siesta–ride–supper. You do not even have to stay overnight, since many of the estancias in Buenos Aires Province incorporate rides into their Día de Campo (country day) programs. Two of the best destinations for riding-oriented day trips are Las Artes (where Arabian horses are trained for competition)

and Estancia Los Dos Hermanos (www.estancialosdoshermanos.com).

Serious riders who are interested in long-distance pack trips or endurance rides should book a stay at an estancia that specializes in equestrian activities. Córdoba's Estancia Los Potreros (www.estancialospotreros.com), for example, organizes rides of up to eight days, crossing the sierras. If that sounds too easy, book a nine-day riding holiday at remote Estancia Huechahue (www.huechahue.com), in Patagonia. The schedule includes a three-day

Skiing on virgin snow in the Andes.

⊘ PENÍNSULA VALDÉS

One of Argentina's key attractions is its wildlife, with the Unesco World Heritage Site of Península Valdés renowned for its wildlife watching. Penguins and elephant seals can be seen along the coast, and it is possible to go by boat to observe southern right whales Puerto Madryn, about 100km (60 miles) from the peninsula, is the main tourist center offering scuba-diving, mountain biking, and trekking. On Valdés itself, Puerto Pirámides lacks the facilities of its larger neighbor (accommodations are limited), but camping by the shore gives you ready access to the rugged coastline and the opportunity to be woken by the sound of whales.

pack trip that will take you and your steed high into the Andean cordillera.

RAFTING

The best – or at least the best-organized – rafting in Argentina is to be had in Mendoza province, on the Mendoza, Tunuyán, Diamante, Atuel, and Grande rivers. Two recommended outfitters in Mendoza City are Kahuak (www.kahuak.com.ar) and Argentina Rafting (www.argentinarafting.com). In Salta, you can shoot the 10 Class III rapids of the Río Juramento with Salta Rafting (www.

saltarafting.com). In Misiones, the lower section of the Iguazú also has a number of Class III rapids. Book an outing in Puerto Iguazú with Rainforest EVT (http://rainforest.iguazuargentina.com/).

FISHING

Argentina is crisscrossed by rivers and lakes (both natural and artificial) and includes more than 4,000km (2,500 miles) of coastline along the Atlantic Ocean. Those features make it a fisherman's paradise, and species such as eel, catfish, trout, salmon, sea bass,

Fishing in Patagonia.

⊘ THE TIP OF THE WORLD

Ushuaia is the world's southernmost town and the obvious center for exploring Tierra del Fuego. Various estancias near the town offer accommodations and an insight into ranch life, horseback riding and hiking. Much of Tierra del Fuego's swampy or forested terrain is best accessed on foot or on horseback. From Ushuaia itself there are daily boat trips to the outlying islands to see cormorants and sea lions. It is also possible, although not always easy, to charter yachts to Cape Horn or to see spectacular glaciers along the coast. Two good outfitters offering both land and water excursions in and around Ushuaia are Rumbo Sur (www.rumbosur.com.ar) and Canal Fun (www.canalfun.com).

shark, swordfish, sole, shad, and dorado are plentiful.

Year-round fishing is available at Argentina's coastal resorts, many of which are between 300 and 500km (180–300 miles) from Buenos Aires. Mar del Plata is a prime fishing spot, as are the nearby resorts at Laguna Brava, where the local authorities regularly stock the waters and boats can be rented.

Quequén Grande, on the banks of the Río Necochea, is noted for its excellent trout fishing. Salmon and trout are also plentiful in the inland rivers and lakes to the south of Buenos Aires in the provinces of Neuquén and Río Negro. However, these regions are under the jurisdiction of the National Parks Board and a fishing license is required.

Most serious international anglers head straight for Patagonia, where some of the best fly-fishing in the world (and some of the best amenities for anglers) can be found. The northern Patagonian Lake District is interlaced by crystal clear rivers like the Chimehuin, the Traful, and the Hua Hum, where salmon and brown and rainbow trout weighing over 5kg (11lbs) are caught on a regular basis. Here, fishing lodges like Tipiliuke (www.tipiliuke.com) and Arroyo Verde (www.estanciaarroyoverde.com.ar) offer luxurious accommodations as well as access to private stretches of river and lake.

For those prepared to travel to the extreme south, Río Grande is the center for trout fishing on Tierra del Fuego. The winds are often fierce but the size of the trout offer due reward. The best-known fishing lodge in this region is María Behety (http://maribety.com).

CYCLING/MOUNTAIN BIKING

Cycling is still something of a niche activity in Argentina, but you will find bike hire services in almost every tourist destination. Owing to the quality of the roads in the area and the several excellent sightseeing circuits (such as the Seven Lakes route), the Patagonian Lake District region is particularly popular with cyclists. Bike Way (www.bikeway.com.ar) and Circuito Chico (www.circuitochicoadventure.com) are two well-established agencies in Bariloche offering mountain bike hire and guided excursions.

Touring wineries on a bicycle is every bit as fun as it sounds. The best place to do this in Maipú, the Mendoza suburb that is home to several of the country's top bodegas. Contact Mendoza Wine Bike Tour (www.mendozawinebiketour.com) or Mr Hugo (tel: 02614-974 067; www.mrhugobikes.com).

GOLF

Golf is another sport that has benefitted from the wide open spaces and the even climate of Argentina. There are nearly 300 golf clubs all over the country, including the prestigious Jockey Club (http://golfclubatlas.com) course in San Isidro, just outside Buenos Aires, the picturesque Mar del Plata course (www.mardelplatagolfclub.com.ar/) on the Atlantic coast, the La Cumbre Country Club (www.lacumbrecc.org) in Córdoba, and the course at the spectacular Hotel

Llao Llao (www.llaollao.com) near Bariloche. We Golf Argentina (www.wegolfargentina.com) organize golfing trips across the country.

SCUBA-DIVING

You can find scuba-diving schools and organized diving expeditions in most of the resorts along the Atlantic coast. In Puerto Madryn and nearby Puerto Pirámides (on Península Valdés), beginners and experts alike can swim with sea lions and explore wrecks. Recommended outfitters include Ocean Divers (www.

Cycling through Mendoza's wine country.

oceandivers.com.ar), Madryn Buceo (www.madrynbuceo.com), and Ushuaia Divers (www.tierradelfuego.org.ar).

SAILING

Argentina has some of the best sailing conditions in the world, with a gentle climate, strong winds, and an abundance of lakes, rivers, and reservoirs. This potential is often still underdeveloped commercially in outlying regions.

However, there are yacht clubs along the banks of the fabled Río de la Plata, where members of the public can hire sailboats, sailboards, and yachts. There are also several rowing clubs clustered around the pleasant delta region of Tigre, on the outskirts of Buenos Aires.

SPECTATOR SPORTS

Argentina takes its sport seriously, and a great footballer or tennis player can unite the country in a way that a politician can only dream about.

It should be an average enough day in Buenos Aires, yet the streets are strangely deserted. The banks are empty, the restaurants are quiet, and an eerie silence has settled over the entire city. The only people in sight are huddled around portable radios or television sets, their attention tightly focused on the latest news.

The outbreak of war? Some national disaster? No, this scenario occurs every time Argentina's national soccer team takes to the field, ample evidence of the sport's hold on the country. Every match commands the nation's rapt attention, and victories are cause for unrivaled celebration.

When Argentina won the 1986 World Cup tournament in Mexico, the highest honor in soccer, several hundreds of thousands of fans flooded the streets of Buenos Aires, Córdoba, Rosario, La Plata, and beyond. Makeshift parades materialized out of nowhere, thousands of cars jammed the avenues and side streets, and the nation found itself swathed in blue and white.

The world championship was the second for Argentina, who had also captured the cup in 1978. But that tournament, hastily staged in Argentina by the ruling military government that had come to power not long before, fostered little of the pride and enthusiasm seen in 1986. The 1978 World Cup was perceived by many as a simple exercise in public relations designed to avert the world's eyes from Argentina's soaring inflation, mounting national debt, and human-rights violations.

The national team (known as *"la selección"*) has subsequently failed to scale the giddy heights reached in 1986. They only made the

Mural of Diego Maradona, considered by many to be the greatest footballer ever, in Buenos Aires' La Boca district.

quarterfinals in 2006 and 2010 (the latter with Diego Maradona as coach), and although they reached the final in 2014, Argentina again underwhelmed in Russia's 2018 World Cup. The team scraped through the group stage to reach the last 16, only to be knocked out by France in a high-octane game that ended 4–3.

EL FÚTBOL

Soccer was introduced to Argentina in the 1860s by British sailors who passed the time in port playing "pick-up" games before the curious local onlookers. The large British community in Buenos Aires finally organized the game officially in 1891, and the balls, goalposts, and nets imported from Europe were checked through customs as "some silly things for the mad English."

But by the turn of the 20th century, Argentina had established its own soccer league. Club Mercedes was formed in 1875, making it the country's oldest soccer team. The Quilmes Atlético Club (1887), Rosario Central (1899), River Plate (1901), Independiente (1904), and Boca Juniors (1905) quickly followed suit.

Argentina's national team also progressed rapidly, as proven by its performance in the

Ellerstina Piaget competing at the Hurlingham Polo Open, Buenos Aires.

inaugural World Cup held in Uruguay in 1930. Although still amateur and not highly regarded, Argentina defeated strong teams such as France and Chile en route to a place in the finals, before losing to Uruguay, 4–2.

Soccer became a professional sport in Argentina in 1931, and league games began to draw large, vociferous crowds. River Plate and Boca Juniors, which emerged from the middle-class Belgrano neighborhood and the working class Italian Boca district in Buenos Aires respectively (see page 165), quickly became the two most popular teams in Argentina. Even today, around 50 percent of the nation's soccer

fans support one of these two clubs. Such unbridled support is not necessarily a good thing – Argentine soccer has been increasingly troubled in recent years by crowd violence at its league matches, especially when rival fans such as River Plate and Boca Juniors meet. Consequently, it's advisable to travel to the stadium as part of an organized tour group.

Thirty teams compete annually in the Argentina First Division. In addition, many of the top clubs compete in international tournaments such as the World Club Cup, the Libertadores, and the South American Cups.

Argentines, like most South Americans, seem to have a special skill for soccer. Diego Maradona was a national hero long before he gained international prominence at the 1986 World Cup. When Maradona threatened to leave his club, Boca Juniors, for Europe in 1982, the government unsuccessfully tried to intervene by declaring him to be part of the "national patrimony."

Among the current cream of Argentina's soccer crop are Sergio Agüero, Gonzalo Higuaín, Ángel Di María and, most notably, Lionel Messi (see box).

POLO PROWESS

Of course, soccer is not the only sport in Argentina. Blessed with a climate that allows for a wide variety of sports year round, the country is also known for its polo, rugby, horse and motor racing, and tennis.

⊘ THE FANTASTIC FLEA

Nicknamed "la pulga" (the flea) for his small stature and sublime elusiveness, Lionel Messi is the world's greatest footballer. Born in Rosario in 1987, Messi began his career with the Newell's Old Boys youth team. Scouts from Barcelona spotted his talent and invited Messi and his family to move to Europe in 2000, at the same time offering treatment for his growth hormone deficiency. There was no looking back. At the time of writing Messi has scored 507 goals in 583 appearances for Barcelona – a staggering goals-per-game ratio. However, with a poor Argentinian display in Russia in 2018, it looks as if Messi's chances of lifting the coveted World Cup are dwindling.

One of the first things many visitors ask is where can they see polo being played. Although it did not originate in Argentina, polo has evolved into an integral part of the national

> Specially trained by petiseros (trainers) at an estancia where polo is played, the short, stocky Argentine polo ponies are prized for their speed, strength, and ability to work with their riders.

The indigenous Argentine sport of pato.

sporting heritage. Many of the world's best players and teams have come from this country. In addition, Argentina has top-flight breeding programs for ponies.

As with soccer, polo was introduced to Argentina by the English in the mid-19th century. The inherent riding skill of the Argentines, as proved by the gauchos, and the abundance of space, helped ensure that the sport flourished. Polo tournaments are held all over Argentina throughout the year, but the majority are played in spring and autumn. The top teams compete each November in the Argentine Open championship in the picturesque polo fields of Palermo, in central Buenos Aires, a competition which began in 1893. There is no distinction between amateur

and professional polo in Argentina, but many of the top players are regularly hired by foreign teams for huge sums. There is also big demand overseas for Argentine-trained polo ponies.

PASSION FOR *PATO*

The game of *pato* has been described by some observers as basketball on horseback, and it is one of the few sports indigenous to Argentina. The earliest references to the game can be dated back as far as 1610, but the game was probably played by the native inhabitants long before that time.

Pato is Spanish for "duck," and the unfortunate duck certainly got the worst of it in the game's formative stages. A duck was placed inside a leather basket with handles, the possession of which was then contested by two teams of horsemen – often farm workers or indigenous people – who attempted to grab the basket and return it to their estancia.

The original duck has been replaced by a more acceptable leather ball with handles, and points are scored by passing the ball through the basket. The annual national open championship is held in mid-December in Palermo, Buenos Aires.

OTHER EQUESTRIAN SPORTS

In a country where horses are plentiful and breeding is big business, horse racing and showjumping are also popular. There are racetracks in most Argentine towns and plenty of opportunities for off-track betting, although the government oversees the official odds. The big races are held in Buenos Aires, often at the Jockey Club in the San Isidro suburb.

Horse shows are staged at numerous clubs in Buenos Aires and other major cities, taking place almost weekly from March to December. There is a fine tradition in this sport – as there is for dressage – and only the regular exportation of top horses has kept Argentina from gaining international stature.

BOOM TIME FOR TENNIS

Tennis has been played in Argentina since the 19th century, but it has always been a game largely for the middle and upper classes – until now. Fueled by the meteoric rise of Guillermo Vilas, an energetic and talented player who gained international prominence on the world's courts in the 1970s, tennis experienced an unprecedented boom.

The driven, dashing Vilas won the Masters in 1974 and the US Open in 1977, and soon became known as an international playboy. Linked romantically with such women as Princess Caroline of Monaco and countless Hollywood starlets, Vilas emerged as a national hero.

Virtually overnight, every young Argentine dreamed of being a professional tennis player. The number of players skyrocketed, as did the sales of rackets, balls, and shoes. Courts sprang up all over the suburbs of Buenos Aires – both municipal and privately owned – and Argentine players flooded the professional circuit.

One of the finest of that boom was Gabriela Sabatini, the teenage sensation who emerged as one of the top women players of the mid-1980s. Dubbed "Gorgeous Gabby" by the international press, Sabatini played her way into the top-10 rankings in 1986, quickly rising to the third seed. Sabatini retired from professional tennis in 1996.

In recent years, a new group of top Argentine tennis players has emerged. On the men's side, Gastón Gaudio won the French Open in 2004 and Juan Martín del Potro the US Open in 2009. David Nalbandian, the only Argentine to ever reach the final of Wimbledon (in 2002; he retired in 2013) has been a consistent performer over the last decade or so. Currently, Juan Martín del Potro and Diego Schwartzman are the highest ranked Argentinian tennis players (world no. 6 and 15 respectively). On the women's side, Paola Súarez and Gisela Dulko became the first Argentines to be ranked no.1 in the world at doubles.

THE RISE OF RUGBY

As with soccer and polo, rugby was introduced to Argentina by the British. But the sport inexplicably failed to catch on until the mid-1960s. That was when the Pumas, Argentina's national rugby team, rose to prominence with a string of international successes. Like tennis, the sport experienced a rapid growth of interest and a massive infusion of young talent. The Pumas have had a string of impressive results since the 1999 World Cup, when they reached the quarterfinals for the first time. In the 2007 World Cup, held in France, they beat the home team twice and went on to

finish third in the tournament – their best result ever, and perhaps the greatest achievement by an Argentine sporting team outside soccer. They played well in the 2011 championship but lost to New Zealand, the eventual winners, in the quarterfinals. On 5 October 2014, the Pumas achieved a major victory, beating Australia (21–17) for the first time in 17 years. The Pumas qualified for the prestigious 2015 Rugby World Cup in England, where they finished an impressive fourth. At the start of 2018, they were ranked ninth in the world.

The Argentina rugby team celebrate a victory.

OTHER GROWING SPORTS

The fastest-growing sports for both spectators and players in Argentina are hockey and basketball. Although neither sports attract the mass following of soccer, the success of Argentine teams internationally has given both of them a huge boost at home. New basketball courts and hockey clubs have sprung up all over Buenos Aires and in the provinces. At the 2004 Olympics in Athens, the Argentine basketball team, led by San Antonio Spurs star Emanuel Ginóbili, won gold. Four years later in Beijing, Argentina finished with bronze medal only to slip down to a fourth place at the London Olympics in 2012. In Rio de Janeiro (2016), the national team lost to the US in the quarterfinals.

A winning combination: steak, wine and chimichurri sauce.

FOOD AND WINE

Still a paradise for carnivores, producing the most succulent beef in the world, Argentina is expanding its gastronomic repertoire and growing into a fine wine superpower.

Irrespective of Argentina's increasingly diverse gastronomy, it remains the case that most travelers land in the country with one overriding ambition: to seek out and devour one of the giant, flavorsome, and butter-tender steaks for which the country is renowned.

It is not a difficult mission. If you are more than five minutes away from a *parrilla* (steakhouse) in an Argentine city, you are probably lost. But once you have had a *bife* or two (or five – life is short, after all) it is time to branch out. Even within the genre of roasted meat there are significant variations, including *cordero patagónico* (Patagonian lamb) and *lechón* (suckling pig).

Beyond the grill, there are comfort food classics like the *milanesa* (a breaded veal cutlet), Italian imports such as pizza, pasta and *gelato* (ice cream), regional favorites like the empanada, and, in Buenos Aires at least, international food from all parts of the world. It would be a challenge to eat badly.

You will drink well too. Long regarded as the sleeping giant of the global fine wine industry, Argentina has woken up with a vengeance, and the traveler on a steak hunt probably knows to accompany it with a full-bodied Malbec.

A STEAK PRIMER

There are any number of environments in which you might find yourself eating beef in Argentina, but two stand out. The first is in a *parrilla* or steakhouse; the second, at an *asado* or barbecue.

Parrillas, as mentioned before, are everywhere (there are several thousand in Buenos Aires alone). In style, price, and comfort levels they vary greatly; in menu and method, hardly at all. There will be a large bed of hot coals and,

The literary café La Poesia, in the capital's San Telmo district, brews its own beer.

above it, a grill. Manning (it is always a man) this furnace will be the *parrillero* or grill master, his apron likely streaked with blood and sweat. Molecular gastronomy this is not.

It would be quicker to list the parts of the cow that are not served than the ones that are. Among the most popular cuts are *vacio* (flank), *tira de asado* (rib), *bife de chorizo* (sirloin), *ojo de bife* (rib), *lomo* (tenderloin), and *entraña* (skirt). Offal, known as *achuras*, is prized, with *chinchulines* (small intestine) and *mollejas* (sweetbreads) among the glands and organs no red-blooded Argentine would think to discard.

If you are unsure what to get, one option is to order a *parrillada* or mixed grill. (A *parrillada* advertised for "two" will likely feed three Argentines or four gringos.) Alternatively, simply ask your waiter what's looking good, or walk over to the grill and see for yourself.

> *If you want to eat empanadas, drink cheap wine from a jug, and listen to terrific folkloric music, go to a peña. You will find many of the best ones in Salta.*

A traditional asado (barbecue).

One thing worth knowing before ordering is that the average Argentine, by default, likes their meat cooked through: not dry, but not sanguine either. So if you like it rare, be sure to insist on *jugoso*.

THE *ASADO*

Whether it be at an estancia, a hotel, or in some new friend's back garden, you will almost certainly experience an *asado* (open-air barbecue) during your stay. It is a ritual whose centrality to Argentine culture can hardly be overstated. *Asados* are where friendships are cemented, and family ties strengthened.

The meal begins with a round of *choripánes*, grilled sausage sandwiches that are usually served with *chimmichurri*, a sauce made from chili flakes, dried herbs and oil. Offal cuts are next off the grill, with steaks and ribs to follow. Bread and salads must be served, along with prodigious quantities of cheap red wine (often cut with soda to calm it down). A fruit salad is the ideal consummation.

Beef is by far the most common component of an *asado*, but not the only one. Supermarkets sell whole chickens that have been squashed flat to make them grill ready. *Lechón* is a beloved delicacy that is reserved for special occasions.

Those traveling south should seek out *cordero patagónico*, which is lean lamb, very savory, and usually roasted whole on an upright spit. *Chivito* (kid) is especially good in Mendoza.

FAST FOOD

Much as Argentines love their *carne*, an *asado* is not the kind of thing you can do every day. This is where *minutas* come in. These are short-order dishes, and they are available in all traditional restaurants and in many cafés too.

The undisputed king of the *minutas* is the *milanesa*, a breaded veal cutlet either baked or fried and often served *a la napolitana*, that is to say, topped with tomato sauce, ham, and cheese. If this sounds too light, you can ask for it *a caballo*: garnished with a pair of fried eggs. When the *milanesa* is made from chicken, it becomes a *suprema*.

Another unhealthy option that comes in a hurry is pizza. Purists tend to disapprove of Argentine pizza, which is thicker and cheesier than its Italian progenitor. But such prejudices rarely survive first contact with a slice of *fugazetta*, a delicious cheese and onion stuffed-crust variation invented in Buenos Aires.

Most pizzerias give you the option to eat *al paso* (literally "on the go"). Walk in, ask for a slice of *muzza* (mozzarella) and a slice of *napolitana* (cheese and fresh tomato) at the counter, catch the plate spun your way, wolf it down, walk out. This is the authentic way to eat pizza in Buenos Aires.

CAPITAL CUISINE

You can eat your way the length and breadth of Argentina without offending your palate, but only in Buenos Aires can you get what you want, when you want it. Alongside the capital's many *parrillas*, pizzerias and *bodegones* (traditional, often family-run establishments that usually offer a wide range of options, from the inevitable grilled steak to pasta, *minutas*, Spanish, and even German dishes), you will find Chinese, Armenian, Japanese, North American, Polish, and Basque restaurants, to name just a few representatives in this United Nations of cuisines.

The trend towards cosmopolitanism should not be overstated, however. It is still the case that the number of *porteños* who adhere mostly

A favorite regional dish in the Argentine northwest is the empanada (stuffed pastries that are either baked or fried).

to the "three Ps"– *parrilla*, pasta, and pizza – vastly outnumber those that do not.

REGIONAL SPECIALTIES

A crude but useful rule of thumb: the farther away you get from the pampas, the more likely you are to find alternatives to grilled steak on the menu.

Fish is an ever-present option, but few Argentines relish it. Fresh fish is available in coastal resorts like Mar del Plata, but it tends to be overcooked and overpriced. Far tastier (if a little oily for some palates) are the river fish available in the Litoral region, such as

pejerrey, *surubí*, and *pacú*. You will find *trucha en escabeche* (pickled trout) on the menu in the Patagonian lakes region; it is a delicious appetizer. Farther south, in Tierra del Fuego, *centolla* (king crab) is both caught and eaten. (Though to call it a regional specialty is to stretch the definition, since Fuegians themselves rarely touch it.)

In the Northwest, by contrast, regional dishes are staples enjoyed by tourists and locals alike. This is the spiritual home of the empanada (here often filled with chunks of potato and peas as well as meat), and of *locro* (a thick stew made with corn, beans, chorizo, and meat), *carbonada* (similar to *locro*, but with added chunks of squash and sweet potato), and *humita* (fresh corn sautéed with onions, wrapped in corn husks and then either boiled or steamed).

For vegetarians reading this litany of mainly flesh-based specialties with an ever heavier heart, it is not all bad news. Many regions produce outstanding fruit and vegetables that arrive in cities soon after being harvested. There are sweet, juicy oranges and grapefruits from San Pedro in Buenos Aires province, luscious melons and plums from Mendoza and San Juan, fat, blood-red cherries from Patagonia, and squash and pumpkin varieties of all shapes, sizes, and colors.

SWEET THINGS

To recap: Argentines love meat, pizza, pasta, and empanadas, enjoy fresh fruit and vegetables, and are ambivalent toward fish. But it would be wrong to call any of these things the national addiction. That is a role reserved for *dulce de leche*.

This impossibly sweet caramel-like concoction, said to have been accidentally invented by a maid working for 19th-century dictator Juan Manuel de Rosas (she forgot about a pan of sweetened milk simmering on the stove), gets loaded onto pancakes, stuffed inside *churros* and croissants, dolloped onto plates beside wobbly flans, sandwiched inside *alfajores* (a type of cookie, and another bona fide national obsession), and quite often eaten straight from the jar in surreptitious night-time refrigerator raids. No more efficient calorie-delivery system has ever been invented.

And then there is *helado*: that warm weather life-saver that is particularly popular in Buenos Aires. Much closer in style to Italian *gelato* than to North American ice cream – which even at its best has some air whipped into it, which *gelato* does not – *helado* is made from fresh ingredients and served in *heladerías*. Some of these ice-cream parlors belong to large chains such as Freddo, Persicco, and Munchies, while others are mom-and-pop operations beloved of their barrios. The most popular ice cream flavor is, naturally, *dulce de leche*.

CAFÉ CULTURE

Despite the fairly recent arrival of a certain well-known North American coffee chain, most Argentines remain traditionalists when it comes to their early morning pick-me-up. Few eat anything substantial for breakfast (a knock-on effect of the late supper hour). A large *café con leche* (milky coffee) often constitutes the whole meal. Alternatives include the *café solo* (black coffee), the *cortado* (with a mere "cut" of milk), and the *lágrima* (mostly milk, with a "teardrop" of coffee). An Argentine will only drink instant coffee in an emergency.

The famous Café Tortoni in Buenos Aires.

⦶ GREEN TEA

Ask an Argentine what they like to eat and drink and they will most likely rattle off 10 products before you have even finished the question. It is unlikely, however, that they will mention yerba mate. That is because the habit of drinking this bitter green tea is so deeply embedded in their daily lifestyles that they have ceased even to notice it.

Mate is made by adding yerba (*Ilex paraguayensis*), a plant grown in the northeast, to a specially seasoned gourd, which is then filled with hot (but not boiling) water.

The gourd is then passed to each participant in turn who drains it through a metal straw (*bombilla*),

before returning it to the original server (known as the *cebador*) who refills it with hot water for the next participant. Occasionally, sugar is added to the yerba, although purists (and people who live in the Northeast) regard this as a bad, Buenos Aires, habit.

The mate may do several circuits before it is deemed washed out (*lavado*). To signal to the *cebador* that you have had your fill – but not before – say "gracias".

Argentines are garrulous by nature, but quite often a mate session is conducted in relative silence. This is a gaucho ritual, after all, and the gaucho is a man of few words but much wisdom.

The most popular accompaniment to coffee, eaten for breakfast or *merienda* (afternoon tea), is the *medialuna* (literally "half moon"), a close relative of the croissant. There are two varieties of *medialuna* – *manteca* (sweet and buttery, with a strong hint of vanilla) and *grasa* (drier and saltier). They are sometimes loaded with cheese and ham and heated under the grill.

MARVELOUS MALBEC

Argentina has had a wine industry for half a millennium, and a fine wine industry for a few

Argentina is known for its Malbec.

decades. The discrepancy is startling, but easily explained. Argentines demanded cheap, simple, just-about-drinkable red wines, and the country's large wine industry, largely based in Mendoza, supplied them with it. Everyone, it seemed, was happy.

Then, in the mid-1980s, a quiet revolution occurred. Winemakers like Nicolás Catena began to modernize their vineyards. They brought in foreign wine consultants to teach them how to make great wines. Most importantly, they discovered that one of Argentina's stock grape varieties, Malbec, previously looked down upon as a poor man's Cabernet, could, with the right methods, be elaborated into *stellar* vintages.

Now it seems that everyone is drinking these deep, dark, full-bodied reds that savor of ripe plums and burnt spices. Argentine wines – and not just Malbecs but Cabernets and Pinots and Bonardas too – are winning awards and turning up on supermarket shelves around the world. If you want to drink the best of what the country has to offer, look out for labels like Catena Zapata, Cobos, Achaval Ferrer, and Carlos Pulenta.

But do not let the hype fool you into thinking that Argentines have turned into wine snobs en masse. Far from it. It is not easy to make a faux pas in this most relaxed of countries, but turning up to an *asado* with a bottle of expensive wine comes close. The Argentine male (for women are fairly abstemious) likes to drink when he eats, and when he eats heavily, he drinks heavily. A cheap to mid-range red is the preferred accompaniment to a grilled steak. If it is too warm, some ice cubes will be added; if it is a little brash, a good squirt of soda will calm it down.

So if you want to drink what most Argentines drink, as opposed to what they export, hunt down brands like Vasco Viejo, Rincón Famoso, López, and Valderrobles. If it costs more than six US dollars, it is too expensive to take to an *asado*.

If there is one thing better than drinking wine at a barbecue, it is drinking wine at a winery. Many of Argentina's best bodegas (not only in Mendoza, but in Salta too) are open to visitors (see page 264).

DRAUGHT PICKS

Quilmes is Argentina's national beer (although, it should be whispered, it is owned by a Brazilian conglomerate). It is sold in bottles and cans tricked out in the blue and white of the Argentine flag, and is cheap, ubiquitous, and rather bland.

There are a number of other options that are becoming increasingly popular, however, particularly with younger Argentines who are not as sold on red wine as their parents are. Labels such as Warsteiner and Isenbeck are better than Quilmes, but still taste like the mass-produced products they are. Much more flavorsome are the ales produced by smaller breweries like Antares and Otro Mundo, as well as those that come from El Bolsón in Patagonia, long renowned as the center of the country's artisanal beer cottage industry.

Purmamarca, Jujuy province.

Ushuaia, the world's southernmost city.

El Teatro Colón interior,
Buenos Aires.

INTRODUCTION

A detailed guide to the whole of Argentina, with principal sights cross-referenced by number to the maps.

Gaucho, San Antonio de Areco.

Some travelers arrive in Argentina with their plans fully formed; others hatch itineraries over espressos in a Recoleta pavement café. Either way, almost everyone starts in Buenos Aires.

You'll need several days to visit the key sights and soak up the atmosphere in this most seductive of cities, more if you want to explore it thoroughly. For most people this is also the best opportunity to visit the great grasslands of the pampas. A day trip – or, better still, an overnighter – to an estancia will give you a taste of the countryside and the gaucho lifestyle.

The rest of the country – the interior, as it's known – is vast and, while all the key destinations are easily reached from the capital by plane, you'll need to be selective. Match places to your interests. Some spots, like the Iguazú Falls in the Northeast and the glaciers of southern Patagonia, resonate with almost everyone. Others, like the Iberá wetlands in Corrientes, the Mendoza wine routes, and the Patagonian Welsh villages have narrower appeal. Hence the attraction of a town like Bariloche in the north Patagonian Lake District, which offers an array of different activities – including the always popular one of doing nothing whatsoever.

The Church of the Sacred Heart, Córdoba.

Consider time as well as place. Argentines travel too, which means that many roads and resorts are clogged during the local summer high season (January and February). Spotting whales off the Valdés Peninsula is the experience of a lifetime, but the whales only come from June to December. Drivers in particular need to take account of seasonal variations. The stunning valleys and uplands of the Northwest are a memorable road trip waiting to happen – just not in the rainy season (December–March), when a suddenly impassable route could make it memorable for the wrong reasons.

Above all, be patient. Argentina's tourism infrastructure is constantly improving but delays, cancellations, unscheduled variations...these things are still facts of life. As is the warmth of the local who offers to share a mate with you while you're waiting for that delayed bus. Such consolations invariably outweigh the inconveniences.

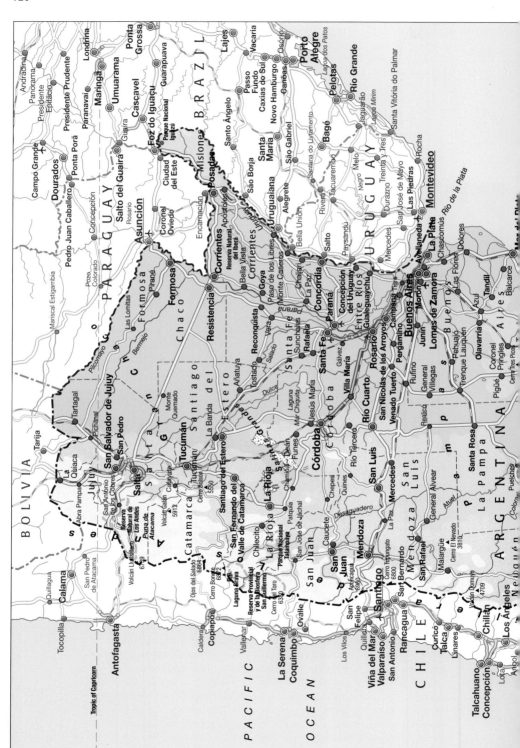

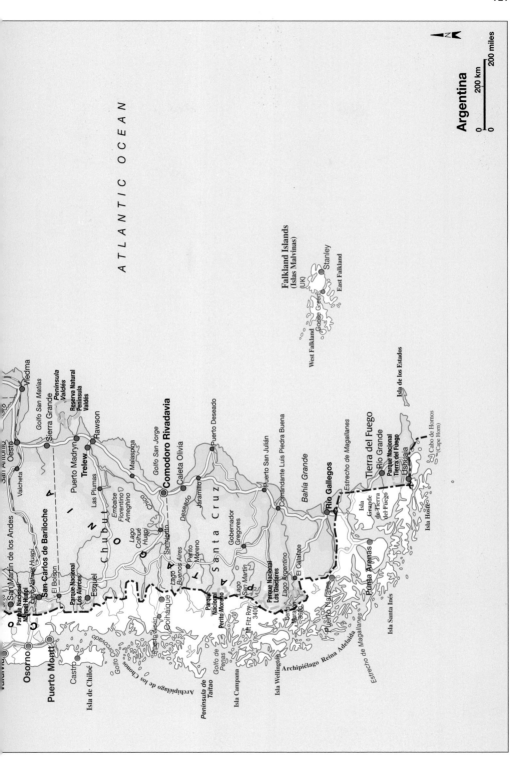

ATLANTIC OCEAN

Argentina

0   200 km
0   200 miles

Falkland Islands
(Islas Malvinas)
(UK)

Stanley
Goose Green
West Falkland   East Falkland

Isla de los Estados

Viedma
Golfo San Matías
Sierra Grande
Península Valdés
Reserva Natural Península Valdés
Rawson
Puerto Madryn   Trelew
Las Plumas
Malaspina
Golfo San Jorge
Comodoro Rivadavia
Caleta Olivia
Puerto Deseado
Jaramillo
Puerto San Julián
Comandante Luis Piedra Buena
Bahía Grande
Río Gallegos
Estrecho de Magallanes
Tierra del Fuego
Río Grande
Parque Nacional Tierra del Fuego
Ushuaia
Cabo de Hornos (Cape Horn)
Isla Hoste

San Antonio Oeste
Valcheta
San Antonio

San Martín de los Andes
Parque Nacional Nahuel Huapi
Lago Nahuel Huapi
San Carlos de Bariloche
El Bolsón
Parque Nacional Los Alerces
Esquel

Chubut

Embalse Florentino Ameghino
Chico
Lago Colhué Huapi
Sarmiento
Deseado

Santa Cruz

Lago Buenos Aires
Perito Moreno
Gobernador Gregores
Lago San Martín
Parque Nacional Perito Moreno
Mt Fitz Roy 3406?
El Chaltén 3600?
Lago Viedma
El Calafate
Lago Argentino
Parque Nacional Los Glaciares
Puerto Natales
Punta Arenas
Isla Santa Inés
Estrecho de Magallanes
Archipiélago Reina Adelaida

Grande Isla de Tierra del Fuego

Osorno
Puerto Montt
Castro
Isla de Chiloé
Golfo Corcovado
Chaitén
Archipiélago de los Chonos
Peninsula de Taitao
Golfo de Penas
Isla Campana
Isla Wellington
Coihaique

N

Buenos Aires

500 m
500 yds

- B Museo de Arte Latinoamericano de Buenos Aires (MALBA)
- A Museo de Arte Popular José Hernández

Palermo

Museo Nacional de Arte Decorativo, Museo Nacional de Arte Oriental

33 Biblioteca Nacional

32 Eva Perón (Evita)

Museo del Libro y de la Lengua

Museo Xul Solar

31 Museo Nacional de Bellas Artes

30 Palais de Glace

Floralis Genérica

Plaza Nacional de Derecho

Facultad de Derecho

28 Basílica de Nuestra Señora del Pilar

29 Centro Cultural Recoleta

27 CEMENTERIO DE LA RECOLETA

RECOLETA

Plaza Francia

Casa de la Cultura

Brick Hotel Buenos Aires

Patio Bullrich

Avenida 9 de Julio

Teatro Nacional Cervantes

Museo de Arte Hispanoamericano Isaac Fernández Blanco

20 Estación Retiro

25 Museo Nacional Ferroviario

Estación Terminal de Ómnibus

FF.CC. General San Martín

FF.CC. General M. Belgrano

FF.CC. General B. Mitre

Casa de Moneda

Adm. General de Vialidad

Plaza Canadá

10 La Torre Monumental

24 Plaza de la Fuerza Aérea

21 Plaza Libertador General San Martín

22 Palacio Paz

Museo de Armas

23 Edificio Kavanagh

Santísimo Sacramento

Dirección General de Migraciones

Antepuerto

Dársena Norte

Dársena B

Dársena C

Dársena D

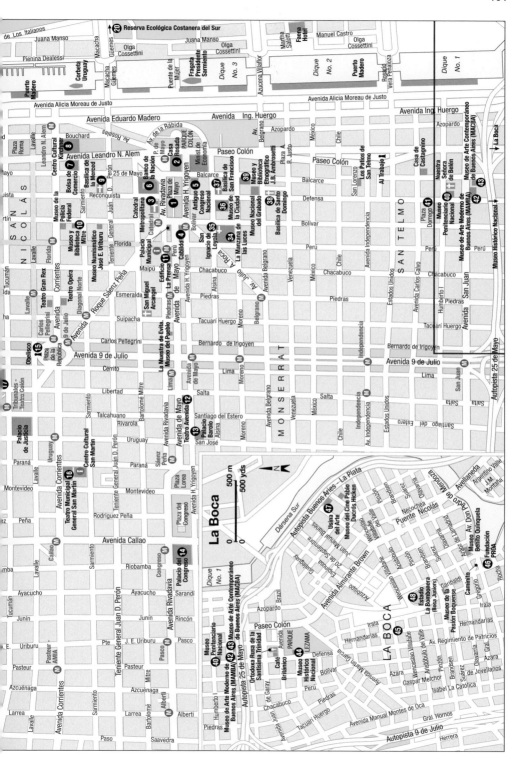

BUENOS AIRES

Grand, edgy, and famously seductive, the Argentine capital continues to earn its right to be counted among the world's great cities.

In terms of size and status, no other Argentine city comes close to Buenos Aires. It is New York, Washington DC, and San Francisco rolled into one, the country's cultural, countercultural, and institutional heart. Its spacious plazas and wide boulevards, laid out a century ago when Argentina was among the world's richest nations, evoke Paris and Madrid. Architecturally, the city is a hymn to eclecticism. Chicago-style skyscrapers overlook British-style railway stations and what should clash in theory, blends in practice.

Travel writer Paul Theroux called the Argentine capital "a most civilized anthill," a metaphor that captures both the city's sophistication and the pace at which its three million inhabitants (known as *porteños*) live their lives. While a quick glance down a list of local surnames will reveal the richness of the city's immigrant heritage, people are unlikely to tell you their (probably tangled) ethnic roots unless pressed into doing so. *Porteños* are justly proud of having synthesized a common culture from such disparate ingredients, and the warmth with which they greet foreign visitors suggests they see this as a work in progress.

FOUNDING AND SETTLEMENT

Historians still argue over who founded Buenos Aires, and when. We can

Street tango.

discount Spanish navigator Juan de Solís whose landing here in 1516 ended with his murder at the hand of tribesmen, though not before he'd named the expanse of brown water on which he had sailed *Mar Dulce* (*Sweet Sea*). This "sea," later renamed the Río de la Plata or River Plate is in fact one of the world's largest estuaries.

A better candidate is Pedro de Mendoza, who established the first settlement here in 1536. Many historians believe he planted the Spanish flag in what is now Parque Lezama, in San

Main attractions

Plaza de Mayo
Museo Xul Solar
Teatro Colón
Plaza San Martín
Cementerio de la Recoleta
Museo Nacional de Bellas Artes
MALBA
La Manzana de las Luces
Plaza Dorrego
Usina del Arte

Maps on pages 130, 156

Street scene in Palermo Soho.

Telmo. After five precarious and, from all accounts, miserable years, Mendoza and crew moved upriver to found Asunción, Paraguay. They left two important legacies: the city's name, Nuestra Señora de Santa María del Buen Ayre, and hundreds of horses and cows that escaped into the pampas where they were to flourish and multiply.

Finally, in 1586, Juan de Garay, a mestizo (of Spanish and indigenous blood) from Asunción, Paraguay, returned with 70 men and established a permanent settlement. A fortress was built facing the river, and the town square, later to be known as Plaza de Mayo, was marked off to the west. At the far end of the plaza they built the Cabildo (town council) and on the northern corner, a small chapel. Although new buildings have been constructed on the ruins, the plaza maintains this basic structure and is still the center of the city's official activities.

Buenos Aires was the last major city to be founded in Latin America. Not only was it geographically cut off from more developed trade routes but

Spanish law prohibited the use of its ports for both the import of European goods and the export of precious metals from Potosí and Lima. The English, Portuguese, and French were quick to exploit this vacuum, and the illegal trade carried out with the connivance of these powers enabled the settlement to survive, if not to flourish.

Porteños traded cow hides, tallow, and silver brought from northern mining centers for manufactured goods from abroad. They also began to import construction materials, since the pampas had neither trees nor stones: homes were originally built of adobe and straw.

INDEPENDENCE AND DEVELOPMENT

Buenos Aires' transition from colonial backwater to regional power began in 1776, when Spain made it the capital of the new Viceroyalty of the River Plate. Lawyers, bureaucrats, and soldiers were needed to execute the city's administrative responsibilities; they came. Slaves were needed to do everything else; they were shipped in. Buenos Aires

experienced its first boom and within a few years was being talked about in the same breath as Lima and Mexico City.

Alarmingly for the Spanish Crown, this rising prosperity had an unintended consequence. The material progress achieved by *porteños* had the effect of throwing their political impoverishment into sharper relief, and the merchant classes, encouraged by intellectuals, began to press for greater autonomy. When, alone, they were able to repel two British invasions in 1806 and 1807, *porteños* were able to add self-defense and security to the list of things for which they no longer needed Spain. These factors, along with Napoleon's invasion of Spain, created the condition for the May Revolution of 1810 (see page 43).

In the subsequent decades, the government of Buenos Aires was consumed with the struggle for control over the rest of the country. The Federalists, represented by Juan Manuel de Rosas, the governor of Buenos Aires from 1829 to 1852, believed each province should maintain considerable power and independence. The Unitarians, who came to power when General Urquiza overthrew Rosas, sought the dominance of Buenos Aires over the rest of the country.

Finally, in 1880, the dispute was resolved in a small street battle, and the city became a federal district, rather than simply the capital of the province of Buenos Aires. This was also to be a decade of intense change for the city. Under President Julio Roca, the mayor of the city looked to Europe and especially Paris as a model for change. Hundreds of buildings were constructed in imitation of the latest Parisian styles. New neighborhoods were created for the wealthy by filling in huge sections of the river, particularly in the northern parts of the city, where Retiro, Recoleta, and Palermo lie.

A CHANGING CITY

The 1880s also saw the beginning of mass immigration from Europe, principally from Italy and Spain but also from Germany, Poland, and Britain, as well as Lebanon and Syria, and later Russia. By 1910 the city had 1,300,000 inhabitants who enjoyed public services such as the tramway, running water, schools, and police protection.

As the 20th century progressed, new architecture in Buenos Aires tended to reflect both home-grown political and cultural movements and the influence of European and North American Modernism. Many buildings from the Peronist 1940s and 1950s are none-too-subtle expressions of state supremacy, while skyscraper blocks of apartment buildings dot the landscape from the following decades.

Thanks in part to the relative political stability of recent years, along with a reorganized city government structure headed by an elected mayor with genuine executive clout, a number of high-profile urban improvement programs have been launched and, what is a rarer thing in Buenos Aires, completed. The shimmering skyscrapers of Puerto Madero house some of the priciest real estate on the continent,

Turkish immigrant with hookah pipe.

Booming trade in a 19th-century dockside warehouse.

Steak sandwich, Buenos Aires-style.

while less affluent citizens can take advantage of the city's growing cycle-lane network. Barrios like San Telmo and, most notably, Palermo Viejo have been transformed, not by government bureaucrats but by a wave of enthusiastic retailers and restaurateurs with a taste for edgy fashions and global cuisine respectively.

GETTING YOUR BEARINGS

Buenos Aires is one of the largest cities in Latin America. The federal district occupies 200 sq km (77 sq miles) and is populated by more than 3 million people. The entire metropolitan area (Greater Buenos Aires) spans 2,915 sq km (1,121 sq miles) and is populated by around 13 million people: a remarkable one-third of the country's population. (Unless stated otherwise, our use of "Buenos Aires" refers to the federal district only.)

The city limits are marked to the west and north by the General Paz orbital road, to the south by the (horribly polluted) Riachuelo waterway, and to the east by the natural boundary of the Río de la Plata across which, on a

clear day, you can glimpse the Uruguayan coast.

Despite its sprawl, Buenos Aires is easy to navigate. Of its 48 *barrios* (neighborhoods), fewer than ten are on what might be called the tourist trail, and these are conveniently stacked one atop the other on the city's eastern edge. Travel north–south following the shoreline of the Río de la Plata (River Plate) and you will pass through the barrios of Palermo, Recoleta, Retiro, San Nicolás (the downtown district, usually known as "el Centro"), Monserrat, San Telmo, and La Boca. Most of the city's great buildings, plazas, and monuments, not to mention its hotels and entertainment venues, are concentrated in this "corridor." However, the ongoing expansion of the city's Subte (subway) network means that several barrios previously ignored by visitors, such as the southern neighborhood of Parque Patricios, are now easily reached from the city center.

Overground, the *colectivo* (bus) network is comprehensive, cheap and efficient, and taxi fares are relatively

affordable. But the cheapest, the most reliable, and in many ways the best form of transport is old-fashioned leg power. The city's *calles* (streets) are laid out in a mostly regular grid pattern, each *manzana* (block) comprising 100 street numbers exactly, so it's hard to get lost. There are few hills to challenge the walker, and the ability to stop and stare whenever you feel like it is priceless.

Locals often talk about the city in terms of "North" and "South", a division that is at once mythical and useful. Below Avenida Rivadavia, which runs 10 miles (16km) east–west from the Casa Rosada to the edge of the city and unofficially divides the city into its two halves, is *el sur* (the south). Here, compared with the north, the streets are narrower and darker, the population more densely packed, and the vestiges of the city's industrial and bohemian past more evident. North of Rivadavia the city opens up into more spacious avenues, plazas, and parks, with monuments, embassies, and Parisian-style apartment blocks replacing the tenements and warehouses of the south.

THE CENTER OF BUENOS AIRES

The center is truly the city's "downtown," and while most *porteños* live in outer barrios, everyone comes here, either to work, to eat, or to find entertainment. Residential barrios have their own mini commercial areas, so that, except to visit friends, many *porteños* never cross the city; they simply head downtown.

As in every big city, there are many hurried, well-dressed businesspeople in the center of Buenos Aires, but there are also Argentines here enjoying the bookstores, the movies, the theater, the café conversations on every imaginable topic, the plazas, the shopping, and the political and cultural street life. Some streets, like Calle Florida, Avenida Corrientes, and Lavalle, are for strolling, and are filled with leisurely visitors who come to see and be seen. A two-hour walk around the center starting at the Plaza de Mayo provides a quick introduction to the government buildings as well as the commercial, financial, and entertainment districts.

Avenida de Mayo stretches 50 blocks, from the Plaza del Congreso to the Plaza de Mayo.

The Cabildo building on Plaza de Mayo.

Casa Rosada or the Pink House.

PLAZA POLITICS

Buenos Aires began with the **Plaza de Mayo ❶**, today a rather down-at-heel square with its tall palm trees (imported from Brazil) and attractive flower beds competing for attention with ever-present political demonstrators and carts loaded with plastic flags and other tat. But the Plaza has been and still is the pulsating center of the country. Since its founding in 1580 as the Plaza del Fuerte (fortress), many important historical events have been celebrated or protested against here.

The most eye-catching structure in the plaza is unquestionably the **Casa Rosada**, the seat of the executive branch of the government (though unlike the U.S. White House, it's not the president's official residence, which is located north of the city, in Olivos). Flanking it are the Banco de la Nación, the Catedral Metropolitana, the Palacio Municipal (City Hall), and the Cabildo (Town Council).

The Casa Rosada was originally a fortress overlooking what is now the **Parque Colón** (confusingly called *parque* but actually a plaza) but was at that time the river's edge. When attacks by the indigenous inhabitants subsided, the plaza became Plaza del Mercado, a marketplace and social center. The name and role of the plaza changed again with the British invasions of 1806 and 1807, when it became the Plaza de la Victoria. Finally, following the declaration of independence, the plaza assumed its present name, in honor of the month of May in 1810 when the city broke with Spanish rule.

The date also marks the first mass rally in the plaza, on this occasion to celebrate independence. Subsequently, Argentines have poured into the plaza to protest and celebrate most of the nation's important events. Political parties, human rights groups, and trade unions regularly ask their supporters to rally in the plaza in order to exert pressure on the government of the day.

HISTORIC DEMONSTRATIONS

Pivotal events in the history of the Plaza de Mayo include the October 17, 1945 workers' demonstration, organized by the General Confederation of Labor to

protest about the brief detention of then vice-president Juan Perón. Ten years later, the air force bombed the plaza while hundreds of thousands of Perón's supporters were rallying to defend his administration from the impending military coup. In 1982, Argentines flooded the plaza to applaud General Galtieri's invasion of the Malvinas/Falkland Islands. A few months later, they were back again, determined to oust the military government for having lied about their chances of defeating the British. In 1987, the plaza was jammed with 800,000 *porteños* demonstrating against a military rebellion, and again at the end of 1989, protesting about President Menem's pardon of convicted generals.

But the most famous rallies have been those of the *Madres de la Plaza de Mayo* – the mothers of the many people who disappeared during the "dirty war" (see page 63). The Mothers now operate from a building close to the Congress, where they continue to put pressure on politicians to uncover the truth about these dark years.

During the last years of the military regime, young people accompanying the Mothers would taunt the menacing army and police units with chants of, "Cowards, this plaza belongs to the Mothers." The white headscarves the Mothers traditionally wear at all the demonstrations have been depicted around the base of the pyramid, marking their weekly route. Despite the prosecution and conviction of many ex-members of the military junta, the Mothers continue to march every Thursday afternoon, protagonists in what they regard as the ongoing struggle for human rights in Argentina.

THE PINK HOUSE

Leaders of the nation traditionally address the masses from the balconies of the **Casa Rosada** ❷ (guided tours in English, Sat–Sun 12.30am and 2.30pm; free, booking essential at https://visitas. casarosada.gob.ar/), an architecturally imbalanced building (originally the city's fort) that has been renovated and rebuilt several times since President Mitre chose it for his office in the 1860s. It was his successor, Domingo Sarmiento, who selected the famous color scheme. There are several explanations for why he had it painted pink, a tone achieved by mixing beef fat, blood, and lime. Some insist that Sarmiento chose pink to distinguish the building from the White House in Washington, DC. Others say that pink was selected as a compromise between Argentina's two feuding factions, the Federalists and the Unitarians, whose colors were red and white respectively. The simplest explanation is probably the most credible: it was the only alternative to white in those days.

The **Museo Casa Rosada** (www.casa-rosada.gob.ar/la-casa-rosada/museo; Wed–Sun 10am–6pm; free) is located behind the Casa Rosada in a space once occupied by the city's fort and later by its customs office. The museum's handsome brick walls and arches date back to the latter construction, built in 1855. Exhibits trace the history of Argentina since

Known for its hip boutiques, art galleries, and cafés, Palermo Soho has become one of the capital's most fashionable areas.

Museo Casa Rosada.

its first cry for independence in 1810 and include posters and portraits of Perón and Evita, a bloodstained headscarf once worn by Madres de la Plaza de Mayo leader Hebe de Bonafini (a security official struck her on the head during a demonstration), and a large mural by the Mexican master David Siqueiros, painted in Buenos Aires in 1930.

The Grenadiers Regiment guards the Casa Rosada and the president. This elite army unit was created during the independence wars by General San Martín, and its soldiers wear the same blue and red uniforms that distinguished them in those times. Between 6 and 7pm each day, they lower the national flag in front of the Casa Rosada. On national holidays the Grenadiers often parade on horseback, and they accompany the president on his public appearances.

CHURCH AND STATE

The **Catedral Metropolitana** ❸ (www. catedralbuenosaires.org.ar; Mon–Fri 7.30am–6.45pm, Sat–Sun 9am–6.45pm; free) is the next historic building on the plaza and the seat of Buenos Aires' archbishopric. The cathedral was erected over the course of several decades and was completed in 1862. It was built, like the Cabildo and the Casa Rosada, upon the foundations of earlier versions. There are 12 severe neoclassical pillars at its front that are said to represent the 12 apostles. The bas-relief on the upper portion of the facade depicts the arrival of Jacob and his sons in Egypt and their reunion with Joseph.

Inside are five naves housing important art relics. The oil paintings on the walls are attributed to the Flemish painter, Sir Peter Paul Rubens (1577–1640). There are also beautiful wood engravings by the Portuguese Manuel Coyto de Couto.

For Argentines, the most important aspect of the cathedral is the tomb of General José de San Martín, liberator of Argentina, Chile, and Peru. San Martín, who died during his self-imposed exile in France, is one of the few national heroes to be revered by Argentines of all political persuasions. An eternal flame burns in his memory on the far right-hand side of the colonnade. The cathedral is also known for its monthly organ recitals concerts and has a small **museum** (Mon–Fri 10am–2pm) containing memorabilia and personal effects of the Cardinal Jorge Mario Bergoglio, now Pope Francis.

Across Avenida de Mayo, on the western end of Plaza de Mayo, is the **Cabildo** ❹ (Town Council), a key historic building and perhaps the greatest patriotic attraction in Argentina. It was here that revolutionaries including Mariano Moreno plotted the break with Spain in 1810. School children are brought here and told how their forebears planned the nation's independence.

The Town Council has been on this site since around the time of the city's founding in 1580, although the present building was constructed in 1751. Originally, it spanned the length of the plaza with five great arches on each

Tomb of General José de San Martín in Catedral Metropolitana.

side. In 1880, when Avenida de Mayo was built, part of the building was demolished. And once again, in 1932, the Cabildo was further reduced, this time to its current size, with two arches on either side of the central balconies.

The Cabildo also houses an historic museum, the **Museo Histórico Nacional del Cabildo y de la Revolución de Mayo** (Tue–Wed and Fri 10.30am–5pm, Thu until 8pm, Sat–Sun 10.30am–6pm; guided tours in Spanish daily, in English only Jan–Feb Sat–Sun at 11.30am), inaugurated in 2010 as part of the country's bicentenary celebrations. Among the exhibits in this spruced-up space are treasures and artefacts from the colonial era, various items related to the "English invasions" of 1806–7, and some (relatively) nifty audio-visual and interactive panels that guide visitors through the events leading up to the 1810 revolution. Behind the museum is a pleasant patio, which is now the site of archeological excavations. Continuing around the plaza, on the southeastern corner is the **Antiguo Congreso Nacional** ❺ (guided tours Thu 3–5pm; library Mon–Fri 12.30–6pm; free), the former House of Congress, built in 1864. It served as the seat of government until 1905 and since 1971 has been used by the National Academy of History (www.anh.org.ar) as a conference center, with a history library and a small museum.

THE MICROCENTRO

The main banking area of Buenos Aires, known as the Microcentro (you may hear some older *porteños* referring to it as "La City") extends four blocks north from Plaza de Mayo to Avenida Corrientes along the parallel streets in between, and west for three blocks as far as pedestrianized Florida. Here you can find the major national as well as international banks.

Opposite the **Antiguo Congreso Nacional**, at the northeastern corner of Plaza de Mayo, is the **Banco de la Nación** ❻ (www.bna.com.ar). The old

Teatro Colón was on this site before it reopened on Plaza Lavalle in 1908. The imposing marble and stone bank was inaugurated in 1888. The building can be visited during bank opening hours and is home to an art gallery and a currency museum with a large collection of coins, notes, and medals.

Nearby, at San Martín 216, in one of the buildings belonging to the Banco Central is the **Museo Numismático José E. Uriburu** (Mon–Fri 10am–3pm; free). With more than 15,000 exhibits, the museum claims to be the biggest of its kind in the Americas.

The **Bolsa de Comercio** ❼ (Stock Exchange; Sarmiento 299; tel: 4316-7065; www.bcba.sba.com.ar; Wed and Fri 3.30pm, Thu 11am; free; booking essential; photo ID required; shorts and sleeveless tops forbidden) is located three blocks from the Plaza de Mayo. The building, which has a fine cupola, was inaugurated in 1919.

Across Avenida Leandro N. Alem, in the former central post office building, is the **Centro Cultural Kirchner** ❽ (CCK; www.cck.gob.ar; exhibitions

The Cabildo, where revolutionaries planned Argentina's independence from Spain.

Wed–Sun 1–8pm), inaugurated in 2015. The biggest cultural centre in Latin America and the third largest in the world, it is home to *La Ballena Azul* (The Blue Whale) concert hall, plus five other auditoriums, 18 halls, and 40 rooms of galleries, spread out over nine floors. It is also the headquarters of the Argentine National Symphony Orchestra.

Also within this area are the **Basílica de la Merced** ❾, at Reconquista and Perón, an 18th-century church and convent with lovely gardens and a restaurant in the patio offering one of the few peaceful oases in central Buenos Aires.

There has been a church on the site since 1712, and there was a convent here from 1600 to 1823. At San Martín 336, between Sarmiento and Corrientes, is the **Museo y Biblioteca Mitre** ❿ (www.museomitre.gob.ar; Mon–Fri 1–5.30pm; library Wed 2–5.30pm), where you'll find oil paintings, the personal effects of President Mitre, and an important historical and map library. Opposite, at San Martín 322, is the **Museo de la Policía Federal** (http://cpf.org.ar/museo-policial; Mon–Fri 2–6pm; free). Dedicated

Café culture in Palermo Soho.

to Argentina's federal police force, which was founded in 1899 and modeled closely on London's Scotland Yard, this small museum exhibits firearms, counterfeit banknotes, and picklocks and is for history-of-crime fanatics only.

AVENIDA DE MAYO

Returning to Plaza de Mayo and facing west, the view down Avenida de Mayo to the National Congress is spectacular, and the 15-block walk is a wonderful introduction to the city. Inaugurated in 1894, the avenue's main function was to link the Casa Rosada and the Congress building (construction on the latter began in 1897 and was largely completed by 1906). It was originally designed to imitate a Spanish avenue, with wide sidewalks, gilded lampposts, chocolate shops, outfitters' emporiums, and old Zarzuela theaters. Today, however, there is a mixture of influences with local adaptations that defy classification. As in much of the city, "neoclassical," "French," "Italian," and "Art Nouveau" are terms that do not adequately describe the potpourri of

☉ CAFE SOCIETY

The social life, and to a great extent the business and cultural life, of Buenos Aires revolves around cafés, or *confiterías*, as they are known in Argentina. "Meet me at the *confitería*" is the typical response to an invitation to go to the cinema or the theater, clinch a business deal, or simply get together for a chat. A coffee or a cognac in a favorite *confitería* is also the standard ritual for ending a night out on the town.

There are cafés on almost every street corner and they range from the most elegant to modest and cozy gathering places where neighbors exchange greetings or employees from nearby offices take a break to read the daily paper. Visitors to Buenos Aires often comment that only Paris rivals Buenos Aires as a true "café society."

Historically, the rise of the café as an institution came from the high proportion of male immigrants, who were either single or whose wives stayed behind. These men came to the cafés for companionship, a smoke, or a game of dominos. Gradually many cafés became associated with a particular clientele. Each political, artistic, and social group laid claim to its own café, so that even today many of the events that mark Argentine history were first discussed among friends or foes over a *confitería* table.

styles seen here. Nor is there a traditional coherence from one building to the next; highly decorative constructions stand cheek by jowl with ones that are functional and austere.

The first eye-catching building on Avenida de Mayo on the way from Plaza de Mayo is the **Edificio La Prensa** ⓫ (Tue–Sun 2–8pm; guided tours in Spanish and English Sat 4pm and 5pm, Sun 11am–4pm on the hour; free) built in the 1890s as the headquarters of the *La Prensa* newspaper, then at the height of its influence. The building, which now houses the city government-run Casa de la Cultura, is a Beaux Arts masterpiece whose facade is a gorgeous medley of sinuous wrought-iron lamp brackets and stucco ornamentation. Crowning it is a bronze lighthouse and on top of that, a statue of Athena, goddess of wisdom, who is depicted brandishing a torch in one hand and a newspaper in the other. (This clarion call for liberty of expression proved too feisty for Juan Domingo Perón, who confiscated the statue, along with the newspaper, in 1951.) The building's interior, and in particular the Salón Dorado (Golden Room), is worth exploring on a guided tour. The basement, once full of printing presses, is now an exhibition space.

At Avenida de Mayo 500 is the Perú subway station. The line from here, Línea A, was South America's first underground railway when it opened in 1913. Some of the station's original features have been preserved.

The Spanish-style **Teatro Avenida** ⓬, inaugurated in 1908, is at Avenida de Mayo 1212. Closed since 1979 as a result of a fire, the building has been renovated and was reopened in 1994. The beautiful 1,200-seat theater offers regular theatrical and musical performances, usually by Spanish companies or with a Spanish theme, and is also used for conferences.

By consensus the Avenida's architectural pièce de résistance is **Palacio Barolo** ⓭ (www.palaciobarolo.com.ar; guided tours in English, some with wine tasting and tango shows, see website for full details), at No.1370. The tallest building in the city when it was completed in 1923 (it held the title until the 1935 inauguration of the Kavanagh Building), the Barolo is nonetheless a triumph of style over size. Italian architect Mario Palanti designed the structure as a tribute to his great compatriot Dante Alighieri, author of the *Divine Comedy*. Like the poem, the building's 22 floors are divided into three chapters – hell, purgatory, and heaven. A lighthouse (restored for the 2010 bicentenary) representing God crowns the final floor and the view from the top is spectacular.

At its western end, Avenida de Mayo empties into **Plaza del Congreso**, the vernacular name for several distinct but contiguous squares which together form a large open space in front of the **Palacio del Congreso** ⓮ building (www.congreso.gob.ar/palacio.php; guided tours Mon–Tue and Thu–Fri at 12.30pm and 5pm, entrance from Hipólito Yrigoyen 1849). The square itself has a rather hangdog aspect, its graffiti-smeared monuments juxtaposed with bouncy

Grand architecture in the city center.

The Quilmes brewery was founded in Quilmes town in Buenos Aires province by a German immigrant.

castles and merry-go-rounds. But the Congress building, a monumental neo-classical construction resembling the U.S. Capitol, is impressive.

COFFEE BREAKS

There are several well-known restaurants and cafés along Avenida de Mayo, including Café Tortoni (www.cafetortoni.com.ar) at No.825, once a talking shop for writers, intellectuals, and other nighthawks, now a cultural heritage landmark mostly frequented by tourists. Marble tables, red-leather seats, bronze statues, and elaborate mirrors create the most regal of atmospheres. In the evenings the café hosts various theater and music shows, the most common being tango or jazz. Across the avenue is the almost equally famous London City café (www.londoncity.com.ar), opened in 1954. It was here that novelist Julio Cortázar wrote one of his early novels, *Los Premios* (*The Winners*).

AVENIDA 9 DE JULIO

Café Tortoni, a cultural heritage landmark.

The reason a stroll along Avenida de Mayo takes longer than you think it ought to is because it involves crossing one of the world's widest streets, Avenida 9 de Julio. Measuring 140 meters (460ft) from sidewalk to sidewalk, and with up to seven traffic lanes in each direction, this asphalt grand canyon can take up to ten minutes to traverse. Everything about it is big – big billboards, big buildings, big *palos borrachos* (silk floss trees) with pink blossoms in the summertime, and, of course, the big Obelisk.

The military government of 1936 decided to demolish rows of beautiful old French-style mansions to build this avenue. Much of the central block is now occupied by parking lots. The only mansion to survive was the **French Embassy**; its occupants refused to move, claiming it was foreign territory. There is a sad view of its barren white wall facing the center of town, testimony to the tragic disappearance of its neighbors.

The **Obelisco** ⑮, which rises sharply up towards the clouds at the intersection of Diagonal Norte, Corrientes, and 9 de Julio, was erected in 1936 in commemoration of the 400th anniversary of the first founding of Buenos Aires. Three years after the monument was erected the City Council voted 23 to 3 to tear it down. However, the order was not taken seriously and the Obelisk still stands today.

AVENIDA CORRIENTES

The Congress building is located at the corner of Rivadavia and Callao. Callao runs north from Rivadavia, and four blocks down is **Avenida Corrientes**, another near-mythical street for *porteños* and one that is namechecked in several tangos. Avenida Santa Fe, which has a more North American feel, has hijacked some of its bustle in recent years but Corrientes appeals to those who are more comfortable with local as opposed to imported culture. So, while there are neon lights, movie theaters, fast-food restaurants serving good local cuisine (a late-night slice of pizza eaten standing at the bar is the classic

Corrientes treat), and, most famously, theaters on Corrientes, the atmosphere is intellectual rather than gaudy.

There are little bookstores everywhere, *kioscos* (newsstands) with a wide selection of newspapers, magazines, and paperbacks, and old cafés where friends gather for long talks. The international and national films on show also reflect the serious interests of the moviegoers; you'll find European art-house cinema here, whereas Santa Fe is more likely to feature the latest Hollywood hit. The bookstores are traditionally one of Corrientes' greatest attractions. They are single rooms, open to the street, selling both secondhand and new books. Some patrons come to hunt for old treasures, or the latest bestseller, while others use the bookstores as a meeting place. The stores stay open until midnight.

CORRIENTES CULTURE

At Corrientes 1530 stands the **Teatro Municipal General San Martín** ⓰ (http://complejoteatral.gob.ar; guided tours available by appointment). This chrome and glass building was inaugurated in 1960 and is the largest public theater in Argentina, with five stages and an estimated half a million spectators each year. The year-round program includes concerts, plays, film festivals, and lectures, and there are permanent companies for theater, ballet, and puppetry. On the 10th floor you'll find the Leopoldo Lugones cinema, which screens mostly avant-garde movies.

In the block behind the theater, at Sarmiento 1551, is the **Centro Cultural San Martín** (http://elculturalsanmartin.org; daily 8am–10pm, exhibitions Tue–Sun 3–9pm), a sister building with an equally important flurry of cultural activity.

Further down Corrientes are the main commercial theaters in Buenos Aires: the Opéra, the Gran Rex, and El Nacional. Also on Corrientes is a plaque that is a must-see for all lovers of traditional tango as it marks the spot where the Corrientes 348 apartment

block once stood (the address is mentioned in the first line of Carlos César Lenzi's classic tango *A media luz*).

The tradition of free concerts, seminars, and other cultural activities is one of the most striking aspects of life in Buenos Aires. If anything, the activity has gained momentum in recent years, despite the economic crisis, and was undoubtedly boosted by the 1980s return to democracy (see page 69). For visitors, both these centers are a fine introduction to the contemporary cultural scene in Buenos Aires and the rest of the country.

Plaza Lavalle is another center of activity in the area. It is two blocks north of Corrientes at the 1300 block. The **Federal Justice Tribunals** are at one end of this historic plaza, and the internationally renowned Teatro Colón is at the other. The plaza first served as a dumping ground for the unusable parts of cattle butchered for their hides. In the late 19th century, it became the site of the city's first train station, which later moved to Once. In the plaza today there is a beautiful

⊙ **Tip**

There are two tourist information booths (https://turismo.buenosaires.gob.ar/en/recorrido/tourist-assistance-centers) at either end of Calle Florida, one being at the junction with Diagonal Roque Sáenz Peña, the other with Marcelo T.de Alvear at the Plaza San Martín.

View along Avenida Corrientes towards the Obelisco.

Shoe-shiner on Avenida de Mayo.

statue and fountain commemorating Norma Fontenla and José Neglia, two dancers from the Colón ballet killed in a plane crash with nine other members of the ballet troupe in the 1970s.

Further down, between Corrientes and Tucumán is the **Museo Casa Carlos Gardel** (Jean Jaures 735, Abasto; www.buenosaires.gob.ar/museocasacarlosgardel; Mon, Wed, Thu, and Fri 11am–6pm, Sat–Sun 10am–7pm; free on Wed), dedicated to the famous tango singer and his work. The museum allows visitors to travel back in time and immerse themselves in Gardel's world.

Just a 15-minute walk away is the **Museo Xul Solar** (Laprida 1212; www.xulsolar.org.ar; Tue–Fri noon–8pm, Sat 1–7pm) that celebrates the work of one of the most original Argentine creators of the 20th century. Xul Solar was a painter, sculptor, writer, and inventor of "Neo Criollo", an imaginary language being a fusion of Portuguese and Spanish.

TEATRO COLÓN

The opulent Teatro Colón.

The **Teatro Colón** ⓱ (www.teatrocolon.org.ar; guided tours in English daily 9am–5pm), Buenos Aires' opera house, occupies the entire block between Viamonte, Lavalle, Libertad, and Cerrito (part of 9 de Julio). It is the symbol of the city's high culture, and part of the reason Buenos Aires became known in the early 20th century as the "Paris of Latin America." The theater's elaborate European architecture, its acoustics (said to be near perfect), and the quality of performers who appear here have made the opera house internationally famous.

Three architects took part in the construction of the building before it was finished in 1908. The original blueprint, however, was respected. It is a combination of styles – Italian Renaissance, French, and Greek. The interior includes colored glass domes and elaborate chandeliers. The principal auditorium is seven stories high and holds up to 3,500 spectators. There is a 612-sq-meter (6,590-sq-ft) stage on a revolving disk that permits rapid scenery changes.

Well over 1,000 people are employed by the theater. As well as its role as an opera venue, it is also the home of the National Symphony Orchestra and the

National Ballet. In a refit that cost millions of dollars, a huge basement was added, creating storage space for the sets, costumes, and props and working space for the various departments. The Colón's season runs approximately from April to November.

One block from the front of the Colón, along the Plaza Lavalle, is the beautiful **Templo Libertad**, the principal synagogue of Argentina's 300,000-strong Jewish community (tel: 011-4123 0832; www.templolibertad.org.ar; visits by prior appointment; photo ID required). In front of the synagogue a series of concrete barriers has been erected, as is the case at most buildings linked to Buenos Aires' Jewish community. This sad precaution was instituted in the aftermath of the 1992 car bombing of the Israeli Embassy and the 1994 car bombing of the AMIA community center, atrocities in which 29 and 85 people were killed respectively.

Turning right off Libertad onto Córdoba brings you to the beautiful Spanish-style **Teatro Nacional Cervantes** ⓲ (www.teatrocervantes.gov.ar), inaugurated in 1921, designated the National Theater in 1933 and declared a national monument in 1995. The theater has three stages – the principal, large hall with red-velvet seats and curtains and abundant gilt decoration; the 150-seat Sala Argentina, used for chamber music; and the slightly smaller Salón Dorado – and has been remodeled on several occasions.

RETAIL THERAPY

Crossing 9 de Julio on Avenida Corrientes you enter the heart of the Buenos Aires business district. Here, it is worth going up to Lavalle, one block north, since the best stretch of Corrientes is back across 9 de Julio, as far as Callao. Lavalle, like Florida several blocks down, is a brash pedestrian street. At night it is filled with young moviegoers, due to having numerous movie theaters in a four-block stretch. This is despite the fact that in recent years, a number have been closed down or turned into

bazaars or evangelical temples. As more cinemas have been built in neighborhood shopping centers, the temptation to go downtown has been reduced. There are also pizza parlors, cafés, restaurants, and several shopping malls.

Calle Florida, also closed to motor vehicles and nicely renovated, is the principal shopping district downtown. The promenade, punctuated occasionally with *kioscos* and potted shrubs, is packed with shoppers throughout the day, as well as folk musicians, human statues, tango dancers, and others passing the hat for cash. There is a leisurely pace here, and, because of the crowds, it is not a good route for anyone in a hurry.

The shopping on Florida is slightly more expensive than in other districts downtown, although the posh end of the street is between Corrientes and Plaza San Martín; between Corrientes and Rivadavia, Florida becomes decidedly more cut-price. As elsewhere, most shops are one-room boutiques, many in interior shopping malls that exit onto adjacent streets. They sell clothes, leather goods (mostly

Looking towards Puerto Madero and the Puente de la Mujer footbridge.

overpriced and poor quality), jewelry, toys, and souvenirs.

Centro Cultural Borges (www.cc borges.org.ar; Mon–Sat 10am–9pm, Sun noon–9pm) on Viamonte and San Martín was constructed in 1995. It is a theater and arts venue that commemorates, rather than features, the great writer.

The most centrally located mall is the **Galerías Pacífico** (www.galeriaspa-cifico.com.ar; guided tours in English Mon–Fri), between Viamonte and Córdoba. It is part of an early 20th-century Italian building that was saved from demolition because of the frescoes on the ceiling of its great dome. These are the work of five Argentine painters: Urruchua, Bern, Castagnino, Colmeiro, and Spilimbergo (see page 99). Renovated in 1990, its spacious, air-conditioned interior provides a welcome relief from the bustle of Florida, with a good selection of shops, cafés, and crafts stalls. There are also cafés along Florida, offering a chance to relax from the busy street. The street ends at the Plaza San Martín and the entrance to **Ruth Benzacar** (Florida 1000; www.

ruthbenzacar.com; Tue–Sat 2–7pm), an excellent art gallery showing mostly Argentine contemporary art.

PUERTO MADERO

The vibrant, renovated docklands barrio of Puerto Madero is just a short stroll east (orient yourself by turning your back to the Obelisk) from the intersection of Avenida Corrientes and Florida. The western side of the former docks, Puerto Madero Oeste, comprises a string of renovated red-brick buildings that runs from Avenida Córdoba at the northern end to the Buenos Aires–La Plata Highway at the southern end. The original waterfront port buildings, constructed by Eduardo Madero in 1887, have been turned into fancy office blocks and restaurants, ideal for a very elegant meal or a coffee. While this is the in-place for business lunches, the restaurants here are among the most expensive in Buenos Aires – and not necessarily the best.

The Puerto Madero neighborhood has a pedestrian walkway extending the length of the port, and includes yacht clubs and most of Buenos Aires' most modern tower blocks and hotels, in addition to the 19th-century port buildings. The most prominent buildings in the area are the Telecom Tower and the Fortabat Tower, both near the Córdoba end of the district. At Dock 4, the **Museo Fortabat** ⓲ (www.coleccionfortabat. org.ar; Tue–Sun noon–8pm) houses an interesting collection amassed by the entrepreneur and art collector Amalia Lacroze de Fortabat. Alongside works by Argentine artists, there are more than 200 masterpieces, including works by Dali, Chagall, Miró, Renoir, Gauguin, Lawrence Alma-Tadema, and William Turner. The two-story, steel and glass building by Uruguayan architect Rafael Viñoly has a roof with mobile awnings that open according to the sun's position.

At Dock 3, the **ARA *Presidente Sarmiento*** (daily 10am–7pm; closed when it rains) is a 19th-century Argentine Navy training frigate now serving as a

Dining at Cabaña Las Lilas, a renowned parrilla in Puerto Madero.

museum. The ship, built in England in 1897, still has its original woodwork and furniture. Nearby, the white **Puente de la Mujer** (Woman's Bridge) was designed by famous Spanish architect Santiago Calatrava, and was inspired by an image of a couple dancing the tango.

On the eastern side, known as Puerto Madero Este, lies the Faena Hotel Universe complex (www.faena.com/buenos-aires/), built from a former grain silo by internationally renowned architect Philippe Starck for local entrepreneur Alan Faena. Other landmark buildings include the Aleph Residence designed by the British architect Norman Foster. A cluster of impressive skyscrapers has risen from the rubble of this former wasteland, and real estate prices in Puerto Madero Este are, by some estimates, the highest in South America. Safe but rather soulless, it is the residential district of choice for Argentina's political and corporate high-fliers.

A short distance away is the **Reserva Ecológica Costanera del Sur ㉑** (www.reservacostanera.com.ar; Tue–Sun 8am–6pm, until 7pm Nov–Mar; free), a large open green space along the river which has been a nature reserve since 1986. Clay paths wind their way around four lakes, making this a great spot for a post-prandial stroll. The reserve, which is very popular at weekends, is home to many species of water birds and mammals. Stretching northwards from the entrance to the reserve is the Costanera Sur (Southern Promenade) itself, where you can buy a *choripán* (grilled sausage sandwich) from one of the many food carts lining the sidewalk while looking across the Río de la Plata towards Uruguay.

NORTH OF THE CENTER

The city's northern barrios, which include Retiro, Recoleta, and Palermo, are where the majority of affluent *porteños* live, shop, and socialize. Elegant mansions built at the turn of the 20th century are immediately reminiscent of Paris, although the architectural styles are actually a mixture of different influences.

Until the end of the 19th century, this area was unpopulated, except for a slaughterhouse on the site of the Recoleta Plaza. Much of the area was under water. In the 1870s, following a yellow fever epidemic, many wealthy families from the south moved north.

Great changes came in the 1880s when President Roca launched a concerted program to modernize Buenos Aires. Prominent Argentines had traveled to Paris and London and were deeply influenced by what they had seen. They brought back materials and ideas for the transformation of Buenos Aires into a cosmopolitan city.

Roca's policies were and still are controversial. Critics supported a more nationalistic policy, oriented toward the development of the interior of the country. And yet, unquestionably, what was called the "Generation of the 80s" was responsible for making Buenos Aires the great city that it became.

Plaza San Martín and La Torre Monumental.

RETIRO

A walking tour of the northern districts begins at the edge of the city center, where the downtown barrio of San Nicolás turns into Retiro. At the northern end of Florida is **Plaza San Martín ㉑**, which is one of Buenos Aires' loveliest squares, putting Plaza de Mayo to shame. Facing the tree-filled plaza (the jacarandas are particularly stunning when they flower in November), at the corner of Santa Fe and Maipú, is the **Palacio Paz y Museo de Armas ㉒**, formerly the residence of the Paz family (founders of the newspaper *La Prensa*) and later, after it became the headquarters of Argentina's military high command, the *Círculo Militar*. Built in the decade leading up to World War I, this stunning – if rather pharaonic – construction was partially modeled on the Louvre and is the grandest private residence ever built in Argentina. The **Museo de Armas de la Nación** (http://museodearmas.com.ar; Mon–Fri 1–7pm) houses a series of uniforms used by the Argentine Army, as well as antique weapons. The only way to visit Palacio

Evita Perón is buried at the Cementerio de la Recoleta.

Cementerio de la Recoleta.

Paz is on a guided tour (in English Thu 3.30am; www.palaciopaz.com.ar).

Across Plaza San Martín at the end of Florida is the **Edificio Kavanagh ㉓**. This iconic Rationalist skyscraper was the city's tallest structure when it was inaugurated in 1935. The building, with 105 apartments, is notable for its narrow front and ziggurated facade. Behind it, at San Martín 1039, is the **Basílica del Santísimo Sacramento**. Opened in 1928, it is the church of choice for many of the city's most traditional families, and one of the venues of choice for "society" weddings.

The lower, eastern end of Plaza San Martín is dominated by the black-marble monument to Argentine soldiers killed in the Falklands/Malvinas war, modeled on the Vietnam war memorial in Washington. Across Libertador is **La Torre Monumental ㉔** (Mon–Fri 10am–5pm, Sat–Sun 11am–6.30pm; free) or "La Torre de los Ingleses," on Plaza de la Fuerza Aérea, donated by the city's Anglo-Argentine community to celebrate the centenary of the 1806 May Revolution. It includes four clocks whose faces measure 4.5 meters (nearly 15ft) in diameter.

On one side of the plaza is the **Retiro** train station, which includes the Mitre, Belgrano, and Sarmiento terminals and, at the far end, the Retiro bus terminal, where most long-distance buses arrive and depart. Opened in 1915, the railway terminals are glorious examples of post-Victorian industrial engineering and architecture. After decades of decline, the ongoing process of renationalizing the Argentinian railway network (started in 2015) has prompted plans to expand the station and renovate its existing buildings.

To one side of Retiro station, at Avenida del Libertador 405, is the **Museo Nacional Ferroviario ㉕** (www.argentina.gob.ar/museoferroviario; Mon–Fri 9.30am–5pm, Sat–Sun 10.30am–6pm; free). This museum is housed in a converted warehouse and contains old locomotives, documents, and other memorabilia

illustrating the former glories of the Argentine railroad network. Outside is an eccentric collection of modern-art sculptures created out of scraps of train and car parts. On the other side of the plaza is the modern, 24-story Sheraton Hotel (www.starwoodhotels.com), and still further to the south, a series of high-rise mirrored glass and chrome office buildings known as the **Torres Catalinas Norte**, completed in the late 1970s.

Just to the west of Plaza San Martín, at Suipacha 1422, in the Palacio Noel, is the **Museo de Arte Hispanoamericano Isaac Fernández Blanco** ㉖ (www.buenos aires.gob.ar/museofernandezblanco; Tue–Fri 1–7pm, Sat–Sun 11am–7pm; free on Wed). Set in a former stately home it includes collections of colonial and post-independence artwork and silver objects from all over South America. Another branch of the museum, at Hipólito Irigoyen 1420, has a collection of 19th- and 20th-century applied arts.

AVENIDA SANTE FE

Before setting off to visit Recoleta, those interested in shopping may want to take a detour to Avenida Santa Fe, one of the principal commercial districts. The busiest area is between Callao and 9 de Julio avenues. Here there are innumerable shopping malls, replete with little boutiques selling clothing, shoes, chocolates, leather goods, linens, china, and jewels. But perhaps the greatest attraction is watching the young *porteños* from Barrio Norte (as the area of Recoleta around Santa Fe is commonly known), decked out in the latest Parisian styles, and simply out for a stroll. The Ateneo bookshop is known as **El Ateneo Gran Splendid** (www.yenny-elateneo.com); located in an old theater, it is the largest bookstore in Latin America.

RECOLETA

Recoleta is the barrio to the north of Retiro. A 20-minute walk from Plaza San Martín, along elegant Avenida Alvear to Recoleta Cemetery, provides a pleasant introduction to buildings that remind one of what some *porteños* call their golden years (1880–1920).

The **Cementerio de la Recoleta** ㉗ (www.cementeriorecoleta.com.ar; daily

Many affluent porteños employ professional dog walkers.

⊘ A DOG WALKER'S LIFE

A city of dog lovers who live in high-rise apartments means only one thing – opportunities for professional dog walkers – and the hound minders of Buenos Aires are among the world's best. Muscles rippling (being constantly pulled in 20 different directions at once does wonders for the upper body), they patrol the streets of affluent *barrios* like Palermo, Recoleta, and Belgrano, picking up and dropping off their well-groomed charges. Dog breeds range from golden retrievers to boxers, huskies to poodles. When the dog walkers need a break from exercising their packs (sometimes up to ten at once), they tie the dogs to a park railing (Barrancas de Belgrano is a popular spot), find some shade, and pour themselves a mate or two.

7am–5.30pm) is the burial ground for the rich, famous and/or powerful, and is probably Argentina's most exclusive patch of real estate. Entering the gates, you have the sense of walking into a city in miniature, and, in fact, it provides an architectural and artistic history of Buenos Aires from its inauguration in 1882. The nation's great leaders, as well as their enemies, are buried here. The schisms of the rest of Argentine society are also reflected, not only in terms of the conflicting architectural styles, but, astonishingly, in disagreement about who is buried here and why. For example, one of the most visited tombs is that of Evita Perón. Nevertheless, despite the fact that she is listed in the cemetery's own map-guide, tourism officials have been known to deny that Evita is buried here, explaining that she is not of the "category" of people entombed in Recoleta. In fact, she is buried here with other members of the Duarte family, nine meters (30ft) underground, in – according to urban myth at least – a booby-trapped tomb built to withstand a nuclear strike. (This sounds fanciful, but Evita's corpse was spirited out of the country in 1955 by the military junta that overthrew her husband, not to return to Argentina until after Perón's death in 1974.)

EXCLUSIVE ENCLAVES

Many of the city's most sumptuous buildings lie along Avenidas Tres Arroyos and Alvear. At Alvear 1300 is **Plaza Carlos Pellegrini**, where two great mansions, the Brazilian Embassy (Palacio Pereda) and the exclusive Jockey Club (Palacio Unzué de Casares), are located.

Some of the best-quality and most expensive shops are situated along **Alvear**. At No. 1777 and No. 1885 there are elegant malls, ideal for window-shoppers, while at the 1900 block is the stately Alvear Palace Hotel (www.alvear-palace.com), which has its own arcade of chic boutiques.

Running parallel to Alvear one block down the hill toward Avenida Libertador is **Posadas**, where at the 1200 block you'll find **Patio Bullrich** (www.shopping-bullrich.com.ar), the city's most exclusive shopping mall. This former slaughterhouse stretches through to the next street, and houses not only stores and boutiques, but a movie theater and cafés. Directly across from it lies the luxurious **Brick Hotel Buenos Aires – MGallery by Sofitel** (www.sofitel.com).

Also parallel to Alvear, but on the other side to Posadas, runs **Avenida Quintana**, which ends at the **Plaza Ramón Cercano** and the Recoleta Cemetery. Browse in more boutiques, or stop for croissants and coffee at **La Biela** (www.labiela.com) or **Café de la Paix**, two of the city's traditional social gathering sites, or one of the other numerous sidewalk cafés and modern American-style theme restaurants overlooking the plaza.

Just to the left, along the pedestrian street **Ortíz** (which merges with **Junín** after a couple of short blocks), are some of the city's renowned restaurants, most with indoor and outdoor seating. Under the shade of a giant rubber tree, you have

The Museo Nacional de Bellas Artes.

a view of the entrance to the Recoleta Cemetery, the handsome bright white **Basílica de Nuestra Señora del Pilar**, the flamingo-pink Centro Cultural Recoleta, and a series of attractive and well-kept parks and gardens.

Despite its modern-day refinement, the Plaza Ramón Cercano has a very gory past. It used to be the sight of a *hueco de cabecitos*, a dumping ground for heads of cattle slaughtered for their hides. As in the case of other *huecos*, a stream flowed past the area, into which other waste was thrown. The meat was not consumed, and slave women were reputedly instructed to drag away the carcasses.

The stream was piped underground in the 1770s and the Recoleta priests began to improve the area, converting it into an orchard and vegetable garden. Until the 1850s, the Río de la Plata ran up to the edge of the plaza, covering what is now Avenida del Libertador. Under Rosas' administration this area began to be filled in. It was not until the 1870s that the population, mostly the wealthy, started to migrate to this northern barrio.

The **Basílica de Nuestra Señora del Pilar** ⓲ was built between 1716 and 1732. Subsequent restorations have been faithful to the original Jesuit simplicity of its architects, Andres Blanqui and Juan Primoli. Many of the building materials, such as wrought-iron gates and stone, were brought from Spain. There is no rock in Buenos Aires, since the city lies on part of the pampas, and it was not until much later that stone was transported from an island in the delta. Among the historic relics contained in the church is a silver-plated altar, believed to have been brought from Peru. Like many other colonial churches, during the British invasions it was used as a hospital by foreign soldiers. Today, it is where some of the city's elite get married. There is a museum in the cloisters (http://basilicadelpilar.org.ar; Mon–Sat 10.30am–6.10pm, Sun 2.30–6.10pm; guided tours in English Sun 3pm).

The **Centro Cultural Recoleta** ⓳ (www.centroculturalrecoleta.org; Tue–Fri 1.30–10pm, Sat–Sun 11.15am–10pm; free), just next door to the church, is housed in a former convent. There is always a flurry of activity inside this large arts center, which features a changing program of photography, painting, and sculpture exhibits, plus theatrical, dance, and music performances. At weekends, grassy Plaza Francia which slopes down towards the river fills with people enjoying one of the largest arts and crafts fairs (www.feriaplazafrancia.com, 11am–8pm) in the city.

AVENIDA DEL LIBERTADOR

Down the hill from the Recoleta is Avenida del Libertador, and on the far side, before you reach Avenida Figueroa Alcorta, lies a series of parks and gardens that are great for joggers interested in seeing more than the pretty woods and fields of Palermo. On the way down the hill is one of the most spectacular of Buenos Aires' monuments, a mounted statue of **General Alvear**.

The trendy menswear store Bolivia in the fashionable barrio of Palermo Viejo.

Interior of the Museo de Arte Latinoamericano de Buenos Aires (MALBA).

ARGENTINE WRITERS AND BUENOS AIRES

Argentina's capital has fascinated generations of authors, from the Romantic works of Esteban Echevarría to the magical realism of Jorge Luis Borges.

One of the earliest Argentine stories, *El Matadero (The Slaughterhouse)* by Esteban Echevarría (written in 1830 during the dictatorship of General Rosas) already pointed up the contrast between the sordid and often bloody reality of the capital and its symbolic dimensions. Perhaps the country's greatest writer, Jorge Luis Borges (1899–1986) once even suggested in a poem that Buenos Aires had such a mythical force it could never have been founded by man. In some of his other poems, however, he wrote of the grimness of its "butcher's shops."

In the 1920s and 1930s Borges looked back to those 19th-century days. In short stories such as *El Sur (The South)*, Buenos Aires is still a frontier town where violence is always close to the surface. In others, he emphasizes the mystery of a vast city in

Julio Borges at home in Buenos Aires, 1983.

which individual identity can so easily be lost. Borges was part of a thriving scene which made Buenos Aires one of the most important centers of literary production in the Hispanic world.

This anxiety of lost individuals comes to the fore in the work of another essential 1930s Buenos Aires writer, Roberto Arlt (1900–42). His novel *Los Siete Locos (The Seven Madmen)* depicts the chaos of an immigrant society with all its crazy dreams of riches and utopias, which often end in suicide and murder. The harshness of life in Buenos Aires was also the theme of many of the best tango lyrics of this decade, written by world-weary men such as Enrique Discépolo, and sung by men whose appearance and voice spoke of danger and the cheapness of life in the turbulent city.

MYTHS AND NOSTALGIA

During the Peronist period, novels such as *Adán Buenosayres* by Leopoldo Marechal again showed Buenos Aires in a heroic, almost mythical light. But writers who were anti-Peronist, such as Julio Cortázar (1914–84), also wrote memorably about their city: nowhere more so than in his greatest novel *Rayuela (Hopscotch)*, which depicts characters divided between living in Paris and a nostalgic love for the street-corner towers of Buenos Aires. Manuel Puig (1932–90) also wrote books full of the voices and predicaments of lower middle-class people in the barrios of the capital, living their circumscribed, disappointing lives in the midst of this vast metropolis.

The dark days of the 1970s and 1980s have still to be adequately explored in Argentine literature, but the late Tomás Eloy Martínez (1934–2010) made fiction out of the myths of Peronism – and indeed Perón himself in *La Novela de Perón (The Perón Novel)* and in *Santa Evita*. Later, Eloy Martínez returned to the streets of Buenos Aires and the city's nostalgic atmosphere in *El Cantor de Tango (The Tango Singer)*.

The newer generations of Argentine writers have been exploring the myriad private worlds that coexist in the city. In his collection of short stories, *La Novia de Odessa (The Bride of Odessa)*, Edgardo Cozarinsky describes the city's 20th-century Jewish heritage, while in *Pasado (The Past)*, Alan Pauls shows how the city is a complex, living world.

Alongside the monument is the **Palais de Glace**  ㉚, an early 20th-century ice-skating rink that became a cabaret venue and nightclub (Carlos Gardel was shot here in 1915, allegedly – and bizarrely – by Che Guevara's father, Ernesto) and is now an art gallery. The complex has housed the National Fine Arts Salon since 1932, and was remodeled as the National Exposition Rooms in 1978. The Palais de Glace offers an ongoing series of temporary exhibitions (closed for renovation until mid-2019).

Two blocks away at Libertador 1473 is the **Museo Nacional de Bellas Artes** ㉛ (National Fine Arts Museum; www.mnba.gob.ar; Tue–Fri 11am–8pm, Sat–Sun 10am–8pm; free). It contains some 10,000 works, including the best collection of 19th- and 20th-century Argentine paintings in the world, as well as some lesser paintings and sculpture by major foreign artists, including Rembrandt, El Greco, Goya, Degas, Gauguin, Rodin, Manet, and Monet. Opposite the museum, on the northern side of Avenida Figueroa Alcorta, is the Floralis Genérica, a giant steel and aluminium flower that opens and closes with the sun.

Almost at the end of this row of plazas is the Chilean Embassy. Behind it lies one of the prettiest public gardens in the area. Nearby is the reconstructed house **Grand Bourg** (http://sanmartiniano.gob.ar; Mon–Fri 10am–6pm; free), from France, where the hero of the independence wars, General José de San Martín, spent the last 10 years of his life. In front of the building a series of statues represents some of the liberation fighter's closest fellow campaigners.

THE NATIONAL LIBRARY

On Avenida del Libertador, between Agüero and Austria, you will find the **Biblioteca Nacional** ㉜ (www.bn.gov.ar), the national library that was under construction for 30 years before its inauguration in 1992. The building is located on the site of the former Unzué Palace, which became the presidential palace and was torn down in 1955 because the military government considered it "contaminated" by the fact that the Peróns had lived there (and Evita died in the building). A statue of Evita was erected in the plaza in 1999.

The concrete library has several million books and a newspaper library, with extensive reading rooms and park space outside with benches for readers. It also contains exhibits such as a first edition of Don Quixote and a desk used by the novelist Jorge Luis Borges, once the library's director. Behind the library lies the **Museo del Libro y de la Lengua** (Book and Language Museum; Tue–Sun 2–7pm), with displays on the history of publishing in Argentina and manuscripts including a log book of *Hopscotch* by Julio Cortazar.

PALERMO

Palermo is the largest barrio in the city and also the most diverse. Densely populated residential zones sit alongside spacious parks and gardens, foreign embassies overlook artificial duck ponds, and trendy global cuisine restaurants

The family-owned Don Julio parrilla in Palermo Viejo.

compete for custom with hole-in-the-wall steakhouses with molded plastic garden chairs for furniture.

Just around the bend from the Biblioteca Nacional are the exclusive sub-barrios of Barrio Parque – one of the few neighborhoods in the city with winding, rather than orthogonal, streets – and the adjoining Palermo Chico, both of which are favored by well-to-do *porteños* and foreign diplomats.

These areas were built up, together with the Recoleta area, in the 1880s. Many of the old French-style mansions are now used as embassies, since the original owners have been unable to maintain such an exorbitant standard of living. There are also many new wood- and brick-built homes with classic red-tile roofs, but apart from their well-kept gardens, they can hardly compete with the great stone palaces.

One of those classic palaces can be found at Libertador 1902. The **Museo Nacional de Arte Decorativo** (www.mnad.org; Tue–Sun 12.30–7pm) and the **Museo Nacional de Arte Oriental** ㉝ (https://mnao.cultura.gob.ar; permanent collection closed to the public but showcased in various exhibitions, see website for details) are located in a French-style mansion, primarily in Louis XVI style, which contains European and Oriental paintings, porcelain, and sculptures.

Also in Palermo Chico, at Libertador 2373, is the **Museo de Arte Popular José Hernández** Ⓐ (www.buenosaires.gob.ar/museojosehernandez; Tue–Fri 1–7pm, Sat–Sun 10am–8pm; free on Wed), with an impressive collection of 19th-century silver pieces, including the traditional gaucho tack and tools of the trade, and an exposition of crafts from the interior of the country on sale to the public. There is also a library specializing in Argentine folklore.

Also in Palermo is Buenos Aires' only world-class museum – the **Museo de Arte Latinoamericano de Buenos Aires (MALBA)** Ⓑ at Figueroa Alcorta 3415 (www.malba.org.ar; Wed noon–9pm, Thu–Mon noon–8pm). Inaugurated in 2001, this strikingly angular building was purpose built to house the private collection of Argentine real estate mogul Eduardo Costantini. The permanent collection is

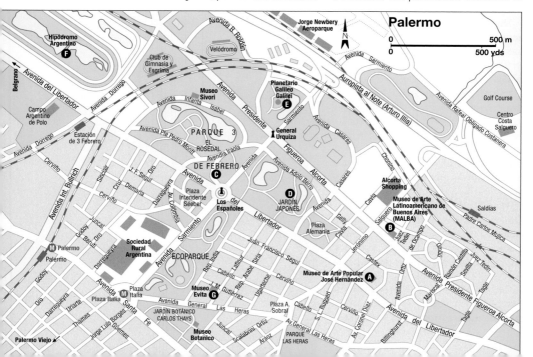

an unrivaled treasury of 20th-century Latin American art, while the temporary exhibitions tend to be top-notch crowd pleasers. MALBA also has a small cinema showing hard-to-catch arthouse flicks, a restaurant with a lovely outdoor terrace, and a gift shop selling hand-selected wares by local designers.

PARQUE 3 DE FEBRERO AND AVENIDA IRAOLA

Sandwiched as they are between major, traffic-choked roads, the parks of Palermo can only loosely be described as places to go for a bit of fresh air; they are, nonetheless, your best bet if you want to escape the frenzy of the city. Here you'll find families picnicking and passing round gourds of yerba mate, runners training for the next marathon, young (and not so young) couples indulging in public displays of affection, and, of course, lots of babies and dogs.

A pleasant but lengthy jaunt through Palermo may begin in Palermo Chico, but the heart of the park area, **Parque 3 de Febrero ⓒ**, is six blocks further down Figueroa Alcorta Avenue from the tip of Palermo Chico.

The park includes 400 hectares (1,000 acres) of fields, woods, and lakes. There are several points of interest near and within it. These include **Museo Sívori** (/ www.buenosaires.gob.ar/museosivori), with a collection of 20th and 21st-century Argentine art); the Jardín Botánico (botanical garden); and the extraordinarily lush **Jardín Japonés ⓓ**, (www. jardinjapones.org.ar; daily 10am–6pm), said to be the largest Japanese garden outside Japan. There are also tearooms and a restaurant, tennis courts, a golf course, and polo and horseback riding facilities. However, many people simply come to sprawl out on the well-trimmed grass to begin work on their tans before hitting the beaches of Mar del Plata or Punta del Este.

Situated to the right on Avenida Sarmiento next to a small artificial lake is the state-of-the-art **Planetario**

Galileo Galilei ⓔ (see www.planetario. gob.ar for information on shows and other activities).

An enormous statue of General Urquiza, who became president after overthrowing Rosas in 1852, marks the intersection of Figueroa Alcorta and Avenida Sarmiento, the wide avenue that crosses the park. Past Figueroa Alcorta is the Costanera Norte, where the metropolitan airport Aeroparque Jorge Newbery is located.

To the left on Sarmiento is **Avenida Iraola**, which leads to the heart of Palermo's parks and lakes. There are paddle boats for hire and a storybook pedestrian bridge that leads to rose-bush-lined gravel paths with stone benches every few yards. Ice-cream vendors also sell candied peanuts and almonds, while others specialize in choripánes (grilled sausage sandwiches) and soda. A café overlooks the most crowded area of the lake.

The enclosed park beside the lake is called **El Rosedal** (Tue–Sun 8am–6pm, until 8pm in summer; free). The heart of Parque 3 de Febrero, this enchanting

Taking advantage of the free Wi-fi at a café in Palermo Hollywood.

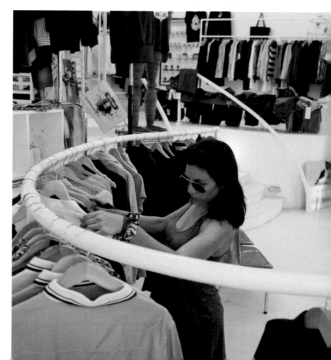

Just one of the trendy fashion stores to have set up shop in Palermo Viejo and San Telmo.

rose garden was laid out between 1910 and 1914 and contains around 8,000 rose bushes of around 93 different species. Once you've stopped to smell the roses you can visit the Jardín de los Poetas (Poets' Garden), where 26 busts of famous literary figures (from Dante to Shakespeare to local hero Jorge Luis Borges) stare solemnly into space. Close by is an Andalusian patio, whose centerpiece is a gorgeous Majolica-tiled fountain.

Iraola wends around the lake and back to Libertador and Sarmiento, an intersection dominated by the Monumento de los Españoles, an elaborate marble and brass confection framed by fountains that was a gift from the Spanish community. Heading back down Avenida Sarmiento and taking a right on Avenida Libertador are two of Palermo's other attractions. The **Hipódromo Argentino** **❻**, or horserace track, is located at the corner of Libertador and Dorrego, and races are usually held on Monday, Friday, Saturday, and Sunday (see http://www.palermo.com.ar for details). Across the street is the **Campo Argentino de Polo**,

Soda siphons on sale at a stall in San Telmo's Sunday market.

the national polo stadium that hosts the Campeonato Argentino Abierto in November and December. Walking down Dorrego you can catch a glimpse through the bushes surrounding the fields.

MUSEO EVITA AND LA RURAL

Avenida Sarmiento continues up away from the parks and toward Plaza Italia. Just past the intersection is the site of the old **Jardín Zoológico**, closed in 2016 and in the process of being converted into a state-of-the-art **Ecoparque** (www.facebook.com/ecoparqueba). Driven by the belief that animal captivity is outdated and at odds with animal welfare, most of the zoo's residents – 1,500 or so animals – have been released into nature reserves; those in need of medical care will remain. The new, interactive Ecoparque will teach visitors about environmental awareness and conservation, as well as featuring artworks by Argentine sculptor Lola Mora.

The **Museo Evita** **❼** (Lafinur 2988; http://web.museoevita.org.ar; Tue–Sun 11am–7pm; guided tours in English by appointment) is located nearby, a comprehensive museum dedicated to the beloved Argentinian heroine, with personal paraphernalia and documents on display.

Across Sarmiento from the Ecoparque is the **Sociedad Rural Argentina** (almost always abbreviated to "La Rural"), an exhibition complex run by the powerful association of Argentina's large-scale farmers. The biggest show held here is July's Exposición Rural, a cattle, horse, and agro-industries show that draws thousands of families as well as professionals, but many other events are held here for the general public, from auto shows to art fairs.

PALERMO VIEJO AND PALERMO HOLLYWOOD

Just beyond Plaza Italia is Palermo Viejo, for many decades a solidly middle-class residential neighborhood that was mainly known for its many car-repair workshops and for the fact that Jorge Luis Borges grew up here. All this changed in the mid-1990s when, drawn by cheap leases and the area's old-world charm, a wave of enterprising young designers and restaurateurs began to snap up attractive properties in the zone and set up shop. As a consequence, Palermo is now the city's trendiest neighborhood and those cheap leases a fond and distance memory.

The heart of the neighborhood is Plazoleta Cortázar, named for the writer Julio Cortázar but often referred to by its former title, Plaza Serrano. To reach the Plazoleta from Plaza Italia, walk along the *calle* named for the other titan of modern Argentine literature – Borges. The streets around the "little square" are lined with hip fashion boutiques, as well as equally hip pit stops in which shoppers can refuel. The area's nickname, Plaza Soho, captures the area's cultural mood and consumer demographic very well.

Walking north and crossing the railway line will land you in another fashionable sub-barrio with an interesting nickname: Palermo Hollywood. This is the center of Buenos Aires' burgeoning television and film industry, and if you're looking for the in-crowd and their hangers-on, this is where you'll find them, hopping between the restaurants, cocktail bars, and nightclubs that make up the area's all-night party infrastructure.

BELGRANO BARRIO

Beyond Palermo to the west (accessible on Line D of the subway) is the barrio of Belgrano, a well-to-do neighborhood that also has a thriving nightlife and social scene, and an important university campus. Belgrano is characterized largely by expensive high-rise apartment buildings, but it also includes the Barrancas de Belgrano, a steep green bluff that stands out amid the general flatness of Buenos Aires, and the interesting **Museo Histórico Sarmiento**

(https://museosarmiento.cultura.gob.ar; Tue–Fri 11am–6pm, Sat–Sun 1–7pm) at the corner of Cuba and Juramento.

SOUTH OF THE CENTER

The initial thrusts of Buenos Aires' expansion in the 17th century were toward the south, making the barrios below Avenida Rivadavia the city's oldest residential areas.

There are three areas of interest to most tourists: Monserrat's La Manzana de las Luces (The Enlightenment Block), one block south of Plaza de Mayo; San Telmo, historically a fascinating barrio and today favored by artists, antiques dealers, and expats; and La Boca, at the southeastern tip of the city, which is famous for the pastel-colored tin houses where dock workers used to live, and for the raucous restaurants where tourists come for a lively evening's entertainment.

HISTORIC MONSERRAT

La Manzana de las Luces ③④ refers to a block of buildings that were constructed by the Jesuits in the early 18th

Gardelito has performed at San Telmo's flea market since it started.

Italian imports such as pizza, pasta, and gelato are easy to find in Buenos Aires.

San Telmo's history and architecture helped kickstart its revival in the 1960s.

century. The church of San Ignacio, the old Jesuit school, and underground tunnels are bordered by *calles* Bolívar, Alsina, Perú, and Moreno.

The area was originally granted to the Jesuits at the end of the 17th century. Relations between the Spanish Crown and the order worsened during the 18th century, however, and in 1767 Charles III threw the Jesuits out of South America. Manzana de las Luces continued to develop, but under the less idealistic eye of the Spanish viceroy. Today, it functions mostly as a cultural center, but guided tours (available in English by prior arrangement) detailing its historical past are available for a small charge.

Despite the repression of the Jesuit order, many of the churches still stand, the oldest of which is **San Ignacio de Loyola** 🟤 (https://sanignaciodeloyola.org.ar), at the corner of Alsina and Bolívar 225. This impressive Baroque church, which is also the oldest of all the remaining six colonial churches in Buenos Aires, was founded in 1675 and completed in 1735.

Walking south on Defensa from the Plaza de Mayo, one finds the **Farmacia la Estrella**, (https://farmaciadelaestrella.com; Mon–Fri 8am–8pm, Sat 8am–1pm) a 19th-century drugstore with marvelous metaphorical murals on the ceiling and walls portraying disease and medicine.

On the second floor of the same building is the **Museo de la Ciudad** 🟤 (daily 11am–6pm; free). The small museum features rotating exhibitions of aspects of the city's past and present, including architectural photo studies and curios, such as old postcards of the city.

On Defensa and Alsina is the **Basílica de San Francisco** 🟤 and the **Capilla de San Roque**. The main church, finished in 1754, is the headquarters of the Franciscan Order. Parts of the neoclassical building were rebuilt at the end of the 19th century, in imitation of the German Baroque styles in vogue at the time. The chapel was built in 1762.

San Francisco was severely damaged in 1955, as were a dozen other churches, when angry Peronist mobs attacked and set fire to them. The violence was a response to the Catholic church's opposition to the Peronist government, and its support for the impending military coup.

The **Basílica de Santo Domingo** 🟤, located at Belgrano and Defensa, is another important church that was partially burned in 1955, with the destruction of much of the principal altar. This former convent contains the mausoleum of independence hero General Manuel Belgrano. The basilica (correctly known as Nuestra Señora del Rosario) was inaugurated in 1783, although there has been a church on the site since 1600, and it is famous for its organ, which is often used for recitals.

One block north, at Moreno 350, the **Museo y Biblioteca Etnográfico J.B. Ambrosetti** 🟤 (http://museo.filo.uba.ar; Tue–Fri 1–7pm, Sat–Sun 3–7pm) has the largest archeological and ethnographic collection in Argentina, including a 1,200-year-old mummy

and ceramics from the pre-Columbian era. The early 19th-century building was formerly the Law Faculty of the University of Buenos Aires.

The **Museo Nacional del Grabado** (https://museodelgrabado.cultura.gob.ar; currently closed) at Defensa 372 offers exhibitions of works by contemporary and 19th-century engravers, and includes a library.

SAN TELMO

Like Greenwich Village in New York, **San Telmo** used to be one of the city's more run-down areas, until its history, architecture, and low rents caught the attention of artists, students, and trustafarians who began to revive the area in the 1960s. Attractive studios, restaurants, and antiques shops began to replace the decaying tenements. An open-air Sunday flea market in the central plaza has brought in enough tourists to nourish the new business ventures. While San Telmo is now one of the principal tourist stops, the neighborhood maintains its authenticity and vitality. **Plaza Dorrego**, the site of the Sunday flea market, is proof of this; on weekdays, it remains a fascinating spot, where old people who have lived all their lives in the barrio meet to talk and to play chess and *truco*.

San Telmo grew during the 18th century as a rest stop for merchants en route from the Plaza de Mayo to the warehouses along the Riachuelo. Next to the Plaza Dorrego was a trading post for imported goods. On adjacent streets, *pulperías* (bar/grocery stores) quickly sprang up to accommodate passers-by.

Except for the Bethlemite priests who had established themselves in the San Pedro Church, the area's first residents were Irish, black slaves or their descendants, and Genoese sailors, whose rowdy drinking habits made the *pulperías* notorious.

In the early 19th century, many important families built their homes along **Calle Defensa**, which connects Plaza de Mayo and Plaza Dorrego. During this period, a typical home had three successive interior patios, and only the facade would change as new architectural styles arrived. The first patio was used as living quarters, the second for cooking and washing, and the third for the animals.

In the 1870s, a yellow fever epidemic swept through San Telmo, killing more than 13,000 people during a three-month period. At the time, it was widely believed that the fog off the Riachuelo carried the disease. Those who could, fled San Telmo and built homes just west of the downtown area, approaching what is now called Congreso, and in the area of Recoleta around Avenida Santa Fe, now known as Barrio Norte.

In the 1880s and the subsequent three decades, San Telmo received poor European immigrants, particularly Italians, who were arriving in Argentina. Many of the old mansions and chorizo houses were converted into *conventillos* (one-room tenements that open onto a common patio), in order to accommodate the flood of new families.

Open-air Sunday flea market in San Telmo.

EXPLORING SAN TELMO ON FOOT

A walk through San Telmo begins at the corner of Balcarce and Chile, the northern edge of the barrio. Several of the city's most popular tango bars are near here.

Crossing Chile on Balcarce, you come to a two block-long cobblestone street called **San Lorenzo**. To the right are beautiful old houses, many now nightclubs. Others, some with interior patios, have been converted into apartments, studios, and boutiques. At San Lorenzo 319 are **Los Patios de San Telmo**, a renovated house open to the public, containing numerous artists' studios and a bar.

Balcarce continues across Independencia and is one of the prettiest streets in San Telmo for strolling, and for more live music venues. The next block is **Pasaje Giuffra**, another narrow cobblestone street, where many of the old *pulperías* used to be.

Further down, Carlos Calvo is an attractive street with numerous restored colonial houses, several of which have been converted into elegant restaurants.

The colorful barrio of La Boca.

Half a block past Carlos Calvo at Balcarce 1016 is the old home of the Argentine painter **Juan Carlos Castagnino**, whose murals from the 1950s adorn the ceiling of the Galerías Pacífico shopping mall on Florida. After he died, his son converted Castagnino's home into an art museum.

On this same block on the right is the **Galería del Viejo Hotel** (Balcarce 1053), another old *conventillo* that has been renovated and now serves as an arts center. Two stories of studios open onto a central plant-filled patio. Visitors may wander through the complex (weekends are the best time to visit) and watch the artists at work.

Calle Humberto 1 is the next block. Turning right, you come upon the **Iglesia de Nuestra Señora de Belén**. The church was built by Bethlemite priests in 1770, and was temporarily occupied by the British invaders in 1807. Next door, at Humberto 1 378, is the ghoulish **Museo Penitenciario Nacional** ⑳ (Wed–Fri and Sun 2–6pm; free), on the site of a former jail which operated until the 1870s. This museum offers such delights as exhibitions of leg irons and other prison paraphernalia. Guided visits of the museum, which hosts occasional art exhibitions, can be arranged on request.

Across the street is the **Escuela G. Rawson**, a former convent that was the first school of medicine in Buenos Aires. Next door is a plaque commemorating the site of an old *pulpería*, operated by a woman named Martina Céspedes. During the British invasion, Señora Céspedes and her daughters enticed British soldiers into their bar, tied them up, and turned them over to the Argentine Army. Although one of her daughters reputedly married a captured British soldier, the mother was eventually rewarded for her brave deeds with the title of Captain of the Argentine Army.

THE HEART OF SAN TELMO

Finally, we are upon **Plaza Dorrego** ㉑, the center of San Telmo's commercial and cultural life and the site of Sunday's

Feria de San Pedro Telmo antiques market (www.feriadesantelmo.com; Sun 10am–5pm), where you can browse junk jewelry, second-hand books, colorful old soda siphons, and some handicrafts. Surrounding the plaza are several restaurants, bars, and antiques shops that are fun to wander through (serious antiques hunters are more likely to find what they're looking for in the shops than in the market). Another charming shopping mall is **Galería El Solar de French** (www.solardefrench.com) on nearby Calle Defensa. It has been redone in a colonial style, with flagstone floors, narrow wooden doors, birdcages, and plants hanging from wrought-iron hooks along the patio.

Located two blocks south of the plaza, at Avenida San Juan 350, the **Museo de Arte Moderno de Buenos Aires ㊷** (MAMBA; http://museomoderno.org; Tue–Fri 11am–7pm, Sat–Sun 11am–8pm; free on Tue), is housed in the former Massalin y Celasco cigarette factory, an attractive building with a brick facade. The permanent collection comprises avant-garde Argentine art from the 1940s onwards and a few international pieces; temporary exhibitions round out the schedule. Next to the MAMBA is the **Museo de Arte Contemporáneo de Buenos Aires ㊸** (MACBA; www.macba.com.ar; Mon–Fri 11am–7pm, Sat–Sun 11am–7.30pm), a modern, glass-fronted space built to house works by Argentine and international contemporary artists, with a special focus on abstract and geometric art.

Parque Lezama is just four blocks south of Plaza Dorrego on Defensa. Many believe that this little hill was the site of the first founding of the city. Later it was the home of Gregorio Lezama, who developed the grounds into a public park. After Lezama's death his family sold the property to the municipal authorities and by the end of the 19th century, it had become an important social center, with many amenities including a restaurant, a circus, a boxing ring, and a theater. Today, the park is somewhat run-down,

and the view is no longer attractive due to the surrounding construction and heavy traffic. There is a fountain built to commemorate one of the city's founders, Pedro de Mendoza, and the old mansion still holds nostalgic memories and has been converted into the **Museo Histórico Nacional ㊹** (https://museohistoriconacional. cultura.gob.ar; Wed–Sun 11am–6pm; guided tour in English Thu and Fri at noon; free), the national history museum at Defensa 1600. One of the museum's highlights is a room decorated with the furniture from the house in France where General San Martín ended his days.

Next to Parque Lezama is one of the city's most extraordinary sights: the onion-shaped domes of the Russian Orthodox Church. The church was opened in 1940 to serve the many Russian immigrants who had settled the area. The facade has a Venetian-style gold mosaic made in St. Petersburg. Nearby at the intersection of Defensa and Brasil streets is the Café Británico, one of the most traditional in Buenos Aires, named in honor of the British builders of the railway system.

Tango-themed mate gourds on sale at a market in Palermo Soho.

San Ignacio de Loyola, the city's oldest Jesuit church, dates back to 1675.

LA BOCA

The neighborhood of **La Boca** ⑮ is at the southern tip of the city, beyond Parque Lezama, along the Riachuelo Canal. The barrio is famous for its houses made from zinc and sheet iron and painted in bright colors, and for its history as a residential area for Genoese sailors and dock workers in the 19th century.

La Boca came to life with the mid-19th century surge in international trade and the accompanying increase in port activity. In the 1870s, meat-salting plants and warehouses were built, and a tramway facilitated access to the area. As the city's ports expanded, the Riachuelo was dug out to permit the entrance of ships. Sailors and long-shoremen, most of whom were Italian immigrants, began to settle in the area. Decline set in when new, deeper ports opened to the north (the Riachuelo was too shallow for the heavier trading vessels of the 20th century), but despite the crime and poverty that have blighted the neighborhood in recent decades, La Boca's residents remain fiercely proud of their unique barrio.

Modern art museum Fundación PROA in La Boca.

BENITO QUINQUELA AND FUNDACIÓN PROA

The famous painter Benito Quinquela Martín took up the theme of color, traditional to his neighborhood, and made it his own. Quinquela was an orphan, adopted by a longshoreman family of La Boca at the turn of the 20th century. As an artist, he dedicated his life to capturing the essence of La Boca. He painted dark, stooped figures set in raging scenes of port action. In one of his works (which Mussolini reputedly tried unsuccessfully to buy from him with a blank check), an immense canvas splashed with bright oranges, blues, and black, men hurriedly unload a burning ship.

Neighborhood residents took pride in their local artist, and were influenced by Quinquela's vision of their lives. They chose even wilder colors for their own homes, and a unique dialogue grew between residents and artist.

Quinquela took over a derelict railway siding, nicknamed it **Caminito** after the famous tango, decorated it with murals and sculpture, and established an open-air market to promote local artists. The

brightly painted homes and colorful laundry hanging out to dry provide the background to this charming one-block alley. There are small stands, manned by the artists themselves, where watercolor paintings and other works of art are displayed for sale.

Overlooking Caminito is **Fundación PROA** ㊻ (www.proa.org; Tue–Sun 11am–7pm), one of the best modern art museums in Buenos Aires. There's no permanent collection on display, but the high-profile and superbly curated temporary shows draw large crowds of art lovers, who might otherwise give La Boca a wide berth.

CALLE NECOCHEA AND AVENIDA ALMIRANTE BROWN

Just past the Avellaneda Bridge is **Calle Necochea**, where rowdy cantinas contrast with the sedate restaurants found in other areas of Buenos Aires. These lively music and dance clubs were originally sailors' mess halls, and their high spirits recall the jazz clubs of New Orleans.

Brightly colored murals of couples dancing the tango, speakers set out on the sidewalk blaring loud music, and somewhat aggressive doormen who compete for the tourist dollar, may combine to frighten off those who are not prepared. But the scene is not as seedy as it might appear. Families from the interior of the country are there for a festive night out, and old people sing their favorite tunes and dance amid balloons and ribbons. And the idea that a night out on Calle Necochea is a celebration of sailors returning home is definitely preserved. Much of the action is concentrated between *calles* Brandsen and Olavarria. Two blocks west is **Avenida Almirante Brown**, the main commercial street in La Boca, renowned for its excellent pizzerias. At the end of the street is the "Ghost Tower," said to be haunted by a local female painter who threw herself from the top. To the east, at the corner of

Pérez Galdós and Pedro de Mendoza, is the **Usina del Arte** ㊼ (Tue–Thu 2–7pm, Fri–Sun 10am–9pm; guided tours Fri 4pm and 6pm, Sat and Sun noon–5pm), a modern art center and concert venue located in a former power station with an ornate Italianate facade. Next door, the **Museo del Cine Pablo Ducrós Hicken** (Mon and Wed–Fri 11am–6pm, Sat–Sun 10am–7pm; free on Wed) has a large collection of cinematographic memorabilia, artefacts, and equipment.

La Boca is also home to the country's most famous soccer team, **Boca Juniors** ㊽. Their stadium, La Bombonera (The Chocolate Box), located in the heart of the neighborhood, draws fans from all over the city. Diego Maradona, the internationally famous soccer star who carried Argentina to victory with his spectacular goals in the 1986 World Cup, played here. The **Museo de la Pasión Boquense** (http://museoboquense.com; daily 10am–6pm) charts the history of the famous club and will be of interest to fans of the beautiful game.

Detail on a house in the Caminito area of La Boca.

Playing el fútbol in La Boca.

📷 THE ARCHITECTURE OF BUENOS AIRES

Its streets flanked with buildings of all shapes, sizes, and styles (often on the same block), Buenos Aires is a mecca for architecture fans.

Buenos Aires has an advantage over many of the European cities it resembles – it survived the 20th century without being bombed or occupied. Most of the great constructions from the city's late-Victorian golden age have, therefore, survived (though plenty are in need of a facelift).

Very few colonial structures are extant – even the city's oldest churches, in Monserrat (see page 159), have been extensively reconstructed. Nineteenth-century *porteños* had no desire to remind themselves of their former Spanish overlords. With little regret, they razed colonial structures and rebuilt them in (mostly) neoclassical styles. Many of the buildings that look colonial – such as Plaza de Mayo's Cabildo – were built in the early 20th century, when Argentines were re-evaluating their Hispanic heritage.

The majority of the buildings that make the city beautiful were built from the 1880s onwards, during Argentina's age of prosperity that continued until at least the 1930s. It was a time of optimism and opulence, when huge sums of money were plowed into both private residences and municipal infrastructure. The sumptuous palaces on Avenida Alvear and around Plaza San Martín date from this era, as do the great landmarks on Avenida de Mayo such as Edificio La Prensa and Palacio Barolo. Where Paris led, Buenos Aires followed; the Beaux Arts, Art Nouveau, and Art Deco styles are all well represented in the Argentine capital. Many of the period's important architects, such as the Italians Vittorio Meano and Francesco Tamburini, were also European, though they were later supplanted by home-grown masters such as Alejandro Bustillo.

Colorful buildings on Calle Caminito in the southern barr of La Boca, whose brightly painted houses recall the first Italian immigrants.

It was from Government House, known as the Casa Rosada, that Perón and Evita addressed their followers in the Plaza de Mayo.

The Monserrat neighborhood still preserves some of the Baroque French-style roofs and cupolas.

MALBA modern art museum in Palermo was designed by an Argentine-US architecture company.

From Modernism to skyscrapers

Modernist architecture, inspired by Le Corbusier and promoted by important local writers like Victoria Ocampo, began to appear in the late 1930s. The Rationalist masterpiece Edificio Kavanagh would be followed in later decades by Brutalist statements such as the Biblioteca Nacional (National Library) and the Banco Hipotecario Nacional (on Reconquista 101), both by the architect Clorindo Testa.

Buenos Aires is far from finished. The MALBA modern art museum, Santiago Calatrava's Puente de la Mujer (a footbridge), and Norman Foster's new City Hall building, are among the superb buildings and structures inaugurated over the past decade. The Puerto Madero Este area of the city has been the focus of intense urban development for some time now, with the Faena Art District, Cesar Pelli's Torre Repsol-YPF, and the Fortabat Museum among the stand-out projects. The Kirchner Cultural Center, opened in 2015 and located in a beautifully converted former post office, has become yet another city landmark and a perfect blend of the glorious past with modern present.

The spectacular Teatro Colón, an acoustically near-perfect temple to music and dance realized in gilt, crystal, marble, and velvet.

The elegant Cabildo, where Argentine independence took its first steps in 1810, sits on the Plaza de Mayo, scene of many protests.

The slim, distinctive profile of the Kavanagh Building, which in the 1930s was Latin America's first skyscraper.

AROUND BUENOS AIRES

Despite the enormous sprawl of the capital city, it's relatively easy to head out for a day or two to a quiet ranch in the country or an elegant riverside resort.

From Buenos Aires there are many possibilities for trips to nearby small towns in the pampas, north along the river to the delta and its islands, or east along the coast as far as the provincial capital, La Plata. Most of the attractions described below can be seen in a day, but if you fancy a longer break from the city bustle, a good range of accommodations is available.

SAN ISIDRO AND ZONA NORTE

Heading north from the federal capital takes you into Zona Norte, a belt of attractive suburbs that is home to some of the country's wealthiest citizens. Most of these neighborhoods are of little interest to tourists, but San Isidro, with its cathedral, handicrafts market, and excellent places to eat and drink, is worth at least half a day of your time. The racetrack Hipódromo de San Isidro is on Avenida Santa Fe, at the junction with Márquez, flanked by the golf course and polo club. Races are generally held on Wednesdays, Fridays, Saturdays, and some Sundays. The **Museo Municipal Histórico** (Tue and Thu 10am–6pm, Sat–Sun 3–6pm; guided tours Apr–Oct Sun 3.30pm, Nov–Mar 4.30pm; free), by the San Isidro cathedral, is part of the **Quinta los Ombúes** (www.quintalosombues.com.ar), a former mansion of the Beccar Varela family, which also houses the municipal archive and library. The

Tigre lies at the mouth of the Paraná delta.

Museo Brigadier General Juan Martín de Pueyrredón (http://museopueyrredon.org.ar; Rivera Indarte 48; Tue and Thu 10am–6pm, Sat–Sun 3–6pm; free) housed in the country house *(quinta)* formerly occupied by the important Pueyrredón family, is also worth a visit. Both **Olivos** and **San Isidro** ❶ are located along the continuation of Avenida del Libertador and have traditionally been home to most of Buenos Aires' English-speaking community.

The quickest way to reach San Isidro is by train from Retiro station, a journey

◉ **Main attractions**
San Isidro
Tigre
San Antonio de Areco
La Plata

Map on page 170

*Gauchos near San
Antonio de Areco.*

*A street in the Old
Town, Colonia del
Sacramento.*

of approximately 35 minutes. An alternative option is to take the popular Tren de la Costa from Maipú station in Olivos. With one ticket, you can get on and off at any of the stations along the route, many of which have their own attractions (Barrancas, for example, has a lovely café and hosts an antiques fair at weekends).

TIGRE

The final stop on the Tren de la Costa is **Tigre ❷** (you can also get here directly from Retiro, albeit on a less scenic route), an attractive, popular town at the mouth of the Paraná delta. Tropical fruit brought by boat from the northern provinces is deposited here en route to Buenos Aires. But the principal economic activity revolves around the summer tourists and weekenders who come to fish, row, water ski, and cruise the winding channels and hundreds of little islands (many of them dotted with summer houses built on stilts) that make up the labyrinthine Paraná delta. While it is only 28km (17 miles) from downtown Buenos Aires, the air is clear, the vegetation subtropical, and the rhythm of

activity less hurried (though be warned that Tigre gets extremely crowded on fine weekends). There's a recommended fruit market, **Puerto de Frutos**, at Sarmiento 160 which takes place daily and is joined by a lively crafts market at weekends.

After strolling around the charming, plant-filled residential area of the town, you should head for the attractive riverside promenade, **Paseo Victorica**, which is lined with steakhouses and rowing clubs. The end of the promenade is marked by a stunning Italian-French-style mansion from 1912 that now houses the **Museo Arte de Tigre** (www.mat.gov.ar/; Wed–Fri 9am–7pm, Sat–Sun noon–7pm). Its permanent collection includes works by important Argentine artists such as Antonio Berni and Raúl Soldi.

Fans of Argentina's ubiquitous green tea, yerba mate, will want to visit the **Museo del Mate** at Lavalle 289 (http://elmuseodelmate.com.ar; Wed–Sun 11am–6pm). The museum displays more than 2,000 pieces of mate paraphernalia, from gourds and *bombillas* (the metal straw through which the drink is sucked) to jars and vintage thermos

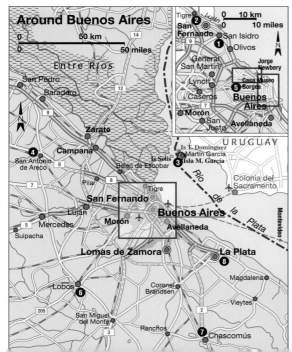

flasks. It's an attraction you wouldn't find anywhere else in the world, which is more than could be said for **Parque de la Costa** (www.parquedelacosta.com.ar; opening times vary, check website), a big, brash theme park with a reasonable selection of stomach-churning rides and a water park.

THE RÍO PARANÁ DELTA

As pleasant as a stroll around Tigre is, it can't compete with a trip on the river (or rivers one might say, since the Río Paraná branches out in countless different directions to form the maze of the delta). To get on a river bus or a tour boat, go to the Estación Fluvial, close to the town center. Several companies operate launches from here and you can browse what they have to offer at their respective booths. There are also stands representing various restaurants and leisure facilities on the islands; talk to the staff, who will help you catch the right boat for each destination. One excellent option is to take the two-hour trip from here back to Puerto Madero; if possible, aim to arrive in Buenos Aires at sunset for memorable views of the city skyline. Boats may also be rented for floating parties, and there is a ferry that crosses over to Carmelo and the Uruguayan beaches.

ISLA MARTÍN GARCÍA

A three-hour boat ride away from Tigre is the **Isla Martín García** ❸, the largest in the delta. The island, which was once a fortress and center of naval battles in the wars of independence, and where presidents Hipólito Yrigoyen, Juan Perón, and Arturo Frondizi were briefly detained, is now a nature reserve with a wide variety of flora and fauna, including water birds and deer. The island also has a small historical museum, a hotel with a good restaurant, and a modern lighthouse. Around 105 people live permanently on the island, which is administered by Buenos Aires Province.

For more information on Tigre, consult the municipal tourism website at http://vivitigre.gob.ar/.

GAUCHO COUNTRY

Some 110km (68 miles) further northwest of Buenos Aires, on RN8, is the town of **San Antonio de Areco** ❹, an especially picturesque country town that these days owes as much to tourism as to cattle raising. San Antonio's fame rose alongside that of the author Ricardo Güiraldes, who grew up in the town and used it as the setting for his novel *Don Segundo Sombra*, one of the canonical works of gaucho literature. The **Ricardo Güiraldes Gaucho Museum** (daily 11am–5pm; guided tours daily 11.30am and 3pm; free) includes extensive grounds on the river with numerous indigenous plants, while the **Museo y Taller Draghi** silver museum and workshop (Lavalle 387; Mon–Sat 10.30am–12.30pm and 5–7.30pm, Sun 10.30am–12.30pm; free) has a wonderful collection of gaucho knives.

Pleasantly sleepy for most of the year, San Antonio roars into life in

⊙ Tip

Cacciola Viajes y Turismo (www.cacciolaviajes.com) operates guided tours to Isla Martín García. The full-day cruises depart from Tigre at 9am, returning at 8.30pm, and include lunch on the island.

Tres Bocas neighborhood in Tigre.

Quirky restaurant El Drugstore in Colonia del Sacramento.

Puerto Viejo in Colonia del Sacramento, Uruguay.

the second week of November, when it hosts Tradition Week, an exciting jamboree of gaucho shows and horse races culminating in the Tradition Day (Día de la Tradición) parade.

While San Antonio de Areco can be visited on a day trip (rent a car or take a bus from Retiro station), for the full gaucho-in-the-pampas experience you should consider spending the night at one of the several estancias (country ranches) within shouting distance of the town.

SOUTH OF BUENOS AIRES

There are also a number of possible outings to the south of Buenos Aires that offer fresh air, green space, and other attractions. Twenty kilometers (12 miles) to the south of the city lies the **Casa Museo Borges** ❺ (Jorge Luis Borges 301; tel: 011-5034-6282; www.fundacionborges.com.ar; Mon–Fri 10am–4pm, Sat 11am–5pm) in the leafy residential district of Adrogué. The former home of the writer Jorge Luis Borges is now a museum with an interesting collection of photographs

and manuscripts, a writer's library, and a study centre.

Southwest of **Ezeiza**, the area which includes both the international airport and the wide-open spaces of the local forests, is the small pampas town of **Lobos** ❻, about 95km (59 miles) from Buenos Aires on RN3. The town is known primarily for its *laguna*, a large lake used for fishing and windsurfing, and for being the birthplace of Juan Domingo Perón.

The house in which Perón was born, located at Buenos Aires 1380, is now the **Museo Juan Domingo Perón** (Wed–Sun 10am–noon and 3–6pm; free) and contains some of the ex-president's personal effects, including a letter written to Evita from his prison cell on Martín García.

Some 120km (75 miles) south of Buenos Aires on RN2, going toward Mar del Plata, is the city of **Chascomús** ❼, located on the largest of the chain of lakes south of the capital. The attractive colonial city is the center of a prosperous agricultural region, and its buildings are well preserved and stand on wide tree-lined streets with green plazas. The Laguna de Chascomús offers fishing, boating, water-skiing, and other water sports, while the Chascomús Riding Center offers horseback rides.

The town has a well-developed tourism infrastructure (the tourist office is located at Av. Costanera, on the *laguna*; daily 9am–6pm) and has a variety of attractive restaurants along the lake front offering fresh fish (primarily river fish such as *pejerrey*) and mixed grills. There are a number of estancias offering accommodations and shows for tourists, as well as the **Fortín Chascomús** fort, scene of battles against the native Araucanian tribes in 1780.

LA PLATA

Despite being only 58km (36 miles) south of Buenos Aires, **La Plata** ❽, the capital of Buenos Aires province, is representative of many of the

country's provincial cities. Life moves at a relaxed pace here, and the city's inhabitants enjoy an independent political and cultural life.

The city was founded in 1882 by Dr Dardo Rocha, and designed by Pedro Benoit, who planned its tidy layout with its numbered horizontal/vertical streets and diagonal avenues. Just off Plaza San Martín is the Legislatura, the Palacio del Gobierno, and the Pasaje Dardo Rocha, a large cultural center. The Gothic Cathedral de La Plata is on the Plaza Moreno, and across the plaza you'll find the Palacio Municipal. One block away, between calles 9 and 10, is the Teatro Argentino.

The **Paseo del Bosque** is a series of pretty parks in the center of the city, with lakes, a zoo, an observatory, and a theater, **Anfiteatro Martín Fierro**. The Paseo del Bosque is also home to the **Museo de Ciencias Naturales de la Plata** (www.museo.fcnym.unlp.edu.ar; Tue–Sun 10am–6pm; free on Tue), which was founded in 1884. This museum has many fascinating geological, zoological, and archeological exhibits, and is considered the best of its kind in South America. The **Museo Provincial de Bellas Artes Emilio Pettoruti** (Tue–Fri 10am–7pm, Sat–Sun 4–7pm), at 525 Calle 51, has an excellent collection of Argentine paintings and sculpture.

URUGUAY'S COLONIA DEL SACRAMENTO

In less time than it takes to get from downtown Buenos Aires to the suburbs, you could be in a different country altogether: Uruguay. Just an hour from Puerto Madero by fast catamaran, **Colonia del Sacramento** is as hushed and laid back as the Argentine capital is loud and brash, making it the ideal destination for a day trip or overnighter.

It's also rich in history. Founded as a Portuguese colony in 1680, the town yo-yoed between Spanish and Portuguese rule for over a century before being incorporated into the new independent state of Uruguay in 1828.

The most interesting area of this compact port town is the Barrio Histórico (Old Town), named a Unesco World Heritage Site in 1996. Its narrow cobblestoned streets wind around well-preserved colonial buildings, many of which have been transformed into restaurants and handicrafts stores. Climb the working lighthouse to get a view of the town and the coastline and be sure to walk down the Calle de los Suspiros (Street of Sighs) with its huge cobbles, which resembles a kind of man-made Giant's Causeway (the rock formation in Northern Ireland).

Bring your driver's license, since the best way to get around Colonia is by golf cart. They can be rented by the hour or by the day and enable you to explore the beaches along the coast (Playa Ferrando is particularly good) as well as the town itself.

To get to Colonia, take a ferry from the Buquebus (www.buquebus.com) terminal at the northern end of Puerto Madero. The journey takes either one or three hours, depending on the type of ferry.

The neoclassical facade of the outstanding Museo de Ciencias Naturales de la Plata.

Estancias such as Villa Maria are within easy reach of Buenos Aires.

The fashionable seaside resort of Pinamar.

Barman at Viejo Lobo bar and restaurant in Pinamar.

MAR Y SIERRAS

The summer holiday destination for millions of Argentines, the Atlantic coast has some excellent beach resorts, while inland in the sierra there is fine countryside to explore.

Main attractions
Pinamar
Cariló
Mar del Plata
Tandil

Like most people, Argentines like to see the sea and will endure congested roads and standing-room-only beaches to do so. No sooner is the New Year's celebration over than large swathes of the Buenos Aires populace pack their buckets, spades, and thermos flasks and set off for their annual summer holidays. The destination? The Atlantic coastline of Buenos Aires province.

"La costa," as it is known, is an attractive riviera where whispering pines and acacias shade the dunes and hills roll down to the sea (giving rise to the popular name Mar y Sierras). But this is not the Hamptons or St-Tropez. Most of the people who own holiday homes and *cabañas* here are middle-class citizens; many of them have been coming here for decades, rain or shine. The Buenos Aires elite, who once regarded the Atlantic coast as their personal playground, increasingly choose to fly to more glamorous resorts such as Miami, Uruguay's Punta del Este, or the more reliably sun-soaked beaches of Brazil. Still, it's dangerous to generalize about the demographics of the Atlantic coast in holiday season, since there are destinations here for all budgets and tastes.

We can, however, generalize to our heart's content about the kind of things people get up to on their summer holidays, since these activities vary little from one person to the next. As usual

in Latin America, children come first; summers on the Atlantic coast are nothing if not family affairs. Parents prefer to play with the kids rather than farm them out to holiday clubs. Somehow they find the energy to play soccer and build sandcastles all day, and eat, drink, and attend cabaret shows for most of the night. Beauty pageants and fashion shows (most resorts elect a summer "queen," and competition is intense) have an unfading appeal. It's a curious fact that while women try to out-do each other in terms of the

Map on page 178

Nautical-themed restaurant, Pinamar.

itsy-bitsyness of their bikinis, topless sunbathing is more or less taboo.

COASTAL DEVELOPMENTS

The main strip of this popular vacation coast extends from San Clemente del Tuyú to Mar del Plata, the hub of the Atlántica area. Though founded late in the 19th century, Mar del Plata was at first a resort for well-to-do *porteños*, for those residents of Buenos Aires who could afford the 400km (250-mile) journey to the then solitary cliffs near Punta Mogotes. This journey was first made by train, then later by car. Only in the mid-1930s did Mar del Plata really start to boom. This was due mainly to two developments: the opening of the casino, with its 36 roulette tables (in those days the largest gambling place in the world), and the paving of the RN2, which brought Mar del Plata to within four hours by car from Buenos Aires. (The road has since been repaved and widened, cutting the journey time further.) With the construction of still another road along the coast (Ruta 11), smaller seaside resorts started to sprout up north and south of Mar del Plata. Before long, each of these places acquired a character of its own, some preferred by the elderly, others by youth,

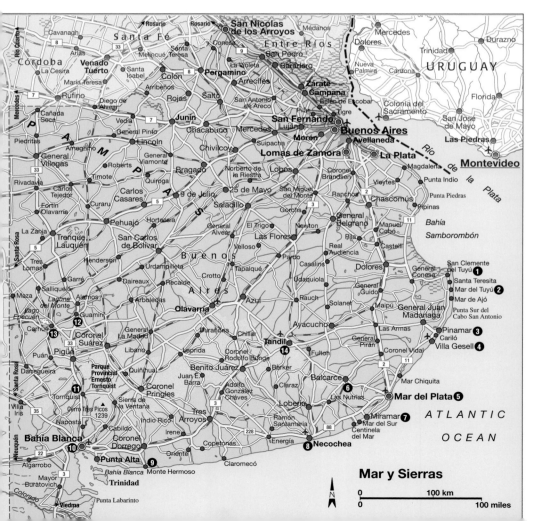

some by those who like rock music, and some by the lovers of tango dancing.

BY PLANE, TRAIN, OR AUTOMOBILE

Until fairly recently, an excursion to the vacation coast was a small adventure. Muddy roads made access to many of the smaller villages very difficult, but today the entire coastline is easily reached. While the roads are now excellent, be warned that there are four toll stops between Buenos Aires and Mar del Plata and the roads can get very crowded during weekends and holidays. There are police checkpoints at regular intervals, so if you do decide to travel to the coast by car, ensure that all your documents are in perfect order. For one person traveling alone, it's cheaper to go by long-distance buses which serve most of Mar del Plata's sprawl, or even by air: in summer (December through February), services are inexpensive and frequent, and you can often pick up special promotional offers. Most flights connect Buenos Aires and Mar del Plata, but some of the smaller resorts can be reached by air, including Santa Teresita, Pinamar, Villa Gesell, Miramar, and Necochea. If traveling by rail, Mar del Plata and Miramar can be reached by the Roca train which departs from Constitución station in Buenos Aires twice a week, taking less than six hours to make the journey south (there is also a daily train which takes a little longer but is also much cheaper).

SAN CLEMENTE DEL TUYÚ TO MAR DEL TUYÚ

Heading south on Ruta 11 from Buenos Aires, the first resort town is **San Clemente del Tuyú ❶**, located at the northern point of **Cabo San Antonio**, the most easterly point of continental Argentina. It is adjacent to Bahía Samborombón, the muddy mouth of the Río Salado and other, smaller rivers of the pampas. The bay is rich with fish that come here to feed.

A further 22km (14 miles) south on Ruta 11 is another well-developed resort town, **Santa Teresita**. In addition to the popular beach, long fishing pier, and many seafood restaurants, there is a

> **⊘ Fact**
>
> To the west of San Clemente del Tuyú is a wildlife sanctuary which is one of the last remaining habitats of the once numerous pampas deer, and an important resting area for migratory birds.

Playing football on the beach at Mar de las Pampas, south of Villa Gesell.

⊘ THE SUMMER SEASON

It's commonly supposed that *porteños* leave Buenos Aires in January and February in order to "escape the city." Closer inspection of the evidence, however, suggests that the city comes with them. The beaches are so crowded that getting from your hotel to the water's edge takes on the aspect of an urban commute. The wait times at restaurants mean you're as likely to get stuck into that airport novel in a queue than you are in a deckchair. And most strikingly of all, the *entire* Argentine entertainment industry seems to move from Buenos Aires to Mar del Plata for the summer "season."

So good luck if you want to attend the theater in the capital. Chances are that both that *revista porteña* (a kind of vaudeville featuring songs, satirical sketches, and scantily clad showgirls known as *vedettes*) and that Brecht revival you wanted to catch have packed up their sets and reassembled them at the coast. For soccer fans, the Torneo de Verano (Summer Tournament) swings into action, with matches held at stadiums in resort towns. Even the national news bulletins get in on the act, with weather forecasts for coastal towns pushing important political developments down the running order. Sanity is restored in March. Or at least it would be if people weren't already making plans for the following January...

golf course, horseback riding, and various campgrounds.

After Santa Teresita, still heading south on Ruta 11, you'll find resort towns one after the other, in a rather developed 26km (16-mile) stretch of coastline. **Mar del Tuyú ❷** is the capital of the so-called Coast municipality, which includes the following towns: Costa del Este, Aguas Verdes, La Lucila del Mar, Costa Azul, San Bernardo, and Mar de Ajó. Mar del Tuyú itself is a small, quiet resort, most popular for its swimming and fishing off the pier. The resorts attract many tourists as the beaches are wide and services abundant. San Bernardo is the largest resort, with high-rise condominiums and hotels.

South from Mar de Ajó, the beach becomes increasingly solitary. The spaces between settlements become wider, and you can find more stretches of isolated pristine shore.

SHIPWRECKS, SAND DUNES, AND LIGHTHOUSES

Horses grazing on the pampas.

Along this part of the coast you can see many old lighthouses made of iron and brick. There is one in San Clemente, called El Faro San Antonio, with another near Punta Médanos, a rather barren and rocky area without many facilities, which also reportedly boasts a number of past shipwrecks at the southern tip of Cabo San Antonio. The lighthouse here, built in 1893, stands 59 meters (194ft) tall amid sand dunes (*médanos*), after which the place is named. The dunes cover an enormous stretch of coastline between Mar de Ajó and Pinamar, some of them now covered in vegetation but others still forming, and reaching up to 30 meters (98ft) high.

Still more lighthouses can be found halfway to Mar del Plata (Faro Querandí), on the southern outskirts of Mar del Plata (Faro Punta Mogotes), and at Monte Hermoso. Some of these towers are over a century old, and many of them have shared in the area's long and fascinating history of maritime adventures and misfortunes. They are well worth a visit, both from an architectural and a historical point of view, although some may be under repair and closed to visitors. In a walk along the beach you will frequently encounter the stranded and disintegrating hull of some old windjammer or steamer.

FROM PINAMAR TO VILLA GESELL

Probably one of the loveliest of all the urban areas along the Atlantic coast is the one that comprises Pinamar, Ostende, Valeria del Mar, and Cariló.

Pinamar ❸ is a very fashionable spot which receives large numbers of tourists in January and February. It is bordered by a pine forest, and the scent of the pines mixed with the salty sea air gives the town a bracing atmosphere. There are no sand dunes at Pinamar, which makes access to the beach easy, even by car. Accommodations range from four-star establishments down to modest, if not budget *hosterías* and *hospedajes* (hostels). Although hotels of all categories are available all year round, most people come for two weeks or a full month and therefore choose to rent an apartment constructed at a price which is much cheaper than that of the most humble hostel. These apartments may be rented on the spot, or in advance in Buenos Aires. Pinamar is the most urban development along this part of the coast, with a number of high-rise apartment blocks and discos, which makes it a good spot for young people. Its range of sporting activities include everything from horseback riding to windsurfing.

The Greater Pinamar area includes **Ostende** and **Valeria del Mar**, where some very high dunes are to be found. A casino is located just outside Valeria, on Ruta 11, the main road running parallel to the coast. A short distance south of Valeria, **Cariló** is a country club-style community dotted with elegant villas and shaded by pines, which also has a wide beach and some of the most beautiful and unspoiled wooded areas left on the coast. Cariló also has a tiny, attractive, and up-market town center, with shops and restaurants constructed in alpine style.

About 20km (12 miles) south of Cariló lies **Villa Gesell ❹**. Founded by Carlos Idaho Gesell in 1940, the town was forested with pines with the intention of maintaining a small and tranquil tourist spot. Except for Avenida 3, its streets are still made of sand, which absorbs water better; trucks pass on a daily basis to water it down. Villa Gesell, with its long and very wide beach, also has a forestry reserve with a museum and archive, containing photos and documents relating to the town's foundation. Outside the center is a horseback riding school, which offers classes and trekking, and there is year-round fishing for shark, mackerel, and other fish from the pier. The town is especially popular with young people, due to its many bars, disco, and skating rinks; it also has several excellent campsites.

Just south of Villa Gesell is Mar de las Pampas, a more exclusive resort which in the space of a few years has gone from being a beach with a couple of cabins next to it to a small town with a beach next to it.

MAR DEL PLATA

Shortly before you reach **Mar del Plata ❺**, the landscape changes dramatically. Approaching the city on the coastal Ruta 11, the high cliffs of Cabo Corrientes and the downtown skyscrapers built upon this rocky peninsula seem to grow from the sea like a mirage. It is a truly striking first impression which, as one gets closer, becomes no less impressive.

Mar del Plata (often shortened to "Mardel") has a permanent population of around 860,000 residents, many of whom are employed looking after the seven million tourists who visit each year. Accommodations range from first-class hotels to apartments available for short-term lease all year round. The city has well-groomed plazas, parks, boulevards, and several golf courses. Beyond the beaches and the sun lies perhaps the biggest attraction for the

Seafood takes the place of beef on the majority of restaurant menus in resorts along the Atlantic coast.

Beachware stall at Cariló.

Lago Epecuén.

3 million summer visitors, the colossal casino where you can try your hand at roulette, poker, *punta banca*, and other games. There are also several theaters, which feature mostly comedies (see page 179); and interesting museums, including the beautifully designed **Museo de Arte Contemporaneo de Mar del Plata** (MAR; www.gba.gob.ar/museomar; Thu–Tue noon–8pm) which showcases works by contemporary Argentinian artists.

INTERNATIONAL EVENTS

Mar del Plata has a number of important events throughout the year, such as the Fiesta Nacional del Mar (National Sea Festival) in February, the International Film Festival (www.mardelplatafilmfest.com) in November, and the International Jazz Festival (www.mardelplatajazz.com) in December. In summer, its beaches are so crowded that the sand virtually disappears, although further from the center the beaches are somewhat less populated. A good place to observe the beautiful people and the locals is the Rambla, a wide pedestrian walkway which runs

Boutique stores, Cariló.

along the Bristol beach in the center of the city, past the Gran Hotel Provincial (www.nh-hotels.com) and the casino.

JUAN MANUEL FANGIO

A visit to Mar del Plata would not be complete without sampling the area's specialties. At the fishing port, with its red and yellow boats bobbing along the quays, a raft of restaurants in the area serve good, fresh fish and seafood. You might also like to take the opportunity to buy well-made inexpensive woolens here, made by the locals during the winter months.

Some 60km (37 miles) inland from Mar del Plata on RN226 is the city of **Balcarce ⑥**, with about 40,000 residents. The area is more hilly than most of the province of Buenos Aires, and Balcarce lies in a valley near La Brava. The city houses a satellite land station, of which a guided tour can be organized with the EMTUR tourist office (www.turismomardelplata.gov.ar) in Mar del Plata. The **Museo de Automovilismo Juan Manuel Fangio** (www.museofangio.com; daily 10am–5pm, until 6pm on weekends and in March) in Balcarce is named for the town's most famous citizen, the five-time world champion racing driver who died in 1995. The museum contains many of Fangio's trophies as well as one of his racing cars, the Mercedes Benz Flecha de Plata. Near Balcarce are the Ojos de Agua caves as well as Laguna La Brava, a well-known fishing spot.

MAR DEL PLATA TO NECOCHEA

From Mar del Plata, the coastal road runs past the Punta Mogotes lighthouse (where there is a popular beach lined with seafood restaurants) toward Miramar. The scenery along this 40km (25-mile) stretch is very different from that at the northern end of the Atlantic coast. Instead of dunes and sandy beaches, the sea is met by cliffs. The road runs along the very edge, offering travelers a splendid view of the ocean, and the spectacle of Mar del Plata disappearing into the distance.

About halfway between Mar del Plata and Miramar is Chapadmalal, where the presidential vacation residence is located. The area has a tourism complex opened in the 1950s by the Eva Perón Foundation for students, pensioners, and low-income families, which has a privileged position on a quiet beach and is still much in demand. There is a small museum, the Museo Eva Perón (www.museoevaperon.com.ar) on site.

Miramar ❼ is less developed and much quieter than Mar del Plata, yet the main beachfront is overshadowed by towering apartment buildings. However, the beach is very wide here and it's not difficult to escape the crowds. There is plenty of open space for many outdoor sports, including bicycling, horseback riding, tennis, jogging, or just walking. For a break from the sand and surf, Miramar boasts a lovely large, wooded park, Vivero Florentino Ameghino, complete with picnic spots and walking trails.

Between Miramar and Necochea, the seaside resorts become sparser. Along this 80km (50-mile) section of shoreline, there are only three places with facilities for vacationers: Mar del Sur (which has beautiful, deserted, and windswept beaches), Centinela del Mar, and Costa Bonita.

At **Necochea** ❽, a pleasant city 125km (78 miles) from Mar del Plata, the Río Quequén empties into the sea. There is a large port, from where fishing excursions depart daily, a developed beachfront, and a proper city center. Beyond the beach, an interesting trip is the 15km (9-mile) journey up the river to the Parque Cura Meucó, where you can relax and enjoy the small waterfalls.

There are even fewer developed beaches south of Necochea. **Claromecó**, about 150km (93 miles) to the south, is one of the most attractive.

MONTE HERMOSO AND BAHÍA BLANCA

One place that is highly recommended is **Monte Hermoso** ❾, some 110km (68 miles) further down the coast. Visited by Darwin during his voyage on the *Beagle*, and since then well known for its wealth of fossils along the shore, Monte Hermoso has a broad beach of fine white sand, shady campsites, and a venerable lighthouse. The lack of crowds make this peaceful place well worth exploring. There is a large YMCA campsite (www.ymcamar.com.ar) just outside Monte Hermoso, which also offers hotel accommodations, and the town has an artisans' market. Sunbathing opportunities may, however, be limited by the fierce wind which sweeps the area most of the time, as the southern coast of Buenos Aires is much less protected from South Atlantic winds than the eastern coast. It is here, at Monte Hermoso, that the Argentine vacation coast ends.

About 90km (56 miles) further along the southern coast from Monte Hermoso, and some 660km (410 miles)

○ Eat

While in Mar del Plata, be sure to try one of the famed *alfajores marplatenses*. These are biscuits filled with chocolate or caramel, and are a favorite for afternoon tea.

Fishermen on the pier in Pinamar.

southwest of Buenos Aires on RN3, is the city of **Bahía Blanca** . Located on the largest bay in southern Argentina, it is a major industrial center and port with more than 300,000 inhabitants. The most important civic buildings are located on the **Plaza Rivadavia**, including the town hall, cathedral, court buildings, library, and the newspaper offices of *La Nueva Provincia*.

The city has several interesting museums. The **Museo Municipal de Ciencias** (Mon–Fri 9am–3.30pm, Sat–Sun 2–6pm, Jan–Feb closed Sat–Sun), on Alsina 425 is a natural history museum with some interesting exhibits, while the **Museo del Puerto de Ingeniero White**, on Guillermo Torres 4180 (Mon–Fri 8am–12.30pm, Sat–Sun 3.30–7.30pm, summer closed Sat–Sun) contains old photographs and other memorabilia of the town's industrial past. In the Mercado Victoria area, formerly the central export market for hides and wool, there remains a British neighborhood of houses constructed in the 19th century by the railway companies for their British employees.

The replacement Piedra Movediza.

INTO THE SIERRAS

Some 80km (49 miles) north of Bahía Blanca, and entering the sierras area of the province, is the small town of **Tornquist** , founded in 1883 and filled with pines and attractive gardens. The Santa Rosa de Lima church is made of stone and especially pretty. Nearby is the former residence of Ernesto Tornquist (an important 19th-century businessman responsible for much of the early development of the Atlantic coastal resorts), for whom it is named. The estate includes a castle of medieval design, a copy of Château d'Amboise in the French Loire Valley. Close to Tornquist is the **Parque Provincial Ernesto Tornquist**, which has an ecology center containing information on its flora and fauna, from where guided tours of the park can be made. The Cerro Bahía Blanca mountain and the Toro cave grotto lie within the park.

GUAMINÍ TO TANDIL

North of Tornquist, on RN33, is **Guamini** , in the southwest of Buenos

Aires province close to the border with La Pampa. The town, a central fortress in the Conquest of the Desert in the 1870s (see page 58), is located on the Laguna del Monte. One of the largest lagoons in the province, it has a beach and fishing clubs, as well as an island with an antelope reserve. In the town itself, the former fort (now the police station) and the **Museo Histórico** are worth a visit. Some 40km (25 miles) further west lies **Carhué** ⓭, also originally a fort and now a spa town. Carhué is located near **Lago Epecuén**, a large saltwater lake known for its curative properties, which swallowed up the nearby town of Villa de Epecuén during the 1985 floods.

The principal city in the sierras is **Tandil** ⓮, located some 360km (240 miles) from Buenos Aires. The city was founded in the early 19th century and is an important tourist center, especially in Holy Week (Easter), when celebrations are held at Mount Calvary and the Passion is enacted. It's also a great base for adventure sports, with mountain biking, hang-gliding, and parachuting among the most popular activities.

Tandil found fame as the site of the "moving rock," a 300-ton stone which perched precariously on the edge of a cliff, and trembled for some 30 years before finally falling in 1912 (see box). Tandil has a large park and lake (Lago del Fuerte) nestling at the foot of the hills in the south of the city, and is home to the **Museo Tradicionalista Fuerte Independencia** (4 de Abril 845; www.museodelfuerte.org.ar/; Tue–Sun 2.30–6.30pm, summer Tue–Sun 4–8pm), which includes exhibits from the history of life in Tandil, such as a hansom cab and carriages, and rooms to rent in the old estancia school.

In the sierras surrounding the city are several estancias, which offer accommodations as well as a range of day visits with outdoor activities. The luxurious **Estancia Acelain**, 50km (31 miles) north of Tandil, has an Andalusian-style mansion, a pool, and gardens.

View over Tandil from Fort Independence.

Gaucho and his horse, Estancia
Los Potreros.

Stunning interior of Córdoba's Catedral.

THE CENTRAL SIERRAS

This landlocked region offers some exquisite Jesuit architecture in and around the historic city of Córdoba, as well as excellent outdoor activities in the surrounding countryside.

Lying about midway between the Andes and Buenos Aires, the province of Córdoba represents much that Argentina is known for, and is often thought of as the country's heartland. Its economy is based not only on farming and ranching, but also on commerce and agro-related and automotive industries. The *cordobeses*, as the inhabitants of the province are known, are renowned throughout the country for their distinctive accents and sophisticated (sometimes surreal) sense of humor.

Approaching Córdoba from Buenos Aires, one traverses miles and miles of flat pampas before reaching the gentle waves of the central sierras. Along the open plains or in the hidden valleys you can stumble upon a variety of characteristically Argentine scenes: a herd of the country's famous grass-fed cattle, an animated scene of gauchos branding cows in a rough-hewn country paddock, or a farm specializing in the breeding and training of world-class racehorses and polo ponies.

Aside from the chance encounters, there is much that the traveler can see and do here. The city of Córdoba, Argentina's second largest, holds some of the country's finest examples of colonial architecture, both secular and religious. But few tourists spend more than a day exploring the provincial capital before heading out into its mountainous backcountry, which is embellished by numerous lakes, rivers, and attractive towns. It's an ideal environment for trekking, horseback riding, water sports, and fishing, among other options.

HISTORIC CÓRDOBA

The city of Córdoba dates back to colonial times. One of the oldest cities in the country, it was founded by Jerónimo Luis de Cabrera in 1573.

Main attractions
Córdoba
The Punilla Valley
The Jesuit estancias
Alta Gracia
Villa General Belgrano

Maps on pages 193, 198

Gaucho at Estancia La Paz, near Córdoba.

When Cabrera arrived in the Córdoba region in 1573, it was populated by three principal indigenous groups: the Sanavirones in the northeast, the Comechingones in the west, and the Pampas in the plains. Though a few confrontations did take place between the Spanish and the indigenous peoples, the latter were labeled "peaceful and cooperative" by the Spaniards. (In other words, and in contrast to the more bellicose tribes of the country's northwest, south, and east, they would not stand in the way of the Europeans and their colonization mission.)

The Pampas were nomadic groups who roamed the plains. The Sanavirones and Comechingones lived in caves or crude adobe houses surrounded by thorny bushes and cactus fences. They were organized in tribes led by *caciques* (chiefs) and they lived by hunting, gathering, and agriculture. Their religion centered around the sun and the moon, and there were three or four main languages and many dialects in the area. It is estimated that there were between 12,000 and 30,000 people in the area at the time of the Spanish conquest.

One hundred years after its foundation, Córdoba manifested the characteristics which are still seen as its trademark. The little village had flourished religiously and culturally. By that time it boasted an astonishing number of churches, chapels, and convents erected by the Jesuits, the Franciscans, the Carmelites, and others. It had a Jesuit-run university, the oldest in the country, erected in 1621 (now called the Universidad Nacional de Córdoba), and the local economy was supported by a variety of agricultural products (corn, wheat, beans, potatoes, peaches, apricots, grapes, and pears), and by extensive and ever-growing herds of wild cattle.

THE SIERRAS

In Córdoba province one finds the stark juxtaposition of the flat pampas with the rolling sierras, the first mountain chain one encounters when moving west toward the Andes. Approaching

Plaza San Martín.

across the plain, the hills appear like great waves breaking on a beach.

There are three chains of mountains in the western part of the province of Córdoba, all of which run parallel to each other, from north to south. They are the Sierra Chica in the east, the Sierra Grande in the center, and the Sierra del Pocho (which turn into the Sierra de Guasapampa) in the west. The highest peak in the province is Champaquí, which reaches a height of 2,884 meters (9,462ft). The Sierras de Córdoba are neither as high nor as extensive as many of the other mountain formations east of the Andes. Their easy accessibility, their beauty, their dry weather, magnificent views, and good roads, as well as the myriad of small rivers and watercourses, have established for Córdoba a strong reputation as an ideal spot for rest and recuperation.

Most of the rain falls in the summer (December through February) and is heavier in the eastern section, where the hills look very green and lush, although it is mostly bushes and low thorny thickets. Toward the piedmont of the eastern hills, larger trees grow in greater abundance. Among these trees, the *algarrobo* (carob) deserves special mention. From prehistoric times right up to the present it has been used by the local populations as a shade-giving tree, and as a source both of fruit and wood for fence posts and for fires. The fruit is used to make various foodstuffs, including *patay*, a hard, sweet bread. The *algarrobo* is also one of the trees most resistant to drought, and because of all these virtues, it is sometimes simply called "the tree" by the locals.

CÓRDOBA CITY

The city of **Córdoba** ❶ has a population exceeding 1.4 million. The basis of its economy is agriculture, cattle, and the car industry. Its key location, at the crossroads of many of the main routes, established its early importance and fostered its rapid growth. Although Buenos Aires, with its excessive absorption of power and people, has always tended to

The sierras surrounding Córdoba city make perfect horseback-riding country – for young and old alike.

Córdoba's architecture ranges from the Spanish colonial to the modern.

Córdoba province's economy is partly based on farming and ranching, and has many beautiful estancias.

Like most colonial cities, Córdoba is centred around a main plaza and a cathedral.

overshadow the rest of the country, Córdoba and its zone of influence is the strongest nucleus found in the vast interior of Argentina.

Córdoba, like most Spanish-settled cities, was designed with a rectangular grid of streets, with the main plaza (Plaza San Martín), the cathedral, and the main buildings in the city center. It is therefore easy for tourists to find the city's different sites of historical, architectural, and artistic interest on a map.

Because many of the early buildings of Córdoba were either religious or educational, time and progress have spared a great number of them, leaving visitors and residents with a rich treasure-trove of colonial chapels, churches, convents, and public buildings amid the modern surroundings.

There are several tourist offices, including in the downtown area, at the airport, and inside the bus terminal. The main office for city tourism is located in the **Recova del Cabildo ⒜** (Independencia 30; daily 8am–8pm).

Here you can obtain maps and information about walking tours, special events, and museum exhibits.

CHURCH CIRCUIT

The religious *circuito* (circuits being the various tours that are recommended by the city tourist office) covers most of the oldest colonial religious buildings. An ideal walking tour around the city center, which you can make unaccompanied or with a guide, begins at Plaza San Martín. Though its site was originally decided on in 1577, the final consecration of the **Catedral ⒝** (daily 8am–noon, 4–8pm) took place in 1784, after collapses, interruptions, and changes. These delays account for the many artistic styles visible in the architecture. It has been described by the architect J. Roca as having a classic Renaissance portico and a Baroque dome and steeple, with influences of indigenous origin in its towers. A large wrought-iron gate completes the picture. The cool, shady interior of the church, located on the western side of **Plaza San Martín**, is divided into three

large naves, separated from each other by wide, thick columns (which replaced the smaller original columns that were not strong enough to support the building). The main altar, made of silver, is from the 19th century; it replaced the original Baroque altar which is now in the church of Tulumba, a small town located 150km (93 miles) from Córdoba city.

The church and convent of **Santa Catalina de Siena** C (daily 8am–6pm) is located behind the cathedral, off the pedestrian street Obispo Trejo and at the end of the Pasaje Cuzco. It was founded in 1613 by a wealthy

widow, Leonor de Tejeda y Mirabal, who converted her home into the province's first convent. The current building dates from the end of the 19th century, and is noted in particular for its dome.

The **Iglesia de Santa Teresa y Monasterio de las Carmelitas Descalzas de San José** D (Church and Monastery of the Carmelite Nuns, also called Las Teresas; open during Mass hours: Mon–Sun 6–8pm) was founded in the early 17th century. It was completed in 1717 but was heavily renovated during the latter half of the 18th century and many of the buildings date to this later

○ **Tip**

If you are planning a trip into the countryside, make sure to visit Córdoba's main tourist office, Agencia Córdoba Turismo (www.cordoba turismo.gov.ar; Avenida Cárcano s/n), or one of the tourist information points, which offers a wide range of information about the nearby sierras.

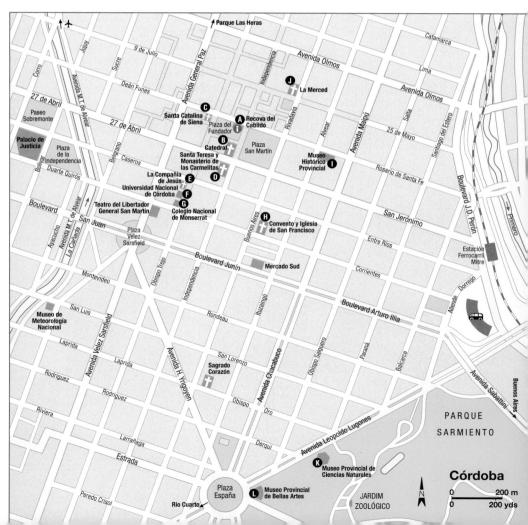

Córdoba

period. The main altar has a large Baroque sculpture of Santa Teresa de Jesús and the wooden choir is an example of fine woodwork. In the monastery there is a religious art museum, the **Museo de Arte Religioso Juan de Tejeda** (Wed–Sat 9.30am–12.30pm) in which many of the objects once belonging to the cathedral are now exhibited. The entrance is on Calle Independencia and the complex is located opposite the cathedral.

The Catedral on Plaza San Martín is one of the oldest colonial religious buildings in the city.

THE JESUIT COMPLEX

Built on the original site of a small shrine, dating from 1589, the Jesuit complex is located on Calle Caseros, two blocks from the cathedral. It was declared a Unesco World Heritage Site in 2000.

The group of buildings is made up of the church, the Capilla Doméstica and the living quarters. Originally it also encompassed the Colegio Máximo and the university, both of which are now national institutions.

The church, **La Compañía de Jesús**

La Compañía de Jesús.

E (Mon–Sat 10am–11.30am and 4–6pm) dates to the 17th century. One of its notable details is an arch made of Paraguayan cedar, in the shape of an inverted boat's hull. The church interior is lined with cedar beams and the roof is made up of beams and tiles. The tiles were joined with a special glue, which after 300 years is still tightly weatherproof. Many of the Baroque altars, including the one made of cedar, date to the 18th century and the Carrara marble work on the walls is 19th century.

The Capilla Doméstica is also from the 17th century. Here, the ceiling was constructed of wooden beams and canes tied with rawhide, which were placed between the beams and then plastered and covered with painted cloth.

Within the Jesuit complex is located the **Universidad Nacional de Córdoba F**. Opened in 1613, it is the oldest university in South America. The rectory includes the university library, as well as cloisters, gardens, and a monument to university founder Bishop Trejo y Sanabria.

Another academic institution located within the Jesuit complex is the traditional **Colegio Nacional de Monserrat** G (Monserrat National College), a secondary school which until 1998 was open only to boys. The college was founded by Ignacio Duarte Quirós in 1687, and since 1907 has been a dependency of the university. The building was reconstructed in 1927 and is primarily notable for the clock tower at one end, as well as a mural by Claudio Boggino in its central salon. It now houses the **Museo del Colegio Nacional de Monserrat** (guided tours only; Tue–Fri at 3 and 4pm, Sat 10 and 11am; free on Wed).

The **Convento y Iglesia de San Francisco** H (Church and Convent of Saint Francis) is located at the corner of *calles* Buenos Aires and Entre Ríos, two blocks from the cathedral. The land for the church was given to the Franciscan Order by the founder of the city, Jerónimo Luis de Cabrera. The first chapel was built in 1575; this original chapel and a second one which replaced it no longer exist. The current structure was initiated in 1796 and finished in 1813. Within the complex, the room named Salón de Profundis is original.

ETHNIC ARTIFACTS

Also worth mentioning is the **Museo Histórico Provincial Marqués de Sobremonte** I (Provincial History Museum; daily 10.30am–5.30pm), an outstanding example of colonial residential architecture, located in the mansion of the Marquis de Sobremonte, the last colonial mansion left in the city, on *calles* Rosario de Santa Fe and Ituzaingó, three blocks from the cathedral. The building was constructed in the 18th century and occupied by the governor of Córdoba. It hosts a large collection of indigenous and gaucho artifacts, old musical instruments, ceramics, and furniture.

Located in the corner of 25 de Mayo and Rivadavia, only three blocks from the cathedral, is the **Basílica de La Merced** J. The present building was finished in 1826 over foundations dating from the 17th century. The main altar, executed in 1890, and the polychrome wooden pulpit from the 18th century, are two of the outstanding attractions of the interior. Just two blocks away lies the **Espacio Cultural Museo de las Mujeres** (Rivera Indarte 55; Tue–Sat 10am–8pm), a concert hall and exhibition space offering a varied programme of events.

In the southern part of the city is the huge **Parque Sarmiento**, near the Barrio Nueva Córdoba and the **Ciudad Universitaria**, which houses all of the university's faculties in buildings of different eras and designs. The park has a lake with two islands, a Greek theater, a zoo, and the Córdoba Lawn Tennis Club (www.cordobalawntenis.com.ar). It was designed in the late 19th century by French landscape architect Carlos Thays.

Tip

A traditional evening out in Córdoba would include attending a *peña*, where locals and visitors gather to drink wine, eat empanadas, and listen to folk music.

Inside La Compañía de Jesús church.

BEYOND THE CITY CENTER

The **Museo Provincial de Ciencias Naturales** Ⓚ (Tue–Sun 10am–5.30pm; free on Wed), located at Poeta Lugones 395, includes exhibits on geology, botany, paleontology, and zoology relating to the history and flora and fauna of the province.

At Parque Sarmiento's main entrance, located on Plaza España, is the **Museo Provincial de Bellas Artes Emilio Caraffa** Ⓛ (www.museocaraffa.org. ar; Tue–Sun 10am–8pm; free on Wed), opened in 1916 and offering special art exhibitions, a library, and cultural activities. Another fine arts museum, the **Museo de Bellas Artes Dr. Génaro Perez** (Tue–Sun 10am–8pm; free on Wed), is located in the Palacio Garzón, on the Paseo de la Ciudad two blocks north of the cathedral and has permanent exhibitions of Argentine three-dimensional art.

Another huge park, located on the western edge of the city, is the **Parque San Martín**, located by the Río Suquía and close to the Córdoba stadium and the University of the Environment. This beautiful park, also designed by Carlos Thays, includes an exhibition center, a campground, and the **Chateau CAC Centro de Arte Contemporáneo** (Tue–Sun 2–7pm), which exhibits permanent and temporary works of modern art. Also by the river is the **Parque Las Heras**, extending from the Centenario Bridge to the Antártida Bridge, which includes a monument to famous tango singer Carlos Gardel.

CONTEMPORARY CÓRDOBA

Córdoba might be better known for its colonial charm, but the modern city also has much to offer visitors. A few blocks from the city center is **La Cañada**, the tree-lined canal that runs through town, a lovely place to walk in the evening or at quiet times of day. On Saturday and Sunday there is an art and crafts fair on the corner of La Cañada and A. Rodríguez. The Rincón de los Pintores (the Painters' Corner) is a gallery devoted to the work of local artists, and can be found inside the Centro Muncipal de Exposiciones Obispo Mercadillo (Rosario de Santa Fe 39). *Peatonales* (pedestrian streets)

The Azur Real boutique hotel was the first of its kind to open in Córdoba city, and has established a good reputation.

La Cañada canal.

in the city center are lined with cafés, bookstores, and boutiques – all popular with university students. This is a good place to sit and relax, window-shop, and people-watch. Also close by are numerous movie theaters showing current releases.

INTO THE SIERRAS

Attractive and interesting though Córdoba city is, few tourists spend more than a day here. It is the sierras which surround the city, far older and therefore smaller and less intimidating than the great Andean peaks, that are the region's real draw. The local tourism authorities have laid out a number of routes which will lead the dedicated traveler up into the hills, along paved and unpaved roads to tiny villages, lakes, streams, campsites, and spectacular views. While these routes can be undertaken by public bus, private transport is necessary to really explore the area.

DAY TRIPS FROM CÓRDOBA

Among the shorter day excursions from Córdoba is **La Calera ❷**, some 15km (9 miles) to the west of the city and now one of the dormitory communities for those working in the city. Located at the foot of the sierras, La Calera stands near the Mal Paso Dam on Río Suquía, which offers attractive views over the reservoir. Within La Calera, surrounded by former limestone quarries started in the 17th century, are the ruins of a Jesuit chapel and of the former lime mills and furnaces. The town also has a municipal beach on the river, which gets extremely busy in the summer.

About 40km (25 miles) to the north of Córdoba is **Río Ceballos ❸**, a delightful town in the sierras that is also home to many of those working in the city. The Ceballos River runs through the center of town, set among green hills, and at the far end of the town is La Quebrada reservoir and park. Slightly farther up (or about two hours' walk on foot) are two waterfalls, the Cascada del Aguila and the Cascada de los Hornillos. Río Ceballos also has a casino and is a popular summer watering hole for those seeking a quieter getaway than the

◉ Tip

Laguna Azul is a popular bathing pool and wakepark converted from a disused quarry, near the Mal Paso Dam on the Río Suquía, outside La Calera.

Central Sierras

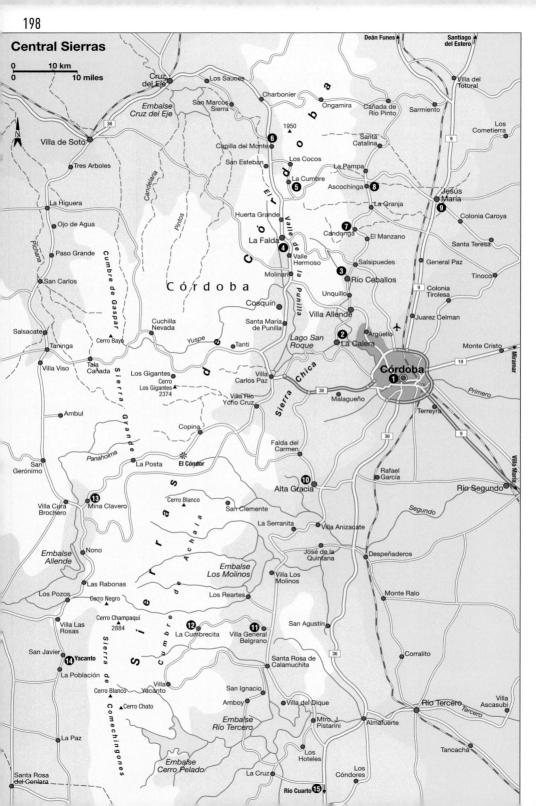

0 ___ 10 km
0 ___ 10 miles

N

Deán Funes

Santiago del Estero

Villa del Totoral

Cruz del Eje

Los Sauces

Charbonier

Ongamira

Cañada de Río Pinto

Sarmiento

Los Cometierra

Embalse Cruz del Eje

San Marcos Sierra

38

Villa de Soto

1950 ▲

6

Capilla del Monte

Santa Catalina

Tres Arboles

San Esteban

Los Cocos

La Pampa

La Cumbre

5

Ascochinga

8

Jesús María

9

La Higuera

Huerta Grande

La Granja

Colonia Caroya

Ojo de Agua

Candonga

7

El Manzano

Santa Teresa

Paso Grande

La Falda

4

Valle Hermoso

Salsipuedes

General Paz

San Carlos

Molinari

3

Río Ceballos

Tinoco

C ó r d o b a

Unquillo

Salsacate

Cosquín

Santa María de Punilla

Villa Allende

Colonia Tirolesa

Taninga

Cuchilla Nevada

Lago San Roque

2

Argüello

Juarez Celman

Villa Viso

Cerro Bayo

Yuspe

Tanti

La Calera

Monte Cristo

Tala Cañada

Los Gigantes

Cerro Los Gigantes 2374 ▲

Villa Carlos Paz

1

Córdoba

19

Ambul

Villa Río Ycho Cruz

Malagueño

Terreyra

Miramar

Copina

El Cóndor

Falda del Carmen

36

Villa María

San Gerónimo

Panaholma

La Posta

Rafael García

Río Segundo

9

Villa Cura Brochero

13

Mina Clavero

Cerro Blanco ▲

San Clemente

10

Alta Gracia

Segundo

Nono

La Serranita

Villa Anizacate

Despeñaderos

Embalse Allende

Embalse Los Molinos

José de la Quintana

Las Rabonas

Villa Los Molinos

Monte Ralo

Los Pozos

Cerro Negro

Los Reartes

Cerro Champaquí 2884 ▲

12

La Cumbrecita

11

Villa General Belgrano

San Agustín

Corralito

Villa Las Rosas

San Javier

14 Yacanto

San Ignacio

Santa Rosa de Calamuchita

36

La Población

Cerro Blanco ▲

Villa Yacanto

Amboy

Villa del Dique

Río Tercero

Villa Ascasubi

Cerro Chato ▲

Embalse Río Tercero

Mtro. J Pistarini

Almafuerte

Tancacha

La Paz

Los Hoteles

Embalse Cerro Pelado

La Cruz

Los Cóndores

Santa Rosa del Conlara

Río Cuarto **15**

nightlife of Villa Carlos Paz. Between La Calera and Río Ceballos are a number of other purely residential towns such as Villa Allende and Unquillo, which are well worth passing through because of their attractiveness.

Some 39km (24 miles) to the west of Córdoba is **Villa Carlos Paz**, famous for its busy nightlife, its casinos, restaurants and clubs, and the sports activities centered around San Roque reservoir. While immensely popular with Argentinians (second only to Mar del Plata as a high-season destination), it's ugly, overdeveloped, and hard to recommend to international visitors.

THE PUNILLA VALLEY

To truly appreciate the magic of this countryside, you need to push further into the sierras and stay overnight (or longer) in one of the many towns, villages, and estancias that give this region its character. One of the most popular visits is to **El Valle de la Punilla**, which extends north from the city of Córdoba, wedged between the Sierra Grande to the west and the Sierra Chica to the east. RN38 cuts through the valley, connecting the key towns of Cosquín, La Falda, La Cumbre and Capilla del Monte.

Cosquín, 50km (31 miles) from Córdoba, is a quaint village famous for its Argentine and Latin American folk music and dance festival in the second half of January. Another 15km (9 miles) north along the narrow, well-paved road brings you to the village of **La Falda ❹**, which holds a festival celebrating the folk music of Argentina's immigrants, along with tango, in the first week of February. At other times of the year, golfing, swimming, horseback riding, and sailing can be enjoyed. Even if you're just passing through, it's worth taking a moment to look around the Parroquia Santísimo Sacramento, an Italianate church inaugurated in 1948.

About 11km (7 miles) further north lies **La Cumbre ❺**, a popular tourist destination of 7,800 inhabitants that grew out of Estancia San Gerónimo, founded here in the late 16th century. It remained little more than a ranch until the 1870s, when British railway engineers, laying the tracks that would eventually link Córdoba and Cruz del Eje, descended on the area. Many of them decided to stay on, constructing lavish clubs and mansions – such as the celebrated La Cumbre Golf Club (www.lacumbregolf.com.ar), opened in 1926 – that gave the town a reputation for "Englishness" which survives to this day. La Cumbre is also known for being (or at least for having been) the Argentine answer to California's Big Sur: a remote haven for writers, painters, and musicians. This is reflected in the town's seasonal events calendar, which has a cultural flavor, with art galleries and theaters open late on summer nights. Nonetheless, anglers are as thick on the ground as artists from November to April, when the Río San Gerónimo is open for trout fishing.

The Southern Crested Caracara is found throughout southern South America, and is usually seen alone or in pairs.

La Cumbre.

There are several interesting detours you can take from La Cumbre. One is to El Mirador, a 400-meter (1,312ft) -high natural platform located 9km (5.5 miles) west of the town. Paragliders regard this as one of the best ridges in the world from which to leap into the void, the air currents allowing them to ascend to a giddying 3,000 meters (9,800ft). Even if you don't fancy doing this yourself, there's a voyeuristic thrill to be had from watching others do it, and the views across the Río Pinto valley are spectacular. Another good side trip from La Cumbre is to San Esteban, a lovely village located 15km (9 miles) to the north. There is some fine colonial architecture to be seen here, including a stone chapel from 1750. A more unexpected but equally delightful sight is the village's windmill, which was designed by none other than Gustave Eiffel and imported from France in 1900.

Former Jesuit estancia Santa Catalina, Ascochinga.

The final stop on the Punilla Valley route is **Capilla del Monte** ❻, 106km (66 miles) from Córdoba city. This photogenic town of 9,000 inhabitants attracts campers, hikers, rock climbers, and… UFO spotters. The latter have been coming here since 1986, when a number of people reported having seen a large and luminous object hovering over Mt Uritorco, 3km (1.9 miles) from the town center. All manner of esoteric and new age services have taken root in the town since then, and people travel here from all over the country to have their minds and bodies "re-energized."

THE JESUIT TRAIL

If you enjoyed touring the Jesuit buildings in Córdoba city, it's worth driving north to see some of the important estancias the order founded among the sierras. Start in Salsipuedes, about 30km (19 miles) north of Río Ceballos. The town is located in an area of great natural beauty and has a riverside beach area for tourists. Passing Salsipuedes, another 20km (12 miles) brings you to the tiny village of **Candonga** ❼, located on the dirt road on the way to Cerro Azul. There is an 18th-century chapel here, the **Capilla de Candonga** (Wed–Sun 9am–7pm; free) which was formerly part of the Santa Gertrudis Jesuit estancia. A larger Jesuit site is located in **Ascochinga** ❽, north of Salsipuedes on a road that offers great natural beauty and a great selection of German pastry shops. Ascochinga has the former Jesuit **Estancia Santa Catalina**, (www. santacatalina.info; guided tours Tue–Sun 10am–1pm and 3–6pm, until 7pm in summer) including a church and cemetery and the ruins of a seminary. The complex is an exceptional example of colonial architecture from the early 18th century.

Cutting across country to the southeast for some 23km (14 miles) on to Ruta 9 brings you to the large town of **Jesús María** ❾, also associated with the Jesuits. The **Estancia Jesuítica San**

Isidro Labrador, one of the earliest vineyards in Argentina, on the outskirts of the town, comprises a church, a residence, and a museum exhibiting religious artifacts and colonial art (Tue–Fri 8am–7pm, Sat–Sun 10am–6pm; free). There is another former Jesuit school in town, the **Casa de Caroya** (Tue–Fri 9am–7pm, Sat–Sun 9am–noon and 5–8pm). The city also has a national festival of folklore and rodeo, held in the first half of January at an amphitheater next to San Isidro Labrador.

FROM ALTA GRACIA TO LA CUMBRECITA

Another former Jesuit settlement is **Alta Gracia ⑩**, some 36km (24 miles) southwest of Córdoba city. This is a charming, prosperous town which welcomes tourists but is not overwhelmed by the kinds of crowds found in Carlos Paz. One of the main attractions is the Jesuit complex, a veritable jewel of colonial architecture, comprising the Iglesia de la Merced (open during Mass hours: Tue–Sat 8pm, Sun 9am, 11am, and 8pm) and

the 17th-century Residencia Jesu-ítica, which now houses a museum displaying religious art and other items relating to the Jesuit presence in the region (Tue–Sun 9.30am–8pm). Alta Gracia is most famous for a more recent inhabitant, however – Che Guevara spent his teenage years here when a doctor recommended the town's dry air for his asthma. His family home is now the **Museo Casa de Ernesto Che Guevara** (Avellaneda 501; Mon–Sun 9am–7pm).

A short excursion into the hills behind Alta Gracia toward La Isla, on the Río Anizacate, leads over a passable dirt road, past small farms with spectacular views of the beautiful river. With luck, somewhere along this route, or another in the sierra region, you just might come upon a group of locals branding their cattle and be invited to eat a barbecue *(asado)*, drink strong red wine, and throw the *taba* (a gaucho game of chance played with the left knee bone of a horse).

Leaving Alta Gracia behind and returning to the main route, continue

Working in the garden of Estancia Los Potreros, an organic ranch employing a number of local people.

Inside the church of Santa Catalina, on the former estancia in Ascochinga founded by the Jesuit order.

⊘ THE JESUITS IN CÓRDOBA

During the 17th and 18th centuries, the city of Córdoba was the spiritual and administrative center of the Jesuit movement in the Americas, whose activities covered all of north and west Argentina and much of central South America.

The chief goal of the Jesuits was a spiritual one – to convert the heathen souls of the local indigenous population and to further the religious education of their brotherhood. However, as they attracted an increasing number of native converts into their missions, the Jesuits proceeded to develop their own economic system, abolishing forced labor and replacing it with a productive, communal economy.

With a steady flow of new missionaries from Europe, together with large donations of money and property, the Jesuit "empire" grew spectacularly. The highly skilled communities built fabulous missions, comprising churches, residences, and estancias filled with finely crafted furniture, ironwork, and silverware. By the time of their expulsion in 1767 by Spain's King Carlos III, the Jesuits had established a network of centers in and around Córdoba, including La Calera, Estancia Santa Catalina, Jesús María, and Alta Gracia, the remains of which can be visited today.

on south and enter the sierras on a well-paved but winding road. Twenty picturesque kilometers (12 miles) later the Embalse Los Molinos appears. This is a favorite spot for the people of the region to practice various aquatic sports, or have a meal by the dam, high above the lake.

Another 20km (12 miles) brings you to **Villa General Belgrano** ⓫, a town with a decidedly German character (see box) – don't leave town without sampling some of the famous home-made cakes. As might be expected, the town celebrates an Oktoberfest during the first week of that month. A bit further to the south is the Embalse Río Tercero, part of a series of seven lakes beginning with Los Molinos, all of which offer beautiful mountain scenery. Embalse Río Tercero is the largest lake in the area. The town of Embalse at the tip of the lake offers reasonable tourist facilities.

The tiny town of **La Cumbrecita** ⓬ nestles at the foot of Las Sierras Grandes, 40km (25 miles) down an unpaved road west of Villa General Belgrano. Visitors will find many nature paths just outside town, crossing small rivers and waterfalls, and meandering among varied plant life, including a small forest of cedar, pine, and cypress trees. La Cumbrecita is relaxing and quiet, with attractive houses and gardens along the side streets. On the road between Villa General Belgrano and La Cumbrecita there's a view of **Cerro Champaquí**, at 2,884 meters (9,461ft), the highest peak in the sierras of Córdoba; it can be climbed on foot or on horseback (in around two hours in the latter case).

THE TRASLASIERRA VALLEY

A more tranquil part of the sierras is the valley of Traslasierra (which means behind the mountains), reached by taking **El Camino de las Altas Cumbres** to the west, on the other side of the mountains from the La Punilla and Calamuchita valleys. On this road there is a panoramic view from a lookout point known as **El Cóndor**. Some of the towns worth visiting

Gaucho on Estancia Los Potreros, in the Sierras Chicas.

in Traslasierra are Mina Clavero, San Javier, and Cura Brochero.

Mina Clavero ⓭ is located at the meeting of the Panaholma and Mina Clavero rivers, and contains the **Museo Piedra Cruz del Sur** (Jan–Feb 9.30am–1.30pm and 4–10pm, Mar–Dec 10am–1pm and 5–8pm), a museum of minerals, which has stone carvings and other crafts for sale. Further south is the former tobacco town of **Villa Las Rosas**, on the Río Gusmara, with a beach area. South of Villa Las Rosas is **Yacanto** ⓮, an upmarket resort built by British railway engineers, with grand summer houses and an exclusive hotel complex, the Hotel Yacanto, with its own golf course. Like Capillo del Monte, Yacanto is also known for a well-documented UFO sighting.

FURTHER EXPLORATION

The sierras of Córdoba offer countless possibilities to explore off the main tourist routes, following dirt roads to quiet villages in the mountains.

In the south of the province is the large city of **Río Cuarto** ⓯, located on the river of the same name, close to the southern lake district around Río Tercero and some 220km (137 miles) from the city of Córdoba. Río Cuarto has a 19th-century cathedral located on Central Julio Roca, as well as the **Museo de Bellas Artes** (Tue–Fri 10am–noon and 4–8pm, Sat–Sun 4–8pm, until 9pm in summer), with an important collection by local and national artists and the **Museo Histórico Regional** (Tue–Fri 10am–noon and 3–8pm, Sat–Sun 4–8pm), housed in a building dating from 1860, covering local history from the pre-Columbian era to the present day.

In the northeast of Córdoba province, on the shore of **Laguna Mar Chiquita**, the largest saltwater lake in Argentina, is the resort town of **Miramar** which offers water sports, a center for balneotherapy, and the Reserva Provincial at Laguna Mar Chiquita, an important wetlands area for overwintering shore birds; the area has been made a Provincial Natural Reserve and Hemispheric Site of the Organization of Reserves for Beach Birds.

Street scene in La Cumbre, a town known for its "Englishness" and as a haven for artists.

⊘ SHIPWRECKED IN THE SIERRAS

"The Mexicans descend from the Aztecs; the Peruvians descend from the Incas; the Argentines descend from the boats," wrote Mexican novelist Carlos Fuentes, in an acidic summation of Argentine immigration. He had a point. But even a boat descent can be dramatic – as was proved by the events of December 1939. Since the outbreak of World War II in September of that same year, the German pocket battleship *Admiral Graf Spee* had been sinking Allied merchant shipping in the South Atlantic. On December 13, however, in what would become known as the Battle of the River Plate, a British naval squadron engaged and damaged the *Graf Spee*, causing her to retire to the neutral port of Montevideo in Uruguay. Deceived by false reports of heavy British reinforcements, the ship's captain, Hans Langsdorff, ordered the vessel to be scuttled. He later committed suicide, leaving around 1,000 of his crew to be interned in Buenos Aires.

In terms of world history, the story ends there. But not in terms of the history of Villa General Belgrano, a mountain village in Córdoba founded in 1930 by German immigrants. Around 125 of the *Graf Spee*'s crew found their way to the village, and some of them settled there. Many of the Bavarian-style, wood-frame constructions you see there today, some of them housing microbreweries or shops selling apple strudel, were built by the shipwreckees.

An inquisitive capybara.

The majestic Iguazú Falls.

THE NORTHEAST

Fed by two great rivers, the Uruguay and the Paraná, Argentina's Northeast is famous for its shimmering wetlands, Jesuit ruins, and, of course, the mighty Iguazú Falls.

Known as the Litoral, Argentina's Northeast comprises the provinces of Misiones, Corrientes, and Entre Ríos (sometimes collectively referred to as Mesopotamia, Greek for "in between rivers") along with the drier provinces of Santa Fe, Chaco, and Formosa. Mesopotamia, as the name suggests, is wedged between the Paraná and Uruguay rivers, with the three other provinces running in a north–south corridor along the western bank of the Río Paraná.

Geographically, the region is diverse, with different types of terrain supporting different industries. The vast plains of Entre Ríos and Santa Fe (the former much greener than the latter) support cattle farming and agriculture. Misiones, nicknamed *tierra colorada* (red earth) for its distinctive iron-rich soil, is home to yerba mate plantations in the south and the remnants of what was once a great Atlantic rainforest in the north, straddling the border with Brazil. Sadly, most of this jungle has been sawn down and milled, though the tracts that remain are impressive enough. Tobacco is grown on the plains of Corrientes, the monotony of which are broken up by the large depression of swamps, lagoons, and floating islands known as Esteros del Iberá. Chaco and Formosa, two of the poorest and least developed provinces

in the republic, are part of the Gran Chaco semi-arid lowland region that stretches from Paraguay to Bolivia.

The Litoral's culture and demographics are diverse, too, though certain generalizations can be ventured. Many of those who immigrated to the Northeast over a century ago were from Germany, Austria, and Poland and, even today, visitors are surprised at the number of pale-skinned and fair haired people who live in the region. There are also many mestizos with Guaraní blood, as well as smaller communities that are

Main attractions
The Iguazú Falls
The Atlantic rainforest
The Jesuit ruins
Esteros del Iberá
Rosario

Maps on pages
209, 210

Palacio de San José, near Colón, Entre Ríos province.

Las Cataratas del Iguazú attract more visitors than the rest of the region's sights combined.

Marvel at the sheer volume of pounding water at Iguazú Falls.

more or less pure Guaraní. Regardless of background or socioeconomic status, most *litoraleños* are easygoing and hospitable, and regard the siesta hour as sacred.

PLANNING YOUR TRIP

Befitting its status as one of the great natural wonders of the world, the Iguazú Falls receive more tourists than all of the other attractions in the region combined. Many people fly from Buenos Aires to **Puerto Iguazú** ❶ (the town that is the gateway to the national park), spend two days looking at the falls (one day on the Argentine side, one day on the Brazilian side), and then fly off again.

While there's nothing wrong with that itinerary, there are many interesting ways to extend it. The Jesuit ruins at San Ignacio Miní are within striking distance of Puerto Iguazú and should be visited by anyone interested in history, architecture, and archeology. If the 270-plus cascades at Iguazú aren't enough for you, try the 2km (1.25-mile) -wide Moconá Falls on the Uruguay River on the border with Brazil. On the way to Moconá are 40 smaller cascades accessible by jungle paths in the Central Highlands, and the charming town of Oberá, a jumping-off point for expeditions to the falls.

In the slow-paced and friendly towns in Entre Ríos and Corrientes, there are churches, modest museums, and even small private zoos to visit. In between the towns, across a variety of terrains, there are provincial and national parks, such as the Parque Nacional El Palmar near Colón in Entre Ríos, with rare palm trees and abundant wildlife.

The most interesting park and nature reserve of all is the Esteros del Iberá lagoon and wetlands in Corrientes province, where intrepid travelers can see hundreds of bird and animal species, and look alligators and boa constrictors in the eye from small boats paddled by former poachers-turned-park rangers.

PARQUE NACIONAL IGUAZÚ

Argentines are so proud of **Las Cataratas del Iguazú** Ⓐ (as the Iguazú Falls

are known locally), they sometimes give the impression they built them from scratch. What they can take credit for is the national park they've built to protect both the falls and the ribbon of Atlantic rainforest it so noisily interrupts. In terms of facilities and infrastructure, the only Argentine national park that can compete with **Parque Nacional Iguazú** (www.iguazuargentina.com; daily 8am–6pm, last entry 4.30pm; ID required) is Los Glaciares in Patagonia.

The falls lie on the Río Iguazú, which runs along the border of Brazil and Argentina. It is often said about this magnificent site that Argentina provides the falls and Brazil enjoys the view. Certainly the 550 meters/yds of walks on the Brazilian side give the visitor a marvelous panoramic view of most of the falls but this is at something of a distance. The simple solution, if you are torn for choice but have enough time, is to visit both sides, which can be done in a day but is better spread over two.

The Iguazú Falls are said to comprise over 270 individual cataracts, though the volume of water gushing over the cliffs at any given moment depends on the height of the Río Iguazú. (If you're unlucky enough to visit the falls after a sustained period of drought, you may, at certain points, find yourself wondering what all the fuss was about.) By far the most famous cascade is the so-called Garganta de Diablo (Devil's Throat), a curved wall of white water 150 meters (500ft) wide and 82 meters (269ft) high. Were it to materialize in central Buenos Aires, it would tower over the Obelisk. Getting as close to the Garganta as the viewing platform will allow, with the spray whipping against your skin and into your lungs and all conversation made impossible by the thunder of water, may be the most heart-quickening experience Argentina has to offer.

GETTING AROUND THE PARK

The temptation after entering the national park is to head straight for

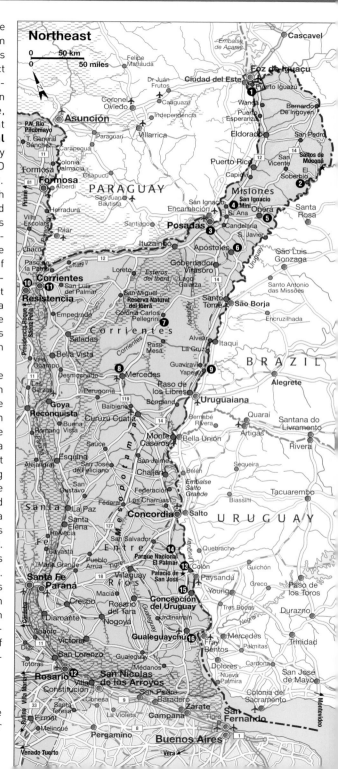

the falls, but it's worth your while to spend 20 minutes in the **interpretation center** near the park's central plaza, where various models, photographs, and vinyl panels shed light on some of the region's defining features.

After that you can decide whether to hop on the park's eco-friendly, natural gas-guzzling "Jungle Train" or to strike out on foot. If you plump for the latter, you can take one of two marked nature trails that disappear temptingly into the forest. The shorter of these, the Sendero Verde (Green Trail), only takes around 15 minutes to complete, though that's probably long enough for you to be approached by a clan of tame coatis, the long-snouted raccoon-like animals that inhabit the park in pest-like proportions. The Sendero Macuco by contrast, is a 7km (4.4-mile) trail that penetrates much deeper into the jungle and gives you the chance to spot a toucan – the most emblematic of the 400 species of bird (around half the total number found in Argentina) that can be spotted in the park.

The train leaves the central station every 30 minutes or so and makes two stops on its way to the falls proper. The first of these is at the Estación Cataratas, which is the place to alight if you want to do one or both of the park's walkway circuits. These are the 1.5km (1 mile)-long Circuito Inferior (Lower Circuit) and the 650-meter/yd-long Circuito Superior (Upper Circuit). Designated viewing stations along the walkways afford stunning views of the falls.

One advantage of doing the Lower Circuit is that it enables you to catch a ferry to **Isla San Martín** , an islet on the Iguazú River that has a balcony looking out towards the Devil's Throat. Boats leave every 30 minutes between 10.30am and 3.30pm.

The end of the line for the Jungle Train is Estacíon Garganta. From here it's a 1km (0.6-mile) walk to the viewing balcony for the Devil's Throat. Late afternoon till dusk is the best time to see the Garganta, both for the lighting at that hour and to watch the flocks of birds that swoop through the billowing mists on their way back to their nests for the night.

Cardo gancho, native Argentinian plant.

CROSSING THE BORDER

Though much larger, Brazil's Parque Nacional do Iguaçu is contiguous with the Argentine national park and easily reached from Puerto Iguazú. Here you can see certain falls from a different angle, and others that can't be seen at all from the Argentine side. The Brazilian park has fewer walkways and forest trails – and no jungle train – but it's equally well laid out, with buses carrying visitors from point to point.

IGUAZÚ AND ITAIPÚ DAMS

The Río Iguazú is some 900km (540 miles) long above the falls and has been dammed. The forest clearing in the watershed permits the immediate run-off of rain, so the river floods, runs dry, runs dirty, "pulses" (due to weekday industrial energy demands), and, in general, behaves in a way unnatural to the trained eye. The stunning natural setting, however, offsets any disappointments.

The **Represa Hidroeléctrica Itaipú** (www.itaipu.gov.py), on the Río Paraná, 20km (12 miles) north of Puerto Iguazú, is a joint enterprise between Brazil and Paraguay. The visit consists of a bus tour (hourly 8am–4pm) and is well worth it, especially if one of the sluice gates is opened, creating a cascade of water to rival that of Iguazú. Free guided tours of the inner section of the dam are available by appointment (see website for details).

THE ATLANTIC RAINFOREST AND THE SALTOS DE MOCONÁ

Although many travelers still treat Misiones and the Iguazú Falls as a one-night stand, an increasing number choose to hang around and penetrate deeper into the forest. One good option is to stay at a jungle lodge, such as the wonderful Yacutinga (www.yacutinga.com/en/). This enables you to get further away from the crowds and school parties that are ever-present at Iguazú, and closer to the flora and fauna of the jungle. As in all rainforest environments, you are far more likely to hear the permanent inhabitants of this ecosystem than you are to see them. Above the relentless chirping of crickets you

Toucan in Parque Nacional Iguazú.

may hear the shrieking of howler monkeys or the less ear-splitting ooh-ooh ah-ahs of black-capped capuchins. Landlubbing mammals are particularly elusive, and that rustling in the lianas (woody vines) could be anything from a coati or a tapir to something extremely rare and endangered, such as a jaguar, an ocelot, or a giant anteater.

Another possibility is to visit the Saltos de Moconá Falls, an extraordinary natural feature whose misfortune it is to be located within striking distance of the more celebrated cataracts at Iguazú. The unique aspect of the Saltos is that the "fall" runs parallel to the river bed rather than perpendicular to it. In other words what you see is one half of the river tumbling into the other half, and doing so for 3km (2 miles). Counterintuitively, it's actually better to visit the Saltos during a period of low rainfall: the more swollen the river, the less pronounced the ridge over which the water spills.

To see the falls, head to the nearest town of **El Soberbio** ❷, which is also known as the national capital of essential oils, its principal export. The

Yerba mate plantation in the south of Misiones province.

tiny town, founded only about 60 years ago by German and Italian immigrants, is located on the Río Uruguay on the site of three river basins and three hill ranges. El Soberbio has both hotels and campsites, and you can arrange trips in small boats to see the falls.

THE JESUIT MISSIONS

Around 300km (186 miles) southwest of Puerto Iguazú is **Posadas** ❸, the provincial capital of Misiones, with some 350,000 inhabitants. Posadas' Paraguayan market is open every day at *calles* San Martín and Roque Pérez, while a bridge crosses the river to Encarnación in Paraguay itself. The tropical spirit of the region is best appreciated at Carnival (Easter) time when it seems the whole city joins in the celebrations.

The Jesuits were the real pioneers in Misiones; indeed, it is from their work that the province gets its name. They arrived early in the 17th century, and proceeded to settle and convert the Guaraní natives in some 30 missions (or "reductions," as they were often known).

⊘ THE CHAMAMÉ

As fast and frisky as tango is leisurely and lugubrious, chamamé is the emblematic folk music genre of the Litoral. The name derives from a Guaraní phrase that simply means "dance songs". The culturally open-minded Jesuits encouraged the locals to play music on their rudimentary instruments, which resembled guitars, flutes, and trumpets (examples can be seen in the visitor's center at San Ignacio Miní). Several centuries later, German and Polish immigrants adapted the chamamé for the accordion (now most closely associated with the dance) and enriched it with influences from their own folk genres, in particular, the polka. Modern masters of the style include Raúl Barboza, who now lives in France and is nicknamed "the ambassador of chamamé", and Horacio "el Chango" Spasiuk.

Their success led to clashes, first with slave traders in the area and then the Iberian governments, first Portugal, then Spain. Overreaching, they were expelled from the Spanish Empire in 1767, leaving the jungle to swallow the mission buildings and less idealistic European colonists to enslave the Guaraní.

Some 20km (12 miles) southeast of Posadas is the small town of **Candelaria**, which has a beach area on the Río Paraná, as well as the Jesuit ruins of Nuestra Señora de Candelaria, which was founded in 1689 and was the Jesuit seat in the area until the order's expulsion. A few kilometers further north on RN12 are the towns of **Santa Ana**, 30km (19 miles) away, and **Loreto**, both of which also have Jesuit ruins dating from the same period. In addition to the ruined missions, Candelaria has natural forests, planted eucalyptus and pine plantations, and the **Parque Provincial El Cañadón de Profundidad**, with a river, waterfall, canyon, and small campsite.

Of the 12 mission ruins that have been restored to date in Misiones, the best-known is **San Ignacio Miní** ❹

(daily 7am–7pm, with a *son et lumière* show at 7pm in winter and 8pm in summer), 55km (34 miles) east of Posadas on RN12. It is best to amble around the ruins at dawn or dusk, when you can be alone and when the light plays wonders on the red stone.

OBERÁ AND APÓSTOLES

There are two other areas of interest in southwest Misiones. **Oberá** ❺, about 90km (56 miles) east of Posadas on Ruta 5, has settlers from many European countries. The second largest city in Misiones, with a population of around 70,000, Oberá has a number of European-style buildings, especially of German influence, and the town hosts the National Festival of the Immigrant each September in its Parque de las Naciones. The city also houses the **Museo Histórico y de Ciencias Naturales** (History and Natural Science Museum; Mon–Fri 8am–noon and 3.30–6.30pm, Sat–Sun 9am–noon and 5–7pm; free), on Barreyro and José Ingenieros streets, and the Wendlinger bird sanctuary (Mon–Fri 9am–6pm,

Atmospheric ruins of the Jesuit mission at San Ignacio Miní.

⊘ THE RUINS OF SAN IGNACIO MINÍ

Among the 30 or so Jesuit missions whose remains have survived in northeast Argentina, San Ignacio Miní is the largest and best preserved. For its historic and architectural importance, the site has been declared a World Heritage Site by Unesco.

Founded in 1610 on what is now Brazilian territory in the north of Misiones province, San Ignacio suffered continual slave raids from the Portuguese colony and was forced to move twice, finally settling in its current location near Posadas, by the Río Paraná, in 1696.

Throughout the 18th century the mission grew to become one of the most important in the region, inhabited by more than 3,000 Guaraní converts. Following the expulsion of the Jesuits in 1767, however, San Ignacio, along with all the missions, fell into decline until, in the 19th century, it was destroyed and its occupants ejected.

Miraculously, much of the original complex has survived today, aided by some careful restoration work. Entering San Ignacio via a wide, tree-lined avenue, visitors are confronted by the towering red sandstone walls of the church and adjoining buildings. Encroaching vegetation drapes some outlying ruins and a nightly *son et lumière* show recreates (daily 7pm in winter, 8pm in summer) the atmosphere of the Jesuits' glory days.

Parrot in the hamlet of Colonia Carlos Pellegrini in the Esteros del Iberá, the second largest wetlands in the world.

Gauchos in a shady plaza in Mercedes.

Sat–Sun 9am–noon and 2–6pm), on Haití and Díaz de Solís, containing native and foreign species.

About 100km (60 miles) to the southwest of Oberá – and founded some 300 years before, in 1638 – lies **Apóstoles** , the capital of the yerba mate industry. The yerba mate tree is of the holly genus *(Ilex)*, though there the similarity ends. Its leaves are used in many South American countries to make a strong tea, sometimes called Argentina's national drink. Apóstoles has the **Museo y Archivo Histórico Padre Diego de Alfaro** (Belgrano 845; daily 7am–noon and 3–7pm), which includes exhibits on prehistoric culture, the Jesuits, the colonial period, and fine arts of the region.

Near Apóstoles are the Jesuit missions *(reducciones)* of **Santa María la Mayor** and **San Javier**. Santa María was one of the most important Jesuit missions in Argentina, after San Ignacio Miní (see page 213), and was also one of the wealthiest, with extensive livestock and crop production. At present, the mission is permanently open to visitors as an archeological site.

San Javier, which was founded first in 1629, was an important cultural center with the first printing press in South America, and later became a fortress against attacks by slave traders from Brazil. The mission, on the outskirts of the small town of the same name, is located on the Río Uruguay. The town also has a sugar mill and distillery.

ESTEROS DEL IBERÁ WETLANDS

The province of Corrientes is easily reached from southwest Misiones. It has one major, though still under-visited attraction, the Iberá wetlands, and several minor ones.

The Esteros del Iberá (the name means "shining waters" in Guaraní) cover almost 20,000 sq km (7,800 sq miles) of Corrientes province, making them the world's largest wetlands after Brazil's Pantanal. Fed by rainfall and by run-off from the Paraná and Uruguay rivers, this untamed, shifting landscape of glinting lagoons and floating islands is fecund with plant and animal life. The area's tourism infrastructure, while excellent, is as small in scale as Iguazú's is massive. That will probably change over the next decade, so if you're a nature lover, visit now.

Only a small proportion of the wetlands can be visited by tourists, and this is contained within the Reserva Natural del Iberá (although there are plans to expand and turn the reserve into a full-fledged national park; see www.proyectoibera.org for details). Apart from a couple of remote fishing lodges that can only be reached by plane or helicopter, accommodations are located in **Colonia Carlos Pellegrini ❼**, a cute hamlet of clay streets on the banks of Laguna Iberá, the most important lake in the reserve. For now, the only way to reach Carlos Pellegrini is via a dirt road from Mercedes, the nearest town of any size. It's a bumpy two- to three-hour transfer which can be arranged through your lodging in Carlos Pellegrini.

To get an introduction to the lie of this very strange land, visit the Agua Brillante Interpretation Center, which can be reached by crossing a Bailey bridge on the edge of town. Here you can chat to the extremely approachable and helpful park rangers (some of whom were poachers before the area was given protected status) and read information panels concerning the region's wildlife. A couple of short and easy marked trails lead off from the Interpretation Center into a patch of forest nearby. A family of howler monkeys call this home, though you're more likely to hear them than see them.

Boat trips on the lake will be arranged by your lodging and are almost always included in the price. The wetlands are home to 85 mammal, 35 reptile, and 45 amphibian species and an astonishing 250 different types of bird. As well as storks, swallows, and southern screamers (you'll know them when you hear them), you will be sure to see capybaras (the world's largest rodent, known locally as the *carpincho*) and yacaré caimans, who spend most of the day basking lazily among the reeds on the floating islands. (At night they feed, their eyes glowing a diabolical red in the darkness.) Among the shyer, more slithery

There are a couple of remote fishing lodges in the Iberá wetlands that can only be reached by plane or helicopter.

Yacare caiman in Esteros del Iberá wetlands.

City council building in Mercedes.

Riding through Colonia Carlos Pellegrini.

denizens of the wetlands are anacondas and boa constrictors, while a rustle in the bushes will often indicate the passage of a marsh deer or a rhea. Ask your lodging to arrange a night-time tour, since many species are nocturnal.

SOUTH OF THE WETLANDS

About 50km (30 miles) south of Iberá is the attractive town of **Mercedes** ❽, a livestock breeding center which hosts an annual livestock exposition as well as regional craft exhibitions. Within the city is the artisans' cooperative **Fundación Manos Correntinas** (on the corner of San Martín and Salta), which sells leather, stone, wood, and woolen crafts, as well as fine work in silver or bone. The city has museums of natural science (the largest in the area) and history, while the Nuestra Señora de las Mercedes church, on the main Plaza 25 de Mayo, includes a collection of fine robes, jewels, and a silver crown.

Some 76km (47 miles) southeast of Mercedes, on the Río Uruguay and the border with Brazil, is **Paso de los Libres**, a main transport route for the Brazilian port of Porto Alegre. The city is located in one of the principal rice-growing areas in Argentina. Its Laguna Mansa (lake) has camping and swimming facilities.

Yapeyú ❾, some 60km (37 miles) northeast of Paso de los Libres, was originally a Jesuit mission and later a Spanish garrison which was burned to the ground by the Portuguese in 1817. It has two claims to fame. First, and most important, Argentine hero and liberator José de San Martín was born here, the son of a Spanish officer stationed at the garrison. The **Templete Histórico Sanmartiniano** (daily 8am–noon and 2.30–4pm), on Alejandro Aguado, displays some of San Martín's personal effects. Second, many music scholars have suggested that Yapeyú, which was known to be a center of music culture during the time of the Jesuits, was the birthplace of chamamé (see page 212).

RESISTENCIA AND CORRIENTES

Resistencia ❿, with almost 300,000 inhabitants, is the capital of Chaco

province on the edge of the Gran Chaco, the heart of South America. These flat swampy lowlands stretch from Argentina into Paraguay and Bolivia, and as far as southwestern Brazil. Resistencia, founded in 1750, grew rich on agricultural produce and through exporting the local quebracho plants for tannin extraction. It is now famous as the "capital of sculpture," with hundreds of pieces scattered throughout the city and displayed in the **Museo de las Esculturas Urbanas del Mundo** (MusEUM; Mon–Sat 8am–1pm). Other highlights include **El Fogón de los Arrieros** (http://fogondelosarrieros.com.ar; Mon–Fri 8am–8pm, Sat 9am–1pm), an art gallery and cultural center with an eclectic collection of paintings, sculptures, and some excellent events; and the Museum of the Chaqueño Man (Mon–Fri 8am–1pm and 4–8pm), which focuses on local history.

The city is linked by bridge to **Corrientes** ⓫, capital of the province of the same name. The latter, on the east bank, sits high, while Resistencia lies among the swamps. In the subtropical heat, Corrientes is one of the most laid-back cities in Argentina, closer in spirit to Asunción in Paraguay. Its central streets, decorated with murals and with stores selling local indigenous handicrafts, make it an interesting place to visit. There has also been a revival in the regional guitar music of chamamé, and there's an increasingly popular carnival during the last days before Lent, with floats, music, dancing, and fancy dress. About 25km (15 miles) inland from Corrientes, the small town of San Luis del Palmar has retained the flavor of colonial times. East of the town is the **Parque Nacional Mburucuyá** which is worth a visit for its quebracho forests.

A short distance beyond Corrientes, you reach the confluence with the Río Paraguay. It is about here, at **Paso de la Patria**, that fishermen from all over the world congregate to try for dorado, the "fightingest fish in the world."

Lodging, boats, guides, and equipment are available from July to November.

ROSARIO

Most tourists, to borrow some North American slang, regard Santa Fe as a "fly-over province." This is understandable: Santa Fe is cattle (and, increasingly, soya) country, largely flat and featureless. The capital, also called Santa Fe, has few attractions for the foreign visitor. But the province *does* have **Rosario** ⓬ – Argentina's third largest city and comfortably the country's most underrated urban destination.

Rosario is not especially geared toward foreign visitors (yet), but therein lies much of its charm. It's a vibrant and, in parts, handsome city populated by one million proud and life-loving *rosarinos*. The city's nightlife is legendary and its restaurants are good too, the best of them specialising in fresh river fish such as *pejerrey* netted from the Río Paraná, on whose banks Rosario sits. Unlike Buenos Aires, Rosario celebrates its riverside location and much of the city's social life

Boats on the Uruguay River which separates Entre Ríos province from Uruguay.

Traditional gaucho belt for sale in Mercedes.

*Parque Nacional
El Palmar.*

revolves around the 5km (3-mile) -long *costanera* (waterfront). Post-siesta it's the place to be, with traders laying out blankets loaded with handicrafts and groups of students passing round mate gourds. It's also the location of the La Fluvial riverboat terminus. From here you can take a catamaran tour around the small islands on the Paraná, several of which have their own restaurants and beaches.

Other places of interest in Rosario include: the city's huge park, Parque de la Independencia, a patchwork of ornamental gardens, sporting stadia and art museums; the **Museo de Arte Contemporáneo de Rosario** (www. macromuseo.org.ar; Tue–Sun 3–9pm; donation), an old grain silo turned contemporary art museum which exhibits more than 300 paintings, sculptures and installations; and, most notably, the Monumento Histórico Nacional a la Bandera (National Flag Monument), a joyless but undeniably imposing 70-meter (230ft) -high tower that pays tribute to the Argentinian flag, which was first raised near here in 1812.

*The bandoneon, used
in tango orchestras.*

ENTRE RÍOS

Entre Ríos (literally "between rivers") is the Litoral's southernmost province. Socioeconomically and geographically it has much in common with Santa Fe as well as with Uruguay, which lies across the river of the same name. The attractive town of **Colón ⓭**, founded in 1863, is one of several resorts on that river. Its sandy beaches draw Argentine holidaymakers who prefer not to face the crowds on the Atlantic coast, while anglers use the town as a base for fishing excursions on the Río Uruguay.

A few kilometers west of Colón is the **Palacio de San José** (Mon–Fri 8am–7pm, Sat–Sun 9am–6pm), former residence of General Justo José de Urquiza, who is famous for having ousted Juan Manuel de Rosas, the 19th-century dictator (see page 55). The house is maintained as a National Historic Monument; its opulence has faded but it is still impressive.

Around 50km (30 miles) north of here is the **Parque Nacional El Palmar ⓮** (www.parquesnacionales.gob.ar/areas-prote gidas/region-centro-este/pn-el-palmar/), which protects the yatay palms (some

of which are two centuries old) for which the park is named. Facilities for staying overnight are limited to campsites in the park and a motel in **Ubajay**, the nearby village. There are a number of interesting walking trails in the park, which is inhabited by animals such as viscachas (a rodent relative of the chinchilla), woodpeckers, and rheas.

Approximately 30km (18 miles) south of Colón is **Concepción del Uruguay 15**, situated on the Río Uruguay. Founded in 1783, it was one of the first provincial cities to join the rebels after the 1810 revolution against Spain, and also saw the beginning of the uprising led by General Urquiza against Rosas in 1851. The pronouncement by Urquiza was made at the pyramid located in the center of the **Plaza Francisco Ramírez**, where the **Basílica de la Inmaculada Concepción** sits. The basilica was constructed in 1857 on the orders of Urquiza, who is buried here, and is noted in particular for its organ.

The city also has the **Museo Casa de Delio Panizza** (daily 9am–noon and 5–8pm), on Galarza and Supremo Entrerriano. Housed in a colonial residence, it contains a collection of colonial exhibits. Close to Concepción is the Banco Pelay beach and campground, with water sports and horseback riding.

Gualeguaychú 16, south of Concepción, is one of the largest cities in Entre Ríos province and is famous for its carnival, the largest in Argentina, which takes place during Lent. The city also has an annual week-long carriage parade starting on October 12, considered a provincial festival, and hosts folklore and horse-breaking shows throughout the year. The colonial city was sacked in 1845 by the Italian nationalist Giuseppe Garibaldi (then residing in Uruguay and a supporter of anti-Rosas forces) and includes a number of interesting buildings such as the cathedral, located on Plaza San Martín, the **Museo de la Ciudad Azotea de la Palma** (City Museum; Wed–Sat 9am–noon and 3.30–6.30pm, Sun 9am–noon), on San Luis and Jujuy, and the **Museo Arqueológico** (Archeological Museum; Wed–Sun 9am–noon, Fri–Sat also 4–7pm), housed in the city's cultural center, on 25 de Mayo 734.

A carnival parade makes its way through the town of Colón.

The resort town of Colón.

A church in the small town of Iruya.

THE NORTHWEST

This is where Argentina's colonial and indigenous cultures collide and mingle, amid some of the country's most magnificent and diverse landscapes.

With the possible exception of Buenos Aires, no region of Argentina is easier to fall in love with than the country's Northwest. Taken together, its colonial and pre-colonial heritage, friendly locals, hallucinatory rock formations, increasingly sophisticated tourism infrastructure, and lush valleys that rise into oxygen-thin, condor-haunted uplands are a brew that most travelers find intoxicating. It doesn't hurt that the region – Salta and Jujuy in particular – is extremely compact, with most places of interest within a few hours of one other. (For those who have experienced the rigors of Patagonia, where getting from one place to the next can take days, it is hard to overstate what a relief this can be.)

The Northwest comprises the provinces of Jujuy, Salta, Tucumán, Santiago del Estero, and Catamarca, and can be (crudely) divided into the three discrete ecosystems. First, the *quebradas*: the arid, high *precordillera* (foothills of the Andes), characterized by multicolored desert hillsides, cacti and dry shrubs, deep canyons, and wide valleys. In stark contrast, the *yungas*, or subtropical mountainous jungle, are identified by dense vegetation, misty hillsides, and trees draped in vines and moss. Finally, there is the *puna*: cold, high-altitude,

Decorative mate gourds.

and practically barren plateaux close to the Chilean and Bolivian borders.

The majority of tourists base themselves in or around Salta, the capital city of the province of the same name and an attractive destination in its own right. From here, either with a rental car (by far the best option) or on organized excursions, one can explore the Valles Calchaquíes (Calchaquí Valleys), named for one of the pre-Inca tribes that settled the region, which occupy a 17,500-sq-km (6,800-sq-mile) area in the provinces of Salta, Catamarca,

○ **Main attractions**
Salta
La Quebrada de
  Humahuaca
Cafayate
Cachi
Ruinas de Quilmes

**Maps on pages
224, 226, 229**

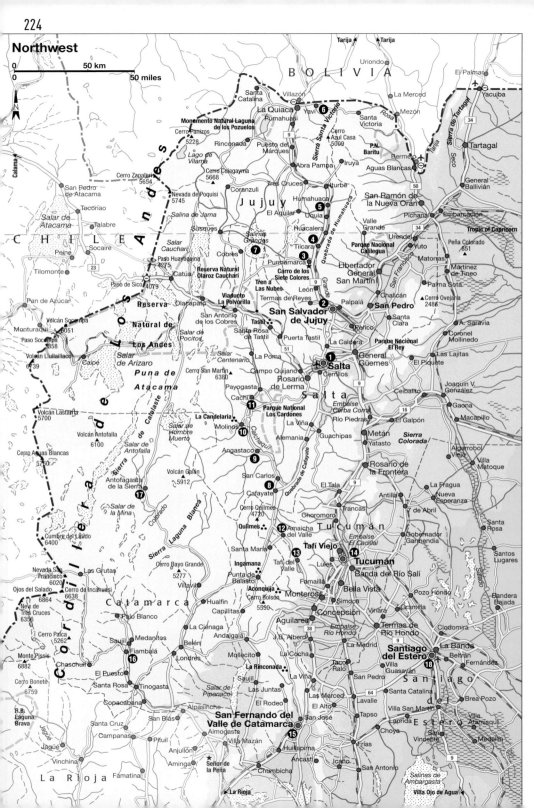

and Tucumán, and the Quebrada de Humahuaca, a stunning mountain valley that cuts north through Jujuy towards the Bolivian border. More adventurous travelers, or those with plenty of time on their hands, can strike out onto the less-beaten tracks of Catamarca and Tucumán.

There are interesting yet modest ruins scattered throughout the Northwest, historical museums and monuments, traditional foods and music, and arts and crafts still made using ancient techniques. This is the most traditional region of Argentina, and the area where the size and influence of the indigenous population are still significant.

SALTA LA LINDA

Salta ❶, also known as "Salta la Linda" or "Salta the Beautiful," is probably the most seductive town of the Northwest, due both to its setting in the lovely Lerma Valley and to the eye-catching contrast of its old colonial buildings with its modern urban architecture. The inhabitants are very proud – some might say snobbish – of the city's colonial heritage, and many *salteños* (as they are known) consider themselves to be the only true criollos (native Argentines of Spanish descent) "untainted" by generations of immigrants. The city is the most formal in dress and behavior in the region, and is the largest in northern Argentina, making it a good base to explore the area, which offers many opportunities for adventure tourism.

Founded in 1582, Salta was an important colonial settlement and several of the most important buildings raised during the era of Spanish rule have survived. One of these is the **Convento de San Bernardo Ⓐ** at Caseros and Santa Fe, established in 1582 (the current structure dates from 1723). Its bright-white adobe walls debar all but the Carmelite nuns who live here, though you can admire the door that indigenous craftsmen carved from carob wood in 1762. (You can also visit the adjoining church for early morning Mass: Mon–Sat 6.30–8.30am, Sun 8–10.30am). Three blocks west is the celebrated **Iglesia y Convento de San Francisco Ⓑ** (museum: Tue–Fri

⊙ Tip

In the whole Northwest region many roads are impassable during the rainy summer season (approximately Christmas to Easter). Fall and spring (Apr–May and Sept–Nov) are the best times for a visit.

Iglesia y Convento de San Francisco.

> **Tip**

An excellent way to pass an evening in Salta is at a local *peña*, where traditional food is served and folk music is performed live by local musicians. Among the city's best places are El Boliche de Balderrama (Av. San Martín 1126; www.bolichebalderrama.com) and La Casona del Molino (Luis Burela and Caseros 2500).

10.30am–12.30pm and 4.30–6.30pm, Sat 10.30am–12.30pm) which seems to grace the glossy side of every other postcard sold in Salta. Built in the late 16th century, it's as exuberant as the Convento de San Bernardo is plain, though the ravishing red and gold terracotta facade that makes it so was only added in the 19th century, along with the 54-meter (117ft) -high bell tower.

Several important buildings surround Salta's main square, Plaza 9 de Julio. The **Catedral Basílica de Salta** Ⓒ (www.catedralsalta.org; Mon–Fri 6.30am–12.30pm, Sat 7.30am–12.30pm, Sun 8am–1pm and 5–9.30pm), on the north side, is an Italianate construction built between 1858 and 1882. It houses the remains of independence heroes such as General Martín Miguel de Güemes. Opposite the cathedral on the plaza is the **Cabildo y Museo Histórico del Norte** Ⓓ (Tue–Fri 9.30am–1.30pm and 3.30–8.30pm, Sat 4.30pm–8.30pm, Sun 9.30am–1.30pm), dating from 1626 (the current structure was completed in the 1780s), which used to house the government of the viceroyalty until 1825. It

was the seat of provincial government until the end of the 19th century. With its graceful double portico, the Cabildo is particularly famous for the 16th-century statues of the Virgin Mary and **Cristo del Milagro** (Christ of the Miracle), washed up from a Spanish shipwreck on the Peruvian coast and credited with having performed miracles such as stopping a 1692 earthquake. The statues are paraded in a colorful procession every September 15. The Cabildo also houses a very fine historical museum, which has nine rooms of archeological and colonial artifacts, including oil paintings and several impressive Baroque wooden pulpits.

MUSEUMS AND MUMMIES

Two blocks from the Cabildo, on the corner of Florida and Alvarado, is the **Museo Casa de Hernández** Ⓔ (Mon–Sat 9am–1pm and 4–8.30pm), dating from 1870 and once the residence of the Hernández family. It now houses the museum of the city of Salta.

Another residence from the colonial period, the **Museo Casa de Uriburu** Ⓕ

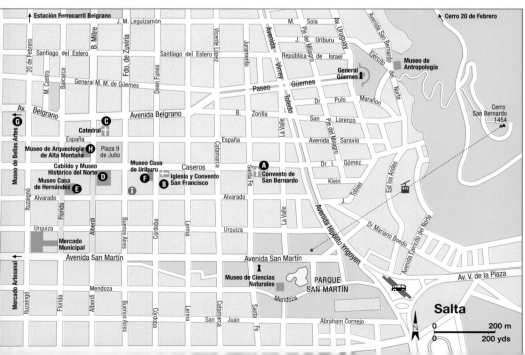

(Tue–Fri 4–6pm, Sat 10.30am–noon), located on Caseros one block from San Francisco, has been renovated and houses a museum of the colonial era. Also in this area are a number of artisans' shops, primarily selling silver and alpaca products of high quality (the locally crafted silver, alpaca, and wooden mate holders are especially beautiful).

A few blocks southeast of the Plaza 9 de Julio is the large **Parque San Martín**, which includes a statue by famous Tucumán sculptress Lola Mora; and at **Mendoza 2**, the **Museo de Ciencias Naturales** (Tue–Sun 3.30–7.30pm) has exhibits of native plant and animal life from Salta and Jujuy, including examples of the tatú, a local type of armadillo, and of fossils of earlier fish and plant species.

The art collection at the **Museo de Bellas Artes de Salta** ⓖ (http://mbas. culturasalta.gov.ar; Tue–Sun 9am–7pm) was first exhibited in 1930. It has lived in various locations since then, moving to its current home, a French-style building from the early 20th century known as Casa Usandivaras (Avenida Belgrano 992) in 2008. The house has been restored, and the museum has a fine collection of American art, in particular from local and Argentine artists, as well as paintings from the Jesuit missions.

The **Museo de Antropología** (Mon–Fri 8am–7pm, Sat 10am–6pm; guided tours in English, tel: 0387-422 2960), on Ejército del Norte and Polo Sur, contains a chronology of the cultural history of the Northwest and, in particular, an exhibition of pieces from Santa Rosa de Tastil, including weavings and a stone on which the "Tastil dancer" was carved. More impressive is the **Museo de Arqueología de Alta Montaña** ⓗ (MAAM; www.maam. gob.ar; Tue–Sun 11am–7.30pm) at Mitre 77. The information panels and artifacts relating to Andean and Inca culture are interesting but most visitors come to see the museum's *raison d'être*, which is the storage and display of the mummified remains of the so-called Niños de Llullaillaco or Children of Llullaillaco. The bodies of these children – six, seven, and fifteen years of age when they died – were discovered in 1999, near the summit of the Llullaillaco volcano in the Andean cordillera. Perfectly preserved by

> **Ⓞ Tip**
>
> In spite of its relatively cool mountain climate, most businesses in the Northwest retain the siesta custom inherited from Spain, and close from noon until about 5pm, although this is often offset by longer opening hours in the evening. Supermarkets, however, may stay open all day.

Dining alfresco on Salta's Plaza 9 de Julio.

Nun praying inside the Catedral Basílica de Salta.

the extreme cold, the corpses have been studied exhaustively by anthropologists who have concluded that the children were sacrificed in a religious ritual 500 years ago, when the Inca empire ruled northwest Argentina. Only one mummy is on display at any one time, and the museum has taken pains to ensure that the atmosphere surrounding the exhibit is one of dignity and respect. The experience is fascinating and moving, and to some, disturbing.

Also well worth a visit is the **Mercado Artesanal** (daily 9am–9pm), three blocks southwest of the Plaza 9 de Julio, with handicrafts by some of the indigenous tribes living in the vast province of Salta.

A superb view of the city can be enjoyed from atop **Cerro San Bernardo**, which can be reached by cable car (www.telefericosanbernardo.com) from Parque San Martín; the cable car runs daily 9am–6.30pm.

TRAIN TO THE CLOUDS

Tren a las Nubes on La Polvorilla viaduct.

The **Tren a las Nubes** (Train to the Clouds; www.trenalasnubes.com.ar), the third highest working railway line in the world, is now run purely for tourists. As well as being one of the highlights of Argentina, it is also one of the last remaining "great railway journeys" of South America. The train, fully equipped with dining car, bar, guide, and stewardess, leaves Salta's main station at 7.05am and enters the deep **Quebrada del Toro** gorge about an hour later. Slowly, the train starts to make its way up. The line is a true work of engineering art, and doesn't make use of cogs, even for the steepest parts of the climb. Instead, the rails have been laid so as to allow circulation by means of switchbacks and spirals. This, together with some truly spectacular scenery, is what makes the trip so fascinating.

After passing through **San Antonio de los Cobres**, the old capital of the former national territory, Los Andes, the train finally comes to a halt at **La Polvorilla Viaduct** (63 meters/207ft high and 224 meters/739ft long), an impressive steel span amid the breathtaking Andean landscape. At this point the train has reached an altitude of

4,197 meters (13,850ft) above sea level. From here the train returns to Salta, where it arrives in the late evening, after a roundtrip of 272km (169 miles), taking about 14 hours.

NORTH TO JUJUY

From Salta, a winding but wonderful mountain road, **La Cornisa**, takes you, in about an hour and a half, to **San Salvador de Jujuy** ❷. Don't miss the extraordinary gilded pulpit in the **catedral** ❹ (Mon–Sat 7.30am–12.30pm and 5–9pm). Carved from cedar and ñandubay wood by indigenous craftsmen, it is the most important colonial-era artifact of its kind in the country. The cathedral dates from 1611, although most of the current building was completed in 1765 after being destroyed by an earthquake late in the 17th century. In addition to the famous pulpit, the cathedral has a beautiful chapel dedicated to the Virgin of the Rosary, as well as an outstanding 18th-century painting of the Virgin Mary. The tourist office is located nearby in the old railway station.

Among the other attractions of this colonial city are the **Casa de Gobierno** ❸, across the **Plaza General Belgrano** from the cathedral. The classical building, completed in 1920, houses the first Argentine flag and coat of arms, created by independence hero General Belgrano and donated to the city in 1813. The Salón de la Bandera, where the flag is on display, is open Mon–Fri 8am–noon and 4–8pm. The front of the Casa de Gobierno has four statues, representing Peace, Liberty, Justice, and Progress, by Lola Mora, the Tucumán artist who was once director of plazas and parks in Jujuy. Facing the Casa de Gobierno is the **Cabildo y Museo Histórico Policial** ❸, a 19th-century building reconstructed after it was destroyed by an earthquake in 1863. The Cabildo houses the city's police department and a small museum (Mon–Fri 8am–1pm and 4–9pm, Sat–Sun 9am–noon and 6–8pm), which includes exhibits on the police's anti-drugs campaign.

Two blocks from the Cabildo, on Belgrano and Lavalle, is the beautiful **Basílica de San Francisco** ❹ (daily

Traditional knives for sale in Salta.

Locally made carpets of llama and alpaca wool on sale at Purmamarca's market.

San Salvador de Jujuy

Parque Nacional Los Cardones is named for the distinctive Echinopsis atacamensis cacti found in the area.

View over the town of Maimara and the Paleta del Pintor (Painter's Palette) hills.

9am–1pm and 4–9pm), situated on the site since the beginning of the 17th century, although the current building, maintaining the traditional style of Franciscan churches, dates from the 1920s. The church has a famous pulpit carved on the basis of traditional designs from Cusco in Peru and a notable wooden statue of St Francis – known locally as San Roque. Behind the church is the renovated **Museo Histórico Franciscano** (daily 9am–1pm and 4–9pm), whose exhibits include Stations of the Cross painted in Bolivia in 1780.

The local religious imagery is particularly notable for its rather gory nature, primarily because life for the indigenous communities who originally inhabited the area was so hard that early missionaries had to depict the sufferings of Christ and other religious figures in exceptionally horrific terms in order to make an impression on the locals. Statues in particular are prone to depict gaping and bloody wounds with more enthusiasm than is usually the case.

Among the other interesting museums in Jujuy are the **Museo Histórico Provincial Juan Galo Lavalle E** at Lavalle 256 (Mon–Fri 8am–8pm, Sat–Sun 8am–noon and 4–8pm), located in a 19th-century residence in which the hero of the Argentine union, General Lavalle, died in 1841 after his defeat by the federalists at the battle of Famaillá. The museum contains exhibits of 19th-century dress, as well as religious works of art, and a room is dedicated to the independence movement, including weapons captured in the battle of Suipacha.

Two blocks away, also on Lavalle, is the **Museo Arqueológico Provincial** (daily 9am–noon and 3–9pm), where exhibits, including stone, ceramic, and metal objects, from the region are on display. The oldest church in Jujuy is **Capilla de Santa Bárbara F** dating from 1777 and including a collection of 18th-century religious paintings. Two blocks away, on Calle Lamadrid, is the **Teatro Mitre**, constructed in 1901. The Italian-style theater was restored in 1979. Two blocks to the east is the Mercado Municipal. The French-style railway station is located two blocks from the Plaza Belgrano, on Gorriti and

Urquiza, while the bus terminal is a few blocks south of the Río Chico Xibi Xibi at the corner of Iguazú and Dorrego.

JUJUY'S PARK AND TERMAS DE REYES

Several blocks to the west of the plaza is the **Parque San Martín**, the city's only park, which, although smaller than those of other Argentine cities, contains a swimming pool as well as a housing complex and a restaurant. Near to the park, on Bolivia 2365, is the **Museo de Mineralogía** (Mon–Fri 9am–1pm), which belongs to the provincial university's geology and mining faculty. The museum includes exhibits of the mineral wealth of the province, detailing the history of its tin- and iron-mining tradition as well as its gold deposits.

A few miles from town, one can visit the **Termas de Reyes** spa (www.termas dereyes.com), located in a narrow valley. The visit offers beautiful views of the city and of mountains and lakes in the area, as well as the opportunity to indulge in thermal bathing. Nearby is the Parque Provincial Potrero de Yala, a quiet spot amid the lakes much favored by residents of the city.

THE COLORFUL QUEBRADA

North of San Salvador de Jujuy, RN9 climbs steadily up, and before long the sun breaks through. Here, a wide and highly distinctive *quebrada* (gorge) is dominated by the Río Grande. This river receives torrential and often destructive rains in the summer, when the colors of the valley wall become more intense and delineated. The **Quebrada de Humahuaca** valley has been used for 10,000 years as an important passage for transporting both people and ideas between the Andean highlands and the plains of Jujuy below. In 2003 it was made a Unesco World Heritage Site.

Purmamarca ❸, which means "Desert Region" in the Quechua tongue, is a tiny village 65km (40 miles) north of San Salvador de Jujuy. The adobe and cactus-wood church in the central plaza dates from the mid-17th century, but most visitors to Purmamarca are here to see – and to photograph

⊙ Tip

A pleasant walk in the northern outskirts of Jujuy is to the road (Avenida Fascio) by the Río Grande, where some of the oldest and grandest homes in the city are located, often with courtyards and ornate window grates.

Propping up a restaurant doorway whilst drinking mate.

⊙ TERRIFIC TORRONTÉS

Mention Argentine wine to someone and if they think of anything at all, they will think of Malbec. But this popular red varietal is not the only grape that flourishes in the world's southernmost vineyards. The lesser-known but increasingly popular Torrontés, for example, is Argentina's most widely planted white variety. It produces potent (14 percent alcohol on average) but very drinkable wines, with hints of grapefruit and melon. The grape is particularly well suited to the high altitude vineyards of Salta, with their sandy soils, hot days, and chilly nights. Etchart, El Esteco, and Colomé are just three of the wineries in the region producing excellent Torrontés, and you'll find their labels in most supermarkets.

Tray of traditional northwestern food – empanadas, locro, and humitas.

Humahuaca.

– a landmark that was here many millions of years before: the Cerro de los Siete Colores (Hill of the Seven Colors). Those celebrated hues – yellow, orange, red, pink, gray, green, and black – were created by marine sediments that accumulated in the rock strata over eons. If time allows, you can hike around the hill following a well-defined trail.

The next stop after Purmamarca is **Tilcara ❹**, some 20km (12 miles) north. With around 4,700 inhabitants, Tilcara is a proper town and can date its origins back to the pre-Inca era. You can find out more about the area's pre-colonial history at the Museo Arqueológico Dr Eduardo Casanova (Belgrano 445; daily 9am–6pm; free on Mon), whose exhibits include some Inca masks, a pre-Inca mummy, and some fine ceramics. Keep your ticket because it also gets you entry to the Pucará de Tilcara, a 1,000-year-old ruined fort a couple of kilometers out of town. The fort was discovered in 1908 and reconstructed in the 1960s. Next to the fort is a botanical garden, with specimens from the *puna* (high plateau).

At **El Angosto de Perchel** the quebrada narrows to less than 200 meters (650ft) and then opens into a large valley. Wherever the available water is used for irrigation, tiny fields and orchards give a touch of fresh green to the red and yellow shades of the river banks.

THE HEIGHTS OF HUMAHUACA

Further up the valley lies the town of **Humahuaca ❺**, which gives its name to the whole gorge. Previously an important railway stopover on the way up to Bolivia, it has suffered badly from the closure of the railway. Humahuaca lies at almost 3,000 meters (9,000ft), so move very slowly to avoid running out of breath. Also avoid eating heavily or drinking alcohol prior to ascending: a cup of sweet tea is more beneficial at this altitude. Here one finds stone-paved and extremely narrow streets, vendors of herbs and produce near the former railway station, and an imposing monument made from 70 tonnes of bronze commemorating the Argentine

War of Independence. The town's church, Nuestra Señora de la Candelaria, dates back to the 16th century. The museum of local customs and traditions is also worth a visit. Humahuaca's top tourist attraction, however, is a life-sized mechanized saint (St Francis Solanus) that emerges from the Cabildo's clock tower each day at noon. Pilgrims gather below to witness this low-tech apparition.

Most travelers pay only a short visit to Humahuaca, but a stay of several days is truly worthwhile, as many side trips can be made from here. Some 9km (6 miles) outside the town are the extensive archeological ruins of **Coctaca**. The true significance of this site is still largely unknown although scientists are studying it, and its secrets may soon be revealed. Other options include a journey to **Iruya**, a hamlet (1,150 inhabitants) of narrow streets and colonial-era buildings cradled amid towering mountains, 75km (47 miles) from Humahuaca. The only way to get there is via RP19, a zigzagging unpaved road that branches off from RN9 25km north of Humahuaca and then passes over the spectacular Abra del Cóndor, a 4,000-meter (13,000ft) -high mountain pass marking the border between Salta and Jujuy. From Iruya you can visit yet smaller villages, some of which are not even on the maps, as well as the Pucará de Titiconte, a pre-Columbian fort.

An even more adventurous trip would be to **Abra Pampa** and from there to the **Monumento Natural Laguna de los Pozuelos** (daily 10am– 3pm; free), where you can see huge flocks of the spectacular Andean flamingo, and vicuña herds grazing near the road. Near Abra Pampa there is a huge vicuña farm.

Here in the heart of the Altiplano or *puna* (with an average altitude of 3,500 meters/11,500ft), are some of the most interesting villages in the Northwest, in a region inhabited for thousands of years before the arrival of the Spanish, and occupied by the Incas during the expansion of their empire southward from Bolivia. Many of the isolated

Images of Che Guevara decorate a restaurant in the Quebrada de Humahuaca.

Salt extraction on Salinas Grandes.

villages have surprisingly large and richly decorated colonial churches, including those at Casabindo, Cochinoca, Pozuelos, Tafna, and Rinconada, which can all be reached by small access roads that wind through the peaceful countryside. RN9 continues all the way to **La Quiaca**, at the Argentine border, opposite the Bolivian town of Villazón. This has also suffered with the closure of the railway, but still has a colorful market.

THE END OF THE ROAD

Finally, as if saved for a happy ending to this excursion, there remains one of the most sparkling jewels of Argentina: the ancient **Iglesia de Nuestra Señora del Rosario y San Francisco**, in Yavi.

The tiny village of **Yavi ⑥**, on the windy and barren high plateau near the Bolivian border, lies protected in a small depression, about 15km (9 miles) by paved road to the east of La Quiaca. Between the 17th and 19th centuries, Yavi was the seat of the Marqués de Campero, one of the wealthiest Spanish feudal possessions in this part of

the continent. Though the chapel here was originally built in 1690, one of the later marquesses ordered the altar and pulpit to be gilded. The thin alabaster plaques covering the windows create a soft lighting that makes the gilding glow (daily 2–9pm).

SALT FLATS

A good day trip (or overnighter) from Salta is to **Salinas Grandes ⑦**, a 12,000-hectare (30,000-acre) salt flat bestriding the border of Salta and Jujuy. Once a highly salinated lake, the water evaporated over millions of years to leave the waxen, cracked moonscape we see today, lifeless save for the activity of workers harvesting salt. It is obligatory – and remarkably easy – to take a "trick" photograph here: the flat, featureless plain erases perspective and causes background and foreground to overlap.

To reach the salt flats from Salta City, take RN51 to Santa Rosa de Tastil, a pre-Inca city discovered in 1903 and dating back to the 14th century. There is a small museum at the site, whose caretaker also offers guided tours around the ruins (Tue–Fri and Sun 9am–4pm, until 5pm in summer, Sat 9am–6pm, until 7pm in summer). Continue to **San Antonio de los Cobres** and then take the unpaved Ex-RN40 to Salinas Grandes. After you've seen the salt, return to the city or continue to Purmamarca on RP52.

EXPLORING THE CALCHAQUÍ VALLEYS

Passing as it does through the captivating landscapes of the Calchaquí Valleys, with their outlandish rock formations, high-altitude vineyards and charming towns, the circular route that begins in Salta and passes through Cafayate and Cachi before returning you to the capital is one of Argentina's great road trips. (You can, of course, do the circuit in the other direction, if you prefer to move counterclockwise).

The Salinas Grandes salt flats.

Doing the circuit clockwise means that the first leg – 185km (115 miles) southwards to Cafayate on paved RN68 – is straightforward. The road cuts through the Quebrada de las Conchas, more commonly referred to as the Quebrada de Cafayate. Towering over the gorge are some of the region's best-known rock formations, whose wind-sculpted contours have inspired various nicknames – el Sapo (the Toad), el Fraile (the Friar), and el Obelisco (the Obelisk), for example.

CAFAYATE

Cafayate ❽ should be earmarked in advance as a place to spend at least one night. There is more to Cafayate than the cathedral, with its rare five naves; its small museums of archeology and wine cultivation; its several bodegas (wine cellars), tapestry artisans, and silversmiths. It is the freshness of the altitude of 1,600 meters (5,300ft) and the shade of its patios, overgrown with vines, that really enchant the visitor. The surroundings of this tiny colonial town are dotted with vineyards and countless archeological remains.

While not yet on a par with Mendoza, wine tourism in and around Cafayate is growing steadily. For a stylish introduction to wine production in the area, head to the **Museo de la Vid y el Vino** (www.museodelavidyelvino.gov.ar/; Tue–Sun 9am–7pm) on the corner of Güemes Sur and Fermín Perdiguero. Wineries worth visiting include Bodega Jose L. Mounier, also known as Finca Las Nubes (www.bodegamounier.com.ar); San Pedro de Yacochuya (http://yacochuya.com.ar/spy/); and Bodega El Esteco (www.elesteco.com), the largest winery in the area. Tour schedules change regularly, so check websites before arranging a visit.

A popular side trip from Cafayate is to the archeological ruins of Quilmes, 55km (34 miles) to the south (see page 236).

NORTH TO CACHI ON RUTA 40

The next leg of the circuit, from Cafayate to Cachi, is on an unpaved stretch of Route 40. It's a tough but rewarding drive that crosses the impressive **Quebrada de la Flecha**. Here, a forest of eroded sandstone spikes provides a spectacle as the play of sun and shadow makes the figures appear to change their shapes. **Angastaco** ❾, the first hamlet worth stopping in, was once an aboriginal settlement, with its primitive adobe huts standing on the slopes of immobile sand dunes. In the center there is a comfortable *hostería*. Angastaco lies amid extensive vineyards, though between this point and the north, more red chili peppers than grapes are grown.

Molinos ❿, with its massive adobe church and colonial streets, is another quiet place worth a stop. *Molino* means mill, and one can still see the town's old water-driven mill grinding corn and other grains by the bank of the Calchaquí River. Across the river is an artists' cooperative, housed in a beautifully renovated colonial home,

> **Tip**
>
> Among the bodegas worth visiting around Cafayate are Etchart and El Esteco, where guided tours and wine tastings are available.

Etchart winery in Cafayate produces Torrontés.

Salamis and cheeses on sale at a stall in Cafayate.

Ruins of Quilmes in Salta province.

complete with a large patio, arches, and an inner courtyard. The local craftspeople sell only handmade goods, including sweaters, rugs, and tapestries. At **Seclantás** and the nearby hamlet of **Solco**, artisans continue to produce the traditional handwoven *ponchos de Güemes*, red and black blankets made of fine wool that are carried over the shoulders of the proud gauchos of Salta.

If you have time, take a side trip from Molinos to Bodega Colomé, where grapes from some of the world's highest vineyards are elaborated into lip-smackingly full-bodied wines. It's also the home of Argentina's most incongruous contemporary art museum: the **Museo James Turrell** (www.bodegacolome.com; Tue–Sun 2–6pm; advance booking recommended). Turrell is a well-known and highly respected conceptual artist from California, and this purpose-built space houses many of his beguiling "light and space" installations, drawn from the personal collection of Donald Hess, Colomé's owner.

CACHI AND AROUND

The loveliest place on the circuit is **Cachi** ⑪, 175km (108 miles) north of Cafayate. The town's main square is as pretty and well maintained as any in Argentina. Flanking it is a church from 1796, San José de Cachi, many of whose furnishings and structural features (altar, confessionals, pews, even the roof and the floor) are made of cactus wood, one of the few building materials available in the area. Across the square lies the excellent archeological museum **Pío Pablo Díaz** (Tue–Sun 9am–6pm), whose information panels and 5,000 exhibits tell the story of the region's inhabitants from 10,000 years ago to the Spanish conquest.

For closer views of Mount Cachi and a glimpse of the beautiful farms and country houses, be sure to visit **Cachi Adentro**, a tiny village 6km (4 miles) from Cachi proper. RN40 at this point becomes almost impassable, although you can visit the sleepy village of **La Poma**, 50km (30 miles) to the north and partly destroyed by an earthquake in 1930. But the main

⊘ QUILMES

This vast stronghold of the Calchaquís, located in the Calchaquí Valley, near Santa María, once had as many as 200,000 inhabitants, and was the last indigenous site in Argentina to surrender to the Spanish, in 1667.

The Calchaquís were farmers cultivating a large area of land around the urban settlement, and they developed an impressively integrated social and economic structure. This undoubtedly helped their long resistance of the Spanish – both the invasion and conversion to Christianity.

Quilmes is a paradigm of fine pre-Hispanic urban architecture. Its walls of neatly set flat stones are still perfectly preserved, though the roofs of giant cacti girders vanished long ago. Local guides take the visitor to some of the most interesting parts of this vast complex – its fortifications (requiring quite a steep climb), its residential area, its huge dam, and its reservoir.

At the foot of the ruins, the Centro de Intepretación de la Ciudad Sagrada de Quilmes (CIQ; daily 10am–6pm) opened in 2018, with four interesting rooms housing interactive displays, audiovisuals, and exhibits dedicated to the history and culture of Quilmes' one-time inhabitants.

tourist route runs to the east over a high plateau called Tin-Tin, the native terrain of the sleek, giant *cardón*, or candelabra cactus. The **Parque Nacional Los Cardones** (daily 9.30am–6pm) was designated a national park in 1997 to protect the endangered and distinctive cactus.

Down the spectacular **Cuesta del Obispo Pass**, through the multicolored **Quebrada de Escoipe** and over the lush plains of the Lerma Valley the road stretches to Salta. From Cafayate to Salta, via Cachi, without stopovers, it is a demanding eight-hour drive.

TOWARDS TUCUMÁN

Only a tiny proportion of visitors to the Northwest venture south of Cafayate, into the provinces of Tucumán, Cata-marca, and Santiago del Estero. In the remoter parts of these regions, the tourism infrastructure dwindles to vanishing point. (For the adventurous this, of course, is the attraction.)

Around 68km (42 miles) south of Cafayate, via RN40 and then RP307 into the province of Tucumán, is the town of **Amaicha del Valle** ⑫, a favorite vacation spot for residents of Tucumán city, many of whom have weekend homes here. Local tradition has it that the sun shines 360 days of the year here. Some hotel owners are so fond of this bit of lore that they reimburse their guests if an entire visit should pass without any sun at all. The local handwoven tapestries and the workshops certainly merit the visit. It has a permanent population almost exclusively of indigenous origin, which is the only indigenous community in Argentina to have been given the titles to its traditional lands (by the Perón government in the early 1970s).

Although Amaicha tends to be hot during the day throughout the year, the high altitude and sparklingly clear air make it cold at night even in summer: a sharp change in temperature which is refreshing and requires warm clothes, even at the height of summer.

Every year, coinciding with Carni-val, the traditional indigenous **Fiesta Nacional de la Pachamama** (Mother Earth Festival) is celebrated here, to

Portrait of a Quechua man in Cachi.

Three on a bike in Cafayate.

Unlike sheep's wool, llama wool contains no lanolin and can be worn by people whose skin is usually irritated when wearing woolly clothes.

Pachamama dolls.

give thanks for the fertility of the earth and livestock. An elderly local woman is chosen to play the part of the Pachamama, dressing up and offering wine to all participants. A recent rise in tourist interest has made the week-long festival somewhat more commercial, but it still sticks to tradition and offers ritual ceremony, music, and dance.

STONE CIRCLES

Tafí del Valle ⓑ, 56km (35 miles) south of Amaicha del Valle, is situated in the heart of the Aconquija range. The area was sacred to the Diaguitas, who, with different tribal names, inhabited the area. The valley is littered with clusters of aboriginal dwellings and dozens of sacred stone circles.

By far the most outstanding attractions at Tafí are the menhirs, or standing stones. These stones, which sometimes stand more than two meters (6ft) high, were assembled at the Parque de los Menhires, close to the entrance of the valley, by the government of General

Antonio Bussi, moving them from their original positions when the La Angostura dam was built. The dam and lake are in an idyllic mountain setting. The town of Tafí itself, with a dry and cool mountain climate, is a favorite retreat for local residents, with beautiful views, coffee houses, and artisan crafts, foods (especially cheeses), and sweets.

TUCUMÁN PROVINCE

The province of Tucumán – the smallest of the 24 Argentine federal provinces – is famous for its citrus fruit and sugar cane production and is popularly known as the Garden of the Republic. This climatic and visual contrast is most vividly marked along the Aconquija range, which has several peaks of more than 5,500 meters (18,000ft). The intense greenery is juxtaposed with snowcapped peaks. The best time of year to visit is in winter (June–Aug), when the weather is usually warm and dry; in the summer months it is often stiflingly hot and heavy rains are common.

Ⓞ THE MOTHER OF ALL DEITIES

If you are traveling Argentina's north country, particularly through the province of Jujuy, do not be surprised to see someone digging a hole in the ground and then filling it with cigarettes, coca leaves, cheap wine, and perhaps a ladle or two of llama stew.

This ritual is known as the *challa* and you are most likely to see people performing it on August 1 and at various intervals throughout the rest of that month. The intended recipient of these offerings is Pachamama or the Earth Mother, the most important deity in the Quechua and Aymara pantheons.

If this does not sound very Roman Catholic, that is because it isn't. But like the Incas in whose conquering footsteps they followed, the Spanish were pragmatic as well as ruthless. They intuited that the pagan Amerindians would be more likely to embrace Christianity if their most treasured cultural rituals were left intact. Furthermore, with a little prodding from Spanish missionaries, these rituals could be given a new spin consistent with the doctrine of the gospels.

And so it has turned out, with the result that it is no longer clear where the Virgin Mary begins and Pachamama ends. So if you are wondering whether that person burying wine in the ground is a Pachamamista or a Christian, the likely answer is that they are both.

TUCUMÁN CITY

In addition to its very visible colonial past, **Tucumán** ⑭, previously known as San Miguel de Tucumán, is the only city in the Northwest with a very large immigrant population, especially of Italian, Arab, and Jewish settlers. As a result, it has traditionally been a thriving commercial center with a pace of life more similar to Buenos Aires than to the slower-paced cities of the north. It was also the first industrial center in the Northwest, which, together with its historical past as the main commercial center between Buenos Aires and Bolivia and Peru, make it a fairly cosmopolitan and very lively place.

The spacious **Parque 9 de Julio**, the Baroque **Casa de Gobierno**, and several patrician edifices, together with a number of venerable churches, are reminders of the town's colonial past. This may best be appreciated by visiting the **Casa Histórica de la Independencia** (https://casadelaindependencia.cultura. gob.ar; daily 10am–6pm). In a large room of this stately house, part of which has been rebuilt, the Argentine national independence ceremony took place on July 9, 1816.

The principal colonial churches in Tucumán are the **cathedral** and **San Francisco Church** (daily), both located on the plaza; **Santo Domingo Church** (Mon–Fri), on 9 de Julio and also operating as a school; and **Basilica de La Merced** (daily), on the corner of 24 de Septiembre and Las Heras, which houses a famous image of Tucumán's patroness, the Virgin of Mercy.

SALT FLATS AND VOLCANOES

The southernmost region covered in this section, **Catamarca** offers stark geographical highlights. This province has the greatest altitude differences imaginable; toward Córdoba and Santiago del Estero in the east, the vast **Salinas Grandes** salt flats are barely 400 meters (1,300ft) above sea level, while in the west, near the Chilean border, the Ojos del Salado volcano reaches the vertiginous height of 6,864 meters (22,520ft), making it the highest active volcano in the world.

> **⊙ Tip**
>
> Running northwest of San Fernando, Ruta Nacional 40 and Ruta Provincial 43 leading to Antofagasta de la Sierra cross some of the remotest parts of the Northwest. Facilities are very limited and road conditions highly variable, so it is vital to seek local advice before you set out.

San José de Cachi church.

In the capital, **San Fernando del Valle de Catamarca** , points of interest include the Catedral Basílica, containing the famous wooden Virgin of the Valley, discovered being worshiped by Amerindians in the 17th century; the convent of San Francisco; archeological and historical museums; and a permanent arts and crafts fair, best known for rugs and tapestries, located a few blocks from the center.

AROUND SAN FERNANDO DEL VALLE DE CATAMARCA

The country around the capital is lovely, and several side trips are worth mentioning. Time permitting, a trip to the old indigenous settlements scattered on RN40 is highly recommended. The road crosses the province through a series of valleys and river beds, surrounded by dusty mountains. These towns still give a strong impression of how they were hundreds of years ago, and their small museums, traditional chapels, and the spectacular landscape make for a worthwhile trip. The most visited of these towns are **Tinogasta**, **Belén**, **Londres**, and **Santa María**. Look for the thermal spas along the route, one of the most developed being at **Fiambalá**, 48km (30 miles) north of Tinogasta. Fiambalá, which is also famous for its woven ponchos, is an oasis surrounded by vineyards. Its thermal spa is located 15km (9 miles) to the east of the town, in a ravine with waterfalls, and has been used for its curative waters since pre-Columbian times.

For the adventurous, there is **Antofagasta de la Sierra**, about 250km (155 miles) north of RN40, located in the *puna* region of northern Catamarca. Remote Antofagasta is 3,500 meters (11,482ft) above sea level and nearby are lagoons, volcanoes, and salt flats. High-quality textiles can be bought here, especially during March, when a craft and agricultural fair is held in the town.

SANTIAGO DEL ESTERO

To the east of Catamarca lie the dusty flats of Santiago del Estero province. Along with Chaco and Formosa, this huge province is one of the least-visited

San Francisco church in Tucumán city.

in the country. It has a proud cultural tradition (it is one of the cradles of Argentine folkloric music) but few obvious points of interest and next to no tourism infrastructure. The capital of the province, bearing the same name, was founded by the Spanish in 1553, making it the oldest continuously inhabited city of the region. The city of **Santiago del Estero** ⑱ is also home to the first university established in Argentine territory, and some very attractive colonial buildings remain near the central plaza.

JUNGLE RETREATS

Although the Northwest is mainly known for its valleys, plains, and uplands, there are several large areas dominated by dense, subtropical forest. A number of national parks have been created to protect these fragile ecosystems, and while they're difficult to get to, jungle lovers may consider it worth the effort.

Parque Nacional El Rey is located in the heart of the *yungas* or subtropical jungle region, 80km (50 miles) east of Salta. It's a natural hothouse with tropical vegetation as dense and green as one can find almost anywhere in South America. Visitors who come to fish, study the flora and fauna, or just to relax, will find ample accommodations; there is a clean *hostería*, some bungalows, and a campground. The park is only accessible by car or pre-arranged transportation from Salta, and the best time to visit is between the months of May and October.

Parque Nacional Calilegua occupies 76,000 hectares (188,000 acres) in the east of Jujuy province. Calilegua is primarily tropical *yunga* forest, like El Rey, although as the altitude climbs the topography changes to mountain jungle, mountain forest, and eventually mountain plains. The park has a campsite, several rivers, and a wide range of wildlife, including wild boar and jaguars, in an exceptionally diverse ecosystem. In 2000, environmental groups lost their fight to stop a gas pipeline being constructed through the park.

Horses graze in Tafí del Valle.

Grape vines in Mendoza province.

Arcade leading to the Basílica de Nuestra Señora de Luján.

THE CUYO

Deserts and vineyards, bustling cities and silent valleys, snow-capped peaks and bone-dry plains – west-central Argentina is a land of extremes.

Argentina's west is not as wild as it used to be. Once a precarious frontier town nervously awaiting the next earthquake, Mendoza, the region's largest city, has grown into a thriving, prosperous metropolis. It is one of several oases kept alive by an irrigation network built up and refined over centuries. Melt water from glaciers high up in the Andean cordillera feeds rivers that cut through the dry plains below and which in turn feed the orchards and vineyards that have made Mendoza and, to a lesser extent San Juan, the country's most important fruit- and wine-producing regions. However, these oases are the exception, not the rule. In places like La Rioja's Valle de la Luna (Valley of the Moon), where the rivers dried up millions of years ago, nothing lives and nothing stirs – except for the wind chipping away at the sandstone cliffs. In these areas you are more likely to see a paleontologist than a viticulturist: Cuyo is a mecca for dinosaur hunters.

In terms of tourism, the region attracts both adventurers and hedonists. For the former there are white-water rafting excursions on turbulent stretches of snowmelt river, treks in the Andean foothills, wind-kart rides on ancient, long-dried-up lake beds, and leaps into thin air on a paraglider. Climbers come from across the globe to lock horns with Mt Aconcagua – at 6,960 meters (22,841ft) the highest peak outside the Himalayas.

For hedonists the attractions of the Cuyo (and Mendoza in particular) can be summed up in one word: wine. (Although it should be said that the food in this part of the country is excellent too.) The receptiveness of the province's many wineries to tourism has increased in proportion with the fame of their wines and, in particular, with the fame of those wines elaborated with the Malbec grape. It is now

Main attractions
Mendoza city
The vineyards of Mendoza
Aconcagua
Valle de la Luna

Maps on pages
246, 248

Harvesting grapes.

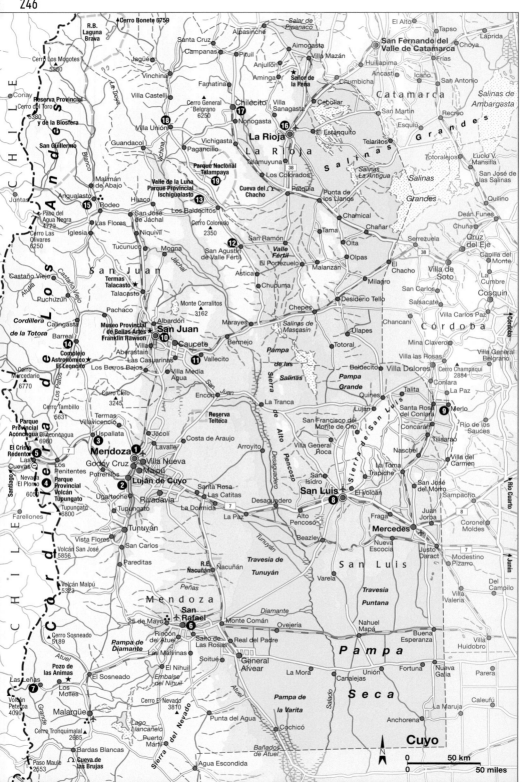

Cerro Bonete 6759

R.B.
Laguna
Brava

El Alto
Tapso
Láprida
Choya

Santa Cruz
Alpasinché
Salar de
Pipanaco
San Fernando del
Valle de Catamarca

Jagüé
Campanas
Pituil
Aimogasta
Villa Mazán
Huillapima
Ancasti
San Antonio

Cerro Los Mogotes
5350
Vinchina
Anjullón
Aminga
Señor de
la Peña
Chumbicha
Icaño
Catamarca

Conay
Reserva Provincial
Cerro del Toro
6380
y de la Biosfera
Famatina

Villa Castelli
Cerro General
Belgrano
6250
Chilecito
Villa
Sanagasta
San Martín
Esquiú
Recreo
Salinas de
Ambargasta

San Guillermo
Villa Unión
Nonogasta
La Rioja
El Estanquito
Telaritos
Totoralejos
Lucío V.
Mansilla

Guandacol
Vichigasta
Pagancillo
La Rioja
Talamuyuna
Los Colorados
38
Salinas
Salinas
La Antigua
Grandes
San José
de las Salinas

Paso del
Agua Negra
4779
Malimán
de Abajo
Huaco
Parque Nacional Talampaya
Parque Provincial
Ischigualasto
Cueva del
Chacho
Patquía
Punta de
los Llanos
Chamical
Grandes
Quilino
Deán Funes

Cerro Las
Olivares
6250
Angualasto
Rodeo
Las Flores
Los Baldecitos
Cerro Colorado
2350
San Ramón
Tama
Chañar
Olta
Serrezuela
38
Chuña
Cruz
del Eje

Castaño Viejo
Iglesia
Niquivil
Mogna
San Agustín
de Valle Fértil
Valle
Fértil
El Portezuelo
Malanzán
Olpas
El Chacho
Villa de
Soto
Capilla del
Monte
Cosquín

Puchuzún
San Juan
Termas
Talacasto
Talacasto
Astica
Chepuma
Miligro
Desiderio Tello
San Carlos
Salsacate
Villa Carlos Paz
La
Cumbre

Cordillera
de la Totora
Barreal
Pachaco
Monte Corralitos
3162
Albardón
Marayes
Chepes
Salinas de
Mascasín
Chancani
Córdoba
Villa General
Belgrano

Complejo
Astronómico
El Leoncito
Museo Provincial
de Bellas Artes
Franklin Rawson
San Juan
Caucete
Bermejo
Ulapes
Totoral
Mina Clavero
Villa las Rosas
Cerro Champaquí
2884

Cerro
Mercedario
6770
Aberastain
Las Casuarinas
Los Berros Bajos
Vallecito
Villa Media
Agua
Pampa
de las
Salinas
Baldecito
Villa Dolores
Conlara
La Paz

Cerro
Tambillo
5631
Encón
La Tranca
Pampa
Grande
Quines
Talita
Merla

Parque
Provincial
Aconcagua
Aconcagua
6960
Termas
Villavicencio
Reserva
Telteca
Lavalle
Costa de Araujo
Arroyito
San Francisco del
Monte de Oro
Luján
Santa Rosa
del Conlara
Concarán
Río de los
Sauces
Tilisarao

El Cristo
Redentor
Las
Cuevas
Jocolí
Villa General
Roca
Naschel
Villa del
Carmen

Nevada
El Plomo
6050
Parque
Provincial
Volcán
Tupungato
6800
Mendoza
Godoy Cruz
Villa Nueva
Maipú
Luján de Cuyo
Rivadavia
Santa Rosa
Las Catitas
La Dormida
San
Isidro
El Volcán
San Luis
La Toma
Trapiche
San José
del Morro
Sampacho

Tupungato
Ugarteche
Tupungato
La Paz
7
Desaguadero
Alto Pencoso
Fraga
Mercedes
Juan
Jorba
Coronel
Moldes

Vista Flores
San Carlos
Tunuyán
La Paz
Beazley
Nueva
Escocia
Justo
Daract
Modestino
Pizarro

Paredites
Tunuyán
Travesía de
Tunuyán
Varela
San Luis
Villa
Valeria
Del
Campillo

Volcán Malpú
5323
R.E.
Ñacuñán
Nacuñán
Peñas
Travesía
Puntana
Nahuel
Mapá
Buena
Esperanza
Villa
Huidobro

Mendoza
25 de Mayo
San
Rafael
Monte Común
Ovejería
Pampa
Seca

Cerro Sosneado
5189
Pampa de
Diamante
Rincón
del Atuel
Salto de
Las Rosas
Real del Padre
Diamante
Fortuna
Villa

Pozo de
las Ánimas
El Sosneado
Las Malvinas
Soitué
General
Alvear
La Mora
Unión
Canalejas
Nueva
Galia
Parera

Los Molles
Embalse
del Nihuil
Pampa de
la Varita
Caleufú

Las Leñas
Cerro El Nevado
3810
Salado
La Maruja

Volcán Payún
4090
Malargüe
Punta del Agua
Cochicó
Anchorena

Cerro Tronquimalal
2685
Lago
Llancañelo
Puerto
Marfil
Bañados
de Atuel

Paso Maule
2653
Cueva de
las Brujas
Bardas Blancas
Agua Escondida
Cuyo
N
0   50 km
0   50 miles

possible to spend day after languid day hopping from one bodega to the other, tasting the latest vintage and touring the facilities. And since many wineries have added board and lodging to their amenities, you could quite easily spend your entire trip among vines.

MENDOZA

The Cuyo comprises the provinces of Mendoza, San Juan, San Luis, and La Rioja. The largest city is **Mendoza ❶**, with a total population of over 1 million inhabitants, located 1,060km (659 miles) due west of Buenos Aires. Little remains today of the town's original colonial architecture.

The whole region is periodically racked by earthquakes, some of them quite severe. One such quake, in 1861, killed 10,000 and completely leveled Mendoza, and rebuilding was done with an eye to averting further disaster. Another in January 1985 left 40,000 homeless. The last major quake happened in 2006.

In spite of Mendoza's relatively modern appearance, it has a long history, of which its residents are very proud. It was from here, in 1817, that General San Martín launched his march with 40,000 men across the Andes to liberate Chile and Peru. The wine industry began in earnest in the mid-19th century, with the arrival of many Italian and French immigrants. This was due in large part to the progressive thinking of a series of Mendozan governors who took positive steps to attract immigrants. Among other things, they paid agents at the port of Buenos Aires for each immigrant transported to the province; in particular, qualified engineers and vintners who were responsible both for designing the irrigation system that made cultivation possible in the desert province, and for the planting of vineyards and the construction of wineries. The strength of the wine industry, which has reached world-class standard for fine wines, is reflected in the annual grape harvest festival (Festival de la Vendimia), held in early March and featuring a beauty contest, fireworks, dances, and *son et lumière* shows in an Andean setting.

Busy street in downtown Mendoza.

Polo player in Luján de Cuyo.

Although wine remains a substantial part of the economy, it was the growth of the petroleum industry in the 1950s that brought real prosperity to the city.

Mendoza is much closer to the Chilean capital, Santiago, than to Buenos Aires, and although the exchange rate is not as favorable as it once was, many Chileans come to Mendoza on weekend shopping trips.

MENDOZA'S CITY

While Mendoza is nothing like the metropolis that is Buenos Aires, it has its own charms, and a wealth of cultural activity. Transplanted residents from the capital boast a happy conversion to the more relaxed pace of Mendoza. *Mendocinos* often claim that the province is the most civilized in the country, with an unusually modernist and democratic tradition based on the concept that the successful development of the province is the result of the efforts of the inhabitants, rather than of the generosity of nature. The city is arguably the cleanest and certainly one of the most modern in the country,

nestled at the foot of the mountains and offering a wide range of cinemas, theaters, concert halls, and other cultural activities.

The waters of the region have been put to good use, and the arid landscape has been transformed into a lush oasis. Some of the irrigation channels dug by the original Amerindian inhabitants are still in use, and many more have been added since. The city's low buildings lie along wide, tree-lined streets where channels of running water keep the temperature an agreeable measure below that of the surrounding dry lands, although in summer Mendoza has an extremely hot, desert climate. Even in winter, when the *zonda* windstorms sweep the city, the temperature can rise to Saharan levels.

Many homes have well-tended gardens, and there are parks throughout the city that serve the dual interests of recreation and safety in case of an earthquake. In the midst of the plentiful shade, it is astonishing to realize that all the millions of trees have been planted by the city's residents

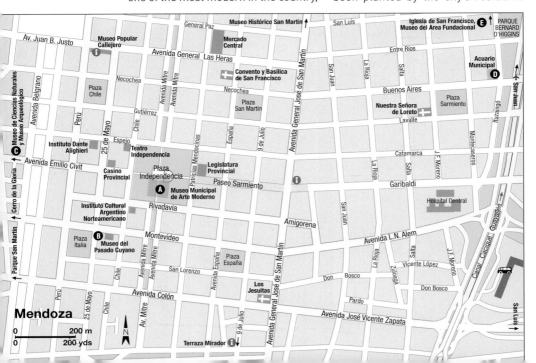

Mendoza

and developers. Not one of the pop-lars, elms, or sycamores is native to the region. Beyond and above all this greenery, to the west, lie the Andes, which provide Mendoza with a spec-tacular backdrop of changing hues throughout the day and night.

THEATERS AND MUSEUMS

At the center of the city of Mendoza is the **Plaza Independencia**. Several important buildings flank the plaza; the oldest is the **Legislatura Provin-cial** (Provincial Legislature), which dates from 1889. Opposite this, on the northwestern corner is the 1925 **Tea-tro Independencia** where theatrical and musical performances are held. In the center of the plaza, located underground, are the **Museo Munici-pal de Arte Moderno Ⓐ** (Tue–Fri 9am–8pm, Sat–Sun 2–8pm), a small gallery exhibiting modern works by local artists, with temporary exhibi-tions; and the **Teatro Municipal Julio Quintanilla**, which puts on theatrical performances at weekends. Around the corner, at Sarmiento and 25 de Mayo, is the provincial **casino**, part of the same complex as the Teatro Inde-pendencia and Park Hyatt Hotel (http://mendoza.park.hyatt.com). There is also an artisans' market on the eastern side of the plaza, facing Calle Patricias Men-docinas, where crafts are on sale Fri-day to Sunday.

Running east from the plaza, past the provincial legislature and the stock exchange, is the pedestrian Paseo Sarmiento, a lively place in the evening, with a number of attractive shops and outdoor cafés, populated by occasional street musicians. This leads to Avenida San Martín, Mendoza's main street.

Mendoza has a good selection of museums and other sites of inter-est. The **Museo del Pasado Cuyano Ⓑ** (Feb–Dec Mon–Fri 9am–12.30pm), located at Montevideo 544, two blocks south of Plaza Independencia and housed in a residence dating from 1873, includes the Historical Studies Board, as well as an exhibition on Gen-eral San Martín, a collection of arti-facts from Mendoza's history, a series of religious art, and an arms collection.

◯ Tip

There are several tourist information offices around Mendoza, including at the bus station. The main Centro Municipal de Información Turística (Mon–Fri 24 hrs), a kiosk at the corner of San Martín and Garibaldi, is quite helpful and organizes themed guided walks round the city.

Passing the time of day in Luján de Cuyo.

Tip

If you are looking for nightlife in Mendoza city, take a stroll along Avenida Villanueva Aristides, to the west of Plaza Independencia. A succession of lively bars, restaurants, and clubs – usually packed – draw the city's young and not so young, and the pace does not start to pick up until after midnight.

Archeology, anthropology, and paleontology buffs should enjoy the **Museo de Ciencias Naturales y Museo Arqueológico** C (Tue–Fri 8am–1pm and 2–7pm, Sat–Sun 3–7pm), outside the city center in Parque San Martín, at Las Tipas and Prado Español. The museum contains some pre-Columbian ceramics, along with a small folkloric collection, and includes archeological and zoological collections. The **Museo Histórico Las Bóvedas** (daily 8.30am–1pm and 4–8pm; free), at Avenida San Martín 1843, houses a collection dedicated to General San Martín and his accomplishments.

Located underground at the junction of Ituzaingó and Buenos Aires, south of Parque O'Higgins, is the **Acuario Municipal** D (daily 9am–7pm). The aquarium has one of the most important collections of fresh- and saltwater fish in Latin America, including species from both the Atlantic and Pacific, and aquatic animals such as giant sea turtles. The aquarium breeds some rare species not usually bred in captivity, and it

makes a very interesting visit, especially for children.

SHADY SQUARES

Mendoza has a number of plazas, of which the **Plaza España** is probably the most attractive. Donated by the Spanish government in the 1940s, the plaza recreates an Andalusian square, complete with fountains and painted tiles imported from Spain; tile scenes include depictions of the founding of Mendoza in 1561. The plaza is one of four that form an extended square some three blocks distant from the Plaza Independencia, the others being Plaza Italia, Plaza Chile, and Plaza San Martín. The latter is located in the heart of the banking district, and has tall, shady trees and a statue of the Liberator. To the east of the city center, located near the aquarium and snake house, and two blocks south of the Parque Bernardo O'Higgins and the Teatro Municipal Gabriela Mistral, is another square, **Plaza Sarmiento**, flanked on its southwestern side by the Nuestra Señora de Loreto Church,

Plaza Independencia.

which was rebuilt after being destroyed by an earthquake in 1861, and renovated in 1957.

North of Plaza Sarmiento, the **Plaza Pedro de Castillo**, formerly the Plaza Mayor, marks the site of the original, 16th-century city center, now preserved as the Area Fundacional. On the northwestern side of the plaza are the ruins of the **Iglesia de San Francisco Ⓔ**. Founded by the Jesuits in the 18th century as the Iglesia de Loreto, the church was destroyed by a massive earthquake in 1861, which flattened the whole city. Also on this plaza is the **Museo del Area Fundacional** (MAF; Tue–Fri 8am–8pm, Sun from 2pm), a comprehensive, modern museum containing exhibits and models of the original city and other archeological objects. It also boasts an underground chamber containing a drinking fountain dating back to 1810, and a café-restaurant serving typical regional dishes.

PARQUE SAN MARTÍN

On the western edge of the city lies **Parque San Martín**, crowned by the Cerro de la Gloria. Lying at the foot of the Andes, the 420-hectare (1,038-acre) park has facilities for a wide variety of sports, including a soccer stadium built for the 1978 World Cup and a yacht club with an artificial lake. Inaugurated in 1906, the park was designed by French landscape architect Carlos Thays. Around 500 different species of plants and 50,000 trees grow in this oasis within an oasis. The park also incorporates a number of fine statues (most of them copies of well-known French sculptures) as well as fountains, an artificial lake, and a rose garden. Just up the hill from the entrance is the former zoo – currently being converted into an Ecoparque, scheduled to open in 2019. The Ecoparque, like the one under construction in the capital (see page 158), will focus on conservation, while the zoo's inhabitants are being transferred to nature parks around Argentina.

At the top of the **Cerro de la Gloria** sits one of Argentina's best-known public sculptures (its fame is helped by the fact that it appears

Outdoor café on Avenida Villanueva Aristides, where Mendoza's best bars and restaurants are located.

Vineyards at the foot of the Andes in Luján de Cuyo.

on the back of the five peso note), the **Monumento al Ejército de los Andes** (Monument to the Army of the Andes). Using 14 tons of bronze, the sculpture celebrates San Martín's liberation of Chile in 1817. The general is depicted in a heroic equestrian pose, while bas-relief around the statue's base depicts various scenes of the liberation campaigns. The site also provides an excellent overview of Mendoza.

Behind the hill, in the southwestern corner of the park, is the **Teatro Griego Frank Romero Day**, an amphitheater built in 1940, and site of many of the city's celebrations, including the grand spectacle of the Festival de la Vendimia (Grape Harvest Festival). First held in 1963, this important festival takes place every year in March, and lasts over three or four days. During the first few days there are street performances and parades, and a queen of the harvest is chosen. The finale is a somewhat overproduced extravaganza, with dancing, fireworks, and moving light shows. This is Mendoza's annual opportunity to show off its hard-earned wealth.

Just to the south of Mendoza, in the town of **Luján de Cuyo ❷**, is the Museo Provincial de Bellas Artes Emiliano Guiñazú, at Avenida San Martín 3651 (closed for renovation). The museum is known as the Casa de Fader, after Spanish painter Fernando Fader, who lived in Mendoza for some years in the early part of the 20th century, and was commissioned by prominent landowner Emiliano Guiñazú to paint some murals for what was at the time his summer residence. The museum was inaugurated on Fader's birthday, and includes formal gardens, as well as collections of foreign and Argentine artists, local landscape painters, and an exhibit of Fader's work.

MENDOZA'S BODEGAS

Scattered across the fertile plains and valleys around Mendoza are hundreds of wineries, ranging from small family operations to huge foreign-owned booze factories. All of this cultivation is made possible through an

Zuccardi winery has several vineyards, two of which are in Valle de Uco and Maipú.

⊘ A DESIGN FOR WINE

Mendoza's wine-growing regions are dotted with structures that appear at first glance to be secret army bases or stranded interplanetary craft but which are revealed on closer inspection to be...wineries. Hugging the ground, as earthquake-proof buildings must do, and devoid of large windows to protect the wine from Mendoza's fierce sun, these bodegas are largely the work of one architecture firm: Bórmida & Yanzón (www.bormidayanzon.com). Through their use of modern engineering solutions to a problem that has plagued winemakers since time immemorial – how to move the grapes from vine to bottle using the minimum of mechanical interference – state-of-the-art wineries like O. Fournier, Salentein, Septima, and DiamAndes are now as likely to appear in architectural journals as they are in wine magazines.

extensive network of irrigation channels, originally laid in pre-Columbian times and extended during the colonial era. The area is blessed with a heady combination of plentiful water, sandy soil, a dry climate, and year-round sunshine, which makes for enormous grape yields.

The first vines were planted in the Cuyo by Jesuit missionaries in the 16th century, but production really took off in the mid-1800s with the arrival of Italian and French immigrants. Many of them simply worked as laborers in the fields, but a knowledgeable few contributed European expertise that greatly refined the industry. Toward the end of the 19th century Mendoza was finally linked by rail with Buenos Aires, and by the 1920s, with the opening up of many more vineyards, the region had become one of the world's leading wine producers. It was not until the 1990s, however, that quality began to catch up with quantity. Then, thanks to the vision of Argentine vineyard owners like Nicolás Catena, the expertise of winemakers like the American Paul Hobbs and the Frenchman Michel Rolland, and a gold rush of foreign investment, Argentine wines began to capture the attention of connoisseurs and critics as well as that of the wider drinking public.

WINE ROUTES

Wine tours can be arranged through a specialist agency, but a more pleasant way to make the rounds is by buying a map, renting a car (or a bicycle), and finding them yourself (see page 264). This provides the opportunity to meander down the lovely country lanes, lined with poplars and wild flowers, and to get a sense of the Cuyo's lifestyle. Local cycling fanatics come out in packs and, with luck, you might even catch sight of old men playing a lazy afternoon game of *bocci* (bowls).

A good starting point for a wine tour is Bodega La Rural, in Maipú, 16km (10 miles) from the center of Mendoza. This huge winery, founded by the Rutini family towards the end of the 19th century, houses an excellent wine museum (www.bodegalarural.com.ar; Mon–Sat 9am–5.30pm) that

Torrontés is Argentina's most widely planted white variety. It produces a strong wine with hints of grapefruit and melon.

Leoncio Arizu winery.

will help you get a feel for how the industry's technology has developed over the past four centuries, from the earthenware jugs, manual corking devices, and horse-pulled carts of the colonial era to the stainless steel tanks, pneumatic pressers, and destemmers used today. Among the other important wineries in Maipú are Familia Zucchardi (www.familia-zuccardi.com), which makes the Santa Julia label; and Trapiche, which was founded at around the same time as La Rural.

Mendoza's most important wine-growing region is Luján de Cuyo, located around 20km (12 miles) southwest of the capital. The area is home to many of Argentina's most respected bodegas – the ones that have done most to transform the image of the country's wine industry from that of a plonk-producing sleeping giant to that of a cutting-edge fine-wine exporter. Key wineries in the region include Achaval Ferrer (http://achaval-ferrer.com), Alta Vista (www.altavistawines.com), Bodega

Sunrise over Aconcagua.

Vistalba (www.bodegavistalba.com), Bodegas y Cavas de Weinert (www.bodegaweinert.com), Catena Zapata (www.catenawines.com), and Ruca Malen (http://bodegarucamalen.com).

Also within an hour's drive of Mendoza City, and growing in status as a wine-producing region, is the stunningly beautiful Valle de Uco. Here, among the poplars that blaze yellow in the fall, are a number of important wineries open to visitors, including Salentein (http://bodegassalentein.com), Lurton (www.francoislurton.com), and Clos de los Siete (www.closdelossiete.com).

CROSSING THE CORDILLERA

One of the most spectacular trips to be made from Mendoza is up the **Uspallata Pass** to the border with Chile. It is an all-day excursion of some 210km (131 miles), passing through the flat, irrigated oases and climbing to over 3,000 meters (9,000ft) beyond Puente del Inca, in the shadow of Cerro Aconcagua. Organized tours are available from Mendoza, but renting a car will allow

you to avoid being herded around. Either way, you should start early in the morning to allow enough time to see all the sights en route. (Unless you are carrying on through Chile, driving independently is only recommended outside the winter months of July–Sept.)

You begin the trip by heading south from Mendoza on Route 7 to **Luján**. Turning right at the town square, you get onto Highway 7, which carries you up into the pass. This stretch of road, the Camino de los Andes, is part of the vast Pan-American Highway. Throughout the centuries, even before the time of the Incas, the pass was used to cross the mountains.

The first spot you will pass in the valley is the **Cacheuta Hot Springs**, located at a lovely bend in the river in the grounds of the Centro Climático Termal Cacheuta (Cacheuta Thermal Springs Center; www.termascacheuta.co/en/home-eng/).

Lying 13km (8 miles) beyond is **Potrerillos**, a scenic oasis where many *mendocinos* have summer homes to escape the heat. Continuing up the valley for another 105km (65 miles), you reach the town of **Uspallata** ③, set in a wide meadow. Farther up again, the valley widens at Punta de Vacas (Cattle Point), where long ago the herds were rounded up to be driven across to Chile. It is at Punta de Vacas that you submit documentation if wishing to continue across the border. About 10km (6 miles) beyond Punta de Vacas lies the ski resort of **Villa Los Penitentes**, which has a ski school, and several hotels and restaurants. Buses bring skiers up for day trips from July through September. Across the valley is the strange formation for which the resort is named: tall rock outcroppings look like hooded monks ("the penitents") ascending toward the cathedral-like peak of the mountain. In winter, windswept ice on the rocks heightens the illusion.

ACONCAGUA

Off to the left of the road, a few kilometers further on, is a melancholy

Wine bar at the eco-friendly, family-owned Finca Adalgisa Hotel and Winery near Mendoza city.

Gauchos riding through Valle de Uco.

sight. The Cementerio de los Andinistas is a small graveyard for those who have died – and a few die every year – in the attempt to scale nearby Cerro Aconcagua. A couple of kilometers beyond this is the **Puente del Inca**, a natural stone bridge made colorful by the sulfurous deposits of the bubbling hot springs beneath it. There is a hostel used particularly by Aconcagua expeditions, as well as gift stalls selling an unusual line in souvenirs – objects solidified in the mineral waters.

Just a few kilometers up the road lies the most impressive sight of the whole excursion. There is a break in the wall of rock and, looking up the valley to the right, you can see the towering mass of **Aconcagua**, at 6,960 meters (22,841ft) the highest peak outside the Himalayas. The mountain is at the center of the Parque Provincial Aconcagua , an important nature reserve. Another major trekking site is **Parque Provincial Volcán Tupungato** , located just south of Puente del Inca and dominated by

the 6,800-meter (22,310ft) Tupungato Volcano, surrounded by glaciers and also served by organized treks.

Aconcagua means "stone watchtower" in the Huarpe dialect. It is perpetually blanketed in snow, and its visible southern face presents a tremendous 3,000-meter (10,000ft) wall of sheer ice and stone. The clear mountain air creates the illusion that Aconcagua lies quite close to the road, but the peak is actually 45km (28 miles) away. You can walk as far as **Laguna de los Horcones**, a green-colored lake at the mountain's base. Most expeditions tackle the northern face. The climb is "straightforward," in the sense that no technical skill is required, but excellent fitness and appropriate equipment are musts. Most of the casualties on the mountain are due to altitude sickness, inadequate equipment, or climbers attempting to summit against the advice of their guides.

The best time to attempt the climb is mid-January to mid-February. Further information can be obtained in

Pickup trucks are a common mode of transport.

Mendoza at the Club Andinista on F.L. Beltrán 357 (http://es-la.facebook.com/clubandinistamendoza; tel: 0261-4319 870), or on the Aconcagua website (www.aconcagua.com).

CHRIST THE REDEEMER

The last sight to see before heading back is the statue of Christ, which marks the border with Chile. On the way there, the road passes the town of **Las Cuevas**, where the road branches. To the right is the tunnel for road and rail traffic to Chile (passenger rail service has been suspended due to lack of customers). To the left is the old road to Chile, which climbs steeply over rock and gravel to **La Cumbre Pass**, at an altitude of 4,200 meters (13,800ft). At the top is the 8-meter (26ft) -high statue of **El Cristo Redentor ❺**, erected in 1904 in commemoration of an international border pact signed with Chile.

SAN RAFAEL

Some 240km (150 miles) south of the regional capital, the city of **San Rafael ❻** is the second most populous oasis in Mendoza. Few tourists would consider it a worthy destination in its own right, but if you are looking for a side trip from Mendoza city, or fancy rafting down the boisterous Río Atuel, it is worth considering.

Like in the city of Mendoza, local residents have kept the desert at bay through planting hundreds of trees and creating parks. There is a park and campsite with a small zoo on an island in the middle of the river, as well as the **Museo Histórico Natural**, a small but eclectic museum with five rooms on botany and zoology, geology, anthropology, history, and local folklore (www.sanrafael.gov.ar/museo/index.html; daily 8am–7pm).

In the city center, on Bernardo de Irigoyen 148, is the **Museo de Bellas Artes**, with a small exhibition of art including works by Antonio Berni and Raúl Soldi (daily 8am–7pm). Some 92km (57 miles) to the south of San Rafael is Mendoza's largest hydroelectric plant, El Nihuil, which has a dam and reservoir where water

Empanadas in the Cuyo tend to contain mince beef, onions, sliced hard-boiled egg, green olives, and spices such as paprika, cumin, and oregano.

Río Atuel, near San Rafael.

sports such as windsurfing and fishing are available.

SKIING AT LAS LEÑAS

To the southwest of San Rafael, in the **Valle Hermoso** (Beautiful Valley), is the ski resort of **Las Leñas** ➐, 2,250 meters (7,400ft) up in the Andes. This is becoming quite the place for the chic set of both hemispheres to meet between June and October. It has 45km (28 miles) of dry powder slopes and accommodations for 2,000 people. Charter flights bring skiers from Mendoza to the nearby town of **Malargüe**, from where buses take them the rest of the way.

SAN LUIS AND WATER SPORTS

Although **San Luis** ➑ does not really merit an extra trip, it lies on the road between Buenos Aires and Mendoza, so those going overland may want to rest here overnight. The town sits at the northwest corner of the pampas, and was a lonely frontier outpost; it retains a faintly colonial atmosphere,

with some interesting buildings, such as the restored 18th-century Convento de San Domingo, on Plaza Independencia. However, industrial promotion schemes offering tax breaks to companies investing in the province have created a significant industrial base in the area around the city.

Several resorts clustered around reservoirs in the San Luis province are popular with anglers and windsurfers. On Ruta 1, which leads to the Sierras de Córdoba, is the spa resort of **Merlo** ➒. With a particularly sunny, dry, and mild microclimate, Merlo offers a range of hotels, holiday chalets, casinos, a river, and attractive surrounding country. It is this region's most popular tourist destination. The resort becomes especially crowded during Semana Santa (Holy Week) and the winter vacation period. While it has few buildings of great architectural or historical interest, the town offers a well-developed tourist infrastructure, with activities such as horseback riding, trekking, climbing, and hang-gliding all available locally.

Building reduced to rubble in San Juan.

⊘ TRAGIC EARTHQUAKE

At 8.52pm on January 15, 1944, the city of San Juan was struck by an earthquake that killed an estimated 100,000 people – the worst natural disaster in Argentina's history. Juan Domingo Perón met his future wife, Evita, at a gala evening to raise funds for the quake victims, but the disaster played another role in shaping the populist and redistributive political philosophy later known as Peronism.

American historian Mark Healey has analyzed the quake and its aftermath in his book *The Ruins of the New Argentina* (2011). According to Healey, the disaster, in revealing the wretched, unsafe conditions in which many people lived, had a galvanizing effect on both the nation and Perón. For better or worse, the San Juan earthquake helped shape Argentine history.

SAN JUAN

The city of **San Juan ⑩**, capital of the province of the same name, is 177km (106 miles) north of Mendoza along RN40. An earthquake on January 15, 1944 leveled the town, and it has been completely rebuilt since then. It was Juan Perón's theatrical and highly successful efforts to raise funds for the devastated town that first brought him to national prominence, and which incidentally first brought him into contact with an obscure radio actress named Eva Duarte. Unfortunately, the town's architecture is on the whole very modern and not especially attractive, with the exception of the **Museo Provincial de Bellas Artes Franklin Rawson** (Avenida San Martín; Tue–Sun noon–9pm), an arts center with an interesting collection of Argentine paintings and sculptures, a library, a concert hall, and a restaurant.

San Juan is a major center of wine production, although the bulk of its production is of the table variety rather than fine wine. The city is most famous for being the birthplace of Domingo Faustino Sarmiento (1811–88), the noted historian and educator who was president of the republic from 1868 to 1874. His former home, on the corner of Avenida San Martín and Sarmiento is the site of the **Museo Casa Natal de Sarmiento** (https://casanatalsarmiento.cultura.gob.ar/; Mon–Fri 9am–8.30pm, Sat–Sun 10.30–4pm; guided tours in English), which has nine rooms around two patios, containing various items of furniture and personal effects. There is also the **Museo de Ciencias Naturales** (Mon–Fri 9am–1pm, Sat–Sun 11am–7pm), which is near the Parque de Mayo, close to the intersection of 25 de Mayo and España. Besides the usual natural history exhibits, this museum also has an important collection of fossils from the Parque Provincial Ischigualasto – better known as Valle de la Luna (see page 260) – which date from 200 million years ago.

On the other side of the city center, to the east, on the corner of Avenida General Rawson and General Paz, is the **Museo Histórico Provincial Agustin Gnecco** (Mon–Fri 8.30am–1pm, Sat 9am–1pm), which houses a large

⊙ **Tip**

If you are travelling to Valle de la Luna, or indeed to any other desert environment, carry plenty of water with you and an extra layer to put on when the temperature drops. In summer the park is prone to sudden storms, which can temporarily cut off the roads – be prepared.

Apartments at the ski resort Las Leñas.

collection, primarily of 18th- and 19th-century crafts and artwork, weapons, silver, furniture, and clothing. Located in the former warehouses of the General Belgrano railroad is the Mercado Artesanal Tradicional (Traditional Artisans' Market; Sun–Mon 9am–1pm and 4–7pm, Sat 9am–7pm), specializing in weaving and other rural crafts.

AROUND SAN JUAN

To the west of San Juan is the Sierra de Tontal, with peaks of around 4,000 meters (13,120ft), which offer less strenuous climbs than those of the Mendoza peaks. You can inquire at the local tourist office about the possibility of white-water rafting on the area's rivers. Some 30km (18.5 miles) away to the west lies the Embalse de Ullum (dam and reservoir) on the Río San Juan, in a pleasantly contrasting green setting. The dam has a hydroelectric plant and the reservoir is used for various water sports.

About 60km (37 miles) to the east of San Juan, on RN20, is the small village of **Vallecito** ⓫ and the shrine to La

La Difunta Correa shrine.

Difunta Correa, one of the most visited religious sites in the whole of South America (see box).

VALLE DE LA LUNA

About 250km (155 miles) to the northeast of Vallecito, along RN141 and Ruta 510, is the Valle Fértil, where the town of **San Agustín de Valle Fértil** ⓬ lies in the middle of a desert oasis surrounded by vineyards and citrus groves, which are irrigated by the adjacent San Agustín reservoir.

For anyone with even a passing interest in geology, Unesco World Heritage Site Valle de la Luna (Valley of the Moon) is an essential part of a Cuyo itinerary, but it is not easy to reach. Agency-run day trips to the valley from San Juan leave at 5am and return 15 hours later. Alternatively, you can break the journey at San Agustín del Valle Fértil, 75km (47 miles) southeast of **Parque Provincial Ischigualasto** ⓭, as Valle de la Luna is officially known.

This extensive park covers a 62,000-hectare (153,000-acre) area and, together with Parque Provincial

---

☉ THE TRUCK DRIVERS' SHRINE

In 1841, in the course of the civil wars between federalists and unitarians, Deolinda Correa was forced to leave San Juan after the death of her husband, and to make the trek north toward La Rioja through the desert with her infant son. Deolinda was later found dead in the desert, although the baby was found to be alive and still able to nurse from his dead mother's breast.

Many years later, at the end of the 19th century, herdsmen stumbled across Deolinda's grave while they were searching for their cattle lost in a storm. They prayed for her assistance in recovering their herd and were astonished when the next morning they found them on a nearby hill. The herdsmen built a crude chapel by Deolinda's grave to show their gratitude and soon the story spread, attracting hopeful pilgrims.

Thus was born the shrine to Deolinda Correa, to whom miracles are popularly attributed, although she has not been canonized by the Catholic Church. A chapel has been erected on the spot, to the east of San Juan, and La Difunta (The Deceased) Correa has become the patron of road travelers and truck drivers, with visitors to the shrine leaving a bottle of water at her grave. At Easter and Christmas it is not uncommon for 200,000 pilgrims to visit the tomb.

Talampaya in La Rioja, forms a Unesco World Heritage Site. Parque Provincial Ischigualasto is set in a large natural depression where constant erosion by wind and water through millennia has sculpted a series of sandstone formations of strange shapes and an abundance of colors. Beyond its beauty, the Valle de la Luna has great geological and paleontological significance. In prehistoric times (even before the birth of the Andes) this area was covered by an immense lake, surrounded, during the Triassic period, by rich fauna and flora. A two-meter (6ft) -long reptile, the Dicinodonte, was one of the most typical inhabitants of the area. Sixty-three different species of fossilized animals have been found here.

In a different direction is the small town of **Barreal** ⑭, lying 94km (58 miles) to the west of San Juan, amid spectacular scenery. The drive there takes some three hours, via Ruta 12, along a difficult mountain road. Barreal lies at 1,650 meters (5,410ft) above sea level, on the banks of the Río Los Patos and flanked by birch trees. It is the region's main tourist center, with trekking and other outdoor activities organized locally, including the increasingly popular, not-as-scary-as-it-looks *carrovelismo* (wind-karting), which takes place on a dried-out lake bed known as La Pampa del Leoncito. North of Barreal, on Ruta 412, is the Calingasta Valley, reached after passing through the Cerros Pintados (Painted Hills), which show a spectacular array of white, green, and red coloration. The town of **Calingasta**, in the middle of the valley at the joining of four rivers, is an important center for local fruit cultivation, primarily apples and tomatoes, and in the past gold, silver, and copper were mined and smelted in the area.

SAN GUILLERMO WILDLIFE RESERVE

Some 200km (120 miles) to the north of Calingasta is the small town of **Angualasto** ⑮, located in a grape- and wheat-growing oasis between two mountain ranges. The town's **Museo Arqueológico Municipal Luis Benedetti**

Valle de la Luna.

Gaucho tending to his horse in the Valle de Uco.

Table football (foosball) game in Luján de Cuyo.

(daily 9am–noon and 3.30–6.30pm) houses a 400-year-old mummy, as well as other archeological exhibits. The town is close to the **Reserva Provincial y de la Biosfera San Guillermo** (www. reservasanguillermo.com), devoted to the preservation of regional fauna, primarily vicuña and guanaco. The park lies at over 3,000 meters (9,840ft) above sea level and is accessible only by 4x4 vehicles. For much of the year, the area is extremely cold and wet, and is best visited in the summer. Information on access and guides can be obtained from the tourist office in Angualasto.

Continuing about 150km (93 miles) farther north, via San José de Jachal on RN40, brings you to the arid province of La Rioja, also a wine-producing province, although on a lesser scale than Mendoza and San Juan. La Rioja is famous as the birthplace of the 19th-century federalist caudillo Facundo Quiroga and of late 20th-century president Carlos Menem.

The provincial capital, **La Rioja** ⓰, a small desert city, whose principal architectural interest lies in the church of **Santo Domingo**, the oldest convent in Argentina. Dating from 1623, it is also the only colonial building left in this city. Occupying an Italian-style 19th-century mansion two blocks from the main plaza is an important artisans' market (Tue–Sun) offering crafts in leather, wood, silver, and ceramics, as well as woven textiles. The city also has a **Museo Folklórico** (Tue–Fri 8am–noon and 4–8pm, Sat–Sun 9am–noon), one block away from the artisans' market along Pelagio Luna, with fascinating exhibits of pre- and post-colonial life in the province, as well as a room devoted to provincial mythology. About 130km (81 miles) northwest of La Rioja, in a valley between the Los Colorados and Sañogasta mountain ranges, is **Chilecito** ⓱, the second-largest city in the province and the center of its wine industry. A cable car leads from a station in the south of the city to the former La Mejicana copper mine. Between 1904 and 1929 the cable car linked the copper refinery with the railroad, although both the mine and the railroad have long since ceased to operate.

CANYONS AND CONDORS

The (relatively) modern town of **Villa Unión** ⑱ lies at the entrance to the Vinchina Valley, parallel to that of Chilecito, and separated by the Sañogasta mountain range. It is reached by the road through the dramatic Cuesta de Miranda pass, and is a popular base for visiting some interesting sites in the vicinity.

Some 65km (40 miles) to the north of Villa Unión is the small town of **Villa San José de Vinchina**, which has been inhabited since pre-Columbian times. It has an old water mill and dotted around the area are six unusual flattened mounds, painted with multicolored, 10-pointed stars, which are thought to have been used as ritual sites. One of the stars can be seen just outside the town, across the Río Vinchina.

Also worth a visit is **Jagüé**, a tiny hamlet 37km (23 miles) to the north of Vinchina, cradled at the foot of the giant **Volcán Bonete** (5,943 meters/19,500ft), on the old mule track that connects the green meadows on the Argentina side with the Chilean mining towns in the southern Atacama Desert.

The main destination from Villa Unión, though, and a suitably dramatic conclusion to this tour of the Cuyo, is the **Parque Nacional Talampaya** ⑲, a 270,000-hectare (667,000-acre) area 65km (40 miles) to the southeast, which has some of the most spectacular scenery in Argentina. The park is set in an impressive gorge with cliffs towering to more than 145 meters (480ft), and is full of amazing rock shapes carved by centuries of wind. The area was occupied by the Diaguita culture, which left behind innumerable rock paintings and engravings that can still be seen on some rock faces, offering a fascinating archeological contrast to the impressive geological formations of the canyon. A wide variety of animals, including foxes, hares, pumas, and guanaco, also inhabit the park; and look for condors soaring high above the gorge, whose nests are perched on the cliffs. Although private vehicles are not allowed within the park, there are guides with their own vehicles who run excursions.

The Río Mendoza near Uspallata.

BODEGA HOPPING IN THE CUYO

Mendoza has vineyards galore, in all shapes and sizes, from enormous industrial plants to friendly, family-based enterprises, and tastings are positively encouraged.

There are more than 1,000 vineyards in the Mendoza region, which produce 80 percent of the country's wines. Many of them offer tours and the chance to sample and buy wine. Local agencies organize excursions to many of the vineyards, some of which are listed here:

Bodegas López
North Ozamis 375, Maipú, tel: 0261-497 2406; www.bodegaslopez.com.ar. Guided tours in English, Mon–Fri 11.30am–3.30pm every hour, Sat 11.30 am.

Museo del Vino Bodega La Rural
Montecaseros 2625, Coquimbito, tel: 0261-497 2013; http://bodegalarural.com.ar/museo. Includes a museum, Mon–Sat 9am–5.30pm.

Bodega Trapiche
Mitre and Nueva Mayorga, Coquimbito, tel: 0261-520 7666; www.trapiche.com.ar. Guided tours daily 10am–6pm (last tour at 4pm).

Museo Nacional del Vino y la Vendimia.
Carril Ozamis 914, Maipú, tel: 0261-497 2448. Mon–Sat 9am–6pm, Sun 10am–1pm.

Antigua Bodega La Giol
Carril Ozamis 1040, tel: 0261-468 7172. Mon–Sat 11am–6pm, Sun 11am–4pm.

Bodega Chandon
Km 29, Agrelo, tel: 0261-490 9968; www.chandon.com.ar. Guided tours daily 9am–6pm (mid-May–June and Aug–mid-Jan Mon–Sat only).

Bodega Catena Zapata
J. Cobos s/n, Agrelo, tel: 0261-413 1124. Visits best arranged in advance, see www.catenawines.com.

Argentina is the world's sixth largest wine producer.

Bodega Luigi Bosca, in Luján de Cuyo, has been established for over a century and is still run by descendants of its founder.

Argentina's first wine producers were 16th-century Jesuit missionaries, who planted the vines to make communion wine.

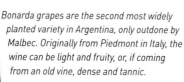

Bonarda grapes are the second most widely planted variety in Argentina, only outdone by Malbec. Originally from Piedmont in Italy, the wine can be light and fruity, or, if coming from an old vine, dense and tannic.

The wine cellar at Bodega Vistalba, near Luján de Cuyo.

The pick of the bunch

The most popular destinations for bodega hoppers are the major, streamlined operations at Peñaflor (producers of Trapiche), and Chandon. The best time to visit is during the March harvest, when the roads are clogged by trucks spilling over with grapes. Visitors are taken on a standard tour through the areas where the various stages of production take place (English-speaking tour guides can also be arranged). Huge oak casks are set on rollers as an anti-seismic precaution.

One of the less-visited but more interesting bodegas is La Rural (www.bodegalarural.com. ar), with a small but fascinating museum. This winery, whose brand is San Felipe, retains a lot of charm, with its original pink adobe architecture.

It is not only Argentina's Malbecs that have won awards – her Cabernets, Pinots, and Bonardas have too. If you wish to sample the best of what the country has to offer, look out for the following labels: Bodegas López, Callía, Carmelo Patti, Catena Zapata, Cobos, Achaval Ferrer, Carlos Pulenta, Zuccardi.

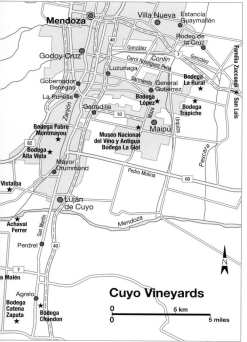

Cuyo Vineyards

0   5 km
0   5 miles

Parque Nacional Perito Moreno.

Hiking on the Perito Moreno glacier.

PATAGONIA

Where the Americas end, great adventures begin – this immense region with its limitless horizons tempts the explorer with everything from primeval landscapes to mountain sports.

Main attractions
San Martín de los Andes
Bariloche
Parque Nacional Los Alerces
Península Valdés
Parque Nacional Los Glaciares
Cueva de las Manos

Extending southwards from the southern banks of the Río Colorado to the icy waters of the South Atlantic, Patagonia is where South America tapers, fragments, and then ends. But like every good magician, the continent has held back some of its most astounding tricks for the finale.

It's important to realize, however, that the Patagonia of the glossy magazines and coffee table books – the Patagonia of primeval forests, crystalline, trout-torn rivers, glaciers as high as apartment buildings, and jewel-surfaced lakes fed by Andean melt water – is only a fraction of the whole. The rest is desert or steppe: a harsh environment in which only straggly bushes and the hardy breeds of sheep that graze on them can eke out a living. It is on the fringes of this tableland, among the Andean foothills in the west and along the Atlantic coast in the east, that the region's exotic scenery and wildlife can be found. Imagine a blank canvas in an ornate frame and you will have a good idea of what Patagonia is really like.

At the top of the wedge-shaped territory are the provinces of Neuquén and Río Negro, the former famed for its ancient *Araucaria araucana* (monkey-puzzle) forests and Mapuche reservations, and the latter for the Alpine-style resort of Bariloche in Parque Nacional Nahuel Huapi. Both provinces border

on beautiful Lago Nahuel Huapi, have their own ski resorts, and offer summer hiking, horseback riding, mountain climbing, and water sports.

Farther south, Chubut flaunts the marine fauna of the Valdés Peninsula and an exotic cultural mix comprising the Mapuches and the customs of the Welsh communities of the Atlantic coast and the hinterland. Puerto Madryn's Golfo Nuevo is Argentina's scuba-diving capital and is home to the southern right whale during the winter and fall months. Santa Cruz,

Maps on pages 271, 278

Patagonian gaucho.

at the tip of the Patagonian wedge, is the country's second largest and least-inhabited province. It harbors some of nature's most imposing glaciers, a large petrified forest that is 150 million years old, and numerous cave paintings more than 10,000 years old.

PATAGONIA DISCOVERED

Ferdinand Magellan, Pedro Sarmiento de Gamboa, Francis Drake, and Thomas Cavendish are just a few of the many explorers who set foot on this land. Here, European law and customs gave way to the most violent passions; revolts, mutinies, banishments, and executions were common. In 1578, in the port of San Julian (now the town of Puerto San Julián in Santa Cruz province), Sir Francis Drake used the same scaffold Magellan had used to hang his mutineers half a century before.

The early inhabitants of this land were, from the start, part of the exotic spell that attracted the first settlers, but soon became an obstacle to their purposes. They had been there long before the white man arrived and they

stood their ground. The bravest were the Mapuches, a nomadic tribe who lived on both sides of the Andes in the northern part of Patagonia. For 300 years they led a violent lifestyle on the plains by stealing and plundering the larger estancias (ranches) of the rich pampas, herding the cattle over the Andes and selling them to the Spaniards on the Chilean side.

In 1879, the Argentine Army, under General Roca, set out to conquer the land from the Amerindians. The campaign, which lasted until 1883, is known as the Conquest of the Desert. It put an end to years of Amerindian dominion in Patagonia and opened up a whole new territory to colonization. The natives vanished: some died in epic battles, others succumbed to new diseases, and others simply became cow hands on the huge estancias. Fragments of their world can still be found in the land, in the features of some of the people, in customs, and in religious rituals still performed on Amerindian reservations.

PATAGONIA SETTLED

When the Amerindian wars ended, colonization began. The large inland plateau, a dry expanse of shrubs and alkaline lagoons, was slowly occupied by people of very diverse origins: Spaniards, Italians, Scots, and English in the far south, Welsh in the Chubut Valley, Italians in the Río Negro Valley, Swiss and Germans in the northern Lake District, and a few North Americans scattered throughout the country.

The Patagonian towns grew fast. Coal mining, oilfields, agriculture, industry, large hydroelectrical projects, and tourism attracted people from all over the country and from Chile, transforming Patagonia into a modern industrial frontier land. Some people came to start a quiet new life in the midst of mountains, forests, and lakes. In the Patagonian interior, descendants of the first sheep-breeding settlers and

Lanín volcano in Parque Nacional Lanín.

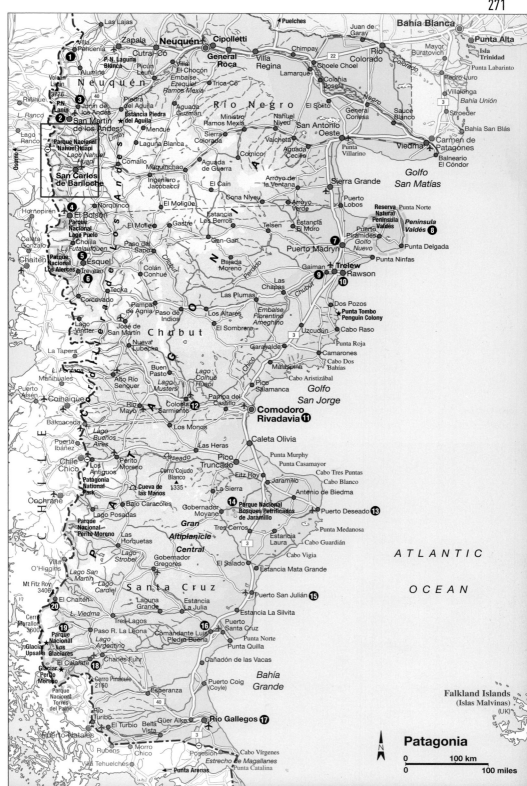

Puelches

Bahía Blanca

Punta Alta

Las Lajas

Juan de Garay

Isla Trinidad

Mayor Buratovich

Villa Pehuenia

Zapala

Neuquén

Cipolletti

Chimpay

Río Colorado

Punta Labarinto

① P.N. Laguna Blanca

Cutral-Có

General Roca

Villa Regina

22

Colonia

Pedro Luro

Alumine

Picún Leufú

Villa El Chocón

Lamarque

Choele Choel

Colonia Josefa

Villalonga

Volcán Lanín 3776

Piedra del Aguila

Embalse Ezequiel Ramos Mexía

Trica-Có

Río Negro

El Solito

General Conesa

Negro

Sauce Blanco

Bahía Unión

Stroeder

N e u q u é n

Bahía San Blás

Riñinue

③ P.N. Lanín

Junín de los Andes

Estancia Piedra del Aguila

Aguada Guzmán

Ministro Ramos Mexía

Nahuel Niyeu

San Antonio Oeste

General

② L. Ranco

San Martín de los Andes

Mencué

Sierra Colorada

Valcheta

Aguada Cecilio

Punta Villarino

Viedma

Carmen de Patagones

Lago Ranco

Parque Nacional Nahuel Huapi

Limay

Comallo

Laguna Blanca

Cómico

Balneario El Cóndor

Osorno

Lago Nahuel Huapi

Maquinchao

Aguada de Guerra

El Cain

Cona Niyeu

Arroyo de la Ventana

Sierra Grande

Golfo San Matías

San Carlos de Bariloche

Ingeniero Jacobacci

Puerto Lobos

④ El Bolsón

Norquinco

El Moligüe

Estancia Los Berros

Arroyo Verde

Reserva Natural Península Valdés

Punta Norte

Hornopirén

Parque Nacional Lago Puelo

El Molle

Gastre

Telsen

Estancia El Moro

Península Valdés ⑧

Caleta Gonzalo

Cholila

L. Futalaufquen

Paso del Sapo

Gan-Gan

Puerto Pirámides

Puerto Madryn

Golfo Nuevo

Punta Delgada

Chaitén

⑤ Esquel

Colán Conhué

Bajada Moreno

⑦

Gaiman ⑨

Trelew

Punta Ninfas

Parque Nacional Los Alerces

⑥ Trevelin

Chubut

Las Chapas

Rawson ⑩

Tecka

Las Plumas

Dos Pozos

Corcovado

Pampa de Agnia

Paso de Indios

Los Altares

Embalse Florentino Ameghino

Punta Tombo Penguin Colony

Lago Vintter

José de San Martín

El Sombrero

Uzcudún

Cabo Raso

La Tapera

Nueva Lubecka

C h u b u t

Chico

Garayalde

Punta Roja

Buen Pasto

Camarones

Cabo Dos Bahías

Maníhuales

Alto Río Senguer

Lago Musters

Lago Colhué Huapi

Malaspina

Cabo Aristizábal

Puerto Aisén

Coihaique

Río Mayo

Colonia ⑫ Sarmiento

Pampa del Castillo

Pico Salamanca

Golfo San Jorge

Balmaceda

Los Monos

Comodoro Rivadavia ⑪

Puerto Ibáñez

Lago Buenos Aires

Las Heras

Caleta Olivia

Chile Chico

Perito Moreno

Deseado

Pico Truncado

Punta Murphy

Los Antiguos

Cerro Cojudo Blanco

Fitz Roy

Punta Casamayor

Cabo Tres Puntas

Patagonia National Park

Cueva de las Manos 1335

La Sierra

Jaramillo

Cabo Blanco

Cochrane

Bajo Caracoles

Gobernador Moyano

⑭ Parque Nacional Bosques Petrificados de Jaramillo

Antonio de Biedma

Puerto Deseado ⑬

Lago Posadas

Parque Nacional Perito Moreno

Las Horquetas

Tres Cerros

Punta Medanosa

Gran

Cabo Guardián

Altiplanicie

Estancia Laura

Cabo Vigia

Central

El Salado

Villa O'Higgins

Lago San Martín

Gobernador Gregores

Estancia Mata Grande

A T L A N T I C

Mt Fitz Roy 3406

Lago Cardiel

S a n t a C r u z

O C E A N

⑳ El Chaltén

L. Viedma

Laguna Grande

Estancia La Julia

Puerto San Julián ⑮

Cerro Murallón 3600

Tres Lagos

⑲ Parque Nacional Los Glaciares

Paso R. La Leona

Estancia La Silvita

Glaciar Upsala

Lago Argentino

⑯ Comandante Luis Piedra Buena

Puerto Santa Cruz

Glaciar Perito Moreno

El Calafate ⑱

Charles Fuhr

Punta Norte

Punta Quilla

Parque Nacional Torres del Paine

Cerro Pináculo 2160

Cañadón de las Vacas

Puerto Natales

Puerto Coig (Coyle)

Bahía Grande

Falkland Islands (Islas Malvinas) (UK)

Esperanza

40

Río Turbio

El Turbio

Bella Vista

Güer Aike

Río Gallegos ⑰

Rubens

Morro Chico

Villa Tehuelches

3

Posesión

Cabo Vírgenes

Punta Arenas

Estrecho de Magallanes

Punta Catalina

N

Patagonia

0 100 km

0 100 miles

○ Fact

Visitors from the crowded parts of Europe and North America often find it hard to comprehend the sheer emptiness of Patagonia. The population density here averages fewer than three inhabitants per square kilometer (less than one per square mile).

their ranch hands still ride over the enormous estancias.

GEOGRAPHY

With defined geographical and political boundaries, Patagonia extends from the Río Colorado in the north, more than 2,000km (1,200 miles) to Cabo de Hornos (Cape Horn) at the southernmost tip of the continent. It covers more than 1 million sq km (400,000 sq miles) and belongs to two neighboring countries, Chile and Argentina. The Argentine part of Patagonia comprises 800,000 sq km (308,000 sq miles), and is usually divided into three definite areas: the coast, the plateau, and the Andes. As these categories are not particularly helpful for tourists, this chapter is organized according to the region's most popular and worthwhile destinations, which are as follows. First, the northern Lake District, which follows the spine of the Andean cordillera southwards from Villa Pehuenia in Neuquén province to Bariloche in Río Negro. This region is well developed for tourism and includes several of the

country's largest and most impressive national parks. Second, the Atlantic coastline, and in particular the whale-watching destinations of Puerto Madryn and Puerto Pirámides. Finally, the deep south or the southern Lake District, where the towns of El Calafate and El Chaltén attract glacier watchers and hikers respectively. (Although Tierra del Fuego is part of Patagonia, it is dealt with in a separate chapter.)

PLANNING YOUR TRIP

Unless you are on a two-year sabbatical and have an all-terrain 4x4 vehicle and a love of strong, persistent gales, you are not going to explore all of Patagonia or even come close. The keys to planning an enjoyable trip to the region are to be selective and realistic. You can always return.

The good news is that, thanks to the distance-obliterating magic of air travel, all of the main destinations mentioned above are suitable for a short break. A weekend in the Lake District, for example, gives you enough time to take a boat trip, do a short hike, and eat your way through many of the local specialties. In El Calafate, farther south, this is plenty enough time to explore Parque Nacional Los Glaciares and perhaps even do a side trip to the trekking capital of El Chaltén. At the Atlantic coast you can be on a whale-watching expedition (in season) within a couple of hours of landing at the airport. The tourism infrastructure at these popular destinations is improving all the time, and getting around Patagonia is often less frustrating than crossing Buenos Aires.

If you want to visit more than one of these places, or to penetrate the region's vast central wilderness, allow yourself at least a week. In the Lake District alone there are many small towns and protected areas worth exploring, most of which are connected by good roads. Cross-country drives, on the other hand, are a serious

San Martín de Los Andes.

undertaking. The state of the roads and weather conditions are both difficult to predict, and fuel is scarce.

WHEN TO GO

Seasons are well-defined in Patagonia. Considering the latitude, the average temperature is mild; winters are never as cold and summers never as warm as in similar latitudes in the northern hemisphere. The average temperature in Ushuaia is 6°C (43°F) and, in Bariloche, 8°C (46°F). Even so, the climate can turn quite rough on the desert plateau. There, the weather is more continental than in the rest of the region. The ever-present companion is the wind, which blows hard all year round, from the mountains to the sea, making life here unbearable for many people.

In spring, the snow on the mountains begins to melt, alpine flowers bloom almost everywhere, and ranchers prepare for the hard work of tending sheep and shearing. Although tourism starts in late springtime, most people visit during the summer (December to March). During this period, all roads are fit for traffic, the airports are open and, normally, the hotels are booked solid.

The fall brings changes on the plateau. The poplars around the lonesome estancias turn to beautiful shades of yellow. The mountains, covered by deciduous beech trees, offer a panorama of reds and yellows, and the air slowly gets colder. At this time of the year, tourism thins out. Parque Nacional Los Glaciares (www.losglaciares.com; see page 289), in the far south, opens later and closes earlier in winter (9am–4pm). While the wide plains sleep, the winter resorts on the mountains thrive. San Martín de los Andes, Bariloche, Esquel, and even Ushuaia attract thousands of skiers, including many from the northern hemisphere who take advantage of the reversal of seasons.

THE NORTHERN LAKE DISTRICT

Going west from Neuquén to the Andes, you come to the northern limit of the Patagonian Lake District, an enormous area of beautiful lakes and

San Martín de Los Andes is set on the banks of Lago Lácar.

Magellanic fuchsia.

⊘ PATAGONIA IN PRINT

Nobody has ever expressed more precisely than British naturalist Charles Darwin the emotions that remote Patagonia stirs in a visitor. Darwin, back in England after sailing five years on the *Beagle*, wrote, "In calling up images of the past, I find that the plains of Patagonia frequently cross before my eyes; yet these plains are pronounced by all wretched and useless... Why then...have these arid wastes taken so firm a hold on my memory?"

Since Darwin's time, Patagonia has attracted a steady stream of foreign writers. In the 19th century, Argentine-born W.H. Hudson wrote *Idle Days in Patagonia*, a poetic narrative of his youth spent discovering the flora and fauna of the region.

But perhaps the best-known modern account of the place and its people is Bruce Chatwin's *In Patagonia* (1977), which captures the essence of Patagonia through his meetings with local inhabitants encountered during his travels: "So next day, as we drove through the desert, I sleepily watched the rags of silver cloud spinning across the sky, and the sea of grey-green thornscrub lying off in sweeps and rising in terraces and the white dust streaming off the saltpans, and, on the horizon, land and sky dissolving into an absence of color."

spectacular mountain peaks, which stretches 1,500km (900 miles) from Lago Aluminé in the north to Parque Nacional Los Glaciares in the south. One can divide this region into two sections, the northern and southern Lake Districts. The zone that lies in between is sparsely populated and traveling is a challenge to be taken on only by the most adventurous.

January and July are the most popular months for visitors, reflecting the vacations in Buenos Aires. However, apart from May and June, which tend to be rainy months, the area has its attractions in all seasons. There are many tours available to local landmarks and abundant opportunities for hiking, climbing, fishing, and horseback riding in summer, or skiing and snowboarding in winter.

The northern Lake District covers the area from Lago Aluminé southward to Lago Amutui Quimei. It encompasses a 500km (300-mile) stretch of lakes, forests, and mountains divided into four national parks. From north to south is the Parque Nacional Lanín and

Demise of the rail network.

the nearby towns of San Martín de los Andes and Junín de los Andes; Parque Nacional Nahuel Huapi and the Alpine-style resort of Bariloche; Parque Nacional Lago Puelo and the village of El Bolsón; and, farthest south, Parque Nacional Los Alerces with the town of Esquel. This region connects to the so-called Lake District in Chile.

Entering the Lake District from the north, the first place of interest you reach is the **Parque Nacional Laguna Blanca**. The park lies just to the southwest of Zapala, which is about 185km (115 miles) west of Neuquén on RN22. It includes a large lake, and is home to hundreds of interesting bird species: the prime attractions are the black-necked swans, which gather in flocks of up to 2,000 birds. Flamingos are also part of the scenery, and the surrounding hills give shelter to large groups of eagles, peregrine falcons, and other birds of prey. There is a visitor's center at the park, and a campsite. There are infrequent buses to the park from the nearest town, Zapala, 35km (22 miles) away, which has an information office.

⊙ RAILROAD TO NOWHERE

It is a fact that can bring tears to the eyes of trainspotters: Argentina's once great rail network, which used to crisscross the length and breadth of the country, is no more. It was "rationalized" out of existence during the great privatization spree of the 1990s (although fortunately there are plans to revive it).

Well, *almost* out of existence. One epic intercity service remains: the Tren Patagónico, which connects Viedma on the Atlantic coast with Bariloche in the Andean foothills. The journey of 850km (528 miles) takes around 18 hours – and apart from the short and scenic approach to (or departure from) Bariloche, that is 18 hours spent crossing the Patagonian desert: a brutal, wind-tormented, almost treeless landscape. The feeling of truly arriving in the middle of nowhere can be both sublime and unnerving, and while this is unquestionably the trip of a lifetime, it is one few people would dare repeat.

Tourists and workers on their weekly commute mix on the train, which offers (for the former at least) pullman carriages and individual compartments with bunk beds. As well as a restaurant car serving an excellent three-course meal, there is a cinema wagon, and even a disco. The train departs from Viedma every Friday evening and returns eastwards on the Sunday. For more information visit www.trenpatagonico-sa.com.ar.

VILLA PEHUENIA

Lying 120km (75 miles) west of Zapala, the lovely mountain village of **Villa Pehuenia** ➊ was founded as a tourist resort in 1989. It sits on the banks of Lago Aluminé, the largest of several lakes in the area, many of which attract canoeists and kayakers. The village's tourism infrastructure is not as sophisticated as that of towns farther south, but most visitors consider this an advantage and welcome the relative lack of crowds. A number of easy and well-marked trails cut through the woodlands encircling the lake, and there are campsites for those who like to carry their accommodations on their backs. Cerro Batea Mahuida (www.cerro bateamahuida.com), a small ski centre located 5km (3.1 miles) from town, is owned and run by a local Mapuche community. It lacks facilities, but beginners will enjoy its accessibility and complete lack of airs and graces.

This area is also home to one of the most peculiar-looking trees in the world, the *Araucaria araucana* or monkey puzzle. The village's name is derived from "Pehuén," the Mapuche word for these strange and ancient conifers.

SAN MARTÍN DE LOS ANDES AND PARQUE NACIONAL LANÍN

The delightful town of **San Martín de los Andes** ➋ is located 208km (129 miles) south of Villa Pehuenia (a five-hour drive on RP23). Set on the banks of Lago Lácar, San Martín has the most beautiful natural harbor in the country, with thickly forested, steep hills rising on three sides, offering a number of vantage points from where you can look down on the town and the colorful skiffs that bob on the waves by the port.

The indigenous Mapuche tribe populated this area long before the town was founded in 1898. The small but interesting Museo de los Primeros Pobladores (Museum of the Original Inhabitants; Mon 8.30am–1.30pm, Tue–Fri 8.30am–1.30pm and 2–7pm, Sat–Sun 4.30–7pm), at Juan Manuel de Rosas 700, exhibits Mapuche textiles, tools, and ceramics along with photographs tracing the town's early history.

⊙ Fact

The 19th-century English explorer George Musters wrote *At Home with the Patagonians* (1871), about his year-long journey through the region with a group of Amerindians. The book earned him a gold watch from the Royal Geographical Society, and is still hailed as the most complete description of the Patagonian interior and its people.

Bariloche's main square.

> **Tip**

Detailed information on all Argentina's national parks can be found at www.parquesnacionales.gob.ar (only in Spanish though).

To explore Lago Lácar, take one of the regular catamaran tours that depart from the town's passenger pier at Avenida Costanera y Muelle. They stop at several hidden coves and beaches around the lake shore, including Playa Catitre (which has a campsite) and Villa Quila Quina. You can also use San Martín as base for exploring **Parque Nacional Lanín**, which covers 3,920 sq km (1,508 sq miles) and gets its name from the imposing Lanín volcano, on the border with Chile. The volcano soars to 3,776 meters (12,388ft), far above the height of the surrounding peaks.

The national park is noted for its fine fishing; the fishing season is from mid-November through mid-April. The rivers and streams around the small town of **Junín de los Andes ③**, 42km (26 miles) northwest of San Martín, are famed for their abundance and variety of trout. Fly-casters come from around the world to fish for the brook, brown, fontinalis, and steelhead. The best catch on record is a 12kg (27lb) brown trout – the average weight for this fish

is 4–5kg (9–11lbs). Although Junín has several good restaurants and hotels, most anglers prefer the fishermen's lodges in the park itself.

Parque Nacional Lanín is also well known for hunting. Wild boar and red and fallow deer are the main prey in the fall rutting season. The national park takes bids for hunting rights over most of the hunting grounds, and local farm owners make their own agreements with hunters. For information, contact the tourist office in San Martín de los Andes.

Cerro Chapelco (www.chapelco.com), at 2,441 meters (8,000ft) and 20 minutes or so by car from San Martín, is one of the country's most important winter sports centers. The ski season here runs from mid-June to mid-October.

SAN MARTÍN TO BARILOCHE

Three roads link San Martín de los Andes with Bariloche. The middle (shortest, but unpaved) road runs across the Paso del Córdoba through narrow valleys where the scenery is beautiful, especially in the fall, when the slopes turn to rich shades of gold and deep red. This road reaches the paved highway at Confluencia. From here, if you turn back inland, you come to the **Estancia La Primavera**, known for its trout farm and owned by US media tycoon Ted Turner. Returning to the paved road to Bariloche, you follow Río Limay through the Valle Encantado, a valley of bizarre rock formations, also skirting the Rincón Grande, a ring of steep escarpments formed by river erosion into a striking natural amphitheater.

The third road from San Martín is the famed **Ruta de los Siete Lagos** (Route of the Seven Lakes). This road, of which about two-thirds is paved, takes you past beautiful lakes and forests and approaches Bariloche from the northern shore of Lago Nahuel Huapi. In summer, all-day tours make the trip

Local grocery shop in Bariloche.

from Bariloche to San Martín, combining the Paso del Córdoba and the Ruta de los Siete Lagos. Another good way of traveling the route is by mountain bike; these can be easily hired in San Martín de los Andes.

BARILOCHE

San Carlos de Bariloche Ⓐ in the middle of **Parque Nacional Nahuel Huapi**, is the real center of the northern Lake District and a year-round destination for hikers, nature lovers, high school students (they come here to celebrate their graduation), and, in winter, skiers. Buses, trains, and planes arrive daily from all over the country and from Chile, across the Paso Puyehue.

Founded in 1902, Bariloche, as it is almost always known, has a very strong Central European influence; most of the first settlers were of Swiss, German, or northern Italian origin. These people gave the city its Alpine atmosphere, with Swiss-style chalets, fondue restaurants, and chocolates. However, something tells you that you are not in Europe; boats are

seldom seen on the huge Lago Nahuel Huapi, the roads are swallowed in the wilderness as soon as they leave the city, and at night there are no lights on the opposite shore of the lake.

The city has grown rapidly in recent decades, spreading along the foot of **Cerro Otto**. This long ridge offers a good introductory walk, or take a cable-car ride to the top, from where there are splendid views of the town, the lake, and the surrounding park, as well as a revolving café. There are also pleasant woodland walks descending the far side of the ridge to Arelauquen and the quiet Lago Gutiérrez.

The best way to begin your tour of Bariloche is by visiting the **Museo de la Patagonia** (www.museodelapatagonia. nahuelhuapi.gov.ar; Tue–Fri 10am– 12.30pm and 2–7pm, Sat 10am–5pm) in the Civic Center. This building and the Hotel Llao Llao were designed by architect Alejandro Bustillo in his own interpretation of traditional Alpine style, and they give Bariloche a distinctive architectural personality. The museum has displays on the geological

Sign for a tea salon in Bariloche.

Native monkey-puzzle tree in Parque Nacional Lanín.

Ⓞ CROSSING THE ANDES

While you are in the northern Lake District there are various options for crossing over to Chile. From Bariloche, if you want to reach Puerto Montt on the Pacific coast, try the old route first used by the Jesuits across the lakes. This day-long journey combines short bus rides with leisurely boat crossings of lakes Nahuel Huapi, Frías, Todos los Santos, and Llanquihue, through marvelous settings of forests and snowcapped volcanoes.

While the lake crossing has the advantage of escaping normal traffic, the road through the Puyehue Pass, northwest of Bariloche, gives views of Lago Correntoso and Lago Espejo. Over the border, the Parque Nacional Puyehue offers the opportunity to sample thermal springs and mud baths, or to explore the temperate rainforest.

Farther north, via San Martín de los Andes, is the little-used Hua-Hum Pass. A small car ferry carries you the length of Lago Pirihueico with its steep-forested sides and glimpses of the Choshuenco volcano, and at the far end a road continues into the village of Choshuenco.

More northerly still, beyond Junín de los Andes, is Paso Tromen (or Mamuil Malal). This road is much higher and sometimes closed in winter, but affords wonderful views of the Lanín volcano and the native *Araucaria* (monkey-puzzle) forests.

origins of the region and of local wildlife. It also has a stunning collection of indigenous artifacts, which chronicle the demise of local tribes.

AROUND BARILOCHE

There are some excellent excursions to choose from in the Bariloche area: 17km (11 miles) southwest is the **Villa Cerro Catedral ⓑ**, South America's largest and most important ski center (www.catedralaltapatagonia.com), also with fine hiking trails on the mountainside and around Lago Gutiérrez. The base of the ski lifts is at 1,050 meters (3,465ft) above sea level, and a cable car and chair-lifts take you up to a height of 2,010 meters (6,633ft). The view from the slopes is absolutely superb. The ski runs range in difficulty from novice to expert, covering more than 25km (15 miles), and there are full facilities. The ski season runs from the end of June to September and peaks in late August with the four-day annual Fiesta de la Nieve, whose highlight is a torch-lit parade down the mountainside.

Nuestra Señora del Nahuel Huapi cathedral in Bariloche.

Snowboarding, bungee jumping, and paragliding are also possible.

Another 10km (6 miles) farther south is **Villa Mascardi ⓒ**, a small tourist resort on the shore of Lago Mascardi. Picturesque boat cruises are available from here across the turquoise waters of the lake toward Monte Tronador, the highest peak in the national park, at 3,478 meters (11,411ft). The mountain can also be visited via a long and winding scenic drive. Between lakes Gutiérrez and Mascardi lies the watershed of rivers draining into the Atlantic and the Pacific oceans. Past Pampa Linda, where there is one hostel, and approaching the mountain, you pass the Black Glacier, so-called because of all the muddy debris churned up onto the surface of the glacier. Another route from Lago Mascardi goes to lakes Fonck and Hess, both popular fishing spots, with campsites. En route, you pass the lovely Cascada Los Alerces, which cascades for some 20 meters (66ft) over drenched, mossy rocks. A number of these routes operate one-way systems allowing only ascent or

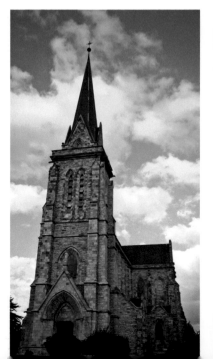

descent within certain times, in order to regulate peak season tourist traffic, so you would be advised to check the details at the Bariloche tourist office if traveling independently by road.

LLAO LLAO PENINSULA

One of the most popular half-day excursions from Bariloche is the so-called Circuito Chico, or small circuit. This takes you westward along the shore of the lake and up to the Punto Panorámico, with its breathtaking views over the water toward Chile. It is a rare building that could blend into, even enhance, such a magnificent landscape, but the **Hotel Llao Llao ⓓ** (http://llaollao.com) at the base of the Península Llao Llao, is equal to the challenge.

Continuing the circuit, farther round the lake is **Bahía López**, a tranquil inlet where it is often possible to see condors circling the huge bulk of Cerro López overshadowing the bay. There is a well-defined path leading up this mountain as far as the mountain refuge, with a more rugged track thereafter up to the summit ridge. On the road back to Bariloche you will pass the Cerro Campanario chair-lift at km 17. Although much lower than lifts at Cerro Otto or Catedral, the views are unrivaled.

At the far end of Lago Nahuel Huapi, en route to Chile, **Puerto Blest ⓔ** is host to much through traffic. Few stay, however, so outside these brief flurries of traffic it is a place of exceptional peace and beauty. There is a small hotel, a pleasant walking trail to the Cascada Los Cantares, and a warden to give directions for more demanding hikes. You can visit Puerto Blest and Isla Victoria by catamaran excursions across Lago Nahuel Huapi from Puerto Pañuelo.

BAMBI'S FOREST

Isla Victoria ⓕ, on Lago Nahuel Huapi, is renowned for its *arrayanes*, rare trees related to myrtles, found only in this area and in the Parque Nacional Los Alerces (see page 281). The story goes that a visiting group of Walt Disney's advisors were so impressed by the white and cinnamon-colored trees here that they used them as the basis for the scenery in the 1942 film *Bambi*. Most visitors to the island come in groups on the catamaran excursions, but you require only a little ingenuity to discover the beauties of the island away from the crowds.

Extending from the northern shore of the lake is the Península de Quetrihue, containing the **Parque Nacional Los Arrayanes ⓖ**, dedicated to protecting the rare *arrayán* trees, some of which are 300 years old and 28 meters (92ft) high. Boat excursions to Isla Victoria often stop at Quetrihue, allowing time to walk in the park. You can also reach the Península de Quetrihue from **Villa La Angostura ⓗ** (www.villala angostura.gov.ar), an increasingly busy chic resort at the far end of the lake. There is a good selection of hotels, campsites, and other amenities in

The chapel in the picturesque town of El Bolsón in Río Negro province.

the vicinity, which has been developed to cater to the tourist overflow of the nearby skiing center of Cerro Bayo (www.cerrobayoweb.com).

Another popular excursion heads east from Bariloche, then north through the Valle Encantado, until turning off at Confluencia for **Villa Traful** ①. The small town is famous for the excellent salmon fishing in Lago Traful, as well as for some inspiring hiking and horseback riding in the surrounding countryside. The road continues through the town, climbing to a commanding viewpoint high above Lago Traful, and takes a scenic route back through Villa La Angostura. This circuit, predictably described as the Circuito Grande (long circuit), covers some 240km (149 miles) and is offered as a full-day excursion from Bariloche. Most travel agencies in Bariloche offer a variety of bus and boat excursions visiting the above-mentioned sites, but if you fancy something a little more energetic to tap this area's vast potential for outdoor pursuits, visit

the Club Andino (www.clubandino.org), the city's specialist mountaineering organization).

EL BOLSÓN

El Bolsón ④ is a small town 130km (80 miles) south of Bariloche, situated in a narrow valley with its own microclimate. Beer hops and all sorts of berries are grown on small farms around the town and made into artisanal beers and preserves respectively. Hippies favored El Bolsón in the 1960s, and today many lead peaceful lives on farms perched in the mountains. Some 20km (12.5 miles) south of El Bolsón, and bordering Chile, is the serene **Parque Nacional Lago Puelo** (237 sq km/92 sq miles), established in 1937 as an annex to nearby Parque Nacional Los Alerces. Another angler's paradise, the park has mountains covered with ancient forests of deciduous beech trees and cypresses and more than 100 species of bird. Basic camping facilities are available by the lakeshore, with some marked trails.

Esquel marks the most southerly point of the Argentine rail network.

CHOLILA VALLEY

Farther south, on the road to Esquel, you come across the beautiful **Cholila Valley**, a little-known area where in early summer the fields are carpeted in blue by wild lupins. This was the place chosen by Butch Cassidy and the Sundance Kid, the US outlaws made famous by George Hill's 1969 movie starring Paul Newman and Robert Redford. Butch and Sundance sheltered temporarily in Cholila while they were on the run from Pinkerton's agents. A letter sent by them to Matilda Davis in Utah, dated August 10, 1902, was posted at Cholila. After their famous hold-up of the Río Gallegos Bank in 1905, they were again on the run, until they were finally killed in Bolivia. Other members of the gang who stayed on in this region were ambushed and killed, years later, by the Argentine constabulary.

From Cholila, the road going south splits in two. RN40 turns slightly to the east, through the large Estancia Leleque, alongside the narrow-gauge railroad, until it reaches Esquel. The other route to Esquel takes you right into **Parque Nacional Los Alerces**. This park covers 2,630 sq km (1,012 sq miles) and is less spoiled by towns and people than other parks are in this region. Summer visitors to the park stay at campsites and fishermen's lodges around **Lago Futalaufquen**. One tour you should not miss is the all-day boat excursion, which leaves in the summer from Puerto Chucao to Lago Menéndez, the largest lake in the national park. There are outstanding views of **Cerro Torrecillas** (2,200 meters/7,260ft) and its glaciers, and be sure to see the huge *Fitzroya* trees (related to the American redwood), some of which are over 2,000 years old.

THE OLD PATAGONIAN EXPRESS

As you get closer to Trevelín and Esquel you begin to leave behind the northern Lake District. This area is strongly influenced by Welsh culture, as a sizeable community of Welsh people settled here in 1888 after a long

Preparing fruit to make a jam. Typical Welsh teas can be had in Trevelín, Esquel, and Gaiman, all settlements of Welsh origin.

trek from the Atlantic coast along the Chubut Valley (see page 284).

Traveling 167km (104 miles) south of El Bolsón on RN40 and RN258 brings you to **Esquel** ❺, an offshoot of the Welsh Chubut colony. The town, with over 36,000 inhabitants, lies to the east of the Andes, on the border of the Patagonian desert – a remote location that gives Esquel the feel of a town in the old American West. You are as likely to see people riding on horseback here as in cars. Sometimes the rider will be a gaucho dandy, all dressed up with broad-brimmed hat, kerchief, and *bombachas* (baggy pleated pants). Several times a year, principally in January, a rural fair is held in Esquel. People come from miles around to trade livestock and agricultural supplies. In town, several stores *(talabarterías)* are well stocked with riding tackle and ranch equipment. Ornate stirrups and hand-tooled saddles sit next to braided, rawhide ropes, and cast-iron cookware. This was once goose-hunting country, but the rare local species have since become protected.

Whale calf seen off Península Valdés.

Esquel's railway station is the most southerly point of the Argentine rail network. The narrow-gauge railway (0.75 meters/2.5ft), used to provide a regular service between Esquel and Ingeniero Jacobacci to the north. The train – La Trochita – was made famous abroad by US author Paul Theroux, in his book *The Old Patagonian Express* (1979). These days it runs only a partial and intermittent schedule largely for the benefit of tourists. Nevertheless, if you happen to arrive at the right time, there is no better way to get acquainted with Patagonia and its people than by a trip on this quaint little train, which is pulled by an old-fashioned steam locomotive. For serious railway buffs, there are workshops open to visitors in El Maitén, providing a further glimpse of the romantic past.

In winter, Esquel turns into a ski resort, with **La Hoya Ski Center** only 15km (10 miles) away. Compared with Bariloche and Villa Cerro Catedral, this ski area is considerably smaller and cozier but a range of rental facilities is available.

⊘ WINDY PATAGONIA

The wind. It is the first thing people notice when they arrive in Patagonia, and the first thing they mention when recounting their trip. It blows across the steppe from the west in a violent, constant stream of air. In a second it can lift a cyclist bodily from their saddle or blow a jeep into a ditch and, over time, it bends trees into submission and clogs machinery with sand and salt.

However, all this power has potential for good as well as mischief. In October 2011, then-President Cristina Kirchner opened the Rawson Aeolic Park in Chubut. It is Argentina's largest wind farm and could eventually power 100,000 homes. As the world's supply of fossil fuels dwindles, Patagonia may find itself on the new energy frontier.

Trevelín ⑥, 23km (14 miles) south-west of Esquel, is a small village, also of Welsh origin. Its name in Welsh means "town of the mill." The old mill has been converted into a museum, the **Museo Regional Molino Andes** or Nant Fach (Mon–Fri 10am–8pm, Sat–Sun from 11am), which houses all sorts of implements that belonged to the first Welsh settlers, together with old photographs and a Welsh Bible. As in all the Welsh communities of Patagonia, you can enjoy a typical tea with Welsh cookies and cakes in sev-eral cafés in Esquel.

THE ATLANTIC COAST: PUERTO MADRYN

Puerto Madryn ⑦ is the gateway for visitors to Península Valdés and the Punta Tombo penguin colony. It is a spruce seaside town with extensive sands and flamingos in the bay. The **Museo Oceanográfico y de Ciencias Naturales** (Mon–Fri 9am–3pm), on the corner of Domecq and García Menén-dez, is worth a visit for its collections of coastal and marine flora and fauna.

Nature lovers will want to visit the **EcoCentro**, Julio Verne 3784 (Wed–Sun 3–7pm), where local marine life is explained in various interactive dis-plays and exhibits.

Punta Tombo, 165km (102 miles) south of Madryn (108km/67 miles of which is dirt road), has the largest colony of Magellanic penguins in the world. The penguins arrive in Sep-tember and stay until March. In this colony you can literally walk among thousands of these comical birds as they come and go along well-defined "penguin highways" that link their nests with the sea across the tourist path, and see them fish near the coast for their meals.

Península Valdés ⑧ is one of the most important wildlife reserves in Argentina and was designated a Une-sco World Heritage Site in 1999. It is the breeding ground for southern right whales, elephant seals, and sea lions, and the nesting site for thousands of shore birds, including pelicans, cor-morants, and oystercatchers. Guanaco, rhea, and mara can all be spotted with sharp eyes. There is an interpretive center and museum at the entrance to the peninsula itself, which is a large wasteland, with the lowest point on the South American continent, 40 meters (132ft) below sea level. Some 40,000 elephant seals are found along a 200km (125-mile) stretch of coastline, the outer edge of the Valdés Penin-sula – the only such colony accessible by land outside Antarctica. Most of the beach is protected but tourists have a chance to observe the wildlife from specially constructed viewing hides at **Punta Norte** and **Caleta Valdés**, where two reserves have been established. About 10,000 elephant-seal pups are born each year from late August to early November.

WHALE WATCHING

Puerto Pirámides, 95km (59 miles) from Puerto Madryn, was once a

Serving a Welsh tea of bread, jams, and scones in a teahouse in Gaiman.

LAND OF THEIR FATHERS

At a time when Argentina was actively seeking pioneers to settle the empty lands of Patagonia, a group of Welsh non-conformists were looking for a new home away from the oppression of the English.

Patagonia is partly pampas, largely desert, and unrelentingly windblown, with only small areas of fertile soil and little discovered mineral wealth. Why would anyone leave the lush valleys and green hills of Wales to settle in such a place? The Welsh came, between 1865 and 1914, partly to escape conditions in Wales which they deemed culturally oppressive, partly because of the promise – later discovered to be exaggerated – of exciting economic opportunities, and largely to be able to pursue their religious traditions in their own language.

The disruptions of the 19th-century Industrial Revolution uprooted many Welsh agricultural workers: the cost of delivering produce to market became exorbitant because of turnpike fees, grazing land was enclosed, and landless laborers were exploited. Increasing domination of public life by

Museo Regional Molino Andes, Trevelín.

arrogant English officials further upset the Welsh. Thus alienated in his own land, the Welshman left.

SPIRITUAL JOURNEY

Equally powerful was the effect on the Welsh people of the religious revivals of the period, which precipitated a pious religionism that continued beyond World War I. For many, the worldliness of modern life made impossible the quiet spirituality of earlier times, and they saw their escape in distant, unpopulated areas of the world then opening up. Some had already tried Canada and the United States and were frustrated by the tides of other European nationalities which threatened the purity of their communities. They responded when Argentina offered cheap land to immigrants who would settle and develop its vast spaces before an aggressive Chile pre-empted them. From the United States and from Wales they came in small ships on hazardous voyages to Puerto Madryn, and settled in the Chubut Valley.

Although the hardships of those gritty pioneers are more than a century behind their descendants, the pioneer tradition is proudly remembered. Some remain in agriculture, many are in trade and commerce. Only a dwindling number of the older generation still speaks Welsh, but descendants will proudly show you their chapels and cemeteries (very similar to those in Wales), take you for Welsh tea in one of the area's many teahouses, and reminisce about their forebears and the difficulties they overcame. They speak of the devastating floods of the Chubut that almost demolished the community at the turn of the 20th century, the scouts who went on indigenous trails to the Andean foothills to settle in the Cwm Hyfrwd (the Beautiful Valley), the loneliness of the prairies in the long cold winters, the incessant winds, and the lack of capital that made all undertakings a matter of backbreaking labor.

Unfortunately, the old ways are being discarded in our modern technological era. The Welsh language will not long be spoken in Patagonia. But traditions are still upheld, and descendants of the Patagonian Welsh still hold *eisteddfods* to compete in song and verse. They revere the tradition of the chapel even when they do not attend, and they take enormous pride in their links with Wales.

major center for whaling and trading in seal skins. In the 19th century there were more than 700 whalers operating in these waters. An international protection treaty was signed in 1935, and since then the whale population has recovered slowly; it currently stands at 700. The whales come to breed near these shores around July and stay until mid-December. Whale watching is concentrated on mother and calf pairs and is organized by a few authorized, experienced boat owners from Puerto Pirámides. On shore, you can observe the sea lions and cormorant colonies from a viewing platform at the foot of the pyramid-shaped cliff that gives this location its name.

There are several good hotels and restaurants and a shore-side campsite where you can wake to the sound of whales blowing in the bay. It is an ideal center for exploring the peninsula's other wildlife sites, too, although if you hire a vehicle, beware of the tricky driving conditions. On the small side road out of the peninsula stands a monument dedicated to the first Spanish settlement here, which lasted only from 1774 to 1810, when the settlers were forced to flee from the native warriors. Here too, is a sea-bird reserve, the **Isla de los Pájaros**.

THE CHUBUT VALLEY AND THE WELSH TOWNS

The lower Chubut Valley was the site of the first settlement established by the Welsh. The towns of Dolavon, Gaiman, Trelew, and Rawson developed here, and today they are surrounded by intensively cultivated lands.

Gaiman ❾ is particularly attractive and makes for an excellent day trip from Puerto Madryn (80km/50 miles away via RN3). It has an interesting museum similar to the one in Trevelín, the **Museo Histórico Regional** (daily 3–8pm), housed in the old train station, with a gift shop. The town is famous for its Welsh teas, which are offered by four leading *casas de té* (teahouses) in somber rooms crowded with evocative memorabilia of the first settlers. An *eisteddfod* – Welsh arts festival – which features singing and reciting, is held here every August. The river meets the sea close to **Rawson** ❿, the provincial capital city. It is worth driving by the fishermen's port here to watch the men unloading their day's catch, a host of lazy sea lions bobbing around their skiffs to grab whatever falls overboard.

Trelew is the most important city in the lower valley, and its airport is the gateway for visitors to the wildlife-rich Península Valdés area. After a program to promote industry was introduced in the 1980s, the population swelled here to more than 100,000. Its Welsh ambiance has faded and, apart from a leafy central square, it is not a particularly attractive city. One point of interest is a paleontological museum marking the important dinosaur remains that have been found in Patagonia: the **Museo Paleontológico Egidio Feruglio** (www.

Southern beech forest in Parque Nacional Los Glaciares.

mef.org.ar; Mon–Fri 9am–6pm, Sat–Sun 10am–7pm). Located on Avenida Fontana 140, it contains fossil remains of dinosaurs such as carnotosaurus, the only known meat-eating dinosaur with horns, and the 65-million-year-old eggs of titanosaurus.

OIL COUNTRY

Some 440km (270 miles) down the coast south of Trelew is Patagonia's major city, **Comodoro Rivadavia** , with a population exceeding 200,000. Its airport has daily flights connecting the Patagonian cities and Buenos Aires.

Colonia Sarmiento ⑫, 190km (118 miles) west of Comodoro Rivadavia, lies in a fertile valley flanked by two huge lakes, lagos Musters and Colhué Huapi, which attract black-necked swans. Heading south from the valley for 30km (19 miles), you reach the Parque Nacional Bosques Petrificados de Jaramillo, which has remains that are more than a million years old. This forest tells us much about the geological past of this land, which a long time ago was covered in trees.

Sheep graze by the Córdoba Pass.

SANTA CRUZ

The province of **Santa Cruz** is the second largest in Argentina but with the smallest population per square kilometer. Most of Santa Cruz is dry grassland or semidesert, with high *mesetas* (plateaux) interspersed with protected valleys and covered with large sheep estancias.

RN3, nearly all of which is paved, is the province's main coastal road. It follows the shoreline of Golfo San Jorge south to the oil town of **Caleta Olivia**, with its huge central statue of an oil worker, then climbs inland. After 86km (53 miles), RN281 branches off RN3 for 126km (78 miles) to the coastal port of **Puerto Deseado** ⑬, named after the *Desire*, flagship of the 16th-century English global navigator Thomas Cavendish.

Virtually unknown for many years, Puerto Deseado is the home base for a number of ships that fish in the western South Atlantic. It is beginning to develop as a tourist center, particularly for its rich coastal wildlife. There are sea-lion colonies at Cabo Blanco to the

⊘ SHEAR PROFIT

The first governor of Santa Cruz, Carlos Moyano, could find no one to settle in the desolate south of Patagonia. In desperation, he invited young couples from the Malvinas/Falklands to try their hand "on the coast," and the first sheep farmers were English and Scottish shepherds. They were soon followed by people from many other nations, mainly in central Europe, who remained behind after the 1890s gold rush. The sheep rearing proved hugely successful, and, by the 1920s, Argentinian wool commanded record prices on the world market.

The sheep in southern Patagonia are mainly Scottish corriedale, although some merinos have been brought from Australia, and two hardy new breeds have been developed for the region. Farm work intensifies from October to April, with lamb marking, shearing, dipping, and moving the animals to the summer camps. In the fall they are moved back to the winter camps and the wool around the eyes is shorn.

Shearing is usually done by a *comparsa*, a group of professionals who travel from farm to farm, moving south with the season. However, each farm has its own shepherds and *peones* (unskilled workmen) who stay year round, tending fences and animals.

north, and Isla Pingüino to the south, of the bay, where you might see yellow-crested penguins and the unusual Guanay cormorant, and where spectacular black and white Commerson's dolphins play with boats sailing in the estuary just outside the town.

Back on RN3, the next important stop is a pristine natural wonder, the **Parque Nacional Bosques Petrificados de Jaramillo** ⑭, just 80km (50 miles) to the west of the highway. This enormous petrified forest occupies over 15,000 hectares (247,000 acres). At the edges of canyons and mesas, the rock-hard trunks of 150 million-year-old monkey-puzzle trees stick out of the ground. Some trunks are 30 meters (100ft) long and a meter/yard thick – among the largest in the world. There are no overnight facilities at the park, and it closes at sundown, but there is a campsite with a store at La Paloma, 20km (12 miles) from the park headquarters.

EXPLORERS' TRACES

About 250km (155 miles) farther south on RN3 is the picturesque port of **Puerto San Julián** ⑮, also awakening to tourism, with several hotels and a small museum. Both Magellan (in 1520) and Drake (in 1578) spent the winter here and hanged mutineers on the eastern shore. Nothing remains there except a small plaque. Not far to the south of San Julián is the little town of **Comandante Luis Piedra Buena** ⑯, on the Río Santa Cruz, which was followed upstream by Fitz-Roy, Moreno, and other early explorers. Its main attraction is the tiny shack on Isla Pavón, occupied in 1859 by Piedra Buena, an Argentine naval hero. The island, on the river, is linked to the town by road bridge.

About 29km (18 miles) downstream lies the sleepy town of **Puerto Santa Cruz**, with its port, Punta Quilla, which is the base for ships that service the offshore oil rigs.

RÍO GALLEGOS

The capital of the province is **Río Gallegos** ⑰, some 180km (112 miles) south of Puerto Santa Cruz. It is a sprawling city of about 110,000 on the south bank of the eponymous river, which has the third highest tides in the world, at 16 meters (53ft). At low tide, ships are left high and dry on mud flats. It is perhaps one of the most austere places in Argentina, and it is unlikely that you will want to linger here longer than you have to.

Moving southwest of Río Gallegos, RN3 enters Chile near a series of rims of long-extinct volcanoes. One of these, Laguna Azul, is a geological reserve, 3km (1.5 miles) off the main highway near the border post.

PENGUINS AND DOLPHINS

Some 11km (6 miles) south of Río Gallegos, Ruta 1 branches southeast off RN3, over open plains to **Cabo Vírgenes** (129km/80 miles from Río Gallegos) and Punta Dungeness (on the border with Chile) at the northeast mouth of the Strait of Magellan. Here

Magellanic penguins at Cabo Vírgenes.

you can see Argentina's second largest penguin colony, home to some 300,000 birds; visit the lighthouse; and perhaps watch dolphins just offshore. Near the cliffs are the meagre remains of Ciudad Nombre de Jesús, founded by the Spanish explorer Pedro Sarmiento de Gamboa in 1584. The road to Cabo Virgenes passes a couple of farms: Estancia Cóndor, one of the larger estancias in the area, and a few kilometers beyond that, Estancia Monte Dinero (www.montedinero.com.ar), which has a separate guesthouse for visitors and which also offers wildlife trips to the penguin colony at Cabo Virgenes.

WESTWARD ON RUTA NACIONAL 40

Western Santa Cruz province is spectacular but desolate. The main route through it is on **RN40** – the longest road in the country, snaking its way up through the Northwest as far as the Bolivian border – and not a road to be taken lightly. Those who have traveled it from top to bottom are full of admiration for the rugged beauty of the country and are proud they have survived it. RN40 is not even accurately detailed on most maps, including those of the prestigious Instituto Geográfico Militar. The best one is the ACA (Automóvil Club Argentino) map of the province of Santa Cruz. In winter, some parts of the road may be inaccessible.

Southern RN40 is a difficult gravel road – rocky and dusty when dry, muddy when wet. Places marked on the map may consist of just one shack or may not exist at all. You must carry extra fuel and/or go out of your way at several places to refill. Sometimes small towns, or even larger ones, run out of gasoline and you may have to wait several days until a fuel truck comes along. In southwestern Patagonia Perito Moreno, Bajo Caracoles, Tres Lagos, El Calafate, and Río Turbio are among the few places which have gas stations.

If you take any secondary roads, remember that there is no fuel available. You also need to carry spare tires, some food, and probably even your bed. There are few places to buy food or even a soft drink outside the larger towns. El Calafate is the main town of the southern Lake District, 313km (194 miles) from Río Gallegos. Halfway there is Esperanza, a truck stop with a gas station and roadside snack bar; nearby is Estancia Chali-Aike, which takes paying guests. Most of the drive is past ranches over the **meseta central**, coming to a high lookout at Cuesta de Miguez, where the whole of Lago Argentino, the mountains and glaciers beyond, and even Mount Fitz Roy can be seen.

THE SOUTHERN LAKE DISTRICT: EL CALAFATE

El Calafate , a town of about 25,000 people, nestles at the base of cliffs on the south shore of beautiful **Lago Argentino**, one of Argentina's largest lakes. An airport constructed in 2000 receives direct flights from Buenos

Ruta 40.

Aires and this is the jumping-off point for the surrounding area, particularly to the Parque Nacional Los Glaciares. On the eastern shore of Lago Argentino, at the edge of town, is Laguna Nimez, a small bird reserve (daily 9am–8pm), which is home to a variety of ducks, geese, flamingos, and elegant black-necked swans. Walking around the lake from here is tricky, however, as the ground is boggy and crisscrossed with wide streams. Accommodations range from campsites and a youth hostel to elegant hotels. There are several tourist agencies and a number of good restaurants. Large tour groups do the circuit – Buenos Aires, Puerto Madryn, El Calafate, Ushuaia, Buenos Aires – every week.

PARQUE NACIONAL LOS GLACIARES

Traveling 51km (32 miles) west of El Calafate, along the south shore of the Península Magallanes, brings you to the **Parque Nacional Los Glaciares** ⑲, one of the most spectacular parks in Argentina. The southern Patagonian icecap, which is about 400km (250 miles) long, spills over into innumerable glaciers, which end on high cliffs or wend their way down to fjords. Just beyond the Península Magallanes, you can cross Brazo Rico in a boat for a guided climb on the Unesco World Heritage Site of the **Perito Moreno** glacier. A few kilometers on, the road ends at the *pasarelas*, a series of walkways and terraces down a steep cliff, which faces the glacier head on. It is a magnificent sight, especially on a sunny day. Visitors line up along the walkways, cameras at the ready like paparazzi at the Oscar awards ceremony, waiting for a chunk of glacier to calve off into the water with a resounding thunderous crack. To get even closer to the glacier, take one of the regular boat tours that leave from the nearby pier and which get you almost within touching distance of the ice wall.

The Perito Moreno glacier advances across the narrow stretch of water in front of it until it cuts off Brazo Rico and Brazo Sur from the rest of Lago

Stunning landscape near El Calafate, with Lago Argentino.

Argentino. Pressure slowly builds up behind the glacial wall until, about every three to four years, the wall collapses dramatically and the cycle begins again. The glacier has not advanced since 1988, however, leading scientists to question whether global warming is to blame: 90 percent of the world's glaciers are retreating. Old water levels can be seen around these lakes. Hiking too near the glacial front is prohibited because of the danger from waves caused by falling ice.

UPSALA GLACIER

The second major trip from El Calafate is a visit to **Glaciar Upsala**, at the far northwest end of Lago Argentino. Boats leave every morning from Punta Bandera, 40km (25 miles) west of El Calafate. In early spring, they cannot get near Upsala because of the large field of icebergs, so may visit Spegazzini and other glaciers instead. Some trips stop for a short walk through the forest to Onelli glacier. On the way back, stop at Estancia Alice (www.estanciaalice.com.ar), on the road to El Calafate. *Asados*

(barbecues) and tea are available here, and shearing demonstrations are held in season. You may also see black-necked swans and other birds.

It is only a short distance across the Sierra Los Baguales from Parque Nacional Los Glaciares, Argentina, to Parque Nacional Torres del Paine, in Chile. From some spots near El Calafate, the Paine mountains can be seen. But there is no road through. Instead, you must backtrack to Puerto El Cerrito (at least that section is paved) and then take RN40 again west and south to enter Chile either at Cancha Carrera or farther south at Río Turbio. You can also fly back to Río Gallegos and fly on to Punta Arenas, in Chile, from where it is still a seven-hour drive north to the Paine National Park.

EL CHALTÉN AND MONTE FITZ ROY

Returning north, up RN40 from El Calafate, at the far northern end of the Parque Nacional Los Glaciares are some of the most impressive peaks in the Andes, including Cerro Torre (3,128 meters/10,263ft) and Monte Fitz Roy (3,406 meters/11,175ft). In good weather Fitz Roy can be seen from El Calafate. The sheer granite peaks attract climbers from all over the world, who describe their experiences in the register at the northern entrance to the park.

The best base for visiting this part of the national park is the village of **El Chaltén ⑳**, some 219km (136 miles) north of El Calafate, via a well-paved stretch of RN40 above the western end of **Lago Viedma**. The village – whose name means "blue mountain," the Amerindian name for Fitz Roy – nestles in a hidden bowl at the foot of the mountain, with its glacier coming down off the Southern Patagonian Ice Field. Founded in 1985, this once tiny village has expanded rapidly in recent years due to its ever-growing popularity with visiting trekkers and mountain climbers (though it virtually closes down in

Monte Fitz Roy.

winter). It has a national park information office, food and souvenir stores, and a gas station. There is a range of accommodations available, including holiday bungalows, hostels, and basic campsites. In summer, there are two daily buses from El Calafate.

Continuing north on RN40, at Tres Lagos, Ruta 31 leads northwest to **Lago San Martín** (called Lago O'Higgins in Chile). Estancia El Cóndor (www.cielos patagonicos.com) is situated on the south shore, offering accommodations, horseback riding, fishing, and trekking.

About 560km (348 miles) north of El Chaltén, the northwesternmost town in Santa Cruz province is **Perito Moreno**, a dusty place with little to offer. From here, however, a paved road leads 57km (35 miles) west to the small town of **Los Antiguos**, on the shore of Lago Buenos Aires. Small farms here produce milk, honey, fruit, and vegetables; the town has a couple of hotels and a campsite. A mere 3km (1.5 miles) to the west, you can cross the Chilean border to the town of Chile Chico and other scenic areas near the Río Baker.

CUEVA DE LAS MANOS

South of Perito Moreno is the **Cueva de las Manos** (Cave of the Hands; www.cuevadelasmanos.org; daily Nov–Apr 9am–7pm, May–Oct 10am–6pm; guided tours only), a national historical monument and World Heritage Site located in a beautiful canyon 56km (35 miles) off RN40 from just north of Bajo Caracoles. Pre-Columbian cave paintings are found all over Santa Cruz, but those at Cueva de las Manos are the finest. The walls here are covered by paintings of hands and animals, principally guanacos (relatives of the llama), which are thought to be anything between 3,000 and 10,000 years old. Numerous lakes straddle the Argentine–Chilean border in this region. RN40 lies well to the east of the mountains. Any excursions to the lakes to the west, such as Lago Ghio, Pueyrredón, Belgrano, and San Martín, must be made along side roads; there are no circuits – you must go in and out on the same road. The road to Lago Pueyrredón leaves from Bajo Caracoles.

Perito Moreno glacier.

📷 PATAGONIA'S WILDLIFE

In the vast and lonely expanses of Patagonia, people are far outnumbered by the region's wild inhabitants, who range from condors to cougars.

Wildlife is predictably more scarce on the Patagonian steppe than in most other regions of Argentina, but that does not mean it's not out there. Grey foxes are a common sight almost everywhere, and the open steppe is home to Patagonian hares or *maras*, to rheas (relatives of the ostrich), and to the elusive puma or cougar. Patches of marshy ground are good places to watch southern lapwings – probably Patagonia's noisiest birds – while to the west, the foothills of the Andes offer a good chance to spot condors as they soar high overhead in search of food. However, for most visitors, Patagonia's biggest attraction is its coastal wildlife, and the best time to see it is during the southern spring and summer, when penguins, seals, and whales all gather along the shore to breed.

WHALE WATCHING

Like seals and penguins, Patagonia's whales are animals of fixed habits, breeding at the same sites year after year. The Península Valdés is one of the most famous of them all, hosting over 10 percent of the world's southern right whale population for three or four months each year. With so many of these huge, docile mammals crowded into the peninsula's bays, the result is a wildlife spectacle not to be missed, and whale-watching boat trips can be organized locally.

Between May and December southern right whales come to the temperate waters off Península Valdés to breed and raise their calves.

Elephant seals come ashore in spring and autumn, the first time to breed, the second to molt. The largest of all seals, they were nearly hunted to extinction by man during the 19th century.

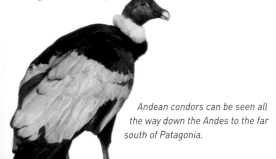

Andean condors can be seen all the way down the Andes to the far south of Patagonia.

Huge rookeries of Magellanic penguins can be seen on Península Valdés and the adjacent coastline.

Where to spot the wildlife

Wildlife tourism is still relatively new in Patagonia, but there are numerous companies in Trelew and Puerto Madryn that can arrange tours to Península Valdés and whale-watching boat trips. Be aware that the distances involved here can be very large: with day trips especially, you may find that you spend a lot of time on the move.

The penguin breeding season runs from about October to March, with the down-covered chicks hatching from late November onwards. The biggest colony – and the most visited one by far – is at Punta Tombo. The colony at Cabo dos Bahías, further down the coast, is more time-consuming to reach, but offers the added attraction of other kinds of wildlife, including rheas and numerous guanacos.

On the Península Valdés, the whale-watching season extends from June to December – roughly from early winter to early summer. To make the most of this spectacular area it is worth staying here for several days.

With its strange bouncing run, the Patagonian hare or mara can speed along at 45kmh (28 mph). True hares – from Europe – are also common here.

The red or Fuegian fox is indigenous. They are hunted mainly for their fur, but still skilfully manage to survive in large numbers.

The puma has one of the biggest ranges of any cat – Patagonia to western Canada.

Les Eclaireurs Lighthouse in the Beagle Channel.

TIERRA DEL FUEGO

Wild and windswept, the uttermost south has been the
ultimate challenge to travelers and explorers since the
early days of global navigation and discovery.

Main attractions
Ushuaia
The Canal Beagle
Estancia Harberton
Parque Nacional Tierra
del Fuego

Tierra del Fuego, the Land of Fire, lies
at the southern tip of the South American continent. The very name evokes
feelings of distance, fear of the elements, isolation, and loneliness. But
the feeling of isolation can be an invig-
orating one, when allied with a spirit of
adventure. You really feel like you have
reached the edge here, a sensation
reinforced by the seemingly endless
number of places and brands whose
names incorporate the phrase *fin del
mundo* (end of the world).

In the days of sail, many people – the
early merchants, explorers, and scientists – were able to claim that they had
rounded Cape Horn. Some were ship-
wrecked there, but few stayed to settle.
With the opening of the Panama Canal
in 1914, fewer ships took the southernmost route. By then, Europeans had
settled parts of Tierra del Fuego, but it
was difficult for tourists to reach.

Transport links to Tierra del Fuego
have improved considerably since
then, and it has become a popular
destination for the discerning traveler.
And although the province can be as
bleak and windswept as it is supposed
to be – or perhaps because of those
things – most visitors enjoy their trip
to the uttermost south. Unless you
have come here to ski (the season runs
from mid-June to mid-September),

the best months to visit are October
through April, before the southern
winter closes in.

GEOGRAPHY AND CLIMATE

About 9,000 years ago, the waters of
the Strait of Magellan broke through
the tip of the continent, isolat-
ing Tierra del Fuego from Patagonia. Technically, Tierra del Fuego
includes all the land south of the
Strait of Magellan and north of the
Drake Passage, although only one
island, the Isla Grande, is actually

Map on page 296

*A testimony to the force of the wind
in Tierra del Fuego.*

called Tierra del Fuego. Locally, the Isla Grande is known simply as "La Isla." It is surrounded, to the south and west, by a maze of mountainous islands, islets, channels, and fjords, most of them uninhabited and many unexplored.

The Fuegian Archipelago is within the Subantarctic Zone. Its cool climate is dominated by the prevailing southwesterly winds that sweep in off the South Pacific and waters farther south. These often gale-force winds can occur throughout the year but are strongest from the end of August to March (spring and summer).

The Andes, curving from northwest to east across the archipelago, ensure high rain over the western and southern islands, leaving less moisture for the northeastern plains. Temperatures along the Canal Beagle range from a record high of 30°C (86°F) in summer to a record low of about -14°C (7°F) in winter. Temperatures in the plains region are more extreme, but all of Tierra del Fuego lives in a perpetual "cool spring."

Eighteenth-century painting of a Yaghan woman.

EXPLORATION AND SETTLEMENT

Humans arrived on the archipelago in two ways. The earliest record is an 11,800-year-old site in northern Tierra del Fuego occupied by nomadic hunters – people who, near the end of the last ice age, crossed the Magellanic land bridge before waters broke through it. In southern Tierra del Fuego, the oldest adaptation to a marine environment is a 6,000-year-old site at Tunel on the Canal Beagle, developed by canoe peoples. On the arrival of the Europeans, four cultural groups populated the area: the Ona (Selk'nam) and Hausch were the guanaco-hunters of the plains, while the Yaghan (Yámana) and Alaculuf were the spear-hunting canoe natives of the islands and channels. Eliminated mainly by white man's diseases, fewer than five pure members remain of the first three groups, although there are many people of mixed race.

The European exploration of Tierra del Fuego – first by Magellan in 1520, then by pirates, explorers, collectors,

scientists, sealers and whalers, missionaries, gold prospectors, and merchants – is one of the great adventure stories in history. Many tourists visit Tierra del Fuego because of childhood memories of hearing stories of the exploits of Drake, Cook, and Darwin, or the arduous, careful surveys of Fitzroy and King. In his book *Uttermost Part of the Earth* (1946), E. Lucas Bridges tells how his father, Thomas Bridges, began the Anglican Mission in Ushuaia (1869), explored unknown areas, worked with and taught the Yaghan, and finally settled the first farm. The missionaries were followed by a coastguards' station, gold miners, sheep farmers, small merchants, oil workers, and all those needed to make up a modern town. In one century, Tierra del Fuego went from a land occupied by near-naked Amerindian hunter-gatherers to a major tourist destination for cruise liners and yachtsmen.

FLORA AND FAUNA

Plant and animal life in this subantarctic climate is less varied than in warmer regions. Only six species of tree are native to Tierro del Fuego, including three kinds of *Nothofagus* or southern beech. Several kinds of shrubs produce beautiful flowers or edible berries. The most famous is the calafate *(Berberis buxifolia)*, a purple berry with a tangy taste that according to legend destines all those who taste it to return to Patagonia. Most wildflowers are small but well worth searching for. Flowering plants and ferns total about 500 species, but some 150 of these have been introduced or naturalized.

Among the few native land animals are guanaco, Fuegian fox (or Andean wolf), bats, tucu-tucu, and mice. An abundance of introduced animals, such as beaver, muskrats, rabbits, and Patagonian foxes thrive (in the case of the beaver, destructively so) here. About 200 species of birds are either resident or migratory. Surprisingly, this cool climate is also home to parrots

(the *Austral conure*), flamingos, and hummingbirds. The sea is fecund with algae, and 27 species of whale visit the archipelago to feed on it.

ACROSS THE STRAIT

Politically, Tierra del Fuego is split between Chile (to the west and south) and Argentina (north and east). The Argentine section is part of the Provincia de Tierra del Fuego, Antártida e Islas del Atlántico Sur, the capital of which is the city of Ushuaia. The rough triangle that is Argentina's part of the Isla Grande covers some 21,340 sq km (8,300 sq miles).

Visitors arrive by several means. Aerolíneas Argentinas, LATAM, and smaller airlines provide daily flights to Ushuaia airport (which involves the most spectacular airplane descent in all Argentina) from Buenos Aires and other areas. Tourist ships visit Ushuaia briefly as part of longer cruises between Río de Janeiro, Buenos Aires, and the west coast of South America. Ushuaia, like Punta Arenas in Chile, is a jumping-off point for ships sailing to Antarctica.

The elusive Fuegian fox.

Sea lions and sea birds on an island in the Beagle Channel.

Visitors coming by land must cross the Strait of Magellan by ferry, either at the Primera Angostura (a 20- to 30-minute crossing) or between Punta Arenas and Porvenir (a 2- to 3-hour crossing) in Chile. There are no regular bus routes between Río Gallegos and Río Grande (charter services may be available), but there are two routes between Río Grande and Ushuaia.

USHUAIA

The city of **Ushuaia** ❶ (pronounced "ooh-SWY-ah") sits in a picturesque bowl on the southern side of the mountains, overlooking Bahía Ushuaia, the Canal Beagle, and Navarino and Hoste islands (both in Chile) to the south. To the east rise the peaks of the spectacular, pointed Monte Olivia and the Cinco Hermanos (Five Brothers). Ushuaia is the home of a large naval base, government offices, and stores for imported goods. It is a base for one or two farms, sawmills, a crab fishery, and a growing offshore fishing industry.

The other growth industry around here is tourism. Ushuaia is easily the best base from which to explore Tierra del Fuego, and most visitors begin and end their time in the province here. There are good accommodations to choose from, some in the city center, others along the coast – with coveted views of the Canal Beagle – and several overlooking the town, Alpine style, from the mountains behind. The tourist office (www.turismoushuaia.com) at Avenida Prefectura Naval Argentina 470 provides information and brochures and has branches at the airport and port.

A simple triangular monument near the airfield marks the site of the **Anglican Mission** (1869–1907). Thomas and Mary Bridges (1870) and John and Clara Lawrence (1873) became the archipelago's first non-indigenous permanent residents. The official founding of the town was the establishment of a sub-prefecture (coastguard) in 1884.

USHUAIA'S HISTORY

Ushuaia's former prison, a forbidding, semi-Panopticon facility that held Argentina's most dangerous criminals in the first half of the 20th century,

A signpost in remote Ushuaia.

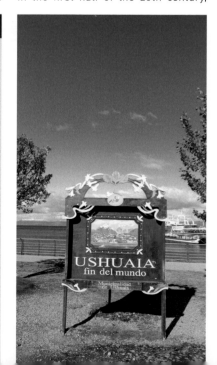

is now part of the naval base. The jail is open to the public as part of the impressive **Maritimo y del Presidio de Ushuaia** museum (www.museomaritimo. com; daily Mar–Dec 10am–8pm, Jan–Feb 9am–8pm). Visitors can peek into several of the 400 cells, once occupied by notorious serial killers and master forgers, some of whom have been resurrected as waxwork models wearing striped jumpsuits. Two other museums (hours as above) to visit in the former prison complex are the Museo Antártico (Antarctic Museum) and the Museo de Arte Marino (Marine Art Museum). For a broader view of Ushuaia's history, take a look around the **Museo del Fin del Mundo** (Mon–Sat Oct–Mar 9am–8pm, Apr–Sept noon–7pm) at Avenida Maipú 173. It has information on the indigenous Yaghan people, explorers' and missionaries' artifacts, and an attractive collection of (stuffed) local birds. Active historical research, especially of the eastern tip of the island, Península Mitre, is carried out from here.

Houses with decorative cornices built by Ushuaia's prisoners are still scattered around the town, and a stroll around the steep streets that branch off from main thoroughfare Avenida San Martín reveals a strange variety of architecture. The early wooden houses covered with corrugated iron (to help prevent fires) with their prisoner-produced gingerbread decorations have a somewhat Russian flavor. They are intermingled with modern concrete structures, imported Swedish prefabs, and hundreds of small, wooden shanties.

THE KING OF CRUSTACEA

Though it is not one of Mother Nature's more comely creations, *centolla* (southern king crab) is good eating. Netted in the Pacific around Cape Horn, most of the crabs are frozen and shipped around the world, but enough are consumed in Ushuaia (though not by locals, who leave them for the tourists) to make *centolla* the region's signature dish. Its meat is incredibly tender but not especially flavorsome, and every restaurant in town serves it – either soused in a thick sauce or, the recommended option, naked

A chair-lift runs from just above the town of Ushuaia to a small teahouse within hiking distance of Glaciar Martial.

Freshly caught centolla (southern king crab).

Fly-fishing on Lake Escondido.

with a slice of lemon. *Merluza negra* (Patagonian toothfish) is another local specialty. Meat eaters who have spent time in Buenos Aires are unlikely to be impressed by Fuegian beef, but the local lamb, while scrawny, is delicious.

Stores in Ushuaia pay only half the import duty that is charged in the rest of the country, and so focus on imported items (sweaters, jackets, and china from Europe; cigarettes, whisky, and radios). There is little to buy that is native to Tierra del Fuego. Avenida San Martín is the main shopping street.

SNOW SPORTS

Located 26km (16 miles) northwest of Ushuaia on RN3, Cerro Castor (www. cerrocastor.com) is the world's southern-most ski resort. Its 32 pistes and snow-park attract Argentines, Brazilians, and a small but increasing number of tourists from the northern hemisphere taking advantage of the inverted seasons. The season runs from mid-June to mid-September.

A lighthouse in the Beagle Channel.

One ice-related activity that can be pursued at any time of year is an excursion to Glaciar Martial, a rapidly retreating tongue of ice located above the town. You can hike or take a taxi to the base of the mountain, 7km (4 miles) out of town. From there a chair-lift (daily, weather permitting) will take you to within hiking range of the glacier. If you do not fancy the 90-minute, quite strenu-ous, footslog, you can simply enjoy a brew in the teahouse and take in the view.

THE CANAL BEAGLE AND ESTANCIA HARBERTON

One of the must-do activities in Ushuaia is to take a cruise on the **Canal Beagle** (Beagle Channel). This lovely stretch of water, as calm as the South Atlantic into which it empties is tempestuous, was named for the Royal Navy brig sloop captained by Robert Fitzroy, which, on its second voyage, brought Charles Dar-win to these parts in 1832. Catamarans leave from the main port, and several itineraries are possible. Wildlife spot-ters will want to visit Isla de los Lobos (Sea Lion Island), the main draw of which is self-explanatory, and Isla de los Pájaros (Bird Island) where cormorants

⊘ CRUISING THE SOUTHERN SEAS

Daily, 3-hour excursions on the Canal Beagle aboard large catamarans visit the islands off Bahía Ushuaia to see colonies of sea lions, southern fur seals, cormorants, gulls, and terns. Longer trips go westward to Lapataia or eastward on the channel to see the Magellan penguins on Isla Yecapasela (Martillo) and visit Estancia Harberton. Several yachts based in Ushuaia's harbor offer a charter service to the Fuegian Channels, Cape Horn, Isla de los Estados, and Antarctica. The northwest arm of the Canal Beagle with its glaciers is only several hours by boat west of Ushuaia. It is possible to get there from Ushuaia on board the Chilean chartered yacht, the *Stella Australis* or one of the larger tourist cruise ships.

Large tourist cruise ships make the circuit of southern South America in summer (Nov–March). They leave from Río de Janeiro or Buenos Aires, visit Ushuaia and Punta Arenas, and go up through the Chilean channels to Puerto Montt or Valparaíso. There are usually only 4 to 6 hours in each port. Cruise ships also visit Antarctica. Regular sailings depart from Ushuaia or from Punta Arenas in Chile during the tourist season, which runs from late November to late February. Antarctic cruises last from seven to 15 days, at least two of which are spent crossing the Drake Passage. Most are intensive learning experiences – naturalists and guest lecturers give talks aboard and guided walks ashore.

and petrels nest. Longer tours visit **Estancia Harberton** ❷ (www.estancia harberton.com), a remote and historically significant ranch located in the rolling hills above the Canal Beagle. Founded by the Reverend Thomas Bridges in 1886, Harberton is the oldest farm in Argentine Tierra del Fuego. Open to the public from October to April, the estancia offers a guided walking tour of the property, which includes Tierra del Fuego's oldest nature reserve: a small wood with native trees. There are also some Yaghan kitchen middens and a model wigwam. Visitors can have tea in the original farmhouse by the bay and take a guided tour of the Acatushún marine life museum. The area around Harberton is ideal for birdwatching, with the opportunity to see steamer ducks, cormorants, oystercatchers, and perhaps an eagle or condor.

TIERRA DEL FUEGO NATIONAL PARK

The **Parque Nacional Tierra del Fuego** ❸ protects 63,000 hectares (156,000 acres) of diverse Fuegian terrain, including stretches of Atlantic coast, lenga forests, ancient peat bogs, and several lakes, though only a small fraction of the park is open to the public. You can reach the park entrance by car or taxi but the best way to get there is on the Tren del Fin del Mundo (www. trendelfindelmundo.com.ar), a steam-powered tourist train whose original function was to take convicts to fell trees in the outlying forests. The train departs from the Estación del Fin del Mundo, located 8km (5 miles) west of the city. Several easy trails can be hiked inside the park. Look out for the brightly colored wild flowers that blanket the forest floor in season, "flag trees" that have been bent double by the incessant Patagonian winds, and red foxes. The best time of year to visit is late April, when the fall brings out the colors of the trees.

NORTH OF USHUAIA

Driving out of Ushuaia along RN3 towards Río Grande provides a crash course in ecology, as you pass through thick forests of evergreen southern

Glaciar Martial.

Tip

A popular site for keen fossil hunters is Cabo Domingo, up the coast just to the north of Río Grande, and close to the Salesian Mission Museum.

beech (coihue or guindo), deciduous forests of lenga or "high beech", valleys filled with sphagnum swamps, and then, as you leave the island's mountainous south, flat sea coast and low bush land. You will also skirt two lakes: tranquil, tiny Lago Escondido and 100km (60-mile) -long Lago Fagnano, in the heart of the island. Be sure to stop at the lookout on Paso Garibaldi to look north over Lago Escondido and Lago Fagnano. This windswept spot attracts many local birds, and you can walk along the rocky lakeshore for a short distance, past beavers' dams and small farmsteads.

Just north of Lago Fagnano is the small town of **Tolhuin** ❹. Its name is a transliteration of the native Ona word "tol-wen," meaning "heart." The town enjoys a relatively clement microclimate and both lake and land tours are available for most of the year. Anglers come to fish the fat rainbow trout that lurk in Lago Fagnano. The region is also home to a number of estancias, several of which offer accommodations and sheep-shearing demonstrations.

Hardy sheep on the plains.

RÍO GRANDE

Founded as recently as 1921, the town of **Río Grande** ❺ (population over 80,000) is the center of the sheep and oil region, as well as the home of a number of companies producing television sets, radios, synthetics, and other products – the result of a special 1972 law designed to bring development and more residents to this far reach of the republic.

Río Grande sprawls over the flat northern coast of the river, and its wide, windblown streets overlook the waters of the South Atlantic. The Río Grande river has silted up, allowing for little shipping. The town was an important center during the 1982 Falklands/Malvinas conflict, and has several monuments to those killed.

The **Museo Histórico y de Ciencias Naturales Monseñor Fagnano** (Mon–Fri 3–5.45pm), located in a Salesian mission, and the **Museo Municipal Virginia Choquintel** cover a wide range of local themes, from aboriginal culture and contemporary history to regional fauna and flora. The **Centro de Veteranos de Guerra Malvinas Argentinas** (Falklands War Veteran Center; Mon–Fri 9am–5pm) at O'Higgins 321 displays photographs and equipment from the 1982 Falklands/Malvinas War.

This is Tierra del Fuego's fishing center. Trout (rainbow, brook, and brown) and salmon were introduced in the 1930s, and reach record sizes. Until recently fishing was open in all areas, permission being needed only to cross estancia land. Now access to this land can be gained only with guides and there is a charge. The Río Grande is ideal for sea-run brown trout. Best fishing times are January to March and upmarket estancias are the ideal choice as a fishing base.

West of Río Grande lies **Estancia María Behety** (http://maribety.com/en/), a picturesque village with an enormous shearing shed (room for 40 shearers), which is reported to be the world's

largest. It is also the site of a world-class fishing lodge.

WEST OF RÍO GRANDE

Roads heading west and southwest from Río Grande branch off into the mountains, and cover steep hills, plains, forest, *vegas* (damp meadows), and estancias. This is a fascinating area to explore, if you have time. **Kautapen Lodge** (www.kautapen.com), on Estancia La Retranca is an exclusive fishing lodge (*kautapen* means "fishing-house" in Ona). To the south, **Lago Yehuin**, favored for camping and horseback riding, and the Río Claro to the west are good fishing areas being developed for tourism.

The eastern point of Tierra del Fuego is a mostly unused wilderness of forest, swamp, and mountain and can be reached only on foot, horseback, or helicopter.

GOLD, FOSSILS, AND SHEEP

Northern Tierra del Fuego is sheep-farming and oil country, where wells dot the grasslands and rolling hills. The western Strait of Magellan, in Chile, is peppered with oil platforms. Oil supply roads run in all directions, while sheep, cattle, guanaco, and wild geese graze among them. In winter, guanaco can be seen along any of the secondary roads. The best way to see them in summer is to drive north along the bay from the San Sebastián border post.

Cliffs along the coast near Cabo Espíritu Santo and the roads near San Sebastián yield both marine and forest fossils while sandstone hills farther south are littered with fossilized shells and crabs. The plains may look yellow or brown and appear to have little life, but this is Tierra del Fuego's best sheep land. If you stop to look and listen, you will discover many birds. A short walk will reveal hidden wild flowers.

Before the days of oil, sheep farming was the main industry of northern Fuegia, with thousands of sheep, mainly Corriedale, covering the plains. The larger farms produced (and still do) world-class, prize-winning pedigree sheep.

Ushuaia and the Canal Beagle.

A young porteña.

ARGENTINA

TRAVEL TIPS

TRANSPORTATION

By air

Most international flights arrive at **Ezeiza International Airport** (EZE; www.aa2000.com.ar), 35km (22 miles) from the center of Buenos Aires.

Avoid the floods of taxi drivers who greet arrivals at the airport and buy a ticket from one of the *remise* (private car) stands in the foyer. A cheaper option is to take the airport bus run by the Manuel Tienda León company (offices on Carlos Pellegrini 509; tel: (5411)-4314 3636/4315 5115; www.tiendaleon.com). Tickets for this comfortable service can be bought at the company's booth in the arrivals area. It runs hourly, takes around 1 hour depending on traffic, and drops you off close to Plaza San Martín. From here, most hotels are a short taxi ride away. Public bus no. 8 stops outside terminal B arrivals and can take you to Plaza de Mayo in two hours.

Another airport, **Aeroparque Jorge Newbery** (www.aa2000.com.ar/aeroparque), is located within the city and is used mostly for domestic travel as well as for travel to and from bordering countries (see page 308).

Flights from Europe

There are flights to Buenos Aires from London, Barcelona, Madrid, Frankfurt, Paris, Amsterdam, and Rome with European and North and South American carriers. Aerolíneas Argentinas flies direct from Madrid, Barcelona, and Rome.

Flights from the US

Aerolíneas Argentinas and other major North and South American airlines fly from Dallas, Atlanta, Miami, Los Angeles, New York, and Houston.

Flights from Canada

From Canada, the cheapest option is to go via the US. At the time of writing, there were no direct flights from anywhere in Canada to Buenos Aires.

Flights from South Africa

There are only a few flights to Argentina from South Africa and most go via Sao Paolo.

Flights from Australasia

Air New Zealand operates direct flights between Auckland and Buenos Aires. It's also possible to fly to Santiago de Chile and from there to Australia and New Zealand with Qantas Airlines.

By sea

There are only a few cruise ships that come to Buenos Aires. Most of these originate in Brazil or Europe and operate from December to March.

A number of cruise outfits operate out of Ushuaia and run cruises around the Antarctic region and South Atlantic islands, with various packages on offer from November to March. Heavily discounted last-minute deals are available from travel agencies in Ushuaia. **Quark Expeditions** (www.quarkexpeditions.com) and **Adventure Smith Explorations** (www.adventuresmithexplorations.com) are both highly recommended.

Australis (www.australis.com) has two cruise ships, *Ventus Australis* and *Stella Australis*, which explore Patagonia and Tierra del Fuego on 3–8-night journeys with a program of activities between October and April.

For more details, contact a travel agency in your home country or a reputable private agency in Buenos Aires.

Regular catamarans run between Buenos Aires and Montevideo (they depart from Puerto Madero in downtown Buenos Aires).

Overland

Few tourists arrive by land. However, for the adventurous type, this can be accomplished by bus or automobile. Bus services are available from Chile, Bolivia, Paraguay, Uruguay, and Brazil. Large, air-conditioned buses are available for long-distance overland travel. Bus tickets do not usually have seat numbers, so it is worth getting on the bus in good time to make sure you have a seat. Also be warned that air conditioning is often very powerful, so take a warm sweater, even during the summer months.

At the time of writing there are no regular international train services to and from Argentina. There are, however, limited connections between Posadas (Argentina) and Encarnación (Paraguay) via the San Roque González de Santa Cruz Bridge, between Zapala (Argentina) and Lonquimay (Chile), and Salta (Argentina) and Antofagasta (Chile), as well as between Villazón (Bolivia) and La Quiaca (Argentina).

Argentina is a vast country that presents numerous logistical challenges to anyone trying to plan a comprehensive itinerary. Don't assume that you can go from A (Buenos Aires) to B and thence to C; it is more likely that you will have to return to A after each leg of your journey. Thus it is better to choose one or two areas to explore in depth rather than try to see everything. The Visit Argentina Pass offered by Aerolineas Argentinas and Austral allows you to travel across the country at preferential rates (www.aerolineas.com.ar).

Public transport in Argentina is generally very good by South

American standards. The major cities all have good – and very cheap – bus networks. The Buenos Aires subway (Subte) is cheap and relatively efficient, though it can get stiflingly overcrowded at peak hours. There is no national train service to speak of (yet), but comfortable long-distance buses cover a wide network of destinations.

Buses

City transport

Buses (colectivos) are a good and speedy way to get around Buenos Aires. The network is rather complex, however, so if you're only in the city for a short time, you are probably better off taking taxis or remises. There are 180 bus lines, which cover most of the city. During the day colectivos come very frequently. They also run all night, when they are required to come at least every 30 minutes.

Colectivo fares vary depending on the destination; the minimum fare is $8 pesos. You can pay either by cash or SUBE card (www.sube.gob. ar). Available from centros de obtención around the city, these cost $20 pesos and are valid on colectivos, city trains, and the subway (Subte) in Buenos Aires. You may find it useful to purchase a pocket-size Guia "T" for a few pesos from a kiosco (newsstand) when you arrive in Buenos Aires. This contains detailed maps of the city and all the bus routes. Alternatively, visit http://mapa.buenosaires.gob.ar for an interactive map of the city.

In most cities, there is a bus service that links the airport to the city center. In addition, some airlines run a minibus service that is coordinated with flight schedules.

Long-distance buses

The network of long-distance buses (known as micros) throughout Argentina is efficient, cheap, and comfortable. Unless you are in a particular hurry, or needing to jump from one end of the country to the other, this is a great way to get around.

Distances involved often mean an overnight journey, but the well-paved roads should not hinder sleep. You can request a semi-cama (reclining seat with plenty of legroom) or the more expensive coche cama (180-degree reclining bed seat). Snacks and drinks are usually included in the price.

Buses for destinations throughout the country leave from the Retiro bus station in Buenos Aires (www.tebasa.com.ar). Dozens of bus companies are located within the terminal and are grouped together by destination. Two of the largest – Andesmar (tel: 0810-122-1122; www.andesmar.com), and Nueva Chevallier (tel: 011-4000 5255; www.nuevachevallier.com.ar) – operate buses to destinations throughout Argentina. Numerous smaller companies serve specific regions, as well as destinations in neighboring countries.

There is an information office on the 2nd floor (tel: 011-4310 0700). Left-luggage lockers are available for a few pesos with payment by tokens on sale at kiosks in the station. The nearest subway station is Retiro on Linea C, and the entrance is in the nearby Retiro train station.

Trains

With the exception of a few (excellent) tourist services, passenger services around the country have been limited since the government privatized the network in 1994. However, following the re-nationalization of the railway network in 2015, it is currently being re-developed, with large amounts of money committed to its restoration and modernization. Buenos Aires is now connected with Tucuman, Córdoba, and Rosario, as well as Bahia Blanca and Mar del Plata. Trains also run to the suburbs of the capital. There are four main train terminals in the city:
Retiro-Mitre: For services to Tigre, Capilla del Señor, and Bartolomé Mitre.
Constitución: Mostly for trains going south.
Federico Lacroze: For northbound services to General Lemos.
Once de Septiembre: For travel around Buenos Aires province.
For information call 0800 222 8736. In addition, the journey from Olivos to Tigre along the coast provides excellent views of the River Plate.

Subway

The Buenos Aires subway system, better known as the Subte, is usually the fastest and definitely the cheapest way to get around the city. The rides are quick, taking no more than 40 minutes, and the waiting time is about 3–5 minutes. There are currently six subway lines in Buenos Aires: A, B, C, D,

E, and H (plans to construct another three have already been approved), plus the Premetro tram line which connects with Line E at Plaza de los Virreyes. The Subte is open 5.30am–11pm (until 11. 30 on Sat), except on Sundays when it is open 8am–10pm. Tickets for travel can be bought from the boletería (ticket office) located in the station and cost $7.50 pesos for one journey. SUBE cards (see left) are also valid on the Subte.

Private transport

Remises

Remises are private automobiles, with a driver, that can be rented by the hour, excursion, day, or any other time period. Journeys are unmetered, so you should agree the fare before setting out. Your hotel or apartment rental contact will be able to recommend you a reputable remise company.

Driving

Argentina's road network is good, but a road trip should never be undertaken lightly. It is best to share some of the driving with others as distances are very long and arduous. Unless you are an experienced – and patient – cross-country driver, flying to an airport close to your destination and then renting a car is a better option than driving from Buenos Aires.

Road safety (or lack of it) is a big problem in Argentina. There are many dangerous roads and careless, hazardous drivers. Although this should not put you off, you should drive extra safely.

Roads in remote areas of Patagonia are ripio (dirt roads with loose gravel), which can be challenging, especially in wet conditions. The maximum speed for cars on ripio is 60kmh (37mph). Paved roads are sometimes covered with potholes, which you also need to watch out for.

☉ Tren de la Costa

Inaugurated in 1891 but reopened after 30 years' closure in 1994, this coastal train runs from Olivos to Tigre in the suburbs of Buenos Aires. Trains leave every 30 minutes, there are 11 stops, and the full journey takes around 30 minutes. See www.trendelacosta.com.ar.

Buenos Aires is very congested, making driving extremely time-consuming, and *porteños* have little discipline on the roads, a cause of frequent accidents. Seat belts should be worn at all times whilst driving, as you can be fined for not wearing one, although this is a law that many Argentines take little notice of. The law also requires that you always carry full car documentation and your driver's license with you.

If you plan to do a lot of driving, you may want to consider a monthly membership with the **Automovil Club Argentino (ACA)**. This has a useful emergency breakdown towing and repair service. You can join in Buenos Aires at the head office on Av. del Libertador 1850 (www.aca.org. ar; tel: 011-4808 4000).

Rutas de la Argentina are national and town maps provided free by tourist offices. **YPF**, the state oil company, also produces good road maps, available from gas stations.

Some main roads have private tolls, which charge US$3–5 for every 100km (62 miles). This fee also covers you for emergency towing. Gas stations are infrequent in remote areas so it is best to top up wherever possible.

Parking

Car theft is more common in Buenos Aires than in the rest of the country. Make sure you park your car in well-lit and busy parts of the city where possible. Often in the tourist areas of the capital, street children will offer to guard your car for a peso or two. Outside busy bars or restaurants

Taxis are black with a yellow roof.

there is usually a man who will guard your car for $3–5 pesos. Finding a parking space in the street is difficult but not impossible in most neighborhoods. Most blocks have a parking lot (*estacionamiento*). Driving downtown is not recommended.

Car rental

You can rent a car at the airport upon arrival, but it is better to book from home, especially during the high season. You must be over 21 (although some places require you to be over 25) and hold an international driver's license to rent a car in Argentina. You will usually be asked to leave your credit card details as a deposit. The following better-known car-rental agencies have offices in Buenos Aires: **Avis** tel: 0810-9991 2847, www.avis.com **Budget** tel: 0810-999 2834, www. budget.com.ar **Europcar** tel: 011-4316 6570, www. europcar.com.ar **Hertz** tel: 0810-222 43789, www.hertz. com.ar

☉ Taxis

Taxis are widely used by *porteños* and are often a cheap way to get around, particularly outside the rush hour and if you are sharing the fare with traveling companions. Taxis can be easily recognized (black with a yellow roof), and in Buenos Aires are readily available 24 hours a day. The meter registers a number that will correspond to the amount of the fare appearing on a list. These must be shown to the passenger by law. Tips are not expected though they are, of course, appreciated. Drivers do not carry much change, so you must (few drivers will accept a $100 peso note unless the fare exceeds $50 pesos).

Radio taxis are ordered by telephone or waved down in the street. The latter method is not recommended for solo travelers; if in doubt, ask your hotel desk staff or the waiter in your restaurant to call a taxi for you. **Remise** is a similar service but the cars are unmarked and the fare is calculated according to the distance traveled.

Premium is an excellent radio taxi company. If you order the cab from your cellphone, they will send you a text message informing you of its ETA and license plate number. Tel: 011-5238 000/4374 6666; www.taxipremium.com.

Domestic air travel

Traveling by air in a country as big as Argentina is a good way to get from one region to the other, saving time on some long and, frankly, mind-numbing journeys. **Jorge Newbery Airport** or **El Aeroparque** is Buenos Aires' airport for national traffic and is 10 minutes' drive from the city center at Avenida Costanera Rafael Obligado, between La Pampa and Sarmiento, Costanera Norte. When traveling to or from the airport it is best to take a taxi, which will cost around $50–100 pesos (US$2.5–5) to/from the city center.

Some regional flights are available. You can, for example, fly from Ushuaia to El Calafate, or from Salta to Posadas. For journeys spanning the country, however, you will almost always have to return to Buenos Aires before proceeding to you next destination. Main domestic carriers are Aerolineas Argentinas, LATAM, Andes, Avianca Argentina, and LADE.

Ferries

Traveling by ferry to Uruguay is a good excursion away from the hustle and bustle of Buenos Aires. The most popular destinations are the historic port of Colonia del Sacramento (see page 173), Montevideo, or the beaches of Punta del Este. **Buquebus** operates fast and slow ferries to Colonia and Montevideo, with bus connections to other destinations along the Uruguayan coast. Find them at Av. Córdoba 867 or Terminal Dársena Norte, Av. Antártida Argentina 821 (tel: 011-4316 6530; www.buquebus. com). Should you wish to stay over in Colonia, a good hotel is the **Hotel Beltrán** (tel: (+598) 45-226260/6738; www.hotelbeltran.com). It has pretty, leafy terraces, and rooms start at US$75 a night.

A – Z

Accommodations

As is the case in most countries, the quality of accommodations in Argentina is extremely variable. The good news is that standards have soared over the past decade or so, and with a little research and planning you should be able to find somewhere that matches your taste and budget.

Most of the major international chains have outposts in Buenos Aires and other major cities, but the number of independent "boutique" hotels has grown over the past few years. These are particularly prevalent in the more fashionable districts of Buenos Aires, such as Palermo Viejo and San Telmo. Wine lodges are an excellent option for those traveling to Mendoza or Salta.

Outside the cities, there are numerous estancias (ranches). These tend to be all-inclusive (full board plus horseback riding excursions) and expensive, but for those wishing to sample rural life and gaucho culture, there is no better option.

Room rates go up and availability goes down during the summer months (December through February) and the winter school holiday in July. If you intend to visit one of the Atlantic coastal resorts during the peak months of January and February, try to book your lodging several months in advance.

Some hotels offer one rate for foreign tourists and a much cheaper one for Argentines. There's nothing you can do about this, but if you do happen to have an Argentine in your party, get them to book all accommodations.

Do not be swayed by the number of stars an accommodation has emblazoned on its facade or website. Many self-proclaimed five-star hotels are nothing of the sort, at least by international standards.

Since January 2017 foreign tourists are entitled to full VAT deduction (21 percent at the time of writing) when paying for hotel services with credit card or via bank transfer.

Admission charges

Admission to many galleries and museums in Argentina is free. Entry for those that do charge is usually less than US$10, with concessions available for students and pensioners. Children (under 12) usually get free admission. Galleries and museums are legally required to be free of charge at least one day a week; that day varies between museums so you may want to plan your visits accordingly.

Budgeting for your trip

The following prices should be taken as an approximate guide.
Accommodations: prices vary throughout the country and according to quality. The north of Argentina offers by far the cheapest accommodations in the country – around US$70 per night for a three-star double room. In Buenos Aires and the south, accommodations are more expensive and a similar room will set you back US$90 or more.
Airport transfer: an authorized taxi or remise from Ezeiza airport into the center of Buenos Aires: US$35. Manuel Tienda León bus service from Ezeiza into the center of Buenos Aires: US$16.
Car rental: (international company) VW Golf: US$100 per day. 4x4 pickup: US$250 per day (prices include insurance, mechanical assistance, and value added tax).
Food: eating out is expensive compared to many other South American countries. A three-course meal in Buenos Aires, including wine, at a good establishment will cost around U$100 for two people.
Petrol: US$1.60 per liter.
Taxis: taxis in Argentina are inexpensive though you may be taken on a "scenic route" if you speak English. Stick to metered taxis which start at about US$1.7. Tips are not expected, though are much appreciated.

Children

As a culture, Argentinians are very family-oriented. It's not uncommon to see entire families out for a late-night weekend dinner with their young children in tow. And of course, that most famous of Argentine cultural offerings, the asado (barbecue), is a get-together that celebrates, above all else, family and fellowship. Visitors will therefore have no problems bringing their children along for the stay. In fact, many locals will be even more inclined to welcome foreigners when they see them with their little ones.

Many high-end hotels offer babysitting services, at an extra charge. But you may find it hard to find a cot available in budget accommodations. Most cinemas, theme parks, national parks, and entertainment venues offer discounts for children, usually around 50 percent of the normal price.

Climate

Argentina, the world's eighth largest country, extends from the deserts of Salta in the north to the glaciers of Patagonia in the south. Most of the country lies in the temperate zone of the southern hemisphere.

The Northeast is humid and subtropical. The Northwest is tropical but has a mild winter. The pampas are temperate. The south has colder temperatures and rain most of the year. The rainfall varies in the humid pampa (which comprises the province of Buenos Aires, and some of the Córdoba and La Pampa provinces) from 99cm (39ins) in the eastern parts to about 51cm (20ins) in the areas near the Andes.

The overpowering heat and humidity of the summer months in Buenos Aires means the city is almost empty during January and February, as the majority of people leave soon after Christmas for the beaches and mountain resorts. Winter (June–Sept) is generally pleasant, although July and August have very cold patches. Torrential rain is also common at this time, but is usually short-lived.

During the summer months (Nov–Mar), the north of the country is one of the hottest parts of Latin America. Many Argentines complain about the heat and humidity, so you'll be most comfortable in light cotton clothing and plenty of sun cream. Argentines are famous for their elegance and style so you may feel out of place and get the odd evil stare if you do not make an effort to dress elegantly, especially when out for dinner in a hotel or restaurant.

If visiting the glaciers in the south, prepare for extreme cold weather. Layers and waterproof jackets are essential.

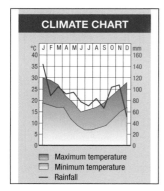

CLIMATE CHART

Maximum temperature
Minimum temperature
Rainfall

Crime and safety

Although cases of violent crime are unlikely to affect tourists, it is best to follow certain precautionary measures. It is inadvisable to walk the streets alone after dark in neighborhoods you are unfamiliar with. Don't flash expensive jewelry, electrical equipment, and expensive watches when walking around large cities, especially in Buenos Aires. Do not take unofficial taxis – always use *remises* or cars that are part of a taxi firm and have a sign reading "Radio Taxi" (see page 307).

To report a crime in Buenos Aires, go to the Comisaría del Turista (Av. Corrientes 436; tel: 0800-999 5000) which is open 24 hours and has English-speaking staff on hand. Alternatively, go to the police station in the area where the incident occurred.

Customs regulations

On entering Argentina you will also be given a customs declaration form. Should you wish to extend your trip past the 90-day limit, you could try leaving the country and returning to get a fresh stamp. This usually works, but is frowned upon if done regularly, and the provision of a stamp is at the discretion of the border guards. When leaving the country you must obtain an exit stamp. Visas for work or study must be obtained prior to your trip from your consulate.

Travelers entering Argentina can bring personal effects, including clothes, jewelry, and professional equipment such as cameras and computers, which value doesn't exceed US$300, without paying duty. In addition, 2 liters of alcohol, 400 cigarettes, and 50 cigars can be brought into the country duty-free.

D

Disabled travelers

Efforts have been made to make buildings more accessible to wheelchair users, such as the recent introduction of ramps in larger cities, but many pavements are still in a bad condition. Very few of the *colectivos* (buses) are *super-bajo* (ultra low), and less than half of the 83 Subte

(subway) stations are accessible to disabled persons. Outside the cities, finding facilities for the disabled is a hit-and-miss affair. Major tourist attractions like Iguazú Falls have made some notable improvements, such as the introduction of ramps and catwalks, making the vast majority of the falls area accessible to disabled travelers.

A few companies specialize in transport and trips for disabled passengers. **Discabus** (tel: 011-4794 4662; http://diskabus.com.ar) run adapted minibuses for wheelchair users, equipped with microphones and guides. The hostel associations, **Red Argentina de Albergues Juveniles** (Florida 835, 3rd floor, Buenos Aires; tel: 011-4511 8723; www.hostels.org.ar), and the **Asociación Argentina de Albergues de la Juventud** (Talchahuano 214, 2nd floor, Buenos Aires; tel: 011-4300 9321) can provide information on access.

E

Eating out

The standard menu in Buenos Aires, and in many other regions too, revolves around the three Ps – *parrilla* (steak), pasta, and pizza. We might also add a fourth P, *postre* or pudding, since Argentines are notoriously sweet-toothed. Empanadas are served everywhere, and in the Northwest, they are a staple. Surprisingly, given the long coastline, many Argentines regard fish as something to be eaten on Good Friday or when there's no meat available.

Restaurants serving international cuisine have become far more prevalent since the turn of the century, particularly in the capital. Trendy Buenos Aires barrios like Palermo Viejo and San Telmo are now chock-a-block with smart sushi restaurants, French-style bistros, Jewish eateries, and even Peruvian-Japanese fusion joints.

Traditional Argentine restaurants come in three flavors: *parrillas*, *bodegones*, and *cantinas*. Parrillas (steakhouses) are ubiquitous and run the gamut from upmarket establishments with prodigious wine lists and bilingual menus to holes in the wall with garden furniture and a binary wine choice (red or white). *Bodegones* and *cantinas* are usually family-run establishments, with a close connection to their neighborhood. Often decorated with football posters and staffed by laconic waiters in tuxedos, these places tend to serve a wide variety of traditional dishes, including, but not restricted to, grilled meat and pasta.

Except for in a few specialist places, vegetarians are tolerated rather than celebrated and will find themselves eating a lot of cheese and pasta.

Restaurants in Argentina open for lunch at noon, though few people sit down to eat before 1pm. In the evening, restaurants start filling up at 9pm and not before, so aiming to arrive at 8.50pm is a good strategy if you want to avoid waiting in line. At the weekends restaurants stay busy into the wee small hours. Many close on Monday. Children and babies are welcome in all traditional restaurants and you should expect everyone from the owner downwards to fuss over them.

Waiters expect to receive a 10 percent tip and are pleasantly surprised if they get more than that. You may notice a surcharge on your bill for *cubiertos*. This is essentially a cover charge, the cost of which varies from place to place.

Electricity

220V/50hz is the standard current throughout the country. Argentina uses the European round two-pin plug and the Australian slanted plugs. Travelers from the UK and US will need to bring an adapter with them.

Embassies and consulates

Foreign embassies in Buenos Aires

Australian Embassy: Villanueva 1400; tel: 011-4779 3500; www.argentina.embassy.gov.au

British Embassy: Dr. Luis Agote 2412, Recoleta; tel: 011-4808 2200; www.gov.uk/world/organisations/british-embassy-buenos-aires

Canadian Embassy: Tagle 2828; tel: 011-4808 1000; www.canadainternational.gc.ca/argentina-argentine/

Embassy of New Zealand: Carlos Pellegrini 1427, 5th Floor; tel: 011-5070 0700; www.mfat.govt.nz/en/countries-and-regions/latin-america/argentina/new-zealand-embassy

Irish Embassy: Av. del Libertador 1068, 6th Floor; tel: 011-4808 5700; www.dfa.ie/irish-embassy/argentina/

US Embassy: Av. Colombia 4300, Palermo; tel: 011-5777 4533; https://ar.usembassy.gov/

Argentine embassies and consulates abroad

Australia
Embassy: John McEwen House, Level 2, 7 National Circuit, Barton, Canberra 2600; tel: (02) 6273 9111; www.ecana.mrecic.gob.ar
Consulate: 44 Market Street, Floor 20, Sydney, NSW; tel: (02) 9262 2993; http://eaust.mrecic.gov.ar/es/node/1338

Canada
Embassy: 81 Metcalfe Street, Suite 700, Ottawa, Ontario, K1P 6K7; tel: (0613) 236 2351; www.ecana.mrecic.gob.ar
Consulate: 2000 Peel Street, 7th floor, suite 710, Montreal, Quebec H3A 2W5; tel: (0514) 842 6582; www.ecana.mrecic.gob.ar/es/content/asistencia-consular-1

Ireland
Embassy: 15 Ailesbury Drive, Ballsbridge, Dublin; tel: (01) 269 1546; www.eirla.mrecic.gov.ar

New Zealand
Embassy: Level 5, 15 Murphy Street, Wellington; tel: (04) 472 8330; www.enzel.mrecic.gov.ar

UK
Embassy: 65 Brook Street, London W1K 4AH; tel: (020) 7318 1300; www.argentine-embassy-uk.org
Consulate: 27 Three Kings Yard, London W1Y 1FL; tel: (020) 7318 1340; www.clond.mrecic.gov.ar

US
Embassy: 1600 New Hampshire Avenue, NW, Washington DC 20009; tel: (202) 238 6400; www.eeeuu.mrecic.gov.ar/
Consulate: 12 West 56th Street, New York, NY 10019; tel: (212) 603 0400; http://cnyor.mrecic.gov.ar/en

Emergencies

General emergencies 91/103
Medical (SAME) 107
Fire 100

Etiquette

Buenos Aires may be a fashionable city, but the culture is an informal, non-conservative one. Still, cultural distinctions do occur. Like in certain European countries, a greeting (whether it's a man and a woman, two women, or two men), involves a kiss on the cheek. In the not-so-unlikely event that a local invites you to his/her home for an *asado*, it is polite to accept, and in turn they will make you feel like part of the family. In most restaurants casual clothing, like shorts, is accepted (especially in summer), but most mid-range bars and restaurants won't allow you in with flip-flops. Do dress conservatively when visiting churches.

F

Festivals and events

The following are just some of the festivals and events that take place in Argentina. Dates vary each year so check with provincial tourist offices (see page 315) for details. For a detailed list of festivals visit www.argentina.gob.ar; for events in Buenos Aires, consult the city government's tourism website at https://turismo.buenosaires.gob.ar/es.

January

Dakar Rally, Argentina. The most challenging rally in the world has been taking place in Argentina (and neighboring countries) since 2009. In 2018, the last stage of the rally was held in Córdoba.

Festival Nacional del Folklore, Cosquín, Córdoba province. Annual folk festival which draws crowds from all over the country with a line-up of top artists from South American and European countries.

Tango en la Usina, Buenos Aires. All month long tango festival in the flagship Usina del Arte cultural centre in La Boca. Tango lessons, concerts, exhibitions, and *milongas* with a live orchestra.

February

Argentina Open. This is Argentina's top tennis event, attracting all of the country's top players along with a host of international stars.

Carnaval. Argentina's carnival takes place mainly in the capital and in Gualeguaychú and Corrientes in the Northeast. There is also a colorful Shrove Tuesday procession in Salta.

Fiesta Nacional de la Chaya, La Rioja. Folk festival which takes its inspiration from pre-Columbian Diaguita legend.

Fiesta Nacional del Puestero, Junín de los Andes. This popular festival celebrates gaucho culture with displays of horsemanship, traditional dance and music, and the chance to sample regional cuisine.

March

Ciudanza, Buenos Aires. A contemporary dance festival featuring free outdoor shows, as well as performances at venues like the Usina del Arte in La Boca.

Festival de la Vendimia, Mendoza. Grape harvest festival culminating in an extravaganza of lights, music, and dancing in an amphitheater set in the Andean foothills.

St Patrick's Day, Mar 17, Buenos Aires. A huge street party takes place in and around the many Irish pubs on Reconquista Street, in the Microcentro.

Fiesta Nacional del Trekking, El Chaltén, Santa Cruz. Second half of the month. Events include a marathon and a bicycle race, as well as team-trekking, horseback riding, and rock-climbing competitions.

April

Festival Internacional de Cine Independiente, Buenos Aires. Latin America's most important independent film festival.

Feria del Libro, Buenos Aires. This three-week-long annual book fair has become one of South America's biggest and most important cultural events.

La Fiesta del Salmón, Camarones. Besides the famous fishing contest, there are performances by local and national music groups, as well as the delicious *Gran Chupín* – a popular free lunch for all participants.

May

Arte BA, Buenos Aires. Contemporary art fair held in the city's sprawling La Rural exhibition complex.

Iguazú in Concert, Iguazú. Children from all over Argentina (as well its neighbors) show off their musical skills during concerts held by the falls.

June

Día de Muerte de Carlos Gardel, Buenos Aires. June 24 marks the death of Argentina's favorite tango hero. A week of events culminates in a pilgrimage to his tomb in the Cementerio de la Chacarita.

A news kiosk in Buenos Aires.

El Año Nuevo patagónico, June 24, San Carlos de Bariloche. Native peoples of Patagonia celebrate the beginning of New Year.

Fiesta Nacional del Folklore Suizo, San Jerónimo Norte, Santa Fe province. A celebration of Swiss culture featuring traditional parades, chocolate tastings, craft expositions, and the election of the beauty queen.

July

Festival Nacional de Tango, La Falda, Córdoba province. Tango aficionados from all over the country come to this tango festival.

Fiesta de San Francisco Solano, July 24, Santiago del Estero. Folk music and dance in the home of the *gato* and *chacarera*.

Festival Nacional e Internacional del Poncho, San Fernando del Valle de Catamarca, Catamarca province. Four days of traditional celebrations.

Exposición de Ganadería, Agricultura e Industria Internacional, Buenos Aires. Known simply as "La Rural," this is Argentina's most important agricultural event, carrying cultural as well as economic significance.

August

Fiesta Nacional de la Nieve, San Carlos de Bariloche. Ski competitions, a snow triathlon, chocolate tasting, parades, and fireworks in Bariloche and at nearby Cerro Catedral.

International Tango Festival and World Cup, Buenos Aires. A two-week cultural feast of concerts, shows, exhibitions, dance lessons, and competitions. A must for tango buffs.

September

Fiesta Nacional del Inmigrante, Oberá, Misiones. Festival celebrating the cultural diversity of this province.

Fiesta del Milagro, Sept 6–15, Salta. Big annual festival in which *salteños* renew their devotion to their two patron saints – "Our Lord of the Miracles" and the "Virgin of the Miracles."

Festival Internacional de Buenos Aires. Organised every two years (next in 2019) by the city's Ministry of Culture, this festival features outdoor performances, workshops, film screenings, and discussions.

October

Semana Musical, Llao Llao, Río Negro. Held in the beautiful Llao Llao Hotel, this festival brings classical music to the Andes.

Oktoberfest, Villa General Belgrano, Córdoba province. German-style beer festival.

Festival de Danza Contemporánea, Buenos Aires. Held in the first half of the month, this 10-day festival celebrates modern dance, with performances and events gracing dozens of venues across the city.

November

Abierto Argentino de Polo, Buenos Aires. The world's premier polo championship, held in the capital's 16,000-capacity Campo Argentino de Polo in Palermo.

Buenos Aires Jazz Festival. This festival features some of the best Argentine and international jazz stars.

Día de la Tradición, Nov 10. A celebration of traditional culture with gaucho displays of horsemanship and enormous *asados* throughout Argentina. The largest festival takes place in San Antonio de Areco.

Festival Internacional de Cine, Mar del Plata. Renowned international film festival.

Fiesta Nacional de la Yerba Mate, Apóstoles, Misiones. Agricultural fair centered around the Argentina custom of drinking yerba mate. Features vintage car parades, sports tournaments, and dance and music presentations.

December

Día del Tango, Dec 11, Buenos Aires. In homage to Carlos Gardel, the day of his birth has been christened "day of the tango." Various tango events take place around the capital.

Argentina Comic-Con, Buenos Aires. International gathering of comic creators and aficionados, plus a celebration of other pop-culture genres including cinema, video games, and music.

H

Health and medical care

Medical services

Health care is generally excellent. In some sections of the country, the hospitals may not have up-to-date equipment, but what is available is adequate for an emergency situation.

A visit to a doctor will cost US$20–50 and cash payment is often expected. Ensure you take out comprehensive travel insurance before traveling to Argentina. In an emergency, go directly to the nearest hospital.

Pharmacies

Many pharmaceutical drugs can be purchased over the counter without a prescription. There is usually a pharmacist on duty, and pharmacists can carry out any injections you are prescribed by a doctor. The pharmacist can also recommend remedies for common ailments, such as colds, stomach disorders, and headaches.

All over the country, pharmacies rotate a 24-hour service. A listing of the ones on duty and nearest to you appears in the local newspaper as "Farmacias de Turno."

Hospitals in Buenos Aires

British Hospital: Perdriel 74; tel: 011-4309 6400; www.hospitalbritanico.org.ar
German Hospital: Pueyrredón 1640; tel: 011-4827 7000; www.hospitaleman.org.ar
Dental Hospital (Hospital Odontológico Dr. Ramón Carrillo): Sanchez de Bustamante 2529; tel: 011-4805 5521; www.buenosaires.gob.ar/hospitalcarrillo
Eye Hospital Santa Lucía (Hospital Oftalmológico Santa Lucía): Av. San Juan 2021; tel: 011-4941 5555; www.hospitalsantalucia.com.ar

I

Internet

Internet cafés are dying out as Wi-Fi becomes more prevalent, although this is more true of Buenos Aires than cities and towns in the provinces. Most hotels offer Wi-Fi, though it's often quite slow, and the signal may not reach the guest rooms. All metro stations in Buenos Aires now have free Wi-Fi access points.

L

Laundry

Laundry services are usually readily available, especially since many people do not own washing machines. Self-service places are unheard of: you leave your laundry and collect it when it has been cleaned. LaveRap (www.laverap.com) is a nationwide laundry chain which is very dependable. Some of them also do dry cleaning. Laundry is either charged by weight or itemized; either way it will be more economical than having it done by your hotel.

LGBTQ travelers

Argentina is rightly considered one of the most LGBTQ-friendly countries in South America. Buenos Aires has become a major global destination for LGBTQ visitors in recent years. The city offers many services and activities directed towards the community, including themed circuits of the city and increasingly popular gay tango and *milonga* nights.

Buenos Aires was the first city in South America to grant gay and lesbian couples the right to a civil partnership union, allowing them to have the same legal rights as heterosexual couples.

In 2012, the right to change gender legally was granted.

Although the capital is generally accepting of homosexuality and signs of affection in public, the rest of the country does lag behind a bit and prejudice may be more prevalent in smaller towns and the countryside. For a gay guide to Argentina, visit www.thegayguide.com.ar.

M

Media

The local papers are *La Nación, Clarín, Ámbito Financiero, La Razón, Crónica, Diario Popular*, and *Página 12* (all in Spanish). There are newspaper and magazine stands on almost every city-center street corner, where foreign papers and magazines can also be found.

There are five network television stations and cable TV is widely available. Many of the programs are bought in from the US and Europe and dubbed into Spanish. A few are in English with Spanish subtitles.

There are numerous radio stations, ranging from rock to tango. Radio Aspen 102.3 FM offers a good selection of international music. You can listen to many radio stations online at www.radioarg.com/.

Fileteado signs are a common sight in Buenos Aires.

Money

Although inflation has picked up again, Argentina is still relatively cheap for foreign tourists, especially those from Western Europe and the US. There are currently two dollar exchange rates in Argentina: the official one used by banks and *casas de cambio* (bureaux de change) and the *dólar blue* (blue dollar) offered by unofficial traders. Both rates can be checked daily on the website of the national newspaper *La Nación* (www. lanacion.com.ar). Since December 2015, when restrictions in dollar purchase and sale were scrapped, the rates differ only slightly. Unofficial operators known as *arbolitos* (little trees) also offer their exchange services, but are best avoided as the risk of getting false notes is greater.

Casas de cambio (bureaux de change) can be found around Plaza San Martín and Lavalle in Buenos Aires. American Express at Arenales 707, near Plaza San Martín, also changes currency and traveler's checks.

Tipping

A ten percent tip is usual in restaurants. Those located in more touristy areas may add this to the bill in the form of a service charge. Taxi drivers do not expect tips but they are appreciated.

Opening hours

From Monday to Friday, the business hours are 9am–7pm (large shopping centers usually stay open seven days a week until 10pm), and the banking hours 10am–3pm. In most of the country outside Buenos Aires, the stores open 9am–1pm and 4–7pm, almost invariably closing for the siesta, although local hours can vary somewhat.

Photography

Take care about where you take photographs. Sensitive border areas and all military installations, including many civilian airports, are no-go areas for cameras – keep a look out for signs. The same is true of synagogues and Jewish community centers.

Postal services

Offices of Correo Argentino (www. correoargentino.com.ar), the national post office, are located in all major towns and cities, with many in Buenos Aires alone.

Public holidays

The summer vacation season, when internal transportation and hotels are heavily booked, runs from January through March. The middle two weeks of July are the school winter vacation, which is also very busy.

Government agencies and banks close on public holidays. With the exception of Christmas, New Year's Day, May 25, July 9, and December 8, holidays are observed on the closest Monday to allow for long weekends.

In addition to national holidays, there are many provincial festivals around the country, which are celebrated with local folklore customs, music, and dancing (see page 311).

Religious services

Like the rest of South America, Argentina is a predominantly Roman Catholic country. The country's main cathedral is the **Catedral Metropolitana** (Rivadavia and San Martín; Mon–Fri 7.30am–6.30pm, Sat–Sun 9am–6.45pm; www.catedralbuenosaires.org.ar) in Buenos Aires.

Argentina is home to the largest Jewish community in South America. Much of Jewish life in Buenos Aires centers around the Once district, where there are several synagogues, including **Yesod Hadat** (Lavalle 2449; www. amia.org.ar), which was founded in 1932. Once also has a Jewish cultural center, which hosts concerts and lectures, and a high school, located at Sarmiento 2233. Argentina's oldest synagogue, the **Congregacion Israelita de la Republica Argentina** (Libertad 769; www.templolibertad.org.ar), houses a small Jewish museum (Museo Judío Buenos Aires; Mon–Fri 11am–5pm; http://museojudio.org. ar/) with a good collection of photographs and Jewish ritual objects.

Buenos Aires is home to the largest mosque in Latin America, donated by the late King Fahd of Saudi Arabia and situated within the **Centro Cultural Rey Fahd** (Av. Bullrich 55 and Cerviño; tel: 011-4899 1144/0201; www.ccislamicorey-fahd.org.ar). The center also houses a school and a library.

Shopping

Frequent peso devaluations resulted in Argentina gaining a reputation for being a cheap place for foreigners to shop. The reputation persists, but thanks to years of steady inflation, the reality these days is very different. Only products like wine and tobacco are consistently cheaper here than in, say, North America. Electronic goods, and anything else that must be imported, are substantially more expensive here than they are elsewhere.

The government runs a tax-refund scheme for foreign tourists on any Argentine-made product purchased for over 70 ARS (about $3.50) from an outlet with a "Global Refund" sticker in its window. You will need to obtain an

⊙ Public holidays

New Year's Day: January 1
Good Friday: Variable
Labor Day: May 1
Rememberance for Truth and Justice Day: March 24
Malvinas (Falklands) Day: April 2
First National Government Day: May 25
National Flag Day: June 20
Independence Day: July 9
Anniversary of the Death of José de San Martín: August 17
Respect for Cultural Diversity Day: October 12
National Sovereignty Day: November 20
Annunciation Day: December 8
Christmas Day: December 25

invoice and appropriate form at the time of purchase. These should be presented at customs when leaving the country. The *puesto de pago* will then reimburse the 21 percent sales tax. For details, consult www.globalblue.com.

The most popular souvenirs brought from Argentina are fine wines, leather products, and regional handicrafts, including alpaca wool clothing as well as other finely crafted textiles.

Student travelers

Student travelers obtaining an ISIC card before departure may be entitled to discounts on museums, hostel accommodations, and bus travel (see www.isic.com.ar for details).

Argentina's travel agency, Almundo (see page 316) has up-to-date information about flights, coach fares, and tours, and offers discounts through its website, http://almundo.com.ar.

T

Telephones

Since the telecommunications service was privatized in 1989, it has been primarily split between Telecom (Personal) and Telefónica de Argentina (Movistar). Claro is the country's third largest telecom company. A fourth one, Nextel, was founded in 2015, while the new kid on the block, Catel, started offering services in 2018. Prices have fluctuated and, although they are becoming more competitive, telephone calls from Argentina are still among the most expensive in the world. However, the service is becoming much more efficient and the line quality is high.

International and national calls can be made from *locutorios* ("call shops") throughout the country.

Local calls can be made from the blue phone booths in the street. Phones accept coins or phone cards, which can be bought from *kioscos* (newsstands).

The cheapest way to use a cell phone if coming from abroad is to bring a handset with you and buy a SIM card once in Argentina. These cost around US$14 and can be

purchased at mobile phone stores in cities around the country.

Dialing codes

Country code (if dialing Argentina from abroad): 54

Regional codes Don't dial the area code if calling the same area you are in. If calling from abroad, drop the initial 0.

Bahía Blanca 0291
Bariloche 0294
Buenos Aires 011
Comodoro Rivadavia 0297
Córdoba 0351
Corrientes 0379
El Bolsón 02944
El Calafate 02902
El Chaltén 02962
Esquel 02945
Jujuy 0388
La Plata 0221
La Rioja 03821
Mar del Plata 0223
Mendoza 0261
Merlo 0220
Neuquén 0299
Posadas 0376
Puerto Iguazú 03757
Resistencia 0362
Río Gallegos 02966
Río Grande 02964
Rosario 0341
Salta 0387
San Fernando 03833
San Juan 0264
San Luis 0266
San Martín de los Andes 02972
Santa Fe 0342
Santiago del Estero 0385
Trevelín 02945
Tucumán 0381
Ushuaia 02901
Viedma 02920
Villa Gesell 02255
International codes
Dial 00, then the country code, followed by the number.
Australia 61
Bolivia 591
Brazil 55
Canada 1
Chile 56
France 33
Germany 49
Ireland, Republic of 353
New Zealand 64
UK 44
Uruguay 598
USA 1

Time zone

Argentina stays at -3 GMT all year round.

Toilets

Apart from the odd exception in the center of Buenos Aires, public toilets are a rarity. Toilets in shopping malls are the best place to head for as they are often spotless. Bars and cafés will usually let you use their toilet facilities, although it is best to bring your own toilet paper as this is often absent. In airports and bus stations there is usually an attendant who keeps the toilets clean for a small fee of around one peso per person. In small towns and rural areas toilet paper is often disposed of in a waste-paper basket (rather than flushed).

Toilets are referred to as *baños* and men should follow the signs that read *hombres, caballeros, señores*, or *varones* and women *mujeres, damas*, or *señoras*.

Tourist information offices

Buenos Aires
Secretaría de Turismo de la Nación
Av. Santa Fe 883, Ground Floor
Tue–Sun 10am–6pm
Tel: 011 4312 2232
www.turismo.gov.ar
The Argentine state tourist board.
Oficina de Información Turística Centro
Paseo 107 corner with Av 2 and 3
Villa Gessel
Tel: 011 478 062
Tourist Information Point
Ezeiza Airport
Tel: 011 4480 0224
Administración de Parques Nacionales
Carlos Pellegrini 657
Tel: 011-3984 7100
www.parquesnacionales.gob.ar
Provides information on Argentina's many national parks.

Addresses to all other offices in the metropolitan area, as well as across the country, can be found at www.argentina.travel

Tour operators and travel agents

Insight Guides
Insight Guides (www.insightguides.com/holidays) offers holidays to numerous destinations around the globe, including Argentina. You can book trips, transfers, and a range of exciting experiences through our local experts, taking in wild Patagonia, the Great Lakes, and much more.

Argentina

Almundo, Florida 825, Buenos Aires; tel: 0810 666 0630; http://almundo.com.ar
One of the largest agencies, primarily aimed at students, but there's no age limit. Bright and cheerful office with noticeboard brimming with items for sale, travel news, and messages from travelers seeking companions.

Cosmopolitan Viajes, Mar del Plata, Alberti; https://cosmopolitanviajes.com.ar/
Organizes trips to popular destinations in Argentina and neighboring countries.

Eurotur, Viamonte 486, Buenos Aires; tel: 011-4312 6077; www.eurotur.com.ar
Tours, transportation, and accommodations throughout Argentina for individuals and groups. English spoken, highly professional, and recommended.

Eves Turismo, Tucumán 702, Buenos Aires; tel: 0800-345 3837; www.eves.com
Helpful and efficient staff can advise you on travel both within Argentina and abroad.

Kallpa Tours, Tucuman 861, 2nd Floor, Buenos Aires; tel: 011-5278 8010; www.kallpatour.com

A young Argentine in Buenos Aires.

Branches in Salta and Ushuaia. Specializes in wine and cultural tours, trekking, and horseback riding.

Nervous Waters, Fernando de las Carreras, Buenos Aires; tel: 011-4801 1008; www.nervouswaters.com
A Patagonian company specializing in fishing trips, with offices in the US and the UK.

Puna Expeditions, Agustín Usandivaras 230, 4400 Salta; tel: 0387-416 9313; www.punaexpeditions.com.ar
Local agency specializing in adventure tours and trekking trips in and around Salta.

Rumbo Sur Excursiones, San Martín 350, Ushuaia; tel: 02901-421139; www.rumbosur.com.ar
Runs catamaran trips to Isla de los Lobos, local penguin colonies, and Harberton.

Swan Turismo, Cerrito 822, 3rd, 4th, 5th, 6th, and 9th floors, Buenos Aires; tel: 011-7078 7926; www.swan-turismo.com.ar
A long-established and high-quality specialist travel agency that organizes trips to a variety of destinations throughout the country.

Tolkeyen Servicios Maritímos, 17 de Octubre 279, Ushuaia; tel: 02901-437073; www.tolkeyenpatagonia.com
Boat excursions to Isla de los Lobos and penguin colonies.

Australia

Adventure Associates, Po Box 246, Blackheath NSW 2785, Australia; tel: (02) 6355 2022; www.adventureassociates.com
Established specialist tour operator, offering tailored trips to numerous destinations in Argentina.

UK

Dragoman Overland, Camp Green, Debenham, Stowmarket Suffolk, IP14 6LA; tel: 01728 861 133; www.dragoman.co.uk
Specializes in South American overland trips.

Jagged Globe, The Foundry Studios, 45 Mowbray Street, Sheffield, S3 8EN; tel: 0114 276 3322; www.jagged-globe.co.uk
Specializes in climbing expeditions, including trips to Argentina and other South American countries.

Journey Latin America, 401 King Street, London, W6 9NJ; tel: 020 8600 1881; www.journeylatinamerica.co.uk

Long-established company offering non-escorted trips throughout Latin America.

US

Anglatin, 4800 SW Meadows Road, Suite 300 Lake Oswego, OR 97035; tel: 503-534-654; www.anglatin.com
Specialized travel agency in Oregon offering trips to destinations throughout Latin America.

Quark Expeditions, 1019 Post Road, Darien, CT 06820; tel 888 979 4073 or 1 802 490 1843; www.quarkexpeditions.com
A wide range of fully inclusive cruises from Ushuaia to Antarctica and the South Atlantic Islands.

Wilderness Travel, 1102 Ninth Street, Berkeley, CA 94710; tel: 1 800 368 2794; www.wildernesstravel.com
Organizes trips throughout Argentina and Chile, including walking trips through Patagonia.

V

Visas and passports

Citizens of Western Europe, the US, Canada, South Africa, Australia, and New Zealand do not need a visa for trips of up to 90 days. A valid passport is required and a landing card must be filled in on arrival.

W

Weights and measures

The metric system is used to calculate distances and weights.

Women travelers

Women travelers shouldn't experience any problems in Argentina, although they are likely to receive plenty of male attention. While some may find this attention annoying, it is unlikely to ever be aggressive. The *piropo*, a flattering comment made in the street, traditionally by a man to a woman, has now become something of a national custom. This is often little more than a whistle, although the more poetic may declare their undying love for you while passing you in the street.

LANGUAGE

GENERAL

Of the many versions of Spanish in South America, the Argentine version is among the most difficult to understand. However, it is much better to know a little Spanish when you arrive. English might be spoken at major hotels and by quite a few Argentinians in Buenos Aires, but don't count on it outside the capital.

PRONUNCIATION AND GRAMMAR TIPS

Argentinians tend to use a local vocabulary with little resemblance to classical Spanish, while the local accent imposes a soft "j" sound on the "ll" and "y" and most people speak very rapidly without enunciating clearly. At the same time, when using the second person familiar, Argentines use the form "vos" instead of the more common "tú". (Note also that in Latin American Spanish the plural form of you is "ustedes" rather than "vosotros," as used in Spain.) The verb form used with "vos" places the accent on the last, rather than the penultimate syllable (for example, "¿que hacÉs?" instead of "¿quÉ hAces?" – what are you doing?).

BASICS

Yes *Sí*
No *No*
Thank you *Gracias*
You're welcome *De nada/Por nada*
Okay *Está bien*
Please *Por favor*
Excuse me (to get attention) *¡Perdón!/¡Por favor!*
Excuse me (to get through a crowd) *¡Permiso!*
Excuse me (sorry) *Perdóneme*

Wait a minute! *¡Un momento!*
Please help me (formal) *Por favor, ayúdame*
Certainly *¡Claro!/¡Claro que sí!/¡Por cierto!*
Can I help you? (formal) *¿Puedo ayudarle?*
Can you show me...? *¿Puede mostrarme...?*
I'm lost *Estoy perdido(a)*
I'm sorry *Lo siento*
I don't know *No sé*
I don't understand *No entiendo*
Do you speak English/French/German? (formal) *¿Habla inglés/francés/alemán?*
Could you speak more slowly, please? *¿Puede hablar más despacio, por favor?*
Could you repeat that, please? *¿Puede repetirlo, por favor?*
here/there *aquí* (place where), *acá* (motion to)/*allí, allá, ahí* (near you)
What? *¿Qué?/¿Cómo?*
When? *¿Cuándo?*
Why? *¿Por qué?*
Where? *¿Dónde?*
Who? *¿Quién(es)?*
How? *¿Cómo?*
Which? *¿Cuál?*
How much/how many? *¿Cuánto?/¿Cuántos?*
Do you have...? *¿Hay...?*
How long? *¿Cuanto tiempo?*
Big, bigger *Grande, más grande*
Small, smaller *Chico, más chico*
I want.../I would like.../I need... *Quiero.../Quisiera.../Necesito...*
Where is the lavatory (men's/women's)? *¿Dónde está el baño(de caballeros/de damas)?*
Which way is it to...? *¿Como se va a...?*

GREETINGS

Hello! *¡Hola!*
Hello *Buenos días*
Good afternoon/night *Buenas tardes/noches*

Goodbye/see you later *Chau/¡Adios!/Hasta luego*
My name is... *Me llamo...*
What is your name? (formal) *¿Cómo se llama usted?*
Mr/Miss/Mrs *Señor/Señorita/Señora*
Pleased to meet you *¡Encantado(a)!/Mucho gusto*
I am English/American/Canadian/Irish/Scottish/Australian *Soy inglés(a)/norteamericano(a)/canadiense/irlandés(a)/escocés(a)/australiano(a)*
Do you speak English? (formal) *¿Habla inglés?*
How are you? (formal/informal) *¿Cómo está? ¿Qué tal?*
Fine, thanks *Muy bien, gracias*
Take care (informal) *¡Cuidate!*

TELEPHONE CALLS

May I use your telephone to make a local call? *¿Puedo usar su teléfono para hacer una llamada local?*
Hello (on the phone) *¡Hola!*
May I speak to...? *¿Puedo hablar con... (name), por favor?*
Sorry, he/she isn't in *Lo siento, no se encuentra*
Can he/she call you back? *¿Puede devolver la llamada?*
Yes, he/she can reach me at... *Sí, él/ella puede llamarme a [number]*
I'll try again later *Voy a intentar más tarde*
Can I leave a message? *¿Puedo dejar un mensaje?*
Please tell him/her I called *Por favor avisarle que llamé*
Hold on *Un momento, por favor*
Can you speak up, please? *¿Puede hablar más fuerte, por favor?*

IN THE HOTEL

Do you have a vacant room? *¿Tiene una habitación disponible?*

I have a reservation *Tengo una reserva*
I'd like... *Quisiera...*
a single/double (with double bed)/a room with twin beds *una habitación individual (sencilla)/una habitación matrimonial/una habitación doble*
for one night/two nights *por una noche/dos noches*
ground floor/first floor/top floor room *una habitación en la planta baja/en el primer piso/ en el último piso*
with a sea view *con vista al mar*
How much is it? *¿Cuánto cuesta?/ ¿Cuánto sale?*
Do you accept credit cards/traveler's checks/dollars? *¿Se aceptan tarjetas de crédito/cheques de viajeros/dólares?*
What time is breakfast/lunch/dinner? *¿A qué hora es el desayuno/ almuerzo/la cena?*
Come in! *¡Pase!, ¡Adelante!*
bath/bathroom *el baño*
dining room *el comedor*
elevator/lift *el ascensor*
key *la llave*
push/pull *empuje/tire*
safety deposit box *la caja de seguridad*
soap *el jabón*
shampoo *el champú*
shower *la ducha*
toilet paper *el papel higiénico*
towel *la toalla*

IN THE RESTAURANT

I'd like to book a table *Quisiera reservar una mesa, por favor*
Do you have a table for...? *¿Tiene una mesa para...?*
I have a reservation *Tengo una reserva*
breakfast/lunch/dinner *desayuno/ almuerzo/cena*
I'm a vegetarian *Soy vegetariano(a)*
May we have the menu? *¿Puede traernos la carta (or el menú)?*
wine list *la carta de vinos*
What would you recommend? *¿Qué recomienda?*
special of the day *plato del día/sugerencia del chef*
main course *segundo/plato principal*
coffee... *un café*
with milk *con leche*
strong *fuerte*
small/large *pequeño/grande*
tea... *té*
with lemon/milk *con limón/leche*
hot chocolate *chocolate caliente*

fresh orange juice *jugo de naranja natural*
soft drink *gaseosa*
mineral water (still/carbonated) *agua mineral (sin gas/con gas)*
with/without ice *con/sin hielo*
cover charge *precio del cubierto*
a bottle/half a bottle *una botella/ media botella*
a glass of red/white/rosé wine *una copa de vino tinto/rosado/blanco*
beer *una cerveza*
I need a receipt, please *Necesito un recibo, por favor*
Keep the change *Está bien/ Quédese con el vuelto*
Cheers! *¡Salud!*

La carne (meat)

crudo *raw*
jugoso(a) *rare*
a punto *medium*
bien hecho *well done*
a la brasa/a la parrilla *charcoal grilled*
a la plancha *grilled*
al horno *baked*
ahumado(a) *smoked*
albóndigas *meat balls*
asado(a)/horneado(a) *roasted*
aves *poultry*
cerdo/chancho/puerco *pork*
chivito *goat*
chorizo *Spanish-style sausage*
conejo *rabbit*
frito(a) *fried*
hamburguesa *hamburger*
jamón *ham*
lengua *tongue*
lomito *tenderloin*
milanesa *breaded and fried thin cut of meat*
morcilla *blood sausage*
pato *duck*
pavo *turkey*
pechuga *breast*
piernas *legs*
pollo *chicken*
riñones *kidneys*
salchichas/panchos *sausages or hot dogs*
ternera *veal*

Pescado/mariscos (fish/seafood)

almejas *clams*
anchoa *anchovy*
atún *tuna*
calamares *squid*
camarones *shrimp*
centolla *kingcrab*
langosta *lobster*
langostinos *prawns*

lenguado *sole or flounder*
mariscos *shellfish*
mejillones *mussels*
ostras *oysters*
pulpo *octopus*
salmón *salmon*
sardinas *sardines*
trucha *trout*
vieiras *scallops*

Vegetales (vegetables)

ajo *garlic*
alcaucil *artichoke*
arvejas *peas*
batata *sweet potato*
berenjena *eggplant/aubergine*
brócoli *broccoli*
calabaza *pumpkin or yellow squash*
cebolla *onion*
chauchas *green beans*
choclo *corn (on the cob)*
coliflor *cauliflower*
ensalada mixta *mixed salad*
espárrago *asparagus*
hongos, champiñones *mushrooms*
lechuga *lettuce*
papa *potato*
pepino *cucumber*
porotos *Lima beans*
puerro *leeks*
remolacha *beets/beetroot*
repollo *cabbage*
zanahorias *carrots*
zapallo *yellow squash*
zapallito *green squash*
zapallito largo *zucchini/courgette*

Frutas (fruit)

banana *banana*
cereza *cherry*
ciruela *plum*
dátil *date*
durazno *peach*
frambuesa *raspberry*
frutilla *strawberry*
higo *fig*
lima *lime*
limón *lemon*
mandarina *tangerine*
manzana *apple*
naranja *orange*
palta *avocado*
papaya *papaya*
pera *pear*
pomelo *grapefruit*
sandía *watermelon*
uvas *grapes*

Miscellaneous

arroz *rice*
azúcar *sugar*
empanada *savory turnover*

fideos *spaghetti*
helado *ice cream*
huevos (revueltos/fritos/hervidos) *eggs (scrambled/fried/boiled)*
manteca *butter*
mermelada *jam*
mostaza *mustard*
pan *bread*
pan integral *wholewheat bread*
pan tostado/tostadas *toast*
pimienta negra *black pepper*
queso *cheese*
sal *salt*
salsa picante *spicy sauce*
sandwich *sandwich*
sopa/crema *soup/cream soup*
tortilla *omelet*

TOURIST ATTRACTIONS/ TERMS

aguas termales *hot springs*
artesanía *handicrafts*
capilla *chapel*
catedral *cathedral*
cervecería *beer hall/pub*
convento *convent*
disco/discoteca boliche *disco or club*
galería *gallery*
glaciar *glacier*
iglesia *church*
isla *island*
lago *lake*
laguna *lagoon*
mar *sea*
mercado *market*
mirador *viewpoint*
montaña *mountain*
monumento *monument*
oficina de turismo *tourist office*
parque *park*
pileta *swimming pool*
playa *beach*
plaza *town square*
puente *bridge*
río *river*
torre *tower*

ROAD SIGNS

autopista *freeway*
carretera *highway, road*
despacio *slow*
entrada prohibida *no entry*
estacionamiento *parking lot*
fuera de servicio *not in service*
gomería *tire repair shop*
no estacione/prohibido estacionar *no parking*
no pare *no stopping here*
¡ojo! *watch out!*
ruta *highway*
salida *exit*

semáforo *traffic light*
sin salida *no exit*

DRIVING

Where can I rent a car? *¿Dónde puedo alquilar un coche?*
Is mileage included? *¿Está incluido el kilometraje?*
comprehensive insurance *seguros comprensivos*
How do I get to...? *¿Cómo se llega a...?*
Turn right/left *Cruzar (or girar, doblar) hacia la derecha/izquierda*
at the next corner/street *en la próxima esquina/calle*
Go straight ahead *Siga derecho*
Where can I find...? *¿Dónde hay...?*
Where is the nearest...? *¿Dónde está el/la... más cerca?*
driver's license *licencia de conducir/ manejar*
service/gasoline station *estación de servicio*
My car won't start *Mi coche no arranca*
My car is overheating *Mi coche está recalentando*
My car has broken down *Mi coche se rompió/no anda*

TRAVELING

airline *línea aérea*
airport *aeropuerto*
arrivals/departures *llegadas/salidas*
bus (urban) *bus colectivo*
bus (long-distance) *bus micro/ omnibus*
bus stop *parada (de colectivo/micro)*
bus terminal *terminal de pasajeros*
car *coche/automóvil*
car rental *alquiler de coche*
ferry *ferry*
first class/second class *primera clase/segunda clase, clase de turista*
flight *vuelo*
luggage, bag(s) *equipaje, valija(s)*
Next stop please *(for buses) La próxima parada, por favor*
one-way ticket *boleto de ida*
platform *el andén*
ship *barco*
subway *Metro/subterráneo/Subte*
taxi *taxi*

Terms for directions

a la derecha *on the right*
a la izquierda *on the left*
abajo de *under*
adelante de *in front of*
al lado de *beside*

alrededor de *around*
arriba/abajo *above/below*
atrás de *behind*
avenida (Av) *avenue*
calle *street*
cerca de *near*
cruce con/con *at the junction of (two streets)*
cruce hacia la izquierda/la derecha *turn to the left/right*
derecho *straight ahead*
edificio (Edif) *building*
en *in, on, at*
en la parte de atrás *in the rear area (as in behind a building)*
encima de *on top of*
entre *between*
esquina (Esq) *corner*
PH – penthouse/PB – planta baja/ PA – planta alta/mezanina/sótano *penthouse/ground floor/upper floor (of two)/mezzanine/basement*
residencia (Res) *small pension*
una cuadra *a block*

AIRPORT OR TRAVEL AGENCY

customs and immigration *aduana y migraciones*
travel/tour agency *agencia de viajes/ de turismo*
ticket *boleto pasaje*
I would like to purchase a ticket for... *Quisiera comprar un boleto (pasaje) para...*
When is the next/last flight/departure for...? *¿Cuándo es el próximo/ último vuelo/para...?*
What time does the plane/bus/ boat/ferry [leave/return?] *¿A qué hora [sale/regresa] el avión/el autobús/la lancha/el ferry?*
What time do I have to be at the airport? *¿A qué hora tengo que_estar en el aeropuerto?*
Is the tax included? *¿Se incluye el impuesto?*
What is included in the price? *¿Qué está incluido en el precio?*
departure tax *el impuesto de salida*
I would like a seat in first class/ business class/tourist class *Quisiera un asiento en primera clase/ejecutivo/ clase de turista*
lost-luggage office *oficina de reclamos*
on time *a tiempo*
late *atrasado*
I need to change my ticket *Necesito cambiar mi boleto*
How long is the flight? *¿Cuánto tiempo dura el vuelo?*
Is this seat taken? *¿Está ocupado este asiento?*

Is this the stop for...? *¿Es ésta la parada para...?*

Help! *¡Socorro! ¡Auxilio!*
Stop! *¡Pare!*
Watch out! *¡Cuidado! ¡Ojo!*
I've had an accident *He tenido un accidente/Sufrí un accidente*
Call a doctor *Llame a un médico*
Call an ambulance *Llame una ambulancia*
Call the... *Llame a...*
...police *la policía* (for minor accidents)
...transit police *la policía de tránsito* (for traffic accidents)
...the fire brigade *los bomberos*
This is an emergency, where is a telephone? *Esto es una emergencia. ¿Dónde hay un teléfono?*
Where is the nearest hospital? *¿Dónde queda el hospital más cercano?*
I want to report an assault/a robbery *Quisiera reportar un asalto/un robo*
Thank you very much for your help *Muchísimas gracias por su ayuda*

Health

shift duty pharmacy *farmacia de turno*
hospital/clinic *hospital/clínica*
I need a doctor/dentist *Necesito un médico/dentista (odontólogo)*
I don't feel well *Me siento mal*
I am sick *Estoy enfermo(a)*
It hurts here *Duele aquí*
I have a headache/stomachache/cramps *Tengo dolor de cabeza/de estómago/de vientre*
I feel dizzy *Me siento mareado(a)*
Do you have (something for)...? *¿Tiene (algo para)...?*
a cold/flu *resfrío/gripe*
diarrhea *diarrea*
constipation *estreñimiento*
fever *fiebre*
aspirin *aspirina*
heartburn *acidez*
insect/mosquito bites *picaduras de insectos/mosquitos*

What time do you open/close? *¿A qué hora abre/cierra?*
Open/closed *Abierto/cerrado*
I'd like... *Quisiera...*
I'm just looking *Sólo estoy mirando, gracias*
How much does it cost? *¿Cuánto cuesta/sale?*
It doesn't fit *No queda bien*

Do you have it in another color? *¿Tiene en otro color?*
Do you have it in another size? *¿Tiene en otro talle?*
smaller/larger *más chico/más grande*

Shops and services

antiques shop *antigüedades*
bakery *panadería*
bank *banco*
barber shop *peluquería*
bookstore *librería*
butcher shop *carnicería*
cake shop *pastelería*
currency exchange *bureau casa de cambio*
delicatessen *delicatessen*
department store *tienda por departamentos*
fish shop *pescadería*
florist *florista*
fruit shop *frutería*
jewelers *joyería*
laundromat *lavadero*
library *biblioteca*
market *mercado*
newsstand *kiosco*
post office *correos*
shoe repair shop/shoe store *zapatero/zapatería*
shopping center *centro commercial/ "shoppings"*
small grocery store *almacén*
stationers *papelería*
supermarket *supermercado, autoservicio*
toy store *juguetería*
vegetable shop *verdulería*

light/dark *claro/oscuro*
red *rojo/colorado*
yellow *amarillo*
blue *azul*
brown *marrón*
black *negro*
white *blanco*
cream *crema*
beige *beige*
green *verde*
wine *bordó*
gray *gris*
orange *naranja*
pink *rosa*

1 *uno*
2 *dos*
3 *tres*
4 *cuatro*
5 *cinco*
6 *seis*
7 *siete*
8 *ocho*
9 *nueve*
10 *diez*
11 *once*
12 *doce*
13 *trece*
14 *catorce*
15 *quince*
16 *dieciséis*
17 *diecisiete*
18 *dieciocho*
19 *diecinueve*
20 *veinte*
21 *veintiuno*
22 *veintidos*
25 *veinticinco*
30 *treinta*
40 *cuarenta*
50 *cincuenta*
60 *sesenta*
70 *setenta*
80 *ochenta*
90 *noventa*
100 *cien*
101 *ciento uno*
102 *ciento dos*
200 *doscientos*
300 *trescientos*
400 *cuatrocientos*
500 *quinientos*
600 *seiscientos*
700 *setecientos*
800 *ochocientos*
900 *novecientos*
1,000 *mil*
2,000 *dos mil*
10,000 *diez mil*
100,000 *cien mil*
1,000,000 *un millón*

morning *la mañana*
afternoon *la tarde*
late afternoon *la tardecita*
evening *la noche*
last night *anoche*
yesterday *ayer*
today *hoy*
tonight *esta noche*
tomorrow *mañana*
now *ahora*
early *temprano*
late *tarde*
a minute *un minuto*
an hour *una hora*
half an hour *media hora*
a day *un día*
a week *una semana*
a month *un mes*
a year *un año*

weekend *fin de semana*
holiday *día feriado*

Months

January *enero*
February *febrero*
March *marzo*
April *abril*
May *mayo*
June *junio*
July *julio*
August *agosto*
September *septiembre*
October *octubre*
November *noviembre*
December *diciembre*

Days of the week

Monday *lunes*
Tuesday *martes*
Wednesday *miércoles*
Thursday *jueves*
Friday *viernes*
Saturday *sábado*
Sunday *domingo*

SEASONS

spring *primavera*
summer *verano*
fall/autumn *otoño*
winter *invierno*

TIME

at nine o'clock *a las nueve*
at a quarter past ten *a las diez y cuarto*
at half past one/one thirty *a la una y media*
at a quarter to two *a las dos menos cuarto*
at midday/noon *a mediodía*
at midnight *a medianoche*
NOTE: Times are usually followed by *de la mañana* (in the morning) or *de la tarde* (in the afternoon). Transport schedules, however, are usually given using the 24-hour clock.

FURTHER READING

HISTORY

Argentina: 1516–1987 by David Rock. The best English-language history book on Argentina.

The Argentina Reader edited by Gabriela Nouzeilles and Graciela Montaldo. A diverse collection of articles, songs, comic strips, essays, and poems from colonial times to the present day.

Buenos Aires: A Cultural and Literary Companion by Jason Wilson. A brilliant description of the history and cultural life of the Argentine capital.

Gauchos and the Vanishing Frontier by Richard W. Slatta. Fascinating account of the cowboys who roamed the pampas hundreds of years before the Wild West existed.

Peron: A Biography by Joseph A. Page. The compelling story of the most remarkable politician in Argentina's history.

The Real Odessa: Smuggling the Nazis to Perón's Argentina by Uki Goni. The shocking and largely untold story of the Perón government's involvement in bringing Nazi fugitives to Argentina.

The Voyage of the Beagle by Charles Darwin. Abridged journal of Darwin's five-year voyage around the world, covering natural history and civil war in Argentina. A classic.

FICTION

Blow-up and Other Stories by Julio Cortazar. A collection of short and often shocking masterpieces from one of Argentina's greatest modern writers.

Ghosts by César Aira. A day in the life of a construction worker's family, who are squatting in a haunted building.

The Invention of Morel by Adolfo Bioy Casares. 1940 novella of suspense and unlikely romance.

Kiss of the Spider Woman by Manuel Puig. Story of two men imprisoned under the dictatorship. Adapted into a film.

Labyrinths by Jorge Luis Borges. Seminal short stories and other writings from Argentina's greatest author.

My Father's Ghost is Climbing in the Rain by Patricio Pron. A largely autobiographical account of the shadow cast over one man's family by the 1970s dictatorship.

On Heroes and Tombs by Ernesto Sabato. Complex and sad tale of a tormented love affair.

The Tango Singer by Tomás Eloy Martínez. The story of a student from New York who travels to Buenos Aires in search of inspiration. A passionate homage to the city and the writer Jorge Luis Borges.

Send Us Your Thoughts

We do our best to ensure the information in our books is as accurate and up-to-date as possible. The books are updated on a regular basis using local contacts, who painstakingly add, amend and correct as required. However, some details (such as telephone numbers and opening times) are liable to change, and we are ultimately reliant on our readers to put us in the picture.

We welcome your feedback, especially your experience of using the book "on the road". Maybe you came across a great bar or new attraction we missed.

We will acknowledge all contributions, and we'll offer an Insight Guide to the best letters received.

Please write to us at:
Insight Guides
PO Box 7910
London SE1 1WE

Or email us at:
hello@insightguides.com

TRAVEL LITERATURE

Bad Times in Buenos Aires by Miranda France. Personal and sometimes generalized overview of life in Buenos Aires through a foreigner's eyes.

In Patagonia by Bruce Chatwin. A combination of fact and fiction, beautifully written by one of the greatest travel writers.

Tales of the Pampas; Far Away and Long Ago; Birds of La Plata; Idle Days in Patagonia all by W.H. Hudson. These delightful memoirs by the 19th-century Anglo-Argentine naturalist blend personal reminiscences with poetic meditations on the flora and fauna (especially the bird life) of the pampas.

The Drunken Forest by Gerald Durrell. Searching for animals in Argentina's tropical north.

Two Thousand Miles' Ride Through the Argentine Provinces by William MacCann. An historical account of the country and people in 1853.

Uttermost Part of the Earth: Indians of Tierra Del Fuego by E. Lucas Bridges. A true story – a mix of biography and adventure.

¡Che Boludo!: A Gringo's Guide to Understanding the Argentines by James Bracken. Highly entertaining but nonetheless informative guide to Argentina.

PEOPLE

Falkland People by Angela Wigglesworth. This portrait of life in the Falklands includes interviews with over 50 islanders and was published to coincide with the tenth anniversary of the war.

Hand of God: The Life of Diego Maradona by Jimmy Burns.

Santa Evita by Tomás Eloy Martínez. A mix of fact and fiction about Argentina's most famous icon.

Angels with Dirty Faces: How Argentinian Soccer Defined a Nation and Changed the Game Forever by Jonathan Wilson. A thrilling history of Argentinian football and its impact on the national psyche.

Pope Francis: His Life in his Own Words by Francesca Ambrogetti and Sergio Rubin. A collection of interviews and conversations with

Argentinian Jorge Bergoglio, who became the first Latin American pope in 2013.

FOOD AND WINE

Argentina Cooks! by Shirley Lomax Brooks. One of the few books covering Argentine cuisine, with recipes from the nine regions.
Food and Drink in Argentina: A guide for Tourists and Residents by Dereck Foster and Richard Tripp.
The Food and Cooking Of Argentina: 65 Traditional Recipes from the Heart of South America by Cesar Bartolini. The ultimate guide to the hearty cuisine of Argentina.
The Vineyard at the End of the World by Ian Mount. The best English-language history of Argentine wine.
Wine Routes of Argentina by Alan Young. Guide to Argentine wines which follows an historical framework. Illustrated with detailed maps.

MISCELLANEOUS

Argentine Trout Fishing by William C. Leitch. Detailed and entertaining, with color photographs.

FILMS

Butch Cassidy and the Sundance Kid (Roy Hill, 1969). Starring Robert Redford and Paul Newman.
Evita (Alan Parker, 1997), starring Madonna.
The Mission (Roland Joffe, 1986). Robert de Niro and Jeremy Irons as Jesuit priests in Argentina and Paraguay.
The Motorcycle Diaries (Walter Salles, 2004) The story of how a young medical student sets out from Buenos Aires to discover Latin America. His name? Che Guevara.
Nine Queens (Fabián Bielinsky. 2000). Engaging thriller about two conmen on the streets of Buenos Aires.

The Secret in Their Eyes (Juan José Campanella, 2009). A retired legal counselor returns to an unresolved homicide which took place decades before.
Wild Tales (Damián Szifrón, 2014). Oscar-nominated film which brings together six short stories of revenge.
The Clan (Pablo Trapero, 2015). Based on a true story, this harrowing thriller sheds light on Argentine's dark side.

OTHER INSIGHT GUIDES

Insight Guides cover nearly 200 destinations, providing information on culture and all the top sights, as well as superb photography. *Insight Guide South America* covers the whole subcontinent from Colombia to Tierra del Fuego. Other Insight Guides on South America include *Brazil*, *Chile*, *Colombia*, *Peru,* and *Ecuador & the Galápagos*.

CREDITS

PHOTO CREDITS

COVER CREDITS

INSIGHT GUIDE CREDITS

Distribution
UK, Ireland and Europe
Apa Publications (UK) Ltd;
sales@insightguides.com
United States and Canada
Ingram Publisher Services;
ips@ingramcontent.com
Australia and New Zealand
Woodslane; info@woodslane.com.au
Southeast Asia
Apa Publications (SN) Pte;
singaporeoffice@insightguides.com
Worldwide
Apa Publications (UK) Ltd;
sales@insightguides.com
Special Sales, Content Licensing and CoPublishing
Insight Guides can be purchased in bulk quantities at discounted prices. We can create special editions, personalised jackets and corporate imprints tailored to your needs. sales@insightguides.com www.insightguides.biz

Printed in China by CTPS

All Rights Reserved
© 2018 Apa Digital (CH) AG and Apa Publications (UK) Ltd

First Edition 1988
Seventh Edition 2018

No part of this book may be reproduced, stored in a retrieval system or transmitted in any form or means electronic, mechanical, photocopying, recording or otherwise, without prior written permission from Apa Publications.

Every effort has been made to provide accurate information in this publication, but changes are inevitable. The publisher cannot be responsible for any resulting loss, inconvenience or injury. We would appreciate it if readers would call our attention to any errors or outdated information. We also welcome your suggestions; please contact us at: hello@insightguides.com

www.insightguides.com

Editor: Helen Fanthorpe
Author: Maciej Zglinicki
Head of DTP and Pre-Press: Rebeka Davies
Update Production: Apa Digital
Picture Editor: Tom Smyth
Cartography: original cartography Colourmap Scanning Ltd updated by Carte

CONTRIBUTORS

This new edition was edited by **Helen Fanthorpe**. It was updated by **Maciej Zglinicki**, a Latin America specialist who has traveled extensively in the region. This new edition builds on earlier versions produced by **Fiona Anderson, Deirdre Ball, Philip Benson, David Burnie, Nick Caistor, Matt Chesterton,** **Elena Decima, Parry Jones, Federico Kirbus,** and **Tony Perrottet**.

Many of the photographs in this new edition were taken by **Yadid Levy**, with others by **Eduardo Gil, Robert Harding,** and **Flora Bemporad**.

The index was compiled by **Penny Phenix**.

ABOUT INSIGHT GUIDES

Insight Guides have more than 45 years' experience of publishing high-quality, visual travel guides. We produce 400 full-colour titles, in both print and digital form, covering more than 200 destinations across the globe, in a variety of formats to meet your different needs.

Insight Guides are written by local authors, whose expertise is evident in the extensive historical and cultural background features. Each destination is carefully researched by regional experts to ensure our guides provide the very latest information. All the reviews in **Insight Guides** are independent; we strive to maintain an impartial view. Our reviews are carefully selected to guide you to the best places to visit, so you can be confident that when we say a place is special, we really mean it.

Legend

City maps

Freeway/Highway/Motorway
Divided Highway
Main Roads
Minor Roads
Pedestrian Roads
Steps
Footpath
Railway
Funicular Railway
Cable Car
Tunnel
City Wall
Important Building
Built Up Area
Other Land
Transport Hub
Park
Pedestrian Area
Bus Station
Tourist Information
Main Post Office
Cathedral/Church
Mosque
Synagogue
Statue/Monument
Beach
Airport

Regional maps

Freeway/Highway/Motorway (with junction)
Freeway/Highway/Motorway (under construction)
Divided Highway
Main Road
Secondary Road
Minor Road
Track
Footpath
International Boundary
State/Province Boundary
National Park/Reserve
Marine Park
Ferry Route
Marshland/Swamp
Glacier   Salt Lake
Airport/Airfield
Ancient Site
Border Control
Cable Car
Castle/Castle Ruins
Cave
Chateau/Stately Home
Church/Church Ruins
Crater
Lighthouse
Mountain Peak
Place of Interest
Viewpoint

INDEX

MAIN REFERENCES ARE IN BOLD TYPE

INSIGHT ⊙ GUIDES

OFF THE SHELF

Since 1970, **INSIGHT GUIDES** has provided a unique perspective on the world's best travel destinations by using specially commissioned photography and illuminating text written by local authors.

Whether you're planning a city break, a walking tour or the journey of a lifetime, our superb range of guidebooks and phrasebooks will inspire you to discover more about your chosen destination.

INSIGHT GUIDES

offer a unique combination of stunning photos, absorbing narrative and detailed maps, providing all the inspiration and information you need.

PHRASEBOOKS & DICTIONARIES

help users to feel at home, when away. Pocket-sized with a free app to download, they go where you do.

CITY GUIDES

pack hundreds of great photos into a smaller format with detailed practical information, so you can navigate the world's top cities with confidence.

EXPLORE GUIDES

feature easy-to-follow walks and itineraries in the world's most exciting destinations, with our choice of the best places to eat and drink along the way.

POCKET GUIDES

combine concise information on where to go and what to do in a handy compact format, ideal on the ground. Includes a full-colour, fold-out map.

EXPERIENCE GUIDES

feature offbeat perspectives and secret gems for experienced travellers, with a collection of over 100 ideas for a memorable stay in a city.

www.insightguides.com

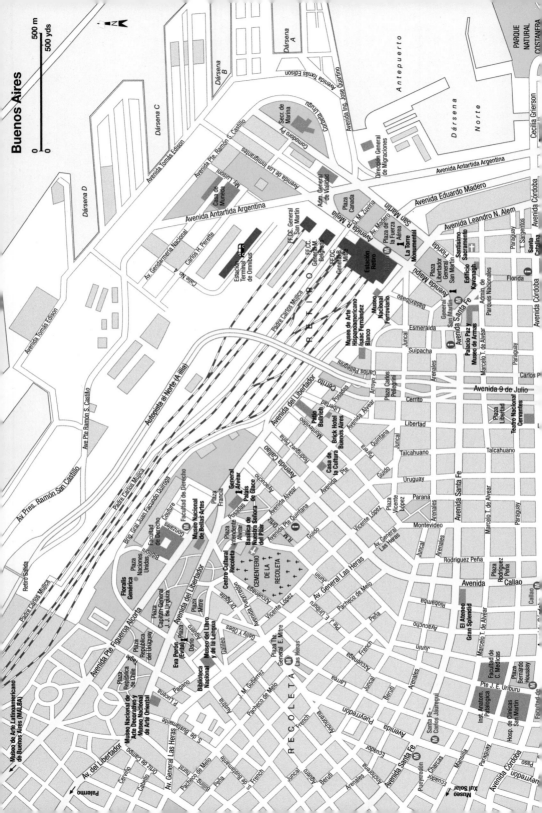